The Interplay of Morphology and Phonology

OXFORD SURVEYS IN SYNTAX AND MORPHOLOGY

GENERAL EDITOR: Robert D Van Valin, Jr, *Heinrich-Heine University and the University at Buffalo, State University of New York*

ADVISORY EDITORS: Guglielmo Cinque, *University of Venice*; Daniel Everett, *Illinois State University*; Adele Goldberg, *Princeton University*; Kees Hengeveld, *University of Amsterdam*; Caroline Heycock, *University of Edinburgh*; David Pesetsky, *MIT*; Ian Roberts, *University of Cambridge*; Masayoshi Shibatani, *Rice University*; Andrew Spencer, *University of Essex*; Tom Wasow, *Stanford University*

The Interplay of Morphology and Phonology

SHARON INKELAS

OXFORD
UNIVERSITY PRESS

OXFORD
UNIVERSITY PRESS

Great Clarendon Street, Oxford, OX2 6DP,
United Kingdom

Oxford University Press is a department of the University of Oxford.
It furthers the University's objective of excellence in research, scholarship,
and education by publishing worldwide. Oxford is a registered trade mark of
Oxford University Press in the UK and in certain other countries

Published in the United States of America by Oxford University Press
198 Madison Avenue, New York, NY 10016, United States of America

British Library Cataloguing in Publication Data
Data available

Library of Congress Cataloging in Publication Data
Data available

ISBN 978-0-19-928047-6

Contents

General preface

Oxford Surveys in Syntax and Morphology provides overviews of the major approaches to subjects and questions at the centre of linguistic research in morphology and syntax. The volumes are accessible, critical, and up to date. Individually and collectively they aim to reveal the field's intellectual history and theoretical diversity. Each book published in the series will characteristically contain: (1) a brief historical overview of relevant research in the subject; (2) a critical presentation of approaches from relevant (but usually seen as competing) theoretical perspectives to the phenomena and issues at hand, including an objective evaluation of the strengths and weaknesses of each approach to the central problems and issues; (3) a balanced account of the current issues, problems, and opportunities relating to the topic, showing the degree of consensus or otherwise in each case. The volumes will thus provide researchers and graduate students concerned with syntax, morphology, and related aspects of semantics with a vital source of information and reference.

The present volume explores the profound interplay between morphology and phonology. It is the only volume in the series that concerns the sound structure of language in relation to morphosyntax, and it provides an excellent and up-to-date overview of contemporary approaches to describing and explaining this interaction.

Robert D. Van Valin, Jr
General Editor

University at Buffalo,
The State University of New York

Heinrich Heine University,
Düsseldorf

Acknowledgments

This book has been in the making since 2005. It draws on courses I have taught in phonology, morphology, and the phonology-morphology interface at UC Berkeley and at the 2009 and 2011 LSA Institutes at UC Berkeley and the University of Colorado. To the students in those courses, I am very grateful for their feedback and for the inspiration they gave me to connect topics that in the literature have not always previously been discussed in the context of one another.

In the long time span during which this book evolved, I received research assistance from four able UC Berkeley graduate students: Ange Strom-Weber, Teresa McFarland, Gregory Finley, and John Sylak-Glassman. Their detective work paid off in the form of many interesting examples in the chapters of this book. For the funding to hire these excellent assistants, I am grateful to the Committee on Research and to the Abigail Hodgen Fund at UC Berkeley.

The thought process that went into this book hinges on intellectual contributions from more talented linguists than I can name. Those who, in discussion or via questions in class or at talks, made particularly salient contributions to my understanding of morphological theory include Geert Booij, Cabriela Caballero, Greville Corbett, and Greg Stump. My understanding of paradigmatic relationships was sharpened by interactions with Andrew Garrett and Donca Steriade. Young-mee Cho, Lev Michael, and Alan Timberlake helped me to better understand the phonology-morphology interactions in Korean, Nanti, and Russian. My former dissertation advisees Yuni Kim, Teresa McFarland, David Mortensen, Mary Paster, Anne Pycha, Alan Yu, and Cheryl Zoll inspired me then and still inspire me now to think in new ways about apparently old issues in the phonology-morphology interface, and their work infuses this book. Through co-teaching a morphology course with Alice Gaby, I found new reasons to be interested in the phonology-morphology interface. Through co-authorship with Cheryl Zoll, I developed a way of thinking outside the box about reduplication that started me on the path to this book. Discussions with Laura Downing and John McCarthy made me realize that there were still new ways to think about the implications of reduplication. During his stewardship of the Exponence Network and his sabbatical in Berkeley,

Jochen Trommer provided stimulating conversations about realizational morphology. And thank you to Paul Kiparsky for sparking my enduring interest in the interplay between morphology and phonology, all those years ago.

Larry Hyman read chapters of this book and gave extremely helpful comments; his innovative work on Bantu phonology and morphology has been instrumental in shaping my views. Andrew Garrett also read chapters and inspired me to think this project might actually culminate in a useful book, during a time when I feared I was becoming permanently stuck in administrative thought patterns.

I am grateful to an anonymous reviewer for very useful feedback, to the editors at the Press for their exceptional patience during the time it took me to complete this manuscript, and especially to series editor Robert Van Valin for reading an early version and encouraging me during all the delays.

The real push to the finish came during a week in Sedona in the summer of 2013. Thank you to my parents for letting me use their timeshare.

Finally, I thank my sons, Jem and Eli, for their love, for their patience, and for always keeping me sharp with their witty banter and penetrating observations.

List of abbreviations

Note that abbreviations for the same category sometimes vary across the sources cited; no attempt has been made to standardize them, other than placing all abbreviations in glosses into small caps, for fear of introducing errors.

1	1st person
1 + 2	1st and 2nd person
2	2nd person
3	3rd person
ABL	ablative
ABS	absolutive
ACC	accusative
ADJ	adjective
ADV	adverbializer
AF	actor focus
AGT	agentive
AOR	aorist
APP	applicative
APPL	applicative
ASSOC	associative
AUG	augmentative
AUX	auxiliary
BEN	benefactive
CAUS	causative
CF	centrifugal
CL	class
CNS	construct state
COM	comitative
COM	comprehensive
COND	conditional
CONS	consequent

CONT	continuative
COP	copular
CP	completive
DAT	dative
DEF	definite
DEN	denominative
DESID	desiderative
DIM	diminutive
DIST	distributive
DL	dual
DU	dual
DUB	dubitative
DUR	durative
DX	deictic
EP	epistemic
ERG	ergative
ESS	essive
EV	evidential
EVID	evidential
EXC.	exclusive plural
FEM	feminine
FUT	future
FV	Final Vowel
GEN	genitive
GON	polygon
GRP	group
IDEO	ideophone
ILL	illative
IMPF	imperfective
IMPRF	imperfective
INAL	inalienable
INC	inclusive
IND	indirect
INESS	inessive
INF	infinitive

INST	instrumental
INT	interrogative
INT	intensive
INTERR	interrogative
INTR	intransitive
IRREAL	irrealis
ITR	intransitive
LOC	locative
M	masculine
MASC	masculine
MIT	mitigative
MOD	modal
N	noun
NEC	necessitative
NEG	negative
NM	non-masculine
NML	nominalizer
NOM	nominative
NOM	nominalizer
NONFUT	non-future
O	object
OBJ	object
OM	object marker
OP.RES	resumptive operator
OPT	optative
P	person
P.P.	past participle
PART	partitive
PART	particle
PASS	passive
PERF	perfective
PL	plural
POSS	possessive
POTEN	potential
PP	past participle

PPL	participle
PRED	predicative
PRES	present
PRET	preterite
PROG	progressive
PROH	prohibitive
PRS	present
PRT	partitive
PST	past
PTCP	participle
PURP	purposive
REAL	realis
REC	reciprocal
RED	reduplication
REFL	reflexive
REL	relative
REP	repetitive
REV	reversive
RPAST	recent past
S	subject
S	singular
S.O.	someone
S.T.	something
SB	subordinate
SEP	separative
SG	singular
SING	singular
ST	stative
SUB	subject
SUBJ	subject
SUBJ	subjunctive
SUP	superlative
TR	transitivizer
TRANS	transitivizer

TRSU	transitive subject
TV	theme vowel
UNSP	unspecified
UR	underlying representation
V	verb
VBL	verbalizer
VBLZ	verbalizer
VOC	vocative
WP	witnessed past

Note on language classifications

Most language classifications (genus and sometimes also subfamily) are taken from the World Atlas of Linguistic Structures (Haspelmath et al. 2005), available online at <http://wals.info>. Bantu languages are classified, following the practice in the literature, with their Guthrie number.

1

Introduction

Phonology and morphology are typically taught in separate courses in undergraduate and graduate Linguistics programs. Books on these two topics are shelved separately in libraries. Theories of one tend to have little to say about the other. Yet any serious study of either ultimately requires expertise in both, because even if phonology and morphology are conceptualized as distinct grammatical modules, they are constantly intermingling.

It is probably safe to say that in every language, at least some of the phonological patterns are conditioned by morphological factors (sensitivity to morpheme boundaries, part of speech, etc.) It is probably also safe to say that in every language, predicting the form of a morphologically complex word requires knowledge of the phonological rules and requirements of the language.

If morphology consisted only of affixation that is "canonical," in the sense of Corbett's (2007) framework of Canonical Typology, then the following statement, adapted from Spencer and Luis (2013), would be true:

The form of a morpheme is constant in all environments

Indeed, this statement probably accurately characterizes the morphologically complex words that are presented to students for analysis in the first week of an introductory morphology class.

However, this criterion does not apply in most real-life situations. Phonologically conditioned allomorphy is pervasive, affecting the phonological form that an affix (or stem) takes in different contexts (Chapters 2, 4). And some morphology is processual, effecting a constant change in the base of affixation rather than assuming a constant affixal form (Chapters 3, 4, 5). Phonological considerations can even interfere with the basic workings of morphology, preventing an affix from attaching (Chapter 9).

Phonological patterns are often introduced to students in a similarly idealized fashion, implying that they apply fully generally to all words in the language. But this is rarely the case. Phonological patterns are often imposed in highly restricted morphological environments (Chapter 2), can be interleaved with the morphological operations that build a word (Chapter 7), and can be prevented (or triggered) in order to ensure well-structured morphological paradigms (Chapter 11).

In order to gain perspective on the degree and nature of the interaction between phonology and morphology, this book presents a phenomenon-oriented overview of the main types of interactions that have been observed. This overview cannot possibly cover every interesting example of phonology-morphology interaction which has been discussed, even prominently, in the literature. But it aims to cover all the *types* of interaction that have been repeatedly noted across languages and which have influenced our understanding of how grammar works.

Although the purpose of the book is not to promote one theory over another, it does have a secondary purpose of highlighting properties any theory of morphology or phonology must possess in order to account for the phenomena covered.

Certain of the phenomena discussed have famously inspired or been cited as support for particular morphological or phonological theories. In conjunction with the presentation of the relevant phenomena, these theories, including Lexical Morphology and Phonology, Prosodic Morphology, A-Morphous Morphology, Construction Morphology, and a variety of subtheories within the general framework of Optimality Theory, are introduced where appropriate and, in cases of competition, compared.

For example, Chapter 7, on the interleaving of morphology and phonology, goes into some detail comparing the predictions of Lexical Morphology and Phonology (Kiparsky 1982b), Stratal Optimality Theory (Kiparsky 2000, 2008), and Cophonology Theory (Anttila 2002; Inkelas and Zoll 2007), which depends on a constructionist morphological theory like Construction Morphology (Booij 2010).

Chapter 5, on reduplication, brings a variety of data to bear on the choice between modeling reduplication with Base-Reduplication Correspondence Theory (McCarthy and Prince 1995) or Morphological Doubling Theory (Inkelas and Zoll 2005).

It is not possible within the scope of this book to give full justice to each morphological theory which is discussed, nor even to give equal treatments of these approaches. The aim is, rather, to present the key insights that different theoretical approaches lend to the phenomena being discussed.

The book assumes some existing knowledge of morphology and phonology, including Optimality Theory. Due to the inclinations of its author, the book has a detectable bias towards construction-based approaches to morphology, including the use of cophonologies. However, the intent is not to argue for this approach over another, but to clearly present the key phenomena that any theory must contend with in order to be successful.

Research in the phonology-morphology interaction is voluminous and rapidly expanding. It is impossible in a single book to include every relevant fact or observation. Very recent literature will necessarily be missing from these pages. An encyclopedia, this book is not. Nor can it be an accurate reflection of the current state of the expanding field, a rapidly moving target. Rather, it is an exposition on and reflection about the interrelationship among the many types of interplay between morphology and phonology that should inform contemporary theories. It is hoped that the connections made between phenomena in and across these chapters will be the legacy of this work.

A brief overview of the chapters follows:

Chapter 2. Morphologically conditioned phonology The book begins, in Chapter 2, with an overview of morphologically conditioned phonology. This is the logical starting point for a discussion of the phonology-morphology interface, since it reveals the many different types of morphological information to which phonological patterns can be sensitive: lexical classes of roots, the difference between roots and affixes, specific morphological constructions. This chapter also addresses the question of what kinds of phonological patterns can be morphologically sensitive, and how many such patterns a given language can have. The theoretical discussion in this chapter focuses mainly on this last question. Morphological conditioning of phonology produces a range of different phonological patterns in the same language. Several theories have been developed which constrain this range in principled ways. Level Ordering theories (e.g. Kiparsky 1982b, 2000, 2008) claim that the morphological constructions of each language will cluster into a small, finite number of sets, each internally uniform in its phonological patterning, which form sequential subcomponents in grammar. By contrast, Cophonology Theory (Anttila 2002; Inkelas and Zoll 2007) and Indexed Constraint Theory (Itô and Mester 1995; Alderete 2001a) predict that the number of different phonological patterns could be significantly larger. Researchers working within each of these theoretical frameworks have advanced hypotheses about the degree of difference tolerated among coexisting morphologically conditioned phonological patterns in the same language; these hypotheses are discussed in Chapter 2.

Chapter 3. Process morphology The counterpart to morphologically conditioned phonology is morphology which is manifested as a phonological process, such as truncation, vowel ablaut, consonant mutation, etc. These processes can either themselves be the sole mark of a morphological category or may form the stems that are involved in the marking of that category.

The existence of process morphology has been cited as evidence for realizational theories of morphology (e.g. A-Morphous Morphology; Anderson 1992) over item-based theories (e.g. Lieber 1980; Kiparsky 1982b), which must treat process morphology as a very different phenomenon from ordinary affixation or compounding.

A potential problem for many theories of morphology, including realizational models, lies in distinguishing process morphology from morphologically conditioned phonology. For example, final consonant deletion alone, as in Tohono O'odham perfective formation, would be described as subtractive morphology, while final consonant deletion in the context of a particular suffix (e.g. Turkish *bebek-cik* → *bebecik* 'baby-DIM = little baby') is normally described as a suffix-triggered consonant deletion rule. As discussed in Chapter 3, this conundrum does not exist in construction morphology frameworks that assume cophonologies; in such approaches, the analyst is not forced to formally distinguish between morphologically conditioned phonology and phonologically manifested morphology.

Chapter 4. Prosodic Templates Prosodic templates lie in the gray area between morphologically conditioned phonology and process morphology. These shape constraints are (associated with) morphological constructions. The constructions in question can be semantically empty stem-formers, or they may perform specific derivational or inflectional functions. The template directly constrains the phonological shape of the output of the morphological construction. This chapter surveys some well-known and lesser-known examples. The main theoretical question addressed in the chapter is whether templates are atomic representational units to which the products of morphological processes are forced to conform, or the emergent effects of a large number of phonological rules or constraints all indexed to the same morphological environment. If the latter, then templates may be simply an extreme case of morphologically conditioned phonology or process morphology.

Chapter 5. Reduplication Reduplication is the duplication of some part, possibly all, of a stem for some morphological purpose. Reduplication has long been of interest to phonological theory because of the apparently restricted set of shapes that characterize partial reduplicants. This chapter surveys partial reduplication, focusing on reduplicant shape and on mismatches between the phonological material in the reduplicant and that in the base from which the reduplicant is largely copied. The theoretical discussion in this chapter focuses largely on the role of identity in reduplication. On some, highly influential, approaches, e.g. Base-Reduplicant Correspondence Theory (McCarthy and Prince 1995), reduplicative identity is strictly phonological, and the imperative to maintain identity between reduplicant and base can cause wrinkles in the otherwise stable phonological system of the language. In Morphological Doubling Theory (Inkelas and Zoll 2005), however, reduplication is treated as a morphological doubling process, not as phonological copying. On either view, reduplication constructions appear to require simultaneous morphological and phonological operations, which is why reduplication is central to any discussion of the morphology-phonology interface.

Chapter 6. Infixation Infixation is often described as being just like affixation except that the affix is positioned within the stem instead of peripheral to it. The phonological interest of infixation lies in the phonological generalizations about where in a word an infix can appear and why infixation occurs at all. On the morphological side, it is interesting to note that only morphemes classified as affixes exhibit infixing behavior; infixation is apparently not a possible property of compounding, modulo several suggestive examples.

The theoretical debate surrounding infixation has to do mainly with whether or not it is a morphological repair for phonological problems. Some (e.g. McCarthy and Prince 1994a, working in Optimality Theory) have argued that infixation is optimizing: an infix will be placed in that location, whether stem-internal or peripheral, which optimizes syllable or other phonological properties of the resulting word. Yu (2007), by contrast, offers a lexicalist approach in which infix position is essentially arbitrary. The key probative data are cases in which the infix appears to occupy a position that results in worse phonotactic problems than if the infix had been adfixed.

Chapter 7. Interleaving Chapter 7 discusses the phonological properties of morphologically complex words, i.e. those formed by more than one word-formation process. What we find in many such cases is clear evidence that phonology is interleaved with morphology in the sense that the output of applying phonology to an inner subconstituent of a word serves as input to the phonology of the next larger constituent in that word. This generalization underlies theories from Lexical Morphology and Phonology (Kiparsky 1982bc) through Distributed Morphology (e.g. Embick 2010). Well-known and lesser-known examples of cyclicity are surveyed; the results put to rest the widespread but inaccurate belief that examples of cyclicity almost exclusively involve stress assignment. This chapter also addresses the question, raised in Chapter 2, of whether restrictive stratal ordering theories make correct predictions for highly affixing languages. Several cases are discussed which pose problems for such approaches.

Chapter 8. Morphologically derived environment effects Phonological alternations which are triggered in morphologically derived environments sometimes fail to apply when the same phonological environment occurs in morphologically nonderived environments. This chapter examines the various definitions of morphologically derived environment that have been proposed in the attempt to cover all of the cases that appear to belong to this category. In the best-known type of example, the trigger and target of a phonological alternation fall on opposite sides of a morpheme boundary, and early theories of nonderived environment blocking (NDEB) effects were designed around exactly this scenario. However, other types of NDEB effects also exist, and have prompted a striking variety of theoretical approaches. By examining several case studies in some depth, this chapter raises the question of whether derived environment effects really constitute an internally uniform and distinct natural class of phenomena, or whether the so-called derived environment condition simply amounts to an acknowledgment that, as seen in Chapter 2, many lexical phonological patterns are morphologically conditioned.

Chapter 9. When phonology interferes with morphology This chapter discusses cases in which word-formation possibilities are constrained by phonology, either because of phonological requirements on inputs to word formation, or because of phonological requirements on the outputs of word formation. Constraints on word formation can result in the choice of one suppletive allomorph over another, or they can result in morphological gaps, where no output (or only a periphrastic output) is possible. This chapter surveys these two phenomena in turn, and then considers two areas in which phonology has been claimed to interfere with morphology, but whose interpretation is more questionable: the Repeated Morph Constraint and phonologically conditioned affix ordering. The main theoretical issue raised in this chapter is the so-called P » M hypothesis of McCarthy and Prince (1994a), according to which phonological considerations ("P") outrank morphological considerations, e.g. affix ordering ("M"). Evidence of the P » M ranking is limited, and there seem to be certain areas in which the phonology does not substantially interfere.

Chapter 10. Nonparallelism between phonological and morphological structure The expectation that the domains of morphologically conditioned phonological patterns are coextensive with the morphological subconstituents of a word is why phonology is considered relevant evidence bearing on the morphological structural analysis of a given word. However, there can be mismatches, i.e. situations in which a phonological domain—termed "prosodic root," or "prosodic stem," or "prosodic word"—does not line up perfectly with a morphological root, stem, or word (see e.g. Booij 1984). This can occur in compounding, with certain affixes that seem to be phonological domains of their own, and in reduplication. A question that naturally arises in a framework that posits coexisting prosodic and morphological domains is whether phonology needs to make direct reference to morphological structure at all, or whether, as has been claimed in the literature on the phonology-syntax interface (e.g. Nespor and Vogel 1986), prosodic structure serves as a proxy for morphological structure. The conclusion of this chapter is that the role of prosodic structure in the morphology-phonology interface is supplementary, rather than a replacement for a direct connection between morphological constructions and phonological patterns.

Chapter 11. Paradigmatic effects It has often been suggested that word formation and the phonological interpretation of words can be influenced not only by properties of the word in question, but also by other words. The main claim of this type is that morphology and phonology can conspire to avoid producing new word forms that are homophonous with some other word in the language (or the paradigm). The issue for anti-homophony principles, addressed in this chapter, is that homophony is quite rampant in languages.

Conversely, it has also been suggested that the phonology conspires to keep the shared portions of morphologically related words phonologically identical (Paradigm Uniformity); the Base-Identity constraints of e.g. Kenstowicz (1996) and Benua (1997) fall into this category. It is unclear whether Base-Identity and cyclicity are both needed as theoretical devices; most formulations of Base-Identity assume that it takes the place of cyclicity. However, not all cases of cyclicity preserve identity, as discussed in this chapter, suggesting that cyclicity is not completely superseded.

The strongest evidence for paradigmatic relationships is not Base-Identity but rather cases in which two words interact phonologically even though neither is a subconstituent of the other (see e.g. Steriade 1999). Clear cases of this sort are not numerous; research has only recently begun to focus on them.

Summary

Phonology-morphology interaction is very different from syntax-phonology interaction. It sheds light on word-internal structure and on the ability for relatively unnatural phonological alternations to be productive, at least within a given morphological niche. Morphophonological patterns are crucial for universalist theories of phonology, and must be taken seriously by morphologists and phonologists, especially those seeking to reduce all synchronic morphological patterns to syntax, or all synchronic phonological patterns to universal phonetic motivations.

2

Morphologically conditioned phonology

Any study of the phonology-morphology interface must begin with the central issue of morphologically conditioned phonological patterns. A topic of intense theoretical interest since well before the inception of generative phonology, morphologically conditioned phonology is the phenomenon in which a particular phonological pattern is imposed on a proper subset of morphological constructions (affix, reduplication, compounding) and thus is not fully general in the word-internal phonological patterning of the language. Such phenomena have been the inspiration for a number of influential theories of the phonology-morphology interface, including Lexical Morphology and Phonology, Stratal Optimality Theory, and Cophonology Theory.

This chapter will survey various facets of the morphological conditioning of phonology, focusing on the types of morphological information that can condition phonological patterns and the types of phonological patterns that can be conditioned by morphology. Also covered will be several of the most influential theories of morphologically conditioned phonology, which aim to capture language-specific as well as cross-linguistic generalizations about the phenomenon.

The chapter will focus specifically on phonological alternations or constraints that affect the surface form of morphemes. A number of closely related topics are taken up in other chapters: process morphology, in Chapter 3; prosodic templates, in Chapter 4; reduplication, in Chapter 5; phonology-morphology interleaving, in Chapter 7; phonology which applies only in morphologically derived environments, in Chapter 8; the interference of phonology with morphology, including suppletive allomorphy, in Chapter 9; the relationship between morphological structure and prosodic structure, in Chapter 10; and the effect of paradigmatic relationships on phonology, in Chapter 11.

2.1 Illustrative examples

We begin with three illustrative examples of morphologically conditioned phonological patterns. These examples are selected fairly arbitrarily out of an enormous set of possibilities; this is a truly vast
phenomenon. The aim of these examples is to show that it is not the
case, as the instructor of an introductory phonology class might tem-
porarily mislead students into believing, that a language has a single
fixed set of general phonological rules or constraints which apply in the
same way to all words. Instead, a large fraction—perhaps the majority, it
is hard to know—of phonological alternations or constraints applying
within words are subject to quite specific morphological conditioning.

Mam Maya exhibits the morphologically conditioned neutralization
of stem vowel length. In Mam, a general constraint in the language
prohibits a word from having more than one long vowel. Some roots
have a long vowel; some suffixes have a long vowel. Suffixes partition
into two classes in terms of the effect that suffixation has on vowel
length in the stem (Willard 2004, based on England 1983). "Dominant"
affixes cause long root vowels to shorten (1a); "Recessive" suffixes
preserve root vowel length (1b). Dominant vs. recessive status is not
predictable; it must be learned individually for each affix:

(1)   a. Dominant suffix: shortens long root vowel   [Mam Maya]
         /liich'-VCVVn/   → [lich'ich'iin] 'break-facilitative resultant'
         /juus-b'een/   → [jus-b'een] 'burn-locative'
         /jaaw-nax/   → [jawnax] 'go up-directional'
         /nooj-na/   → [nojna] 'fill-participial'

      b. Recessive suffix: preserves root vowel length
         /muq-oo/   →   [muqoo]   'bury-intransitive.verbalizer'
         /b'iitz-oo/   →   [b'iitza] 'song-intransitive.verbalizer'
         /luk-b'il/   →   [lukb'il] 'pull up-instrumental'
         /waa-b'an/   →   [waab'an] 'eat-remainder'

In Malayalam (Southern Dravidian), consonant gemination applies
at the internal juncture of Subcompounds, which are noun-noun compounds with head-modifier semantics (2b). Gemination does not apply,
however, at the internal juncture of Cocompounds, which are noun-noun
compounds with coordinate semantics (2c) (Mohanan 1995: 49):

(2) a. meeša   'table'   [Malayalam]
        peṭṭi   'box'
        -kaḷ   (plural suffix)

     b. [meeša-**ppeṭṭi**]ₛ -kaḷə   'boxes made out of tables'

     c. [meeša-peṭṭi]_C -kaḷə   'tables and boxes'

In English, suffixes fall into two classes (e.g. Chomsky and Halle 1968; Siegel 1974; Allen 1978; Kiparsky 1982bc, 1985): those which shift stress (3a) and those which do not (3b):

(3) Base   a. Stress-shifting suffix   b. Non-stress-shifting suffix
-------------------|---------------------------|-----------------------------
     párent   parént-al   párent-ing
     président   prèsidént-ial   présidenc-y
     áctive   àctív-ity   áctiv-ist
     démonstràte   demónstrative   démonstràtor

In all three of these examples, some morphological constructions in the language (affixation, compounding constructions) are associated with a pattern that other constructions (other affixation, other compounding constructions) are not.

2.2 Approaches to morphologically conditioned phonology

Approaches to morphologically conditioned phonology can be grouped into two main types: Single Grammar Theories and Multiple Grammar Theories. In Single Grammar Theories, each language has a single phonological grammar, but that grammar includes, along with fully general phonological rules or constraints, other rules or constraints which are indexed to particular morphological environments and take effect only there. Under this umbrella are *The Sound Pattern of English* (Chomsky and Halle 1968) and Optimality-theoretic models employing morphologically indexed constraints (e.g. Itô and Mester 1995b; Benua 1997[2000]; Alderete 2001ab; Coetzee 2009), to name two of the most prominent theories of this kind.

In Multiple Grammar Theories, a language has multiple subgrammars, each indexed to one or more morphological constructions or lexical strata. Each subgrammar is composed of fully general rules and constraints. Under this umbrella are Cophonology Theory (Orgun 1996; Inkelas, Orgun, and Zoll 1997; Anttila 1997, 2002; Inkelas 1998; Inkelas and Zoll 2005), Lexical Morphology and Phonology (Kiparsky 1982abc,

1984, 1985; Mohanan 1982, 1986; Mohanan and Mohanan 1984; Pulleyblank 1986), and Stratal Optimality Theory (Kiparsky 2000, 2008).

Any individual morphologically conditioned phonological pattern can easily be modeled in either of these two general ways. Consider, for example, Mam vowel length alternations (1). Let us assume, for sake of discussion, an Optimality Theory analysis in which stem vowel shortening is attributed to a constraint against long vowels (*VV); when ranked above FAITH(fulness) to input vowel length, *VV induces vowel shortening.[1]

In a Single Grammar Theory, the fact that only some suffixes are associated with stem vowel shortening in Mam could be handled by assuming that in general in Mam, FAITH outranks *VV, but that the Mam grammar also contains a constraint specific to stems formed by dominant suffixes:

(4)   FAITH_DominantSuffixStems » *VV » FAITH

By contrast, a Multiple Grammar Theory would posit two subgrammars (called "cophonologies," "levels," or "strata"), each with opposite ranking of the *VV and FAITH constraints. Each suffix construction would be associated with one of these subgrammars:

(5)   Recessive subgrammar: *VV » FAITH
      Dominant subgrammar: FAITH » *VV

The Single and the Multiple Grammar approaches are equally capable of handling the distinction between dominant and recessive suffixes in Mam. In general, when looking at any single morphologically conditioned phonological alternation, there is no way to distinguish between the approaches, both of which are in wide use in the literature. The only way to distinguish between the Single and Multiple Grammar Theories is to look at a language as a whole, taking all of its morphologically conditioned alternations into account, and asking questions such as these: how many different morphologically conditioned phonological effects can a single language have? How different from one another can the morphologically conditioned phonological patterns in the same language be? If the morphological constructions in a language can vary in their phonological patterning, what captures the overall phonological unity of a language?

---

[1] For a basic introduction to Optimality Theory, see Archangeli and Langendoen (1997); Kager (1999); Prince and Smolensky (2003, 2004); McCarthy (2002, 2004, 2008).

Some of these questions will be addressed later in this chapter in section 2.7. Others, specifically having to do with the interaction of morphologically conditioned patterns when they are triggered in the same morphologically complex word, will be dealt with in Chapter 7. The evidence marshaled there suggests that Multiple Grammar Theory has a slight edge over Single Grammar Theory in terms of accounting for morphologically complex words.

In the next sections we will take a tour of the types of morphological conditioning that phonology can display cross-linguistically, moving from the general to the specific. Section 2.3 surveys sensitivity to lexical class, section 2.4 looks at phonological asymmetries between roots and affixes, and section 2.5 explores the degree to which individual morphological constructions can be associated with unique phonological patterns. Section 2.6 addresses the phonological substance of morphologically conditioned phonology.

2.3 Phonological sensitivity to lexical class

Some patterns are sensitive to lexical class, applying differentially across classes of lexical items. Lexical classes can be defined in terms of part of speech (sections 2.3.1, 2.3.2), or transparent etymological origin (section 2.3.3), or may seem completely arbitrary from a synchronic point of view (section 2.3.4).

2.3.1 Part of speech

It is not uncommon to find examples in which morphemes from different parts of speech, usually nouns and verbs, differ in their phonological patterning. Accent assignment in Tokyo Japanese is one well-known case of this. Japanese has a system of pitch-accent, phonetically realized as a drop from High to Low pitch (McCawley 1968; Haraguchi 1977; Poser 1984; Pierrehumbert and Beckman 1988, among others). A word can surface with at most one accent. However, not all words are accented. Some roots are lexically accented, while others are not; some affixes are accented and/or assign accent to stems. The distribution of accent is different in nouns and verbs. As pointed out by McCawley (1968), Poser (1984), Tsujimura (1996), Smith (1999) (for the Fukuoka dialect), and many others, the location of accent in lexically accented non derived nouns is unpredictable and must be learned individually for each such noun. Examples from Poser

(1984: 46) are given in (6a). By contrast, the location of accent in an accented verb follows strict rules, falling on the first mora of the syllable containing the penultimate mora of the verb. Examples from Poser (1984: 52) are given in (6b). In (6), syllables are separated by dots, and the accented mora is underlined:

(6)

	Accented			Unaccented		[Japanese]
a. Nouns	fu.ku.<u>ro</u>	'bag'		hasira	'pillar'	
	ta.<u>ma</u>.go	'egg'		kusuri	'medicine'	
	su.to.<u>rai</u>.ki	'strike'		udoN	'noodle dish'	
b. Verbs	ka.k<u>e</u>.ru	'hang'		kakeru	'be broken'	
	su.k<u>uu</u>	'build a nest'		sukuu	'rescue'	
	<u>ue</u>.ru	'starve'		ueru	'plant'	

Smith (2011) calls attention to the example of Lenakel (Oceanic), in which secondary stress assignment is sensitive to part of speech (Lynch 1978; see also Hayes 1995: 167–78 for discussion). Polysyllabic words usually exhibit primary stress on the penultimate syllable. In verbs and adjectives, secondary stress falls on the first syllable and every other syllable thereafter, up to but not including the antepenultimate syllable (avoiding the situation where the antepenultimate and penultimate syllable would both bear stress). In nouns, by contrast, secondary stress is assigned to alternating syllables to the left of the primary penultimate stress. As Lynch (1978) observes, the result is that verbs and adjectives with four or more syllables always have initial (secondary) stress, but nouns of similar length do not. Data from Lynch (1978: 19)[2]:

(7) a. Verbs (four or more syllables)   [Lenakel]

    /r-ɨm-olkeikei/   [řɨ̀.mɔl.gɛ́y.gɛy]   'he liked it'

    /n-ɨm-ar-olkeikei/   [nɨ̀.ma.řɔl.gɛ́y.gɛy]   'you (pl.) liked it'

    /n-ɨm-am-ar-olkeikei/   [nɨ̀.ma.mà.řɔl.gɛ́y.gɛy] 'you (pl.) were
                                                                liking it'

    /t-n-ak-am-ar-olkeikei/ [tɨ̀.na.gà.ma.řɔl.gɛ́y.gɛy] 'you (pl.) will be
                                                                liking it'

          ~[dɨ̀.na.gà.ma.řɔl.gɛ́y.gɛy]

---

[2] Lynch notes that under certain circumstances, e.g. when a long vowel occurs in final position, verbs will take final stress. In that event, the antepenultimate syllable always takes secondary stress. Otherwise, the normal secondary stress rule then applies: secondary stress on the initial syllable, and every other syllable thereafter. This can only be seen in very long verbs, of eight syllables or more, e.g. /na-t-i-ep-ai-ukɨranɨmw-ín/ → [nà.dʸɛ.bà.yu.gə.řà.nɨ.mʷín] ~ 'we (exc. pl.) will be ready to drown it' (Lynch 1978: 20).

b. Nouns (four or more syllables)
/nɨmwakɨlakɨl/   [nɨ.mʷɒ̀.gə.lá.gəl]   'beach'
/tupwalukaluk/   [tu.bʷɒ̀.lu.gá.lʊkʰ]   'lungs'
                   ~[du.bʷɒ̀.lu.gá.lʊkʰ]

In several languages, as Smith (2011) points out, nouns are singled out for augmentation and required to assume a particular minimal prosodic size which verbs are not required to reach. In Chuukese (Trukese; Micronesian), for example, nouns must be minimally bimoraic, a condition which a monosyllabic noun can satisfy by possessing an initial (moraic) geminate (8a) or by undergoing vowel lengthening (8b). (Coda consonants are not moraic in Chuukese.) By contrast, verbs are allowed to surface in monomoraic CVC form (8c). Note that the data in (8a, b) show the effects of vowel apocope, an independent phenomenon (Smith 2011, citing Muller 1999: 395 and Goodenough and Sugita 1980: xiv–xv):

(8)   a.   [kkej]   'laugh'   (< /kkeji/)   [Chuukese]
           [tʃar]   'starfish'   (</tʃtʃara/)

      b.   [faːs]   'nest'   (</fasa/)
           [fæːn]   'building'   (</fæne/)

      c.   [fan]   'go aground'
           [mær]   'move, be shifted'

In her cross-linguistic survey of noun vs. verb phonology, Smith (2011) calls attention not just to the fact of noun-specific or verb-specific phonological patterns but to pervasive cross-linguistic asymmetries across languages in the types of patterns that are observed. Smith finds overall that nouns tend to exhibit more contrasts, while verbs are more prone to neutralization. This finding is clearly consistent with the Japanese example in (6), though it is not as clearly applicable to the Lenakel or Chuukese examples. Smith's generalization will be discussed further in section 2.7.2.1.

2.3.2 Ideophones

Ideophones are a phonosemantic class of words whose meanings typically include color, smell, sound, intensity, or (often vivid) descriptions of unusual appearance or activity. Ideophones can belong to various parts of speech, most often adjectives, adverbs, or verbs. They are of interest to the present discussion because in many languages they constitute a class of words with distinctive phonology, often departing from prosodic or segmental norms. For useful surveys of ideophones, see Hinton et al. (1994) and Voeltz and Kilian-Hatz (2001).

The rich (ca. 500) collection of ideophones in Hausa (Chadic) employs the standard Hausa consonant and vowel inventory but departs from the language's phonological norms in two ways (Newman 1995, 2000: 242–59, 2001). The first involves syllable structure. Ideophones are usually consonant-final, in contrast to the Hausa norm of vowel-final words. Furthermore, ideophones can end in obstruent consonants, including plosives, which is impossible in the other sectors of Hausa vocabulary (Newman 1995: 776; Newman 2000: 244, 250):[3]

(9) fát   fáríː fát   'white IDEO = very white'   [Hausa]
     ʃár̃   kóːrèː ʃár̃   'green IDEO = very green'
     kút   àbóːkíː ƙút   'friend IDEO = very close friend'
     ták   d̃ájá ták   'one IDEO = exactly one'
     r̃úf   jáː r̃úfè ƙóːfár̃ r̃úf   '3SG.MASC close door IDEO = he closed
                                           the door tight'
     fár̃át   táː táːʃì fár̃át   '3SG.FEM get_up IDEO = she got up very
                                           fast'
     túbús   yáː gàjí túbús   '3SG.MASC become_tired IDEO = he
                                           became very tired'
     gàràrà súnàː jáːwòː gàràrà   '3PL walk IDEO = they roamed
                                           aimlessly'

A third characteristic of Hausa ideophones is that they are pronounced with exaggerated intonation. Hausa has three lexical tones: H(igh), L(ow), and Falling (a combination of H and L). Ideophones also exhibit these tones, but with a difference: H on ideophones is realized as extra-H, and L as extra-L. These differences are most noticeable when the ideophone is in phrase-final position (Inkelas and Leben 1991; Newman 1995, 2000). In summary, ideophones in Hausa push the envelope of what is permitted phonologically in the language. This situation is very common. However, as Childs (2001: 182) points out, it is not universal. In some languages, ideophones may exhibit fewer phonological contrasts than are found in other parts of speech. A case

---

[3] Transcriptions are given in IPA (with H tone and L tone marked with acute and grave accents, respectively), rather than the standard Hausa transcription used by Newman.

of this kind in Guarani is discussed in Chapter 4; Guarani noise-word ideophones conform to a rigid template that exceptionally enforces vowel harmony and allows only about one third of the consonants in the Guarani inventory (Langdon 1994).

2.3.3 Etymological classes

Lexical class distinctions to which phonology is sensitive can be etymologically based. A common manifestation of this phenomenon is that certain phonological patterns are imposed or licensed in loanwords but not in native vocabulary items.

In a case study of lexical classes in Japanese, Itô and Mester (1999: 62) point out that the lexical distinction between native vocabulary, Sino-Japanese vocabulary, and loans from other (mainly European) languages is well-recognized by speakers of Japanese, due in part to its reflection in the writing system and in part to phonological differences between the sets of words, which Itô and Mester term vocabulary strata. Itô and Mester point to three phonological properties that distinguish the strata. As depicted in (10), the constraint No-DD bans voiced geminates; No-P bans singleton (onset) [p], and No-NT bans sequences consisting of a nasal consonant followed by a voiceless consonant:

(10)   [Japanese]

	No-DD	No-P	No-NT
Yamato			
Sino-Japanese			violated
Assimilated foreign		violated	violated
Nonassimilated foreign	violated	violated	violated

The native, or Yamato, vocabulary in Japanese adheres to the strictest phonological conditions of the strata, enforcing all three constraints. DD, P, and NT structures are not found in native roots, and when they arise through the concatenation of native morphemes, they are repaired, e.g. /yom-te/ 'read-GERUNDIVE' → [yonde], which converts an illegal NT sequence to a legal [nd] cluster. Sino-Japanese vocabulary items do not heed No-NT. Some contain NT sequences morpheme-internally, e.g. *keŋka* 'quarrel', and NT sequences created by the morphology in Sino-Japanese compounds are not repaired. The "Foreign" strata are the most permissive, including surface voiced geminates (DD), singleton [p]'s (P), as well as NT sequences. In order to capture the differences among the strata, Itô and Mester (1999) propose that the phonological grammar of Japanese is sensitive to the stratal classification, either by means of postulating different sub-grammars (cophonologies) for the different strata or by indexing specific constraints to specific strata. Observing that the strata differ in a scalar fashion in the subset of constraints (No-DD, No-P, No-NT) which they obey, Itô and Mester (1999) propose the constraint ranking for Japanese given in (11). The only constraints which are indexed to strata are the Faithfulness constraints mandating identity between underlying and surface representations. The higher these are ranked, the more strongly lexical items will resist conforming to the phonological well-formedness constraints No-DD, No-P, No-NT (Itô and Mester 1999: 73):

(11)   FAITH-UnassimilatedForeign
                  |
             No-NT
                  |
        FAITH-AssimilatedForeign
                  |
             No-P
                  |
           FAITH-SinoJapanese
                  |
             No-DD
                  |
           FAITH-Yamato

Itô and Mester (1999: 70) observe that the classification of lexical items into strata is not always technically etymologically accurate. For example, the native item *anata* 'you' has contracted to *anta*, which violates *NT. Based on its phonological characteristics, *anta* should belong to one of the non-native strata, but it is etymologically native. Despite occasional counterexamples of this kind, however, the different classes of phonological behavior in Japanese hew quite closely to etymology.

2.3.4 Arbitrary lexical classes: patterned exceptions

Sometimes lexical class distinctions are purely arbitrary, with one set of morphemes simply resisting a phonological pattern that others conform to. For example, in Sacapultec (Mayan, Guatemala), some nouns undergo final-syllable vowel lengthening in combination with possessive prefixes (12a), while others do not (12b) (DuBois 1985: 396):[4]

(12)		Plain		Possessive	
	a.	ak	'chicken'	w-a:k	'my chicken'
		¢'eʔ	'dog'	ni-¢'i:ʔ	'my dog'
		ab'ax	'rock'	w-ub'a:x	'my rock'
		tiʔb'al	'stinger'	ri-tiʔb'a:l	'its stinger'
		mulol	'gourd'	ni-mulu:l	'my gourd'
	b.	oč'	'possum'	w-oč'	'my possum'
		am	'spider'	w-am	'my spider'
		weʔ	'head hair'	ni-weʔ	'my head hair'

DuBois observes that the difference is lexically conditioned, and not reliably predictable from other factors. However, he also notes a weak semantic effect; many of the stems resisting possessive lengthening "do not often occur in possessed constructions, e.g., wild animal names" (p. 396).

In the recent literature, much attention has been paid to finding statistical generalizations of this sort that might shed some light on seemingly arbitrary lexical class distinctions. Zuraw (2000) applies the term "patterned exceptionality" to the phenomena that this line of research seeks out. For example, when the Tagalog prefix *paŋ-* combines with a following (consonant-initial) stem, the environment is created for the Tagalog rule of Nasal Substitution to apply (Zuraw 2000). Nasal Substitution merges a nasal consonant and following stop into a single nasal consonant. As seen in (13), the rule does not apply systematically throughout the lexicon. Some roots undergo it when prefixed, and others do not (Zuraw 2000: 30):

---

[4] Transcriptions have been converted to IPA. The vowel alternations are due to an independent phrase-final lowering process. The 1st person prefix displays suppletive allomorphy, conditioned by whether the stem is vowel- or consonant-initial. On suppletive allomorphy, see Chapter 9.

(13) Lexical conditioning of Nasal Substitution in Tagalog, in environment of prefix *paŋ-*

Undergoer of Nasal Substitution		Non-undergoer of Nasal Substitution	
bugbóg	pa-mugbóg	bigáj	pam-bigáj
'wallo'	'wooden club used to pound clothes during washing'	'gift'	'gifts to be distributed'
búlos	pa-múlos	buʔóʔ	pam-buʔóʔ
'harpoon'	'harpoon'	'whole'	'something used to produce a whole'

In a thorough study of the Tagalog lexicon, Zuraw shows that while Nasal Substitution can never be completely predictable from phonological form, it is also not completely random. A number of factors influence the probability of application of Nasal Substitution. Voicing is one factor. Zuraw shows that, statistically, stems beginning with voiced consonants undergo Nasal Substitution in a much higher proportion than do stems beginning with voiceless consonants (Zuraw 2000: 29). Place of articulation is another factor. A greater-than-average proportion of labial-initial stems undergo Nasal Substitution; with velars, the situation is the opposite, and a lower-than-average proportion undergo the alternation. Dentals fall somewhere in between. In a psycholinguistic experiment in which native Tagalog speakers rated the acceptability of novel derived words in Tagalog, Zuraw was able to show that acceptability judgments paralleled the distribution of Nasal Substitution in the lexicon. Speakers were more likely to accept Nasal Substitution in the environment of a voiced consonant and, with some exceptions, mirrored in their ratings the place of articulation effects as well. Zuraw concludes from this study that speakers are highly sensitive to lexical patterns, even when imperfect, and proposes a model of grammar learning which incorporates and even gradually sharpens and enhances statistical lexical patterns.

On this model, it is to be expected that any dimension of similarity along which lexical items can be grouped is fodder for the conditioning of a phonological pattern: semantic, syntactic, morphological, or phonological.

Whether or not to follow this approach to its logical extreme in describing the grammar of a language is an open question. The argument in favor of recognizing statistical subpatterns in grammar is the mounting evidence from corpus studies and psycholinguistic experiments, like Zuraw's, that speakers are highly sensitive to the statistical profile of the lexicon. The argument against doing so is that the number of lexical subpatterns that could conceivably be identified is dauntingly large, making it impossible to summon psycholinguistic evidence for each one. As a thought experiment, Inkelas et al. (1997) raise the possibility of separate grammars for roots containing at least one closed syllable vs. those containing only open syllables, or separate grammars for roots beginning with consonants vs. those beginning with onsets; cross-cutting these and other imaginable phonological dimensions will, if followed consistently, end up producing as many distinct subgrammars in a language as there are phonologically distinct lexical items.[5]

Phonologists have generally limited themselves in practice to accounting for the phonological generalizations holding over subclasses of lexical items that form independently identifiably natural classes, such as those discussed in this section. However, it is important when working with morphologically justifiable subgrammars not to overlook the potential importance of subterranean statistical patterns in the lexicon.

2.4 The root-affix distinction

The distinction between roots and affixes is relevant to many phonological generalizations. Roots are often subject to phonological size constraints that affixes can flout; conversely, affixes are often limited to smaller segmental inventories than roots exhibit.

In a discussion of root-affix asymmetries, McCarthy and Prince (1995: 116) cite as examples the fact that Sanskrit roots may contain consonant clusters but affixes never do; the fact that Arabic roots may contain pharyngeal consonants, but affixes cannot; and that English suffixes favor coronal consonants, thought to be unmarked phonologically (e.g. Yip 1991). These are all statistical distributional generalizations, similar to those which hold between function and

---

[5] See Golston (1997) for a related proposal, namely that instead of being listed with a phonological underlying form, morphemes are lexically represented as that set of phonological constraints which they violate.

content words. In stress languages in which, as in English, content words are required to have a lexical stress, function words (e.g. prepositions, pronouns, conjunctions, auxiliaries) are typically exempt from this requirement.

There are certainly numerous exceptions to these generalizations. Many languages contain individual roots which are smaller than individual affixes in the same language. The Turkish words *de-mek* 'say-INF' and *gel-ecek* 'come-FUT' are just two of a huge number of examples that can be found across the world's languages. It is well known that most affixes derive historically from free-standing elements (like roots), and that the process of grammaticalization often involves reduction and erosion of the segmental material of the affix. This alone would account for the tendency for affixes to be smaller than roots.

The most interesting development in the literature on phonological root-affix asymmetries is the claim that the root-affix asymmetry extends beyond statistical distributional asymmetries to the phonological behavior of roots and affixes when combined in words. In short, roots are claimed to be more resistant to undergoing alternations than affixes are. McCarthy and Prince (1995) raise root-controlled harmony processes as an example. In vowel harmony systems, one of the basic parameters is the directionality of harmony (see e.g. Rose and Walker 2011 for an overview). In some languages harmony is purely directional (progressive or anticipatory); in other, so-called "dominant" harmony systems, a particular value of the harmonizing feature will spread bidirectionally throughout a word or stem containing it. In still other cases, harmony is triggered by particular morphemes, usually the root. In Ekegusii (also known as Gusii, Bantu; Cammenga 2002), for example, mid vowels in affixes harmonize in [ATR] with mid root vowels (*o, e, ɔ, ɛ*). This is true of prefixes as well as suffixes. In (14), trigger root vowels are single-underlined and harmonizing affix vowels are double-underlined:

(14)   Ekegusii vowel harmony
    o̲-mo̲-te̳   'tree'
    ɔ̳-rɛɛnt-ir-e 'he has brought'
    e-ñu̲ɔ̲m-ɔ̳   'marriage'
    tɔ̳-ɣɛɛnr-ɛ̳ 'let us go'

To account for this type of root-affix asymmetry, McCarthy and Prince (1995) propose a universal constraint ranking which asserts that

THE ROOT-AFFIX DISTINCTION

preserving root structure is more important than preserving affix structure:

(15)   Root-Affix Faithfulness Metaconstraint (RAFM; McCarthy and Prince 1995):
       Root-FAITH >> Affix-FAITH

2.4.1 Examples of root faithfulness

The RAFM predicts that lexical contrasts found in roots may be neutralized in affixes, with the result that affixes either surface with unmarked phonological structure or assimilate to roots (e.g. in vowel harmony). Urbanczyk (2006) makes use of the RAFM to account for asymmetries in reduplication in Lushootseed (see also Downing 2006). Urbanczyk compares two coexisting reduplication constructions: the Diminutive, with a CV reduplication pattern, and the Distributive, with a CVC reduplication pattern. In the Diminutive, the reduplicant vowel defaults to unmarked [i] under most circumstances (16a). By contrast, in the Distributive, the reduplicant vowel is a stressed schwa (16b), a vowel normally found only in roots (and not affixes). Data are from Urbanczyk (2006), citing Bates et al. (1994):

(16)   a. Diminutives   [Lushootseed]
          'foot'   ǰə́səd   → ǰí-ǰəsəd   'little foot'
          'animal hide'   s-kʷə́bšəd   → s- kʷí-kʷəbšəd 'small hide'

       b. Distributives
          'foot'   ǰə́səd   → ǰə́s-ǰəsəd   'feet'
          'bear'   s-čə́txʷəd   → s-čə́t-čətxʷəd   'bears'

Urbanczyk (2006) analyzes the Distributive reduplicant within Generalized Template theory (see also Chapters 4, 5), in which each reduplicant is classified as a Root or as an Affix. In Lushootseed, Urbanczyk classifies CVC Distributive reduplicants as morphological Roots, with all the phonological privileges—stressed schwa, syllable coda contrasts—accorded to Roots but not affixes. Diminutive reduplicants, by contrast, are of type Affix, characterized by the smaller size and vowel inventory of affixes generally.

The RAFM also predicts that the nature of the repair of illicit phonological structures will be affected by whether the segments in question belong to roots or affixes. In a survey of 87 languages, 68 of them in the very large and diverse Niger-Congo family, Casali (1997) finds two strong preferences in the case of vowel hiatus that is resolved via vowel deletion: one is for the first of two consecutive vowels to delete, and the other is for affix vowels to delete. These two interacting preferences add up to the prediction that stem-initial vowels should never delete in order to resolve a VV hiatus and the prefix-stem boundary. Casali identifies 21 cases in which a root vowel deletes if it occupies V1 position (17a), and 41 cases in which the affix vowel deletes, whether it is in first (17b) or second position (17c).

(17) a. Stem vowel deletes before suffix vowel: Turkish progressive suffix (Lewis 1967)

   i. 'understand'   /anla/   [an'la]
   ...+/-dI/ PAST   /anla-dI/   [anla'dɯ]
   -...+/-Ijor/ PROG   /anla + Ijor/ [an'lɯjor]

   ii. cf. 'take'   /al/   ['al]
   ...+/-dI/ PAST   /al-dI/   [al'dɯ]
   -...+/-Ijor/ PROG   /al + Ijor/   [a'lɯjor]

   b. Suffix vowel deletes after stem vowel: Chichewa (Mtenje 1992, Casali p. 521)

   i. /mwana-uyɔ/ → [mwanayɔ]
      'child-that = that child'

   ii. /bambɔ-wa/ → [bambɔwa]
      'man-this = this man'

   iii. /ɲimbɔ-izi/ → [ɲimbɔzi]
      'songs-these = these songs'

   iv. /khasu-ili/ → [khasuli]
      'hoe-this = this hoe'

   c. Prefix vowel deletes before stem vowel: Ndebele (Sibanda 2004: 124, 132)

   i. li-elaph-a   → lelapha 'it (Cl. 5) treats...'
   ii. bu-akh-a   → bakha 'it (Cl. 14) builds'
   iii. si-elaph-a → selapha 'it (Cl. 7) treats...'
   iv. uku-os-a   → ukosa 'to roast' (cf. *uku-misa* 'to stop')
   v. a-a-elaph-a   → elapha '3PL-REMOTE.PST-cure-FV=they
                                       treated/cured'

Casali found no case in his database of a stem-initial vowel deleting following a prefix-final vowel. This outcome would violate not only the phonetically-based preference to preserve the second of two consecutive vowels but also the root faithfulness preference that RAFM encodes.

Accent is another domain in which special faithfulness to roots is in evidence. Alderete (2001b) has drawn recent attention to cases like the following, from Cupeño, in which root accent is treated preferentially. When an accented root and accented affix co-occur in the same word, and one must delete, it is root accent that prevails:

(18)   Accented root + accented affix(es): accent surfaces on root [Cupeño]
    a. /pə́ + √míʔaw + lu/   pə-míʔaw-lu
        3SG + come + MOTION   'He came'

    b. /√ʔáyu + qá/   ʔáyu-qa
        want + PRES.SING   'He wants'

Unaccented root + accented affix(es): accent surfaces on affix, not root

    c. /pə́ + √yax/   pə́-yax
        3SG + say   'He says'

    d. /nəʔən + √yax + qá/ nəʔən ya-qá?
        1SG + say + PRES.SING   'I say'

2.4.2 Counterexamples to the RAFM

McCarthy and Prince's (1995) hypothesis that all languages conform to the ranking in (15) is consistent with the evidence we have seen so far. However, the RAFM is not exceptionless. For example, many alternations occurring at the stem-affix boundary target stem segments and not affix segments, in violation of Root-Faith » Affix-Faith. In a comprehensive study of root vs. affix strength, Pycha (2008a: 52) cites, among other cases, the example of velar deletion in Turkish. As seen in (19), stem-final velars (/k/ and /g/) delete when rendered intervocalic by suffixation (see also Lewis 1967; Zimmer and Abbott 1978; Inkelas and Orgun 1995; Inkelas 2011, among many others who have discussed this phenomenon). Examples are from Inkelas 2011:[6]

---

[6] The deleted velar is represented in the orthography as "ğ". In some dialects of Turkish and even for some speakers of standard Istanbul Turkish, "ğ" manifests as a weak labial glide between round vowels or as a weak palatal glide between front vowels (e.g. Lewis 1967: 5; Göksel and Kerslake 2005: 8).

(19)

	nominative	3rd possessive	dative	[Turkish]
'baby'	bebek	bebe-i	bebe-e	
'street'	sokak	soka-ɯ	soka-a	
'cow'	inek	ine-i	ine-e	
'catalog'	katalog	katalo-u	katalo-a	
'mathematics'	matematik	matemati-i	matemati-e	
'go-REL'	git-tik	git-ti-i	git-ti-e	
'understand-INF'	anla-mak	anla-ma-ɯ	anla-ma-a	

Suffix-initial velars do not delete, even in the same intervocalic phonological environment as the deleting stem-final velars. Examples below are from Inkelas (2011) and Göksel and Kerslake (2005: 62):

(20)   *-gen*   /altɯ-gen/   [al.tɯ.gen]
               'six-GON = hexagon'
               /jedi-gen/   [je.di.gen]
               'seven-GON = septagon'

       -gil-ler /bakla-gil-lAr/   [bak.la.gil.ler]
               'beans-GRP-PL = pulses'
               /amca-sI-gil-lAr/   [am.dʒa.sɯ.gil.ler]
               'uncle-3POSS-GRP-PL = his/her uncle
                   & family'

       -ki   /sene-ki/   [se.ne.ki]
               'year-REL = this year's'
               /ada-DA-ki/   [a.da.da.ki]
               'island-LOC-REL = the one on the island'

The question of why alternations at the stem-affix juncture so commonly target the stem rather than the affix is discussed at greater length in Chapter 8, which focuses on derived environment effects. Here, however, the example simply illustrates the fact that the repair of an ill-formed configuration does not always preferentially target affixes over roots.

Even the otherwise robust generalization of Casali (1997) is not without exceptions, showing that the tendency toward preferential root faithfulness can be overridden. A case of VV hiatus resolution in Nanti in which the affix 'wins' will be discussed in section 2.5.1. Here, we examine the case of Karuk (Karok), which resolves VV hiatus across the boundary between a monosyllabic vowel-final prefix and a vowel-initial root by deleting the root vowel (Bright 1957; see discussion in Kenstowicz and Kisseberth 1979, Koutsoudas 1980). The verb and noun roots in (21b) are underlyingly vowel-initial; CV prefixation produces a VV hiatus which is resolved by V2 deletion.[7] Root allo-morphs are bolded in (21) to make the V~∅ alternations easier to observe. Data and page numbers are from Bright (1957): [8]

(21)   a.   Vowel-initial stems: VV hiatus resolved by deletion

[Karuk]

gloss	No (or C-final) prefix	V-final prefix	gloss
'cook' (33)	**imniš**	ní-**mniš**	'I cook' (33)
'to be cooking' (62)	**imní·štih**	ʔú-**mniš**	'he cooks' (33)
'they're cooking' (62)	kun-í**mni·štih**	ʔú-**mni·štih**	'he's cooking' (62)
'head' (50)	**axvâ·h**	mú-**xvâ·h**	'his head' (50)
'mouth' (49)	**ápma·n**	mú-**pma·n**	'his mouth' (49)
'money' (44)	**išpuka**	mú-**spuka**	'his money' (44)
'jump' (44)	**iškak**	ʔú-**skak**	'he jumps' (44)
'make' (343)	**ikhav**	ʔú-**kyav**	'he makes' (124)
'they make' (126)	kun-í**kyav**		
'leg' (33)	**ʔápsi·h**	naní-**psi·h**	'my leg' (33)
		mú-**psi·h**	'his leg' (33)

b.   Consonant-initial stems

gloss	No (or C-final) prefix	V-final prefix	gloss
'to bleed' (62)	**ʔá·xhi**	ná-**ʔá·xhi**	'I bleed' (62)
		ʔu-**ʔá·xhi**	'he bleeds' (62)
'walk' (61)	**ʔáho·**	ni-**ʔáho·**	'I walk' (61)
'child' (50)	-**ʔáRamah**	mú-**ʔáRamah**	'his child' (50)
'enemy' (49)	**vá·san**	mú-**vá·san**	'his enemy' (49)
'upriver' (57)	**káruk**	nani-**kkáruk**	'upriver from me' (57)
'to like' (DUR) (63)	**ta′pku·puTih**	nu-**tápku·puTih**	'I like you' (63)
		ni-**tapkû·puTih**	'I like him' (63)

---

[7]   If, however, V1 is /a(·)/, vowel contraction (to a lengthened vowel) occurs instead, e.g. /pa-akva·t/ → pa·kva·t 'DEF-raccoon = the raccoon' (Bright 1957: 34), /va-ápsu·n/ → vá·psu·n 'IMPERSONAL.POSS-snake = its snake' (p. 57), /pa-úkra·m/ → pó·kra·m 'DEF-lake = the lake' (p. 34).

[8]   Vowel-initial words undergo /ʔ/ epenthesis, which is transcribed inconsistently in the forms in (21). These forms are all taken directly from Bright (1957), who gives some forms in morphophonemic transcription and others in phonetic transcription. This does not matter as long as it is understood that epenthetic /ʔ/ is not present at the stage at which VV hiatus is created and resolved. The contrast between epenthetic and underlying /ʔ/ can be observed by comparing 'leg', in (21a), with that of 'child', in (21b), which begins with an underlying /ʔ/. 'leg' patterns with vowel-initial stems; 'child' patterns with consonant-initial stems.

Clearly, VV hiatus resolution does not give preference to root vowels in this case.

In the domain of accent, as well, preferential root faithfulness is not universal. In the Yakima dialect of Sahaptin (Penutian; Hargus and Beavert 2006), accent is affix-controlled. The following examples show that the root (underlined) retains its lexical accent only when it combines with unaccented affixes (22a,b). Otherwise, an accented affix draws accent away from the root (22c,d) (Hargus and Beavert 2006: 181):[9]

(22)   Accented root + unaccented affix(es): affix   [Yakima Sahaptin]
        surfaces on root

   a. ʔiʔatɬʼáwiʃa
       /ʔi + ʔatɬʼáwi + ʃa/
       2SG.NOM + beg + IMPRF

   b. 'he's begging him'
       wánpanim
       /wánp + ani + m/
       sing medicine song + BENEFACTIVE + CISLOCATIVE
       'sing for me'

        Accented root + accented prefix(es): accent surfaces on prefix

   c. páʔatɬʼawiʃa
       /pá + ʔatɬʼáwi + ʃa/
       INVERSE + beg + IMPRF
       'he's begging him'

        Accented root + accented suffix(es): accent surfaces on suffix

   d. wanpáwaas
       /wánp + áwaas/
       sing medicine song + INSTRUMENTAL
       'sing medicine song'

The complex morphological sensitivity of accentuation processes will be discussed in more detail in section 2.5.7.

In sum, there are clear cases in which roots are immune to alternations that affixes undergo; it may be the case, though statistical investigation

---

[9] The accentual system is more complicated than what is presented here; Hargus and Beavert (2006) also distinguish a class of "strong" roots, which retain their inherent accent under more conditions than regular accented roots do. Hargus and Beavert posit the overall faithfulness ranking FAITH-SUFFIX » FAITH-ROOT$_{strong}$ » FAITH-PREFIX » FAITH-ROOT.

has not yet been undertaken, the majority of asymmetries are in this direction. However, there are certainly clear examples that go in the opposite direction.

One issue that arises in the study of root vs. affix faithfulness, even in cases where FAITH-root » FAITH-affix is descriptively appropriate, is whether the correct dichotomy is root morpheme vs. affix morpheme, or whether it is bases of affixation vs. the affixes that attach to those bases. The substantive difference between these dichotomies lies in whether complex stems pattern with roots. If they do, then what passes for a FAITH-root » FAITH-affix ranking may instead be reducible to Base-Identity effects of the kinds discussed in Chapter 7 (Interleaving) or Chapter 11 (Paradigmatic effects).

It is also important to observe that the examples cited in the literature in support of FAITH-root » FAITH-affix tend to involve general phonological processes, as opposed to morphologically conditioned alternations associated with specific affixation constructions. The latter will be explored in section 2.5 of this chapter. We will see that they tend to single out roots, or bases of affixation, as targets of alternations. The same is true of process morphology, the topic of Chapter 3. Further research is needed to determine how many counterexamples to the RAFM fall into this category.

2.5 Beyond roots: Morphological construction-specific phonology

The discussion up to this point has focused on static patterns and on root-affix asymmetries, for the most part tacitly maintaining the fiction that the phonological patterns applying within a language are quite general, sensitive only to such large-scale dimensions as root class or morpheme type (root vs. affix).

However, any in-depth investigation inevitably confronts the fact that the bulk of morphologically conditioned phonology resides in the association of phonological patterns with the individual morphological constructions which derive and inflect words. In this section we embark on a broader survey of morphologically conditioned phonology which illustrates that virtually every type of phonological alternation or constraint that can be imposed upon words can be associated with this type of morphological conditioning, in one language or another.

2.5.1 Segment deletion

Segment deletion commonly occurs as a morphologically conditioned phonological process. In Turkish, vowel hiatus arising at stem-suffix boundaries is repaired in most cases by glide epenthesis, as illustrated in (23) by the facilitative suffix /-Iver/. But vowel hiatus created by suffixation of the progressive /-Ijor/ is resolved by vowel deletion:[10]

(23)   [Turkish]

	C-final root		V-final root	
	'do'	'come'	'understand'	'say'
	jap	gel	anla	søjle
Facilitative /-Iver/: epenthesis	jap-ɯver	gel-iver	anla-jɯver	søjle-jiver
Progressive /-Ijor/: deletion	jap-ɯjor	gel-ijor	anl-ɯjor	søjl-yjor

In Nanti (Kampan; Michael 2008), morphological conditioning determines how VV hiatus is resolved across the prefix-stem boundary. In the case of most prefixes, VV hiatus is resolved by deletion of the prefix vowel (24a) (Michael 2008: 149, 241, 243, 268). This is consistent with Casali's (1997) observation that VV hiatus, cross-linguistically, is resolved either by deletion of V1 or by deletion of the affix vowel; in the case of prefix-stem VV hiatus, these descriptions amount to the same thing:

(24) a. /no=am-e/   →   name   [Nanti]
          1S=bring-IRREAL.I   'I'm going to bring'

     cf. /no=keNkitsa-ak-i/   →   nokeNkitsatake
          1S=tell.story=PERF-REALIS.I   'I told a story'

     b.   /pi=ogi-aratiNk-e=ro/   →   pogaratiNkero
          2S=CAUS-stand.up-IRREAL.I=3NMO   [pogaɾatiŋkseɾo]
                                               (*piogiaratiNkero)
          'You will stand it up (e.g. a housepost) (polite imperative)'

     cf. /pi=n-kem-e/   →   pinkeme
          2S=IRREAL-hear-IRREAL.I   'You didn't hear it'

[10] Uppercase letters in underlying representation indicate vowels whose surface quality is determined by progressive vowel harmony; this is the standard convention in analyses of Turkish.

    c. /pi=oog-eNpa=ro/   →   poogeNparo
       2S=consume-IRREAL.A=3NMO   'Please eat it'

    d. /pi=arateh-an-ak-i/   →   paratehanake
       2S=wade-BL-PERF-REAL   'You waded away'

However, in the case of the first person inclusive subject prefix /a-/, VV hiatus is resolved via deletion of the second vowel (Michael 2008: 270, 242). V2 deletion applies straightforwardly in (25a). In (25b), a regular process of intervocalic N-deletion produces a hiatus between /a-/ and the following vowel, and feeds V2 deletion:

(25) a. /a=   obiik -eNpa/   → abiikeNpa
       1PL.INC.S drink -IRREAL.A   (*obiikeNpa)
       'Let's drink!'

    b. /a=   N-   obiik -eNpa oburoki/   → abiikeNpa
                                     oburoki
       1PL.INC.S IRREAL- drink -IRREAL.A manioc.beer (*obiikeNpa
                                     oburoki)

       'Let's drink manioc beer!'

Michael suggests that the root vowel deletion in this case could be attributed to the need to preserve the monovocalic prefix. The 3rd person masculine /i-/ and 3rd person non-masculine /o-/ agreement prefixes in Nanti are also monovocalic. A general $V \rightarrow \emptyset$ / __V rule would delete all three before vowel-initial roots, resulting in homophony that could contribute to confusion (Michael 2008: 268–9). Instead, VV hiatus produced by the three prefixes is resolved differently in each case. The 3rd person non-masculine /i-/ does delete, as (26a), but 1st person inclusive /a-/ triggers root vowel deletion (as seen in (25)), while 3rd person masculine /i-/ glides (26b):[11]

(26) a. /o=   arateh -an -ak   -i/   → aratehanake
       3NMS= wade -ABL -PERF -REAL.I   (*oratehanake)
       'She waded away'

    b. /i=   arateh -an -ak -i/   → yaratehanake
       3MS= wade -ABL -PERF -REAL.I (*iratehanake, aratehanake)
       'He waded away'

---

[11] Michael notes (p. 269) that the 3rd person masculine /i-/ does delete before the only two /i/-initial verb roots in the language, namely *irag* 'cry' and *irak* 'be ripe'. Thus the verb *irigaka* is ambiguous between 'he cried' (/i-irag-ak-a/) and 'she cried' (/o-irag-ak-a/).

Anti-homophony considerations of this kind are discussed in more detail in Chapters 9 and 11. Regardless, the fact that the three vocalic prefixes all behave differently in hiatus situations is in itself evidence of morphological conditioning of vowel deletion.

2.5.2 Gemination

In Hausa, prefixing pluractional verb (27a) and intensive adjective (27b) reduplication are both associated with a process of morphologically conditioned stem-initial gemination that other prefixing constructions do not exhibit (Newman 2000: 16, 47, 234–5, 365, 425). Historically, the gemination arose from CVC reduplication with assimilation across the prefix-stem boundary. Hausa does not tolerate obstruent codas. However, it does generally permit nasal and liquid codas, as illustrated by the words in (27c) which involve prefixes other than those in (27a,b). The gemination in (27a,b) is not forced by the general phonotactics of Hausa; it is morphologically conditioned phonology:

(27) a. 'beat'   búgàː   →   búbbúgàː
          'press down, oppress'   dánnèː   →   dáddànnéː
          'be well repaired'   gʲàːrú   →   gʲàggʲàːrú
          'follow'   bí   →   bíbbí
          'drink'   ʃáː   →   ʃáʃʃáː

      b. 'brittle'   gáutsíː   →   gàggáutsáː
          'strong'   ƙárfíː   →   ƙàƙƙárfáː
          'salty, brackish'   zářtsíː   →   zàzzářtsáː

      c. 'DIM-work'   ɗǎn-táɓà
          'hair-LINKER-mouth= mustache'   gàːʃì-n-bàːkí
          'PROHIBITIVE-2M.SG = don't you!'   ƙář-kà

We saw another case of morphologically conditioned gemination, earlier in (2), in Malayalam, in which gemination serves as a phonological accompaniment to subordinate compounding, but not to coordinate compounding.

2.5.3 Vowel lengthening

It is very common for individual affixes to trigger lengthening on an adjacent syllable. In Turkish, for example, the place name-forming suffix *-iye* triggers lengthening of the vowel /a/ in a stem-final open syllable:[12]

(28)	Orthography	UR	Nominative	Accusative (/-I/)	as place name in /-Ije/
a.	*Murad* (name)	/murad/	[murat]	[muraduɯ]	[muraːdije]
	refah 'comfort'	/refah/	[refah]	[refahɯ]	[refaːhije]
	Ümran (name)	/ymran/	[ymran]	[ymranɯ]	[ymraːnije]
b.	*sultan* 'sultan'	/sultaːn/	[sultan]	[sultaːnɯ]	[sultaːnije]
	zaman 'time'	/zamaːn/	[zaman]	[zamaːnɯ]	

(Although vowel length is phonemic in Turkish and some /a/ vowels in stem-final syllables are underlyingly long (28b), that is not the case for the words in (28a).)

2.5.4 Truncation to a prosodic constituent

Truncation is often associated with specific affixes. Swedish nicknames, in (29), provide one illustration (Weeda 1992: 121, citing original sources):

(29)	a.	alkoholist	→	alk-is	'alcoholic'	[Swedish]
		laboratoriːum	→	labb-is	'lab'	
	b.	mats	→	matt-e	(proper name)	
		fabian	→	fabb-e	(proper name)	

Truncation is most commonly found in hypocoristic or vocative constructions (see e.g. Weeda 1992, Kurisu 2001 for surveys). Germanic nicknames, represented by Swedish in (29), are well known, as is the Japanese nickname-forming pattern in which a longer name is (optionally) truncated to a bimoraic base to which the suffix /-ʧan/ is attached (Poser 1984, 1990; Itô 1990). In Japanese, short vowels count as one mora, and long vowels count as two; coda consonants also count

---

[12] Data, presented in IPA, are from the Turkish Electronic Living Lexicon (TELL): <http://linguistics.berkeley.edu/TELL>. Note: of the two speakers represented in TELL, one has an underlyingly short /a/ vowel in *sultan*, and the other has an underlyingly long vowel, as represented in (28b).

as a single mora. The options are illustrated in (30a–c). Individual bases can vary in how they truncate to two moras, as seen in (30d) (Poser 1990: 82–3, 84, 87):

(30) Girls nickname formation: [Japanese]
      a. (C)VCV
         akira   →   aki-tyan
         megumi   →   megu-tyan
         wa-sabu-roo   →   wasa-tyan

      b. (C)VV
         syuusuke   →   syuu-tyan
         taizoo   →   tai-tyan

      c. (C)VC
         kinsuke   →   kin-tyan

      d. Variation in instantiation of 2-mora "template"
         midori   →   mii-tyan, mit-tyan, mido-tyan
         kiyoko   →   kii-tyan, kit-tyan, kiyo-tyan

      e. ti   →   tii-tyan

Example (30e) illustrates that truncation is a side effect of requiring the base to conform to a bimoraic template. The occasional base that is less than two moras long, as in (30e), has to lengthen, rather than truncate, in order to conform to the size condition.

An example of truncation in a suffixed vocative (used to address others or attract attention) comes from Tswana (Bantu), cited by Weeda (1992: 84–95). In this construction, the base is reduced to a monosyllable and suffixed with -í:

(31) 'blessings'   màtlhɔ́xɔ̀nɔ́lɔ̀   →   tlhɔ̀x-í   [Tswana]
      'trash (female)' màtlàkàlà   →   tlàk-í
      'payer (male)'   mòlèfɛ́   →   lèf-í

Affix-triggered truncation does occur in constructions other than hypocoristics, but is not common, plausibly for the functional reason that truncation eliminates a lot of the segmental structure that distinguishes lexemes from one another. Ambiguity is less important in nicknames than in many other morphological constructions.

Caballero (2008: 123–6) discusses an interesting case of non-hypocoristic truncation in Rarámuri (Uto-Aztecan) which is associated with the denominal suffix -tá and with a noun incorporation construction. As seen, the verbalizing suffix -ta (with allomorphs -ti, -ra) 'make/

become' combines straightforwardly with disyllabic nouns to form verbs (32a,b). If the noun is trisyllabic, however, truncation applies to reduce it to a disyllabic base (32c) (Caballero 2008: 125–6, 310):

(32) a. nori-rá-ma   ré   (cf. *nori* 'cloud') [Rarámuri]
          cloud-VBLZ-FUT:SG   DUB
          'It will get cloudy'

      b. nihé aka-rá-sa   sapato (cf. *aka* 'sandal')
          1SGN sandal-VBLZ-COND   shoes
          'I will wear shoes'

      c. sipu-tá-a   čukú   (cf. *sipúča* 'skirt')
          skirt-VBLZ-PROG   bend
          '(She is) putting on a skirt'

      d. komá-ti-ma   (cf. *komáre* 'comadre')
          comadre-VBLZ-FUT:SG'

Not all Rarámuri suffixes trigger truncation, as the following examples show (Caballero 2008: 59, 139, 141). Truncation is morphologically conditioned.

(33) a. tiyópi-či   < /tiyopa-či/
          church-LOC

      b. banisú-ki-ni-ma
          pull-APPL-DESID-FUT:SG
          'will want to pull for'

      c. wikará-n-čane
          sing-DESID-EV
          'it sounds like they want to sing'

Rarámuri also exhibits base truncation in body part noun incorporation, illustrated in (34), from Caballero (2008: 193). Disyllabic nouns incorporate without incident, but trisyllabic nouns shorten to two syllables by losing their final syllable:

(34) a. /busí + kási/   → busí-kasí
          'eye + break'

      b. /čaméka + repú/   → čame-répu
          'tongue + cut'

      c. /čerewá + bi'wá/   → čere-bíwa
          'sweat + clean'

As Caballero observes (p. 193), this pattern could be analyzed as directly imposed by the incorporation construction, or it could be the indirect result of a three-syllable initial stress window, coupled with the morphologically conditioned phonological requirement that the second member of this construction must be stressed. Regardless, this type of truncation is specific to this construction, exemplifying morphologically conditioned phonology.

Other examples of affixation-associated truncation which is not hypocoristic in nature occur in Japanese denominal verb formation, to be discussed later in this chapter (60), and in Guarijio inceptives, discussed in Chapter 5.

Truncation has played an especially important role in the literature on the phonology-morphology interface because of the light it sheds on phonological representations. The output of truncation usually matches one of the following shapes, identified in the theory of Prosodic Morphology developed by McCarthy and Prince (1996, 1999b):

(35)   prosodic word
       foot
       syllable (heavy or unrestricted)
       mora

The Swedish and Tswana truncation + suffixation constructions shown in (29) and (31) truncate input stems to a (heavy) syllable; the Japanese and Rarámuri constructions in (30), (32), and (34) truncate input stems to a foot. Somewhat more unusual is truncation to one mora. This pattern is illustrated in (36) by Zuni, in which it is associated with the "familiar" suffix -*mme* (36a) and with the first member of compounds (36b) (Newman 1965, via McCarthy and Prince 1996: 49, 1999b):

(36) a. kʷ'alasi kʷ'a-mme   'Crow'   [Zuni]
         suski   su-mme   'coyote'
         kuku   ku-mme   'father's sister'

      b. tukni   tu-mokʷkʷ'anne 'toe-shoe = stocking'
         melika   me-ʔoše   'Non-Indian-be:hungry= hobo'
         pačɥ   pa-lokk'a-akʷe   'Navajo-be:gray = Ramah Navajo'

A contribution of the theory of Prosodic Morphology is the observation that the shapes that truncated stems assume are the same as those featured in prosodic templates (Chapter 4), in reduplication (Chapter 5), and in morphologically conditioned truncation which is not associated with affixation (Chapter 4).

2.5.5 Ablaut and mutation

Vowel ablaut or consonant mutation can accompany overt affixation. These terms refer to alternations in vowels (ablaut) or consonants (mutation) that are too complex or opaquely conditioned to be treated as simple assimilation, dissimilation, or contextual neutralization. Very familiar examples of vowel ablaut include German plurals, such as *Buch* 'book' ~ *Büch-er* 'books', *Koch* 'cook' ~ *Köch-e* 'cooks', which are understood to result historically from assimilation to a front suffix vowel which has since lost the property that originally transparently triggered the alternation.

A less well-known case of vowel ablaut is found in the Papuan language Hua (Haiman 1972, 1998), in which certain suffixes trigger the fronting of stem-final /o/ and /u/ to /e/ and /i/, respectively. Other phonologically similar suffixes do not do this. Data and page numbers from Haiman 1972:

(37)	Basic stem	Suffixed stem	gloss	[Hua]
'eat'	do-	de-ra-'e	'2 DL. have eaten' (1972:41)	
		de-na	'when I eat (in the future)' (1972:37)	
	cf.	do-ga	'when (non-1ˢᵗ, non-singular) eat (in the future) (1972:37)	
	cf.	do-bai-na	'when I eat (in the future)' (1972:37)	
'do'	hu-	hi-s-u (<hu-s-vu)	'may do' (1972:36)	
	cf.	hu-re-s-u (<hu-ro-s-vu)	'may do (perfective)' (1972:36)	
	cf.	hu-bai-s-u (< hu-bai-s-vu)	'may do (progressive)' (1972:36)	

The term "consonant mutation" often evokes the phrasally regulated consonant alternations famously found in Celtic or Mande languages (see e.g. Rice and Cowper 1984; Conteh et al. 1985; Fife and King 1998). However, consonant mutations are also frequently tied to specific word-internal morphological constructions. One example to which we will return in a different context in Chapter 7 is the consonant mutation triggered by the short causative suffix in several Bantu languages. In Cibemba, the short causative /-i/ triggers mutation of the preceding consonant (Hyman 1994, 1995, 2002; see also Zoll 1995). Before the causative, stem-final /p b/ spirantize to *-f-*, and /d t k g/ and /l/ spirantize to *-s-*. The causative /-i/ itself surfaces as an offglide or surfaces as the vowel [i], depending on the place and manner of the surrounding segments. Data from Hyman 1994 (the hook under the causative suffix /i/ indicates that it is a mutation trigger):

(38) a. lub-   'be lost'   luf-į-   'lose'   [Cibemba]
      b. leep-   'be long'   leef-į-   'lengthen'
      c. cind-   'dance'   cins-į-   'make dance'
      d. fiit-   'be dark'   fiis-į-   'darken'
      e. buuk-   'get up'   buus-į-   'get (s.o.) up'
      f. lúng-   'hunt'   lúns-į-   'make hunt'

The Cibemba applicative, which also begins with a high front vocoid, does not trigger mutation, pointing to morphological conditioning of the alternations in (38):

(39) a. sit-   'buy'   sit-il-   'buy for/at'
      b. kak-   'tie'   kak-il-   'tie for/at'
      c. sek-   'laugh (at)'   sek-el-   'laugh (at) for/at'

Among all morphologically conditioned phonological alternations, ablaut and mutation are particularly amenable to analyses in which the apparent need for morphological conditioning is replaced by a phonological representational difference between the constructions which undergo mutation and those which do not. In Hua, for example, we stated that the ablaut triggered by the subjunctive suffix was morphologically conditioned, since the ablaut is not phonologically natural and other phonologically similar suffixes do not trigger it. However, it might be possible to avoid reference to morphological conditioning and instead say that the mutation-triggering suffixes underlyingly possess a floating [-back] feature which links to the stem-final vowel and fronts it. This is the type of analysis developed by Zoll (1995) for Cibemba mutation. Zoll treats the short causative as a subsegment (floating feature) which coalesces with a preceding consonant in a way that the fully segmental vowel of the long causative does not.

If the apparently unpredictable behavior of mutation-triggering morphology could always be attributed to the particulars of the underlying phonological representations of the affixes involved, it might be possible to eliminate mutation and ablaut from the category of morphologically conditioned phonology. The phenomena might instead be analyzed as purely phonologically conditioned. The success of such ventures depends on the ability of phonological theory to contrast abstract representations.

2.5.6 Dissimilation and "exchange" rules

Morphologically conditioned phonological processes include effects where one segment surfaces with a value opposite either to its own input value ("Exchange rules," "toggles") or to the output value of another segment in the same word ("dissimilation"). For useful surveys, see Weigel (1993), Kurisu (2001), Baerman (2007), and DeLacy (2012).

In Kɔnni, Class 1 nouns form their plurals by means of a tonally polar suffix *(-a~ -e)*; its tone dissimilates with respect to the preceding stem tone (Cahill 1998).[13] In (40a), singular noun stems bear H(igh) tone and the plural suffix is L(ow); in (40b), singular stems bear L and the plural suffix is H. (The surface tones of the singulars is affected by the suffixation of H-toned *ŋ*, which is not a tonally polar suffix.) Data adapted from Cahill (1998: 21, 23), with morpheme breaks added.

(40)		gloss	stem tone	singular	plural	[Kɔnni]
	a.	'fish'	H	sí-ŋ	sí-à	
		'house'	H	tígí-ŋ	tíg-è	
		'face mark'	H	wí-ŋ	wí-è	
	b.	'breast'	L	bììsí-ŋ	bììs-á	
		'stone'	L	tă-ŋ	tàn-á	

According to Cahill (1998: 20–21), plural suffixes for all other noun classes are H toned; the polarity exhibited by the Class 1 plurals is morphologically conditioned.

Phenomena similar to this have been documented in a number of other languages; see e.g. Newman (2000) on Hausa, and Pulleyblank (1986) on Margi.

Affix-specific dissimilation can also target stems, as in example (41) from Dholuo, representing the West Nilotic family. In Dholuo, plural suffixation (with *-e*) is associated with voicing dissimilation in the stem:

---

[13] Cahill (1998: 23, fn. 4) attributes the *a~e* variation in suffix vowel quality to root-controlled vowel harmony.

voiced consonants devoice (41a) and voiceless consonants voice (41b). The following data, due to Tucker (1994), are discussed in a survey of morphophonological polarity by DeLacy (2012):

(41)   gloss   singular   plural   [Dholuo]

a.   'open space'   alap   ælæbe
     'hill'   gɔt   gɔdɛ
     'chest'   agɔkɔ   agɔgɛ
b.   'book'   kitæbu   kitepe
     'twig'   kɛdɛ   kɛtɛ
     'year'   hɪga   hike

Dissimilation alternations are a challenge for item-based theories of morphology because of the difficulty in positing a single representation for the affix in question that would unambiguously result in dissimilation; see e.g. Trommer (2012) for a proposal to handle Dholuo polar alternations with devoicing and truncation. Even if one posited both H and L tone in Kɔnni suffixes, or both [+voice] and [-voice] autosegments as part of the Dholuo plural suffix, it would still be necessary to posit a morphologically specific phonological statement to ensure that the dissimilatory option is chosen.

The robustness of morphophonological polarity has been called into question by DeLacy (2012), who carefully examines the Dholuo case and shows that the data which appear to illustrate the morphophonological polarity are only a subset of the data that should be considered; examining the full set of plurals reveals four different morphologically conditioned mutation patterns: devoicing, desonorization, devocoidization, and vowel deletion. Which pattern a given morpheme will exhibit is not predictable. While some singular-plural pairs exhibit polar differences, this is not the overarching pattern in the language. DeLacy suggests that the cross-linguistic rarity of convincing examples of morphophonological parity may be due to historical factors such as susceptibility to reanalysis.

2.5.7 Stress/pitch-accent (re)assignment

Stress and accent shift are very frequent morphologically conditioned concomitants of affixation and other overt morphological processes, as in the example of English stress-shifting suffixes in (3).

An example from Hausa, a lexical tone language with H and L tone, is given in (42). In Hausa, a number of morphological constructions, including some of the plural classes, trigger the replacement of base stem tone with a new tonal melody, whose H and L tones associate to the syllables of the base in a predictable manner (Newman 1986, 2000):

(42)   a. Example suffixes with tone replacement

[Hausa]

máːlàm	→	màːlàm-ái	'teacher-PL'	-LH
rìːgáː	→	ríːg-únàː	'gown-PL'	-HL
tàmbáyàː	→	támbáy-óːyíː	'question-PL'	-H

b. Example suffixes without tone replacement

dáfàː	→	dáfàː-wá	'cook-PPL'	-LH
gàjéːréː	→	gàjéːr-ìyáː	'short-FEM'	-LH
hùːláː	→	hùːlâ-r̃	'hat-DEF'	-L

In Japanese, morphological constructions, which include prefixation, suffixation, zero-derivation, and compounding, come in two essential varieties: those which preserve lexical stem accent and those which erase it. Poser (1984) terms the two types "recessive" and "dominant," respectively, building on terminology introduced in Kiparsky (1973) (see also Kiparsky and Halle 1977, Halle and Mohanan 1985). Japanese pitch-accent is subject to strict distributional regularities: each word has at most one accent, and in cases of conflict between two lexically accented morphemes in the same word, the general principle is that the leftmost accent wins (Poser 1984). Recessive suffixes, as shown in (43), behave according to the "Leftmost Wins" principle. An unaccented suffix, e.g. past tense -ta, leaves stem accent unaffected (43a), while an accented recessive suffix, e.g. conditional -tára, surfaces with its accent only if the stem is not already lexically accented (43b). Otherwise, Leftmost Wins results in the elimination of suffix accent (43c). Page numbers are from Poser (1984):

(43)   Recessive affixes   [Japanese]

a. Unaccented (p. 49)

yóm-	→ yóN-da	'read'
yob-	→ yoN-da	'called'

b. Accented (p. 48)

yóm-	→ yóN-dara	'if he reads'
yob-	→ yoN-dára	'if he calls'

c. Preaccenting (p. 54)

áNdoo	→ áNdoo-si	'Mr. Ando'
nisímura	→ nisímura-si	'Mr. Nishimura'
matumoto	→ matumotó-si	'Mr. Matsumoto'

In contrast to recessive affixes, dominant affixes trigger deletion of stem-accent. Some suffixes are purely accent-deleting, as in (44a), so that the words they produce are unaccented, regardless of base accent. Other dominant affixes are associated with accentual patterns that wipe out any accent the stem brings along. Accented dominant suffixes, as in (44b), surface with accent, instead of succumbing to Leftmost Wins (cf. the behavior of recessive accented suffixes in (43b)). Still other dominant suffixes place accent on the final or penultimate stem syllable, as illustrated by the family naming -*ke* suffix (44c), or the girls' name-forming -*ko* (44d). The "true" prefix *ma(C)-* is dominant post-accenting, putting accent on the stem-initial syllable (44e):

(44)   Dominant affixes

    a. Unaccented suffix (p. 72)

kóobe	→	koobe-kko	'an indigené of Kobe'
nágoya	→	nagoya-kko	'an indigené of Nagoya'
nyuuyóoku	→	nyuuyooku-kko	'an indigené of New York'

    b. Accented suffix (p. 49)

abura	→	abura-ppó-i	'oil, fat/oily'
yásu	→	yasu-ppó-i	'cheap/cheap, tawdry'
adá	→	ada-ppó-i	'charming/coquettish'

    c. Pre-accenting suffix (p. 55)

nisímura	→	nisimurá-ke	'the Nishimura family'
ono	→	onó-ke	'the Ono family'
hára	→	hará-ke	'the Hara family'

    d. Penult-accenting suffix (p. 58–9)

haná	→	hána-ko		'flower/name'
kaede	→	kaéde-ko		'maple/name'
mídori	→	midóri-ko	~ midorí-ko	'green/name'

    e. Post-accenting prefix (p. 57)

futatu	→	map-pútatu	'two/exactly half'
sáityuu	→	mas-sáityuu	'amidst/in the very midst of'
syoozíki	→	mas-syóoziki	'honesty/downright honest'

Affixes that McCawley (1968) and Tsujimura (1996) call "preaccenting" and which Poser calls "dependent" have an accent that "is realized only if the base form to which they are attached is accented" (Poser 1984: 50). These affixes cause stem accent to shift to a designated syllable, but have no effect on unaccented stems.

(45)   Dependent affixes
    a. Accent shifts to suffix (p. 50)
        a'u   →   ai-te'   'meet/companion'
        ka'ku   →   kaki-te'   'write/writer'
        kataru →   katari-te 'recount/narrator'
    b. Accent shifts to stem-final (p. 55)
        kona'   →   kona'-ya   'flour/flour seller'
        ku'zu   →   kuzu'-ya   'junk/junk man'
        kabu   →   kabu-ya   'stock/stockbroker'

Example (46), compiled from Tsujimura (1996: 90–92), illustrates how the accentuation of the same noun stem can vary according to what kind of suffix it combines with.[14] The lexical accent patterns of the noun stems surface in combination with the recessive suffixes. Boldface is used to draw attention to stems and suffixes that surface with accent other than what is in their underlying representation:

(46)

	Recessive, unaccented	Recessive, accented	Dominant, accented	Dependent
stem	-ga (NOM)	-ma'de 'even'	-gu'rai 'about'	-sika 'only'
i'noti 'life'	i'noti-ga	i'noti-**made**	**inoti**-gu'rai	i'noti-sika
koko'ro 'heart'	koko'ro-ga	koko'ro-**made**	**kokoro**-gu'rai	koko'ro-sika
atama' 'head'	atama'-ga	atama'-**made**	**atama**-gu'rai	atama'-sika
miyako 'capital'	miyako-ga	miyako-ma'de	miyako-gu'rai	**miyako'**-sika

Thus for each affix, or more generally for each morphological construction, since in Japanese, compounding and zero-derivation are subject to similar accentual parameters (see Chapter 3), it is necessary to know which of several possible accent placement patterns the affix triggers (none, stem-initial, stem-final, stem-penultimate) and whether those patterns preserve or delete lexical stem accent (dominant vs. recessive).

---

[14] Recall that Tsujimura uses the term "preaccenting" for the column labeled here "dependent".

2.6 Substance of morphologically conditioned phonology

As far as is known, any kind of phonological pattern, other than the most low-level allophonic alternations, may be associated with a morphological construction; most so-called "unnatural" phonological alternations (such as *ki* → *tʃi*, or post-nasal devoicing) are morphologically conditioned in this way (see e.g. Spencer 1998).

Seeking finer-grained generalizations, Smith (2001, 2011) has offered the interesting observation that the majority of phonological phenomena which are specific to part of speech (nouns or verbs) are prosodic in nature. A similar observation has been made for prosodically optimizing suppletive allomorphy (Paster 2008) and common infixation sites (Yu 2007). Yu suggests, for infixation, that this pattern has to do with breadth of generalization; prosodic parameters are ones for which all words have a value (since all words have syllables and, in certain languages, stress or pitch-accent), permitting generalizations for which all words are probative.

2.7 Generalizing over the morphological conditioning of phonology within a language

An interesting question that has been addressed for decades in the literature is the degree to which morphologically conditioned phonological patterns can differ from one another within the same language.

Both qualitative and quantitative answers have been suggested. On the quantitative side, it has been proposed that the number of distinct morphologically conditioned patterns in a given language may be strictly limited to two or three. On the qualitative side, it has been suggested that distinct morphologically conditioned patterns in the same language differ from one another in a principled way, namely the relative degree of faithfulness to lexical entries. We will examine these and other hypotheses in the next sections.

2.7.1 How many types of morphologically conditioned phonological patterns can there be in a language?

The question of how many distinct morphologically conditioned patterns a given language may have is the topic of much discussion in the literature. It is the main parameter differentiating Cophonology Theory (Orgun 1996; Inkelas et al. 1997; Anttila 2002; Inkelas and Zoll 2005,

2007) from Level Ordering theories, i.e. Lexical Morphology and Phonology (LMP; Kiparsky 1982abc, 1984, 1985; Mohanan 1986) and its successor, Stratal Optimality Theory (Stratal OT; Kiparsky 2000, 2008). In Cophonology Theory, each individual morphological construction is associated with its own phonological subgrammar, or "cophonology." In Level Ordering theory, the morphological conditioning of phonology is accomplished by assigning each morphological construction to one of 2, 3, or 4 distinct levels or strata, each associated with its own phonological subgrammar.

For example, Mohanan (1982) proposes the following level ordering schema for Malayalam:

(47)   Stratum 1: Derivation (negative, unproductive causative, among others)
       Stratum 2: Subcompounding, productive causative suffixation
       Stratum 3: Cocompounding
       Stratum 4: Inflection (case and tense)

The division of the morphology into four levels is motivated, on the phonological side, by different characteristic phonological patterns that each level exhibits.

In Level Ordering theory it is necessary to know only the level to which a morphological construction belongs to predict which phonological patterns it will conform to. In this family of theories, the subgrammars, called "levels" or "strata," are assumed to be ordered, such that all the morphological constructions associated with Level 1 phonology apply first, all those associated with Level 2 phonology occur next, and so on. Stratal OT is the latest theory to incorporate claims of this kind.

However, Level Ordering theory has typically attended only to the most general phonological patterns, leaving the more narrowly conditioned ones aside; thus it is not a very good fit with the data from many languages with complex morphology and considerable morphophonemic alternations.

In part this deficiency is due to the claim that levels are strictly ordered. For example, Czaykowska-Higgins (1993) observes that Level Ordering theory would require at least ten levels to account for morphologically conditioned stress patterns in Moses-Columbia Salish (Nxa'amxcin). Suffixes in Nxa'amxcin are either dominant (stress-shifting) or recessive (stress-preserving), in terms of their effect on base stress. Yet, as Czaykowska-Higgins observes, there is no way to predict this phonological difference from the morphological properties of suffixes. Dominant and recessive suffixes are freely interspersed among each other in Nxa'amxcin words.

In part the deficiency of Level Ordering theory is due to the fact that in many languages, the sheer number of distinct phonological patterns exceeds the number of levels posited as universally available in existing stratal models. For example, although nobody has proposed a level ordering system for Hausa, data like that in (42) show that Hausa requires a number of cophonologies simply to account for the numerous different tonal effects that constructions can have on the stems they apply to. Hausa would require more phonologically distinct levels than Level Ordering theory has ever proposed, if all of its lexical phonology is to be accounted for.

In a genetically balanced survey of 70 typologically diverse languages, Bickel et al. (2009) counted the number of "phonological word" domains in each language. Bickel et al. define phonological word domains as "sound pattern domains that are delimited by some morphological structure but do not include more than one lexical stem." Their definition is narrower than the criteria defining a stratum, in Level Ordering theory, in that they exclude compounding, but is otherwise comparable; they specifically exclude from consideration phonological words which would be defined only by a subset of affixes, such that their phonological word domains are much more general (and fewer in number) than the cophonologies of Cophonology Theory. Even with this highly restrictive definition, Bickel et al. found between 1 and 19 phonological word domains in 63 of the languages. Half of those languages had 1–5 phonological word domains, and the other half had more. (Of the original 70 languages in the survey, seven didn't have any phonological word domains general enough to meet the criteria of Bickel et al.)

Level Ordering theory focuses attention on broad generalizations within a language. However, a more flexible model like Cophonology Theory is necessary to fully describe any individual system.

Even in Malayalam, an original poster child for the restrictive model of Lexical Morphology and Phonology, Mohanan and Mohanan (1984: 588) observe that the rule of Palatalization is not accommodated by the Level Ordering model:

[T]he effects of Palatalization being blocked in plurals and across the "compound boundary" cannot be derived by restricting its domain of application in any fashion: it is clear that the rule must apply at least at stratum 2 and stratum 4. At stratum 2, however, it applies to causative and verbalizing suffixes and not to compounds, and at stratum 4 it applies to the dative and not the plural. Perhaps the right solution is to say that Palatalization is blocked when the segment has some ad hoc diacritical feature [-P]...the plural has [-P], but not the causative and verbalizing suffixes. This leaves the problem of accounting for the absence of Palatalization in compounds. It is important to note that the stem-initial velar of a compound does not undergo Palatalization, even if a medial consonant in the same morpheme does. Thus, the second velar in *kanak'am* 'gold' palatalizes, but the initial one does not, in the compound *paccakkanak'am* 'green gold'. Therefore, the exceptionality is a feature of the segment, not the morpheme. What we need, in these cases, is a lexical redundancy rule that marks all stem-initial segments as [-P], thereby preventing palatalization across the stems of a compound (or across words).

2.7.2 How different can morphologically conditioned patterns in the same language be from one another?

The question of quantitative differences among phonological subgrammars, or cophonologies, in the same language is no more vexing than the question of qualitative differences. The essential challenge faced by any model of morphologically conditioned phonology is in characterizing the "genius" of a language, i.e. of capturing the phonological generalizations that the language hews to despite other internal variation, and of constraining language-internal diversity so that it is in some principled way more limited than the kind of diversity that distinguishes languages from one another.

This challenge has been met in several different ways.

(48)   Proposed means of constraining language-internal phonological variation
   • Strong Domain Hypothesis (Lexical Morphology and Phonology; Kiparsky 1984)
   • Stratum Domain Hypothesis (Lexical Morphology and Phonology; Mohanan 1986)
   • Grammar Dependence (Alderete 1999, 2001a)
   • Grammar Lattice (Anttila 1997, 2002)

Within Lexical Morphology and Phonology, Kiparsky (1984) and Mohanan (1986) advanced the Strong Domain Hypothesis and the Stratum Domain Hypothesis, respectively. Both are defined in terms of ordered levels and are formulated within rule-ordering theory. The Stratum Domain Hypothesis holds that if a phonological rule applies within two different levels (e.g. 1 and 3), it must also apply at all intervening levels (e.g. 2). It prevents rules from turning "on" and "off" willy-nilly in a level ordering system. The Strong Domain Hypothesis takes this restriction one step further, requiring all rules in a level-ordered system to apply at level 1, so that rules may "turn off" at different levels, but must all apply from the beginning.

These proposals, while restrictive and interesting, have fallen out of favor. As has been mentioned in this chapter and is discussed in more detail in Chapter 7, level ordering has been challenged by counter-evidence; without level ordering, the Strong and Stratum Domain Hypotheses are not coherent. Furthermore, the approaches do not translate straightforwardly into Optimality Theory, another reason that they are no longer front and center in the theoretical literature.

Within Stratal Optimality Theory, Kiparsky (2008) has suggested that the phonologies of strata in the same language differ in restricted ways: the constraint ranking of one level, e.g. Word, may differ from the constraint ranking of a lower level, e.g. Stem, only by "promotion of one or more constraints to undominated status." For example, Kiparsky (2008) argues that alternating secondary stress in Finnish is optional at the Stem level but obligatory at the Word level, due to the promotion of *Lapse above *Stress at the Word level. Without a more elaborated theory of how many constraints can be undominated and whether constraints can leapfrog over one another into undominated position in successively higher strata, however, this proposal is not sufficiently explicit to generate substantive predictions about stratal variation within a language.

The most explicitly worked out proposals for restricting language-internal variation are Grammar Dependence, formulated within the mono-stratal Indexed Constraint Theory, and Grammar Lattices, formulated within Cophonology Theory.

Grammar Dependence is the hypothesis, developed in work by Fukazawa et al. (1998), Itô and Mester 1999, Alderete (1999, 2001a), and Kawahara (2001), that morphologically conditioned phonological patterns in the same language may differ from one another only in the degree to which they preserve underlying structure from the effects of the language's general phonological requirements. The term "Grammar Dependence" reflects the claim that the "genius" of a language lies in its fixed ranking of markedness constraints. Only the ranking of faithfulness constraints can vary across morphological environments, predicting greater and lesser degrees of compliance with the basic phonology of the language.

This approach works very effectively for cases like the Japanese stratal differences discussed by Itô and Mester and illustrated earlier in (10). The ranking in (49), repeated from (11), illustrates the differential ranking of morphologically specific faithfulness constraints within the fixed markedness hierarchy (Itô and Mester 1999: 73):

(49) FAITH$_{\text{UnassimForeign}}$ » No-NT » FAITH$_{\text{AssimForeign}}$ » No-P » FAITH$_{\text{SinoJapanese}}$ » No-DD » FAITH$_{\text{Yamato}}$

Adhering to Grammar Dependence reduces the overall number of distinct phonological patterns that a language can enforce. Grammar Dependence is also intended to rule out markedness reversals, in which the reranking of markedness constraints could allow cophonologies to differ in the unmarked structures that they impose when faithfulness permits. The Grammar Dependence view is that all languages should be like Japanese, with a series of successively stricter patterns imposed in different morphological environments.

However, as Itô and Mester (1993, 1995ab, 1999) have observed, even Japanese does not conform to this expectation. The mimetic vocabulary stratum in Japanese allows /p/ but bans voiceless postnasal obstruents; the No-NT » FAITH$_{\text{Mimetic}}$ » No-P ranking is inconsistent with the No-P » No-NT ranking required for the Sino-Japanese stratum (49), which obeys No-P but allows voiceless postnasal obstruents. Further discussion of the predictions of Grammar Dependence can be found in Rice (1997), Fukazawa et al. (1998), and Inkelas and Zoll (2008), among others.

An approach to understanding language-internal variation which affords more flexibility than Grammar Dependence is the Grammar Lattice approach, formulated within Cophonology Theory by Anttila (1997, 2002; see also Anttila and Cho 1998). On this view, generalizations over cophonologies in the same language are captured by organizing cophonologies in an inheritance hierarchy according to the similarity of the patterns they impose. Anttila models his Grammar Lattice theory in the Optimality framework, so that cophonology similarity is defined by the partial constraint ranking that two cophonologies share. Cophonologies inherit shared constraint rankings from a subordinate metaconstruction defined by the shared properties. All cophonologies inherit from the top node in the lattice; the partial constraint ranking there, or what Inkelas and Zoll (2008) term the "Master Ranking," is what corresponds to the "genius" of the language.

To illustrate with a very simple example, consider the case of Turkish VV hiatus resolution, illustrated earlier in (23). As analyzed by Inkelas and Zoll (2008), all suffix constructions in Turkish share the imperative that hiatus be resolved, i.e. the ranking *VV » {Dep-C, Max-V}, which both cophonologies conform to. This partial ranking of constraints is fixed in the Master Ranking which all individual constructions inherit (must conform to). It is left to the individual cophonologies to further specify the relative ranking of DEP-C (which bans glide insertion) and Max-V (which bans vowel deletion):

(50)

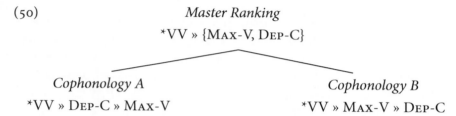

Master Ranking

VV » {MAX-V, DEP-C}

Cophonology A
*VV » DEP-C » MAX-V

Cophonology B
*VV » MAX-V » DEP-C

In this very simple grammar lattice, only one node (the top) has a partial constraint ranking. It is, however, also possible for subordinate nodes to themselves be associated with partial constraint rankings, as Anttila has demonstrated, based on larger fragments of Finnish grammar (see in particular Anttila 1997, 2002, 2009).

To wrap up this discussion, theories of morphologically conditioned phonology share the goal of capturing generalizations about what the internal patterns of a language have in common, while still allowing for observed variation. Frameworks vary greatly in detail, perhaps because the empirical generalizations about degree of language-internal variation are still not clear. Future research is needed to illuminate this corner of the phonology-morphology interface.

2.7.2.1 Noun privilege   Approaching the issue of qualitative variation from a different angle, Smith (2001, 2011) has proposed that languages tend to be restricted in the ways in which part-of-speech-sensitive phonology can differ. In a survey of languages in which phonological patterns are specific to nouns or to verbs, Smith found that the majority pattern is "noun privilege," in which nouns exhibit more contrasts and are less subject to phonological neutralization than verbs. Smith also observes that most of the patterns of this kind that turned up in the survey involved prosodic properties: size, stress, tone.

An example from Rarámuri illustrates the tendency Smith has documented. According to Caballero (2008: 76), vowel hiatus (VV) in Rarámuri is treated differently in nouns and verbs. VV occurs, and is tolerated, in nominal roots (51), but is not found inside verb roots:

(51) čo.ké.a.ri   'mountain dove'   [Rarámuri]
      ko.čí.a.-ra   'eyebrow-POSS'
      wí.a   'rope'
      a.wa.kó.a.ni   'scorpion'

According to Smith, this type of asymmetry follows from a potentially universal ranking of faithfulness constraints:

(52) FAITH-Noun » FAITH-Verb

When a markedness constraint, e.g. *VV in Rarámuri, is ranked between the two category-specific faithfulness constraints, contrast asymmetries between the two parts of speech are the result.

The ranking in (52) is not universal; for example, in Turkish, the productive alternation whereby intervocalic stem-final /g/ and /k/ delete between vowels applies only to nouns (53a,b), and not to verbs (53c,d):

(53) a. [be.bek] [be.be.i]   b. [ba.dem.dʒik] [ba.dem.dʒi.i] [Turkish]
         /bebek/ /bebek-I/   /badem-CIk/ /badem-CIk-I/
         'baby' 'baby-ACC'   'almond-DIM' 'almond-DIM-ACC'

      c. [bi.rik] [bi.ri.ken]   d. [ge.rek]   [ge.re.ki.jor]
         /birik/ /birik-En/   /gerek/   /gerek-Ijor/
         'gather' 'gather-REL'   'be necessary' 'be necessary-PROG'

Many of the most often-cited cases in which phonology is sensitive to lexical class, including most those cited by Smith, resemble the Rarámuri example in that the asymmetry is observed to hold among monomorphemic roots. It is much harder to find a language in which one phonological generalization holds of all nouns, whether monomorphemic or derived, and different phonological generalization holds of all verbs, whether monomorphemic or derived. In Turkish, for instance, while verb roots differ from noun roots in resisting velar deletion, verb suffixes ending in /k/ do undergo it (e.g. /gel-ECEK-E/ 'come-FUT-DAT' → [ge.le.dʒe.e]. The Turkish noun vs. verb asymmetry is limited to roots and does not extend to complex stems.

The same is true of Rarámuri, in which Caballero (2008: 76) observes a double asymmetry in the distribution of VV hiatus. Root-internally, only nouns, and no verbs, exhibit underlying VV hiatus. Some examples are given (54a).[15] Across morpheme boundaries, however, the situation is

---

[15] Caballero (2008: 77) observes that optional semivowel deletion can produce surface VV sequences even within verb roots, e.g. *rejéniri ~ raéniri* 'sun', *kajéni-ri ~ kaéni-ri*

reversed: only verbs—and not nouns—permit vowel hiatus. Junctural hiatus in verbs is illustrated in (54b) (data from Caballero 2008: 75–6, 61):

(54) a. čoké.ari   'mountain dove'   [Rarámuri]
         koči.a-ra   'eyebrow-POSS'
         awakó.ani   'scorpion'

      b. reté.a   'play-PROG'
         ča'.í.-a   'grab-PROG'
         niká.-o   'bark-EP'
         bo.ti.wí.-o   'sink-EP'
         lamú-ami   'purple-PTCP'

      c. pó-a-ra   'cover-PROG-PURP' = 'lid', lit. 'for covering'
         osí-a-ra   'write-PROG-PURP' = 'pen', lit. 'for writing'

      d. ika-méa   'be windy-FUT.SG'
         nori-méa   'be cloudy-FUT.SG'

Interestingly, as illustrated in (54c) (Caballero 2008: 61, 433), it is possible for a VV-containing verb stem (*po-a-*) or *(osí-a)* to be nominalized via suffixation, in which case the inherited internal VV hiatus is preserved. And in (54d) we see that a verbal suffix, marking future singular, itself exhibits VV hiatus (Caballero 2008: 116). Thus it is not generally the case that only verbs permit VV hiatus across junctures, nor that verbs permit VV hiatus only across morphological junctures. The asymmetry appears simply to consist of the fact that verb roots themselves do not exhibit VV hiatus.

The difficulty in finding a pervasive noun phonology in a language, which contrasts with a pervasive verb phonology in the same language, is undoubtedly related to the fact that it is common to find a great deal of phonological variety among the individual morphological constructions into which noun and verb roots can enter, as seen in section 2.5. To illustrate the complication this poses for testing the hypothesis of noun privilege, we turn to a case study of Japanese.

2.7.2.2 Case study: Japanese   Even Japanese, perhaps the most-cited example in the literature of a noun-verb asymmetry because of its accentuation patterns, does not generalize the asymmetry to complex nouns and verbs. In example (6) we saw that the location of monomorphemic noun

---

'harvest-PAST'. However, this is arguably a postlexical process, not one that falls within the scope of morphophonology.

accent is contrastive, while the location of monomorphemic verb accent is predictable and not contrastive. This is a clear example of a case in which noun faithfulness outranks markedness constraints enforcing the location of accent, while verb faithfulness is outranked by markedness. However, the morphological constructions deriving new nouns and verbs, or inflecting existing nouns and verbs, exhibit wide variety and do not conform overall to a simple generalization of noun faithfulness outranking verb faithfulness.

As seen earlier, Japanese affixes differ along several basic accentual parameters. Dominant affixes trigger the erasure of base accent; recessive affixes do not. Some affixes are inherently accented; others are not. Some affixes are associated with accentuation patterns placing accent on the stem-final syllable; others are not.

In assessing the noun privilege hypothesis, we may consider dominant suffixes to neutralize the contrast between accented and unaccented inputs, while recessive suffixes and dependent suffixes preserve that contrast. The question for the noun privilege hypothesis, or more generally for the question about how broadly part-of-speech-sensitive phonology is applied through a lexicon, is whether it applies to derived parts of speech or pertains only to nonderived stems.

In the case of Japanese, the noun privilege hypothesis would predict that nominal morphology would be recessive (preserving contrast), whereas contrast-neutralizing dominant or preaccenting (dependent) accentual patterns would be associated with verbal morphology.

To test this hypothesis, we look first at part-of-speech-preserving constructions. These include derivational constructions (deriving nouns from nouns, or verbs from verbs) as well as inflectional ones. Here we see considerable accentual variety (Poser 1984: 55, 72):

(55) Accentual variation among nominal affixes   [Japanese]
    a. Recessive (see 43c, 46a,b), e.g. unaccented nominative -*ga*

i'noti	→ i'noti-ga	'life-NOM'
koko'ro	→ koko'ro-ga	'heart-NOM'
miyako	→ miyako-ga	'capital-NOM'

    b. Dominant (see 44a,c,d), e.g. unaccented -*kko*

nágoya	→ nagoya-kko	'an indigené of Nagoya'
nyuuyóoku	→ nyuuyooku-kko	'an indigené of New York'

    c. Dependent (see 45b), e.g. pre-accenting -*ya*:

ku'zu	→ kuzu'-ya	'junk/junk man'
kabu	→ kabu-ya	'stock/stockbroker'

A comparable range of accentual variation is observed with verbal morphology. Recessive verbal morphology includes the unaccented past tense -ta, seen in (43a), as well as accented suffixes such as the conditional (43b) and the provisional -re'ba, as seen in (56a). Dominant verbal morphology is illustrated in (56b) by a politeness suffix, accented -ma's, which deletes base accent. Several dependent verbal suffixes are illustrated in (56c,d). Both the causative -(s)ase and passive -(r)are trigger the regular verbal accentuation rule, but only if the input stem is itself accented, in which case accent shifts to the syllable containing the penultimate mora. The verbal negative suffix -na'i is dependent preaccenting. It shifts stem accent, if any, to the stem-final vowel; otherwise, i.e. if the input stem is unaccented, the inherent accent of -na'i surfaces. Data and page numbers from Poser 1984:

(56) Accentual variation among verbal affixes
   a. Recessive (see (43a,b), as well as -re'ba (creates provisional form of verb) (p. 71)
      kake'ru 'be broken'   → kake'-reba
      kakeru   'hang'   → kake-re'ba

   b. Dominant: -ma's 'politeness to addressee' (p. 49)
      yo'm-   'read'   → yomi-ma'si-ta (PAST -ta = recessive, unaccented)
      yob-   'call'   → yobi-ma'si-ta (see (43a))

   c. Dependent preaccenting: -(s)ase (causative), -(r)are (passive) (p. 72)
      yo'm-   'read'   → yom-a're-ta
                             → yom-a'se-ta
      yob-   'call'   → yob-are-ta
                             → yom-ase-ta

   d. Dependent preaccenting: -na'i (negative) (p. 99)
      kake'ru 'hang'   → kake'-nai
      kakeru   'be broken'   → kake-na'i
      sukuu   'rescue'   → sukuwa-na'i

In sum, the accentuation asymmetry between nouns and verbs almost disappears under affixation. The main residue of the stem asymmetry occurs under recessive affixation, in which the asymmetric accentual properties of noun and verb roots are preserved. As Poser points out, the gerund, participle, and past tense forms of the verb fall into this category. The details of morphologically conditioned accentuation in

Japanese are intricate and interesting, and full justice cannot be done to them here. The crucial observation is that it does not seem to be the case, as a simple noun privilege hypothesis might predict, that contrast preservation is limited to nouns, or that contrast neutralization is limited to verbs. Both types of accentuation are found in both parts of speech.

A second point of comparison between derived nouns and verbs is compounding. Here, the parts of speech differ noticeably in their accentuation patterns. Verb-verb compounds are always accented, regardless of the accentual status of the input members. In (57a), both members are accented; in (57b), neither member is. (57c) and (57d) illustrate compounds in which one member is accented. Accent in verbal compounds is assigned according to the default rule for verbs, i.e. to the syllable containing the penultimate mora (Poser 1984: 53):

(57)   Verb-verb compounds in Japanese

     a. bu't   ko'm   buti-ko'mu
       'hit'   'be full'   'throw into'

     b. hik   mekur   hiki-meku'ru
       'pull'   'strip off' 'peel'

     c. yo'm   oe   yomi-oe'ru
       'read'   'finish'   'finish reading'

     d. kari   tao'su   kari-tao'su
       'borrow' 'cheat'   'bilk'

By contrast, noun-noun compounds follow a more complex pattern. In "long" nominal compounds, namely those in which the second member of the compound is more than 2 moras long, the compound is always accented, with the location of accent depending on the location of accent (if any) in the second member. According to Poser (1984), if the second member of the compound "is unaccented or accented on the final syllable, the compound is accented on the first syllable of the second member. If the second member is accented elsewhere, its accent becomes the accent of the whole compound."[16] Data are from Tsujimura (1996):

(58)   "Long" noun-noun compounds in Japanese
     a. Unaccented second member (p. 81)
       ni'   kuruma   ni-gu'ruma
       'load' 'car'   'cart'

---

[16] Tsujimura (1996) modifies the generalization about final-accented second members in such a way that either final- or penultimate-mora accent qualifies; see pp. 85–6.

    b. Final-accented second member (p. 80)

hanari'	musume'	hanauri-mu'sume
'flower selling'	'girl'	'girl who sells flowers'

    c. Second member with non-final accent (p. 80)

yama'	hototo'gisu	yama-hototo'gisu
'mountain'	'quail'	'mountain quail'

This comparison supports the noun privilege hypothesis in that at least some noun-noun compounds preserve the contrast between presence and absence of input accent, while verb-verb compounds do not. However, the location of accent in noun-noun compounds is not contrastive, any more than it is in verb-verb compounds. The details of compound accentuation are, like the details of nominal and verbal suffix accentuation, intricate and interesting; much more detail can be found in McCawley (1968), Poser (1984), Tsujimura (1996), and others.

    A third point of comparison between the accentuation of nouns and verbs in Japanese is the fate of deverbal nouns or denominal verbs. This is a particularly interesting comparison: will category-changing morphology trigger the accentuation pattern of the base or that of the derived category? In Japanese, verbs are converted to nouns by zero-derivation, if the verb is vowel-final, or by the addition of a suffix -i, if the verb is consonant final. (Poser 1984 analyzes this suffix as epenthetic.) When verb-verb compounds are converted to nouns in this manner, accent is always deleted (59a). Thus neither verb-verb compounds (which are always accented) nor their noun counterparts (always unaccented) exhibit any accentual contrast. For non-compound verbs which are converted to nouns, accentuation is input-dependent. If the input verb is unaccented (59b), so is the resulting deverbal noun, but if the input verb is accented (59c), the deverbal noun has final accent, with a few exceptions (Poser 1984: 62).

(59)   Accentuation of deverbal nouns in Japanese

    a. Nouns formed from compound verbs: accent deleted (Poser 1984: 96)

hiki-ge'ru	'pull up'	→	hikiage	'pulling up'
ii-'u	'quarrel'	→	iiai	'quarrel'
mi-oto'su	'overlook'	→	miotosi	'oversight'

    b. Nouns formed from unaccented non-compound verbs: noun is unaccented (Poser 1984: 60)

kariru	'borrow'	→	kari	'borrowing'
kasu	'lend'	→	kasi	'lending'
utagau	'doubt'	→	utagai	'doubt'

c. Nouns formed from accented non-compound verbs: noun
has final accent (Poser 1984: 61)
haji'ru   'be ashamed'   → haji' 'shame'
neba'ru   'be sticky'   → nebari 'stickiness'
sonae'ru 'furnish, prepare' → sonae' 'provision, preparation'

In summary, the existence and location of output accent in Japanese
deverbal nouns is not uniformly faithfully preserved from input.

Denominal verbs in Japanese are created by a variety of strategies,
varying in detail according to whether the input is an obvious loanword, Sino-Japanese, a mimetic vocabulary item, or a proper name. All
share the property that the original noun is clipped, suffixed with -ru,
and accented on the penultimate syllable, regardless of the location of
input accent, if any (Tsujimura and Davis 2011: 800):

(60)   a. (non-Chinese) loanword based: *kopiru* (<'copy'), *kaferu*
(<'café'), *teroru* (<'terrorism')
b. Sino-Japanese-based: *kokuru* (<*kokuhaku* 'confession'), *jikoru*
(<*jiko* 'accident')
c. mimetic-based: *nikoru* (<*nikoniko*: 'for smiling'), *chibiru*
(<*chibichibi*: 'for little by little')
d. proper name-based: *makuru* (<'McDonald's'), *sutabaru*
(<'Starbucks')

According to Tsujimura and Davis (2011: 809), "Regardless of the locus
of the accent of source nouns, all the innovative verbs pattern in exactly
the same fashion, having their root accent on the root final vowel.... the
accent of [these verbs] is not predictable from any part of the verbal forms
nor the nouns from which they are derived." In the forms in (61)
(Tsujimura and Davis 2011: 809), underlining represents accent:

(61) gloss	Source noun	Gerundive form of denominal verb
'copy'	kopii	kopi-tte
'accident'	jiko	jiko-tte
(mimetic for smiling)	nikoniko	niko-tte
'Starbucks'	sutaabakkusu	sutaba-tte
'linguistics'	gengogaku	gengogaku-tte
'café au lait'	kaɸeore	kaɸeore-tte

A naïve interpretation of noun privilege might predict that deverbal
nouns would invoke noun faithfulness and preserve input accent, while

denominal verbs would be default to unmarked accentuation and undergo default verbal accent assignment. In the data we have just seen, this prediction is borne out in that denominal verbs obliterate input accent contrasts. However, the prediction is only weakly borne out, in that most deverbal nouns also neutralize input accent contrast, with the exception of nouns formed from accented verbs (59c).

In summary, this case study of some of the better-known facts of Japanese accentuation suggests that the accentual asymmetry often observed between noun and verb roots is a piece of the puzzle, but does not reflect a broader asymmetry between the behavior of nouns and verbs in the language as a whole.

If this is generally true in other languages as well—and the research has not yet been done, so we can only speculate—then it becomes even more acutely important to ask why the faithfulness asymmetry seems so well established in roots across languages.

In some cases, the tighter restrictions on verbs can be epiphenomenal, due to morphological restrictions. This is what Hargus and Tuttle (1997) say about the well-known size asymmetry between nouns and verbs in most Athapaskan languages. While nouns can be monosyllabic or polysyllabic, verbs must be polysyllabic. Previous accounts attributed this difference to a minimality condition holding on verbs but not nouns; however, Hargus and Tuttle attribute it to the morphological requirement that verbs be tensed, and to the fact that all tense marking is accomplished by affixes that bring even monosyllabic verb stems up to the observed disyllabic minimum (p. 192). For example, cognates of the Witsuwit'en prefixes in (62b) have been analyzed as phonologically epenthetic, in other Athapaskan languages, in service of disyllabic minimality, but Hargus and Tuttle argue convincingly that the prefixes are present even in longer verbs and are morphological in nature, not phonological. Examples below are from Hargus and Tuttle 1997, pp. 181–2.

(62)   a. Monosyllabic nouns   [Witsuwit'en]
           ʔa   'fog'
           ʔaç   'snowshoe'
           ts'o   'spruce'
           tl'oɬ   'rope'
           ye   'louse'
           bet   'mittens'

b. Monosyllabic verb stems
   hə-tsəɣ   's/he is crying'
   hə-tl'et 's/he is farting'
   hə-bəl   's/he is swinging'

One likely factor behind the observed noun-verb root asymmetries is language contact as a source of marked structures in languages. It is a truism of language contact that languages are more likely to borrow nouns than verbs, and this alone could account for a larger segment and syllable type inventory, as well as a greater variety in size, among nouns than verbs. This cannot be the whole story, by any means, and in particular it cannot account for the noun augmentation patterns that Smith (2001, 2011) observes. (These patterns do not conform to the FAITH-Noun » FAITH-Verb ranking either; as Smith notes, they instead support a more over-arching generalization of noun robustness or complexity.) However, in light of borrowing as a potentially significant contributing factor to the noun root - verb root asymmetry, it becomes especially important to look beyond roots to test the robustness of the generalization.

2.7.3 Interaction between morphologically conditioned patterns, in complex words

An important question to address is the interaction between phono-logical patterns associated with different morphological constructions co-occurring in the same morphologically complex word. This is the topic of Chapter 7, which focuses on the important question of the interleaving of phonological patterns and the morphological construc-tions that trigger them within the same word.

2.8 Summary

The primary focus of this chapter has been on allomorphy governed by phonological alternations which are not general in the language but are specific to particular morphological constructions, such as com-pounding, truncation, affixation, or reduplication (see e.g. Dressler 1985; Spencer 1998). Insofar as a morphological construction is pro-ductive, any phonological pattern associated with it is a crucial com-ponent of a speaker's knowledge of his or her language. In Chapter 3, we turn to the closely related phenomenon of process morphology, in which a phonological process (other than overt affixation or com-pounding) is sufficient to realize a morphological category.

3

Process morphology

The counterpart to morphologically conditioned phonology, discussed in Chapter 2, is morphology which is manifested as a phonological process other than concatenation of morphemes. When such a process is the sole mark of a morphological category, the interchangeable terms "realizational morphology" and "process morphology" apply. This phenomenon, and its relationship to morphologically conditioned phonology, will be the focus of the present chapter. It is of great relevance to theories which are highly item-based (can every case of process morphology be reanalyzed as additive?) as well as to theories of multiple exponence. Sometimes more than one phonological process is associated with a morphological category. How a particular phonological process is characterized—as morphologically conditioned phonology or process morphology—is highly relevant to the diagnosis of multiple exponence. Finally, the close study of process morphology potentially informs theories of morphologically conditioned phonology. Whether a particular phonological process is characterized as morphologically conditioned phonology or as process morphology is relevant to the testing of hypotheses, discussed in Chapter 2, regarding the range of variation within a given language in its phonological patterns.

We begin with three illustrative examples of process morphology.

3.1 Three illustrative examples

In Tohono O'odham, a well-known process of subtractive morphology derives perfective verbs from imperfectives by deleting a final segment. Before a final coronal consonant, a high vowel deletes as well. Examples come from Yu (2000: 129–30), citing Zepeda (1984), and Anderson (1992), citing Zepeda (1983):

(1) gloss   Imperfective   Perfective [Tohono O'odham]

'hoe object'	síkon	síko
'rub against object'	híwa	híw
'bark'	hiːnk	hiːn

In Keley-i (Malayo-Polynesian), nonperfect aspect is marked by consonant gemination, providing a coda to what would otherwise be the leftmost light syllable (Samek-Lodovici 1992, citing original sources) (2a–d). (In words with no eligible light syllables, e.g. the first three forms in (2c, d), gemination is blocked.)

(2)

	(a)	(b)	(c)	(d)
Base:	pili	duyag	ʔagtu	duntuk
Subject focus:	um-pilli	um-duyyag	man-ʔagtu	um-duntuk
Object focus:	pilli	duyyag	ʔagtu	duntuk
Access focus:	ʔi-**pp**ili	ʔi-**dd**uyag	ʔi-**ʔʔ**agtu	ʔi-**dd**untuk
				[Keley-i]

English provides a familiar third example: stress shift marks the conversion from verbs to nouns (e.g. Kiparsky 1982bc):

(3) condúct   →   cónduct
     abstráct   →   ábstract
     recórd   →   récord

Process morphology is important to study for several reasons. One is that its nature and prevalence can inform theories of morphology. Approaches to morphology have historically divided themselves into two kinds, those which are "item-based" and those which are "realizational" or "process-based." Item-based approaches (e.g. Lieber 1980; Selkirk 1982; Kiparsky 1982c) treat morphology much like syntax, linearly arranging phonologically stable form-meaning pairings in conformity with the hierarchical structure governing complex words. Distributed Morphology (Halle and Marantz 1993) is a recent example of such a theory. By contrast, realizational approaches treat morphology as rule-based; many of these approaches assume that morphological rules operate on words and eschew postulating word-internal structure. A-Morphous Morphology (Anderson 1992) and Paradigm Function Morphology (Stump 2001) are well-known examples of this kind of approach (see also Bochner 1992). Still other approaches, like Construction Morphology (e.g. Riehemann 2001; Gurevich 2006; Booij 2010), are hybrids of the two, postulating general morphological construction schemas which can combine existing "items" (words, stems, roots) as well as perform the phonological operations that encompass clear cases of process morphology, like those seen earlier in this chapter. Insofar as process morphology poses a serious challenge for purely item-based theories of morphology, it is important to be aware of the extent to which process morphology exists in the world's languages.

A second reason to study process morphology is that it sheds light on the nature of morphologically conditioned phonology. Process morphology and morphologically conditioned phonology overlap substantively to a very high degree. The more similar in form they appear, the more evidence there is for embracing a theory of morphology that can treat them, formally, in the same way. The overlap between them tends to favor constructional approaches to morphology, as argued in Orgun (1996), Inkelas (1998, 2008b), and Inkelas and Zoll (2005).

In Chapter 2 we examined seven different types of phonological effects, each of which is conditioned by morphological context in some language or another. In this chapter we will follow a similar itinerary, demonstrating (in section 3.2) that the same types of phonological effects which can be morphologically conditioned are also capable of instantiating process morphology. Because process morphology has been a controversial topic in the past, many attempts have been made to analyze these effects as additive, more in line with item-and-arrangement morphology; attention will be drawn to these proposals, where relevant.

After this review, we will turn to several empirical questions, all grounds for future research: whether all kinds of phonological operations can realize morphological constructions (section 3.2), whether all kinds of morphological constructions can be realized via phonological processes (section 3.3), how and/or whether to distinguish between morphologically conditioned phonology and realizational morphology (section 3.4), and, finally, to the theoretical question of how morphologically conditioned phonology and process morphology should be modeled (section 3.5).

3.2 Phonological substance of process morphology

The survey of process morphology in this section is designed to enable a comparison, in section 3.4, between process morphology and the kind of morphologically conditioned phonology discussed in Chapter 2.

3.2.1 Segment deletion: Lardil, Nanti, Hausa

We saw in (1) the case of Tohono O'odham, in which final segment deletion encodes the perfective category in verbs. Along similar lines, final vowel deletion has been argued to mark nominative case in Lardil (4) (Blevins 1997: 249, citing original sources for the Lardil data):

(4)	gloss	UR	Nominative	cf. NonFuture Accusative (/-n/)
a.	'dugong'	/kentapal/	kentapal	kentapal-in
	'storey'	/ngaluk/	ngalu	ngaluk-in
b.	'rainbow'	/mayarra/	mayarr	mayarra-n
	'sea'	/mela/	mela	mela-n [Lardil]

Initial vowel deletion marks imperative formation in Nanti (Kampan; Michael 2008: 243, 245):

(5) a. /oog   -eɴpa   =ro/   →   genparo   [Nanti]
         consume -IRREAL.A   =3ɴмO
         'Eat it!'

     b. /ahirik   -e   =ro/   →   hirikero
         hold   -IRREAL.I   =3ɴмO
         'Hold it!'

     c. /ag   -e   =ro/   →   gero
         take   -IRREAL.I   =3ɴмO
         'Take it!'

     d. /am   -ak   -e   paryanti/   →   make paryanti
         bring -PERF -IRREAL.I   plantain
         'Bring plantains!'

While the irrealis suffixes /-eɴpa/ or /-e/ are required in Nanti imperatives, and seen in (5), they are not dedicated markers of the imperative construction. Irrealis marking is also found, for example, in negative declaratives, where imperative truncation is not applicable (pp. 145, 399):

(6) a. /teɴkaɴki o=   irag -e/   →   teɴkaɴki irage
         NEG.FOC   3ɴмS=   cry   -IRREAL.I
         'She didn't cry at all'

     b. /te   o=   irag -e/   →   te irage
         NEG.REAL   3ɴмS=   cry   -IRREAL.I
         'She didn't cry'

In Hausa, a final long vowel is shortened to form derived adverbs
(Newman 2000: 39–40):[1]

(7) 'ground'   ƙásáː   ƙásá   'on the ground, below' [Hausa]
    'forehead' gòːʃíː   gòːʃí   'on the forehead'
    'wing'   fíffíkèː fíffíkè   'on the wing'
    'hands'   hánnàːjéː hánnàːjé 'in/on the hands'
    'fingers'   jáːtsúː jáːtsú   'on the fingers'

A whole syllable rime (VC) is the target of deletion in Alabama
(Muskogean; Hardy and Montler 1988; Broadwell 1993), which
encodes pluralization of some argument, or repetitive action, in verbs.
Alabama verbs fall into two classes with respect to the truncating stem
alternations they undergo. One class undergoes syllable rime truncation (8a) and the other undergoes coda truncation (and vowel lengthening) (8b). Stems are shown with the classifier suffixes -ka or -li
(Broadwell 1993: 417):

(8) | gloss | singular | plural | [Alabama] |
|---|---|---|---|
| a. 'lie down' | bal-ka | balaa-ka | |
| 'hit' | bat-li | batat-li | |
| 'join together' | ibacas-li | ibacasaa-li | |
| 'cut' | kol-li | kolof-li | (→ koloffi) |
| b. 'slide' | salaa-li | salat-li | |
| 'turn around' | haatanaa-li | haatanat-li | |
| 'scrub' | kayoo-li | kayof-li | (→ kayoffi) |

Parallel phenomena occur in other Muskogean languages; on Koasati,
see especially Kimball (1991), Martin (1988); on Chickasaw, Choctaw,
and Mikasuki, see Broadwell (1993) and the references cited therein.

Subtractive morphology has served as the strongest argument that
morphological constructions are, at least in some cases, processual, in
the sense that they cannot be analyzed by means of the addition of a
morpheme. This argument is laid out particularly clearly in chapter 4
of Anderson (1992). There have been serious attempts to reanalyze
subtractive morphology as additive; for instance, Trommer and
Zimmerman (2010) suggest that subtraction could be the phonological

---

[1] Derived adverbs also commonly drop a feminine suffix, except in the case of body parts
like 'hands' or 'fingers'; in some cases an all-H tone pattern is imposed. Some derived
adverbs take a suffix -à.

response to the addition of an abstract empty mora, citing Tohono O'odham as an example. But most theoretical treatments capture subtraction directly, either through deletion rules (e.g. Martin 1988; Anderson 1992), prosodic circumscription rules (e.g. Lombardi and McCarthy 1991), or anti-faithfulness constraints (e.g. Horwood 2001; Kurisu 2001).

3.2.2 Gemination

In Woleaian, denotatives are formed by geminating the stem-initial consonant (Kennedy 2003: 174). No overt affix accompanies gemination, which is the sole exponent of the denotative construction:

(9) fili   → ffili   'choose it/to choose'   [Woleaian]
     βuga   → bbuga   'boil it/to boil'
     tabee-y → ttabe   'follow it/to follow'

In Alabama, consonant gemination can be (along with high tonal accent) the sole mark of what Hardy and Montler (1988) characterize as an imperfective aspectual construction, illustrated in (10) (pp. 402, 408). The pattern is for the onset of the penultimate syllable to geminate and for the antepenultimate syllable to receive a high tonal accent:

(10) | stem | Imperfective gloss | [Alabama] |
|---|---|---|
| ilakallo | ilákkallo | 'strong' / '(getting) stronger' |
| hayooki | háyyooki | 'deep' / '(getting) deeper' |
| abaali | ámbaali | 'high' / '(getting) higher' (< ábbaali) |
| kasatka | kássatka | 'cold' / 'cool' |
| litihka | líttihka | 'dirty' / 'a little dirty' |
| hopaaki | hóppaaki | 'far' / 'not as far' |
| lamatki | lámmatki | 'straight' / 'pretty straight' |
| acanaaka | acánnaaka | 'lean against' / 'be leaning' |
| conotli | cónnotli | 'bend over' / 'be bent, stooped' |
| wataali | wáttaali | 'put around neck' / 'wear around neck' |
| acaapa | átcaapa | 'object to, oppose'   (< áccaapa) |

Gemination, because it augments input structure in an additive way, has often been analyzed as the addition of a timing unit to the input. Thus, Hardy and Montler analyze imperfective aspect in Alabama as mora augmentation; the added mora is assigned to the antepenultimate syllable, and is fleshed out via the gemination of the following onset consonant:

(11)   μ + ilakallo   →   ilákkallo

In some cases, support for an additive analysis of consonant gemination is found in the fact that vowel lengthening is also an available
strategy for realizing the affixed mora. This is the case in Alabama, as
will be seen in the next section.

However, it is important to point out that even on an additive,
affixation-style analysis of consonant gemination in which the morphology adds an empty mora and the phonology supplies segmental
content to it, not all added moras are automatically fleshed out in the
same way. The Alabama imperfective construction comes with strict
phonological instructions on the realization of the added mora (antepenultimate syllable, filled with consonant). Mora affixation itself is a
very incomplete description of the construction.

3.2.3 Vowel lengthening

Imperfective aspect in Alabama is realized as vowel lengthening when
the syllable whose onset would be the target of penultimate consonant
gemination is word-initial (12a) or when the antepenultimate syllable is
closed (CVC), preventing the following onset consonant from geminating (12b). Alabama does not permit initial CC clusters or intervocalic
CCC clusters. In such cases, the onset of the following syllable cannot
geminate; instead, the penultimate syllable undergoes vowel lengthening and receives tonal accent (Hardy and Montler 1988: 403, 404, 408):

(12)		stem	Imperfective	gloss	[Alabama]
	a.	hofna	hóofna	'smell'	
		isko	íisko	'drink'	
		noci	nóoci	'fall asleep'	
	b.	campoli	campóoli	'taste good'/'be sweet'	
		ibakpila	ibakpíila	'turn upside down'	

In a discussion of mora augmentation in several languages, Álvarez
(2005) cites the case of Huallaga Quechua, from Weber (1989). (Additional data can be found in Weber and Landerman (1985).) As seen in
(13), vowel lengthening realizes first person possessive in nouns ending
in a short vowel (13a); otherwise, the suffix -ni: is used instead (13b)
(Weber 1989: 54):

(13)	gloss	noun	1SG.possessive	cf. 2SG.possessive
a.	'head'	uma	umaː	uma-yki
	'house'	wasi	wasiː [~ waseː]	wasi-ki
b.	'older (sibling)'	mayur	mayur-niː	mayur-nin

[H. Quechua]

Vowel lengthening also realizes first person marking in verbs (Weber 1989: 10, 81, 340; Weber and Landerman 1985: 98):

(14)   a. aywa   'go'
          aywa-paːku-n   'go-PL-3
          aywa-sha   'go-PRTC
          aywa-nan   'go-3>3SUB'

       b. aywa-ː   'go-1SG'
          aywa-ː-chu   'go-1SG-NEG'

Estonian is known for a complex set of grade alternations that affect both vowel and consonant length (e.g. Prince 1980: 538):

(15)		Strong grade	Weak grade	[Estonian]
a.	'other'	teiːse (ILL.SG.)	teise (GEN.SG.)	
	'eat'	sööːma (INF.)	söönut (P.P.)	
	'weight'	kaaːlu (PART.SG.)	kaalu (GEN.SG.)	
b.	'sin'	patːtu (PART.SG.)	pattu (GEN.SG.)	
	'town'	linːna (PART.SG.)	linna (GEN.SG.)	

In sum, vowel lengthening can be the sole marker of a morphological category. It is generally possible to analyze vowel lengthening as the addition of a mora, making it formally resemble affixation rather than a non-additive phonological process. Mora affixation is clearly motivated in cases where vowel lengthening alternates contextually with conson-ant gemination, affixation, or in some cases reduplication; see e.g. Yu (2005a) on Washo. From a larger perspective, however, the point of these examples is to show that the cases of vowel lengthening accom-panying affixation, standardly attributed to morphologically condi-tioned phonology (Chapter 2), are parallel in their phonological behavior to the cases described in this section.

3.2.4 Truncation to a prosodic constituent

Truncation, observed acting in Chapter 2 as a concomitant of several cases of affixation, can also serve as the sole exponent of a morphological category. The difference between subtractive morphology (section 3.2.1) and truncation is whether the phonological constant in the process describes the unit deleted ("subtractive morphology") or the unit resulting from deletion ("truncation"). As mentioned in Chapter 2, a large literature on truncation has produced a consensus that truncation is guided by a small list of prosodic constituent types: the syllable, the foot, the phonological word. Weeda (1992) and Kurisu (2001) are useful surveys.

Truncation as the sole marker of a morphological category is particularly common in the case of nickname formation and vocatives. (Truncation which accompanies affixation also commonly features these types of constructions, as discussed in Chapter 2.) In the (Peninsular) Spanish nickname formation process illustrated in (16), proper names are truncated to their first two syllables, the second of which must be open (Piñeros 2002: 439):

(16)   ga.briél   →   gá.bri   *Gabriel*   [Pen. Spanish]
       da.niél   →   dá.ni   *Daniel*
       a.drián   →   á.dri   *Adrián*
       dio.ní.sio   →   dió.ni   *Dionisio*
       χer.trú.dis   →   χér.tru   *Gertrudis*
       mont.se.r̃át   →   mónt.se   *Montserrat*

In the often-cited case of Yapese vocatives (17) (Jensen 1977), names are truncated down to a heavy syllable at the beginning of the word. (This case is discussed in McCarthy and Prince 1996, 1999b and much related work.)

(17)   name   vocative   [Yapese]
       ─────────────────────
       luʔag   luʔ
       bajaad   baj
       maŋɛfɛl   maŋ

As is typical of truncation in general, and illustrated in the Spanish and Yapese examples just seen, the prosodic constituent which results from truncation is not necessarily identical to a foot or syllable in the longer name. Rather, the truncatum is a foot or syllable that can be constituted from the segments at the beginning (in these cases) or end (in other cases) of the original word. Sometimes the truncatum is the largest prosodic constituent of the relevant type that can be constructed; this is true of Yapese (17). Sometimes it is the most optimal or unmarked prosodic constituent; this characterization applies to the Spanish nicknames in (16). A comparison is given in (18):

(18)   Yapese: Spanish:
              maximal syllable   optimal foot
Full name: (lu)$_\sigma$(ʔag)$_\sigma$ (ri)$_\sigma$(kar)$_\sigma$(do)$_\sigma$
Truncatum: (luʔ)$_\sigma$ [(ri)$_\sigma$(ka)$_\sigma$]$_\Phi$
              vs. minimal *(lu)$_\sigma$ vs. maximal *[(ri)$_\sigma$(kar)$_\sigma$]$_\Phi$

For surveys of truncation in forming hypocoristics, see e.g. Lappe (2003).

In addition to its use in hypocoristic formation, truncation is also commonly invoked on its own to produce casual or colloquial variants of longer words. Examples of trisyllabic truncation from Peninsular Spanish (Piñeros 2002: 438, 440) and Japanese (Itô and Mester 1992) are given in (19):

(19) a. 'ecologist'   ekoloχísta   > ekólo   [Spanish]
         'proletariat'   proletário   > proléta
         'amphetamine'   aɱfetamína   > aɱféta
         'anarchist'   anarkísta   > anárko
         'masochist'   masokísta   > masóka

      b. 'trichloro-ethylene' torikuroroetireN > torikuro [Japanese]
         'rehabilitation'   rihabiriteesyoN > rihabiri
         'asparagus'   asuparagasu   > asupara
         'Hysterie (Ger.)'   hisuterii   > hisu
         'hunger strike'   haNgaa sutoraiki > haNsuto
         'Akasaka Prince (hotel)' akasaka puriNsu > akapuri

In general, truncation as the sole marker of morphological constructions is identical to truncation that accompanies affixation (Chapter 2). The main phonological difference between the two is that a truncated base to which suffixes attach does not itself have to be syllabified exhaustively, while bare truncata must be syllabifiable. Thus, for example, the Australian English colloquial or slang clippings that are suffixed with -o in (20) are disyllabic in the output, but the truncata themselves (e.g. conv-, aggr-) are not necessarily well-formed syllables. (For discussion of similar examples, see Lappe 2003.)[2]:

---

[2] Data from <http://www15.uta.fi/FAST/US1/REF/aust-eng.html>, 10/16/2013.

(20) aggressive, aggravation   >   aggr-o
     compensation   >   comp-o
     evening   >   ev-o
     garbage collector   >   garb-o
     journalist   >   journ-o

The *aggravation* → *aggr-o* example, in particular, contains a consonant cluster, the second consonant of which syllabifies as the onset of the syllable headed by suffixal *-o*, but which would not be able to syllabify otherwise. This pattern differs from the German truncation pattern analyzed by Itô and Mester (1997), which is otherwise formally similar except that the truncatum is the largest possible syllable that can be formed from the beginning of the base; this truncatum is then suffixed with *-i*, as seen in (21). (Note that consonant doubling is orthographic only.):

(21)   Gabriele   >   Gab-i   (*Gabr-i)   [German]
     Dagmar   >   Dagg-i   (*Dagm-i)
     Gorbatschow   >   Gorb-i
     Klinsmann   >   Klins-i

The German pattern has a counterpart *-y* construction in English, where the truncatum can either surface on its own as a nickname (true truncation) or can combine with *-y* (truncation + affixation), e.g. *Daniel~Dan~Dann-y*, etc.

3.2.5 Ablaut and mutation

Morphological operations can consist of a change in the features of a segment in the base. As mentioned in Chapter 2, the term "mutation" covers a wide variety of complex or opaque effects on consonants; language families which are famous for this process include Celtic and Atlantic languages. An illustrative example is provided by Seereer-Siin (Atlantic; McLaughlin 2000: 338):

(22)	gloss	infinitive	singular	plural	[Seereer-Siin]
a.	'want, like'	bug	bugu	mbugu	
	'be ill'	ɟir	ɟir	ɲɟir	
	'stutter'	duʔ	duʔa	nduʔa	
b.	'look for'	waaɗ	waaɗa	mbaaɗa	
c.	'do'	fiʔ	fiʔa	piʔa	
d.	'pour out waste water'	ɓaf	ɓafa	ɓ̥afa	
	'cut'	ɗeg	ɗega	fega	

Plural forms of the Seereer-Siin verb are prenasalized if they begin with a voiced (non-implosive) consonant (22a,b), stopped if they begin with a continuant (22b,c), and devoiced if they begin with an implosive consonant (22d). Mutation effects are generally assumed to be the historical residue of an earlier affixation process which triggered junctural alternations at the prefix-stem boundary (e.g. Greenberg 1977). From a synchronic perspective, mutation must either be handled by a set of rules or constraints enforcing change, in which case it is clearly process morphology, or by floating features representing a nonsegmental affix, in which case it could be classed with ordinary prefixation, differing only in that its segments are phonologically defective (see e.g. Zoll 2001).

Note, however, that it is often a challenge to posit a straightforward phonological representation for a single mutation prefix that would predict, through the application of the general phonology of the language, all the attested effects upon combining with the base of affixation. In Seereer-Siin, the mutations in plural forms of verbs involve prenasalization in some cases, stopping in others, and devoicing in still others. These effects can be made to follow from the prefixation of a fixed representation (McLaughlin suggests [+nasal]) only if a number of highly specific phonological rules and constraints are invoked to account for the full complexity of the alternations. Whether or not mutations qualify as process morphology depends on the degree to which researchers are prepared to go in positing abstract representations and associating them with the morphologically conditioned phonological mappings necessary to produce correct surface forms.

3.2.6 Dissimilation and "exchange" rules

Both process morphology and morphologically conditioned phonology include effects where one segment surfaces with a value opposite either to its own input value ("Exchange rules," "toggles") or to the output value of another segment in the same word ("dissimilation"). For useful surveys, see Weigel (1993), Kurisu (2001), Baerman (2007), and DeLacy (2012).

Among the more surprising effects of this kind are the "toggle" effects seen in Nilotic languages, where a binary phonological parameter— voicing, in some languages; vowel length, in others—takes on its opposite value to form a new word. Discussions of exchange rules from a theoretical perspective can be found in Anderson (1992), Alderete (1999), Kurisu (2001), and Anttila and Bodomo (2009), among others. An example from Dinka (Nilotic; Sudan) is given in (23). In Dinka, singular and plural nouns usually have opposite vowel lengths: if one is short, the other is long. Data below are from Malou (1988: 66–71):

(23)		gloss	Singular	Plural	[Dinka]
	a.	'dorsal fin of fish'	ñiim	ñim	
		'mahogany'	tiit	tit	
		'razor blade'	rëët	rët	
	b.	'bell'	löṯ	lööṯ	
		'kind of bread'	tak	taak	

These kinds of effects have been cited for other West Nilotic languages as well, including Dinka's close relative Nuer (Frank 1999). In Dinka and Nuer, vowel length "toggles" are not the only pattern relating singulars and plurals, but form a recognizable subpattern within the nominal morphology.

An interesting toggle effect occurs with first person singular possession in Itnunyoso Trique: a stem-final /h/ is deleted (24a), and /h/ is suffixed to all other stems (i.e. those ending in a vowel or /ʔ/, which is replaced) (24b). The result is an /h/~/Ø/ toggle (Christian Dicanio p.c.).[3] (Alienably possessed nouns also have prefixes.):

(24)		gloss	base noun	1st person possessive	[I. Trique]
	a.	'foot'	ta^{3}koh^4	ta^{3}ko^{43}	
		'petate'	ββeh^5	tu^3-ββe^{43}	
		'money'	sã^{3}ʔãh^2	si^3-sã^{2}ʔã^2	
		'corn'	ʔnih^5	si^3-ʔni^{43}	
	b.	'face'	ri^{3}ã^{32}	riãh^3	
		'head'	tʃa^{31}	tʃah^3	
		'tongue'	ya^{32}	yah^3	
		'breath, air'	na^{3}ne^1	si^3-na^{1}neh^1	
		'candle'	kkaʔ^3	si^3-kkah^3	

Effects like those in Dinka and Trique can be analyzed in terms of phonological dissimilation, qualifying straightforwardly as process morphology. However, dissimilation might not be the right analysis,

---

[3] The /h~Ø/ toggle is also discussed by Baerman (2007). Note that alienably possessed nouns also take possessive prefixes; inalienably possessed nouns do not. Superscripts in (24) encode tone. /h/-deletion and /-h/ suffixation are accompanied by systematic tonal alternations; see later discussion.

given the existence of what Weigel calls "toggle morphology," Baerman (2007) calls "morphological reversals," and DeLacy (2012) and Anttila and Bodomo (2009) call "polarity morphology." These cases involve affixes which have a constant phonological form but which appear to toggle the value of a morphological feature of the base.

In Dagaare (Gur), for example, the overt suffix -*ri* switches the value of number encoded by the stem between singular and plural (Anttila and Bodomo 2009). For the stems in (25a) and (25b), plurals are marked with -*ri*; a bimoraic minimality condition forces vowel epenthesis on mono-moraic singular stems (25b). Other stems, however, form their plural with the [-round] vowel suffix (25c); these stems form singulars by taking the suffix -*ri*[4] (Anttila and Bodomo 2009: 56, 57, 61):

(25)

	gloss	stem	singular	plural	[Dagaare]
a.	'forest'	tùù-	túú	túú-rí	
	'police'	pòlísì-	pòlísì	pòlísì-rí	
	'moon'	kyúú-	kyúù	kyúú-rì	
b.	'log'	wég-	wégè	wég-rì	
	'child'	bì-	bíé	bíí-rí	
	'farm'	wè-	wìé	wè-rí	
c.	'rock'	pì	pìì-rí	pì-é	
	'book'	gán-	gán-í	gám-à	
	'seed'	bí	bí-rì	bí-è	
	'rope'	mí	mí-rì	mí-è	

In a survey of morphological toggle effects, Baerman (2007: 42) cites the example of Tübatülabal (Voegelin 1935), which encodes the distinction between telic and atelic verbs by means of a reduplicative vocalic prefix. For some verbs, the telic stem is basic and the atelic verb is derived by reduplication. For other verbs, the atelic stem is basic and the telic stem is derived by the same reduplicative process:

(26)

	gloss	telic	atelic	[Tübatülabal]
a.	'jump'	e-ʔela	ela-	
	'eat'	i-tɨk	tɨk-	
	'get down'	a-ndana	tana-	
	'be tired'	aː-baːabɨ	paːabɨ	

---

[4] Anttila and Bodomo (2009) argue, based on its different phonological characteristics, that the final vowel in the plurals in (25c) has a morphological source, and is not the same epenthetic vowel that appears in the singulars in (25b).

b. 'pound'   nʊŋ   ʊ-nʊŋ-
   'shell nuts'   patsaːh   a-patsaːh-
   'kick'   taŋ   a-ndaŋ-
   'yell'   tsaːyaːu   aː-dzaːyaːw-

No known semantic basis distinguishes the two verb classes; they simply differ arbitrarily, according to Voegelin (1935) and Baerman (2007), in whether the basic verb stem is telic or atelic, and derive the other via a morphological construction that toggles the value for [telic] to its opposite.

3.2.7 Stress/tone/pitch-accent (re)assignment

Stress and accent shift commonly expone morphological categories on their own, as seen earlier in the English verb-to-noun conversions. In Somali, gender is marked on nouns by means of tonal morphemes. Masculines exhibit H tone on the penultimate vocalic mora, while feminines exhibit H tone on the final vocalic mora (Hyman 1981; Saeed 1999):

(27) masculine   feminine   [Somali]

ínan	'boy'	inán	'girl'
náʕas	'stupid man'	naʕás	'stupid woman'
góray	'male ostrich'	goráy	'female ostrich'
darmáan	'colt'	darmaán	'filly'

Hausa (Chadic) uses full-scale tone melody replacement in the formation of imperative verbs. Each verb in Hausa exhibits the characteristic tone melody of its lexical grade. Tone melody distinctions are neutralized in the imperative, which imposes a LH tone pattern. As illustrated in (28), H is realized on the final syllable and L on all preceding syllables (Newman 2000):

(28) Declarative   Imperative   gloss   [Hausa]

káːmàː	kàːmá	'catch'
rúfèː	rùféː	'close'
bíncìkéː	bìncìkéː	'investigate'
káːwó	kàːwó	'bring'
nánnéːmó	nànnèːmó	'seek repeatedly' (cf. néːmó 'seek')
sòːyú	sòːyú	'be fried'

Rarámuri (Uto-Aztecan) also marks imperatives accentually, by shifting stress to the stem-final syllable (Caballero 2008: 119):

(29)　a. ra'amá 'give advice!'　ra'amá-bo　'. . .-FUT:PL'　[Rarámuri]
　　　　　　　　　　　　　　　　ra'ámi-ri　'. . .-PST'

　　　b. ra'ičá　'speak!'　　ra'ičá-ma　'. . .-FUT:SG'
　　　　　　　　　　　　　　　　ra'íči-ki　'. . .-PST:1'

In Upriver Halkomelem (Salishan), as documented by Galloway
(1993) and discussed by Urbanczyk (1999) and Kurisu (2001), stress
shift is one of several complementary processes for realizing the continuative aspect on verbs. As seen in (30), CV reduplication (30a), hə-
prefixation (30b), and vowel lengthening (30c) are the realizations of
continuative aspect for initially stressed stems; which method is
selected depends on phonological properties of the base. For bases
that are *not* initially stressed, however, continuative aspect is realized
simply: stress shifts to the first syllable (30d) (Kurisu 2001: 143):

(30)　　　　　　　Noncontinuative Continuative [Upriver Halkomelem]

　　a. 'sing'　　't'iləm　　　　't'ilələm
　　b. 'swallow'　'məqət　　　　'hə-mq'ət
　　c. 'walk'　　'ʔiməx　　　　'ʔiiməx
　　d. 'soak'　　ɬɛl.'qi　　　　'ɬɛlqi
　　　'bark'　　ƛ'ə'wəls　　　'ƛ'əwəls
　　　'bleed'　　caa'ləxʷəm　　'caaləxʷəm

Stress shift alone is sufficient to encode continuative aspect in
Upriver Halkomelem.

3.2.8 Summary

As suggested by the examples shown earlier, process morphology
overlaps substantially with morphologically conditioned phonology.
We saw in Chapter 2 that morphologically conditioned phonology
also overlaps to a large degree with "regular" word-internal phonology,
i.e. phonology which is not morphologically conditioned. However,
morphologically conditioned phonology strongly tends to include less
phonetically natural, historically older processes. The same is true of
process morphology.

　The phonological operations used to realize morphological constructions are essentially the same operations that can accompany overt
affixation, reduplication, and compounding. A more comprehensive
survey might well find that certain types of phonological effects are
much more rarely found as the sole markers of morphological categories
than others are, and that certain types of phonological effects are more

likely to be morphologically restricted (in any way) than others are. The reasons for this would be interesting to explore.

3.3 Morphological substance of process morphology

No extensive cross-linguistic survey of process morphology has yet been undertaken, but even a casual review suggests that process morphology is widely distributed in grammar, occurring in derivation and inflection alike. Most of the examples discussed to this point in this chapter have been inflectional (encoding aspect, number, case), but several (English, Hausa, Woleaian) have been derivational.

3.4. Distinguishing between morphologically conditioned phonology and process morphology

The survey in section 3.2 suggests that the phonological operations used to realize morphological constructions are essentially the same operations that can accompany overt affixation, reduplication, and compounding. In terms of substance alone, there is no clear basis for distinguishing the two (cf. Anderson 1975). This overlap creates a potential problem of discriminability. Theories which offer separate treatments of process morphology and morphologically conditioned phonology require some criteria for telling the two apart, even when they resemble one another in form.

The practical criterion seems to be that a phonological alternation is classified as "process morphology" if it is the sole exponent of a morphological construction, whereas it is classified as "morphologically conditioned phonology" if it accompanies something else which is judged to be the primary exponent of a morphological construction (affixation, reduplication, compounding). All of the examples discussed in section 3.2 were selected according to this criterion.

(31)   Process Morphology Diagnostic Criterion (PMDC): the phonological alternation in question is the sole marker of the morphological construction

Classifying cases according to the PMDC, process morphology appears to be far less common than morphologically conditioned phonology. For example, it is extremely easy to find examples of stress shift conditioned by affixation; it is much more difficult to find examples in which stress shift is the sole marker of a morphological construction. This is also true of gemination, vowel length alternations, and the other effects discussed in section 3.2. The explanation for this asymmetry could be diachronic; for example, insofar as process morphology is the result of the phonological erosion of the affix that originally triggered a morphologically conditioned phonological effect, process morphology would be a proper subtype of morphologically conditioned phonology, and about as common as entire affix erosion.

A problem for the PMDC is that many morphological constructions exhibit multiple phonological alternations, making it difficult or impossible to determine which phonological effect is the primary marker of the morphological construction (i.e. process morphology), and which is the secondary phonological correlate (i.e. morphologically conditioned phonology).

In Hausa (Newman 2000), for example, the dimensions of whether a morphological construction is tone-replacing and/or has overt affixation are independent:

(32)

	base tone replaced	base tone preserved
zero derivation	✓	✓
overt affixation	✓	✓

The same tone-replacement phenomenon in some cases classifies as process morphology (33a) and in others as morphologically conditioned phonology (33c).

(33) a. No affixation; tone replacement   [Hausa]
         (imperative formation)
         ká:mà: → kà:má: 'catch (!)'
         bíncìké: → bìncìké: 'investigate (!)'
         nánné:mó: → nànnè:mó: 'seek repeatedly (!)' (< né:mó: 'seek')

      b. No affixation, no tone replacement (Grade 2 verbal noun
          formation)
          fànsá: → fànsá: 'redeem/redeeming'
          tàmbáyà: → tàmbáyà: 'ask/asking'

      c. Overt affixation, tone replacement (various plural classes)
          má:làm   → mà:làm-ái   'teacher-PL'   -LH
          rì:gá: → rí:g-únà: 'gown-PL'   -HL
          tàmbáyà: → támbáy-ó:yí: 'question-PL'   -H

d. Overt suffixation, no tone replacement (various)

dáfàː	→	dáfàː-wá	'cook-PPL'	-LH
gàjéːré	→	gàjéːr-ìyá	'short-FEM'	-LH
hùːlá	→	hùːlâ-r̃	'hat-DEF'	-L

The same analytical conundrum is posed in the familiar case of truncation in nickname formation, e.g. the English pattern alluded to in section 3.2.4:

(34)

Full name	(a) Truncation	(b) Truncation + affixation
Daniel	Dan	Danny
Elizabeth	Liz	Lizzy
Michael	Mike	Mikey
Rebecca	Beck	Becky
Robert	Rob	Robby

Truncation must be analyzed as process morphology in the (34a) nicknames, but accompanies suffixation in (34b). Must truncation be reclassified as morphologically conditioned phonology in the (34b) examples?

Two reductionist solutions to this problem present themselves. One is to analyze all apparent cases of process morphology as morphologically conditioned phonology which happens to accompany zero derivation. In this way, English *Dan* and *Danny* would both have truncation as a morphologically conditioned phonological side effect; the primary morphological process would be zero derivation (for *Dan*) and affixation of *-y* (for *Danny*). The alternative reductionist approach would be to analyze all apparent cases of morphologically conditioned phonology as process morphology, treating forms like *Lizz-y* as containing two different nickname-forming constructions, or exhibiting multiple exponence. This approach is taken by Kurisu (2001) for cases in which overt morphology (affixation) is accompanied by morphologically conditioned phonology; for more discussion, see Chapter 11.

(35) PHONOLOGICAL REDUCTIONISM: all constructions consist of one primary morphological operation (affixation, compounding, reduplication, zero-derivation) and an associated phonological pattern, possibly complex

MORPHOLOGICAL REDUCTIONISM: morphologically conditioned phonology is actually process morphology; multiple exponence is more common than thought

Multiple or "extended" exponence is a well-known phenomenon (see e.g. Matthews 1972; Stump 1992), existing completely independent of the question of morphologically conditioned phonology or process morphology. In Fox (Algonquian), for example, subject person is marked twice on plural verbs (36c,d), once by an inner suffix encoding both person and number of the subject, and one by an outer prefix which encodes subject person (Dahlstrom 1997; see also Crysmann 1999). In (36), the black box '■' represents the root:

(36)   sg   pl   [Fox]
       ─────────────────────────

       1   ne-■   ne-■-pena
       2   ke-■   ke-■-pwa

       a. ne-   nowiː
          1   go.out
          'I go out'

       b. ke-   nowiː
          2   go.out
          'you (sg) go out'

       c. ne-   nowiː   -pena
          1   go.out   -1PL
          'we go out'

       d. ke-   nowiː   -pwa
          2-   go.out   -2PL
          'you (pl) go out

In Hausa, in which nouns fall into many different classes for purposes of pluralization, the formation of class 13 noun plurals shows triple exponence; suffixation, reduplication, *and* tone replacement (with a LH melody) take place (Newman 2000: 458):

(37)   tsíròː   → tsìr-é+tsìr-é   'shoot, sprout(s)'   [Hausa]
       kwánàː   → kwàn-é+kwàn-é   'corner, curve(s)'
       hábáicì   → hàbàic-é+hàbàic-é 'innuendo(s)'

Barasana (Tucanoan) presents a case similar to the Hausa example, in that one of the exponents is an overt affix and another is a tonal effect that would, according to the PMDC, be classified as morphologically conditioned phonology, rather than process morphology. But there is an interesting twist in the Barasana example that supports an analysis of multiple exponence. Contra the PMDC, in Barasana both the affixation and the tonal effect meet the diagnostic criteria for morphology, rather than phonology. Barasana is a tonal accent language in which a number of suffixes exert effects on stem tone (Gomez-Imbert and Kenstowicz 2000, also discussed in Pycha 2008b). For example, the non-3rd person subject (Non3rdSubj) suffix -bɨ causes H tone to align all the way to the right in words containing it (38a), while the Interrogative suffix -ri causes H to align all the way to the left (38b):

(38) a. baa-bɨ 'swim-NON3RDSUBJ = I/you/we swim'   [Barasana]
         HH   H

       b. baa-ri   'swim-INTERR = did he/she/they swim?'
          H

These suffixes cannot co-occur; one might say they belong to the same position class, so that the presence of one excludes the other, even though the morphosyntactic functions they encode seem compatible. While position class blocking is not uncommon in languages (see e.g. the discussion of Turkish suffix incompatibility in Chapter 9), the Barasana suffixes in (38) are unusual in exhibiting what Pycha (2008b) calls "mutual partial blocking." In words where both meanings are desired, we find the segments of the Interrogative -ri and the tones of the Non3rdSubj (39a):

(39) a. baa-ri   'did I/you/we swim?'
          HH   H

       b. *baa-ri-bɨ, *baa-bɨ-ri   (Intended: 'did I/you/we swim?')

Pycha's interpretation of the facts in (38)–(39) is that both the Non3rdSubj and the Interrogative categories achieve exponence in (39a) by using the segments of one and the cophonology of the other. This poses a paradox for theories that, in accordance with the PMDC, distinguish process morphology from morphologically conditioned phonology. The tone pattern of the Non3rdSubj must, per the PMDC, be analyzed as morphologically conditioned phonology based on the fact that it co-occurs with a "primary" exponent, namely the suffix -bɨ; yet the ability of tone to expone Non3rdSubj, even when -bɨ is absent, identifies it as process morphology.

At a minimum, the impossibility of classifying the segmental and tonal components of Barasana suffixes absolutely as morphologically conditioned phonology, or as process morphology, supports proposals that process morphology and morphologically conditioned phonology should be analyzed in the same way (Ford and Singh 1983, 1985; Poser

1984; Dressler 1985; Singh 1987, 1996; Anderson 1992; Bochner 1992; Orgun 1996; Inkelas 1998, 2008b).

3.5 Theoretical approaches to process morphology

Any documented instances of process morphology that cannot readily be reanalyzed as affixation of abstract phonological structure lend strong support to theories of morphology other than those involving pure item-and-arrangement. However, as we have seen, the Phonological Reductionism approach (35) makes it possible for any theory to handle such cases, since all apparent process morphology can be classified as the phonological accompaniment to zero derivation if desired (ignoring the suggestive Barasana example). Therefore, the existence of process morphology is not technically probative when it comes to choosing between item-and-arrangement and realizational morphological frameworks.

However, process morphology is highly relevant to the choice of a framework for capturing the phonology-morphology interface, if one is committed to capturing the substantive overlap between it and morphologically conditioned phonology.

In Chapter 2, we reviewed several different theoretical approaches to the morphology-phonology interface with respect to their ability to capture morphologically conditioned phonology: Cophonology Theory, Indexed Constraint Theory, and Level Ordering theory. The reason for selecting this set of theories for discussion is that they form an explicit comparison set regarding their predictions as to the range of potential phonological variation across morphological constructions in a language.

In Cophonology Theory (e.g. Anttila 2002; Inkelas and Zoll 2007) and Indexed Constraint Theory (e.g. Alderete 2001), there is essentially no formal distinction between morphologically conditioned phonology and process morphology; both are captured easily, and in the same formal way. Even if researchers working in these frameworks have classified particular effects one way or the other, the dichotomy is not required by the architecture of the theory, and is only an informal attribution. In Cophonology Theory, both morphologically conditioned phonology and process morphology result from the association of a phonological mapping (cophonology) with a semantic/syntactic mapping between input and output. Example (40a) illustrates the constraint ranking that imposes the LH tone melody which is the sole marker of the Hausa imperative (examples (28) and (33), this chapter) and which is a concomitant of the *-ai* plural suffix (example (42) in Chapter 2 and example (33), this chapter). Example (40b) illustrates the opposite constraint ranking, characterizing the cophonologies of morphological constructions in which the tones of the input stem are *not* replaced by the LH melody. The point is that the constraint ranking in (40a) exists independently of the presence or absence of an overt affix:

(40)   a. Cophonology for imperative,   Tone=LH » IDENT-Tone
          -ai plural constructions:

       b. Cophonology for tone-   IDENT-Tone » Tone=LH
          preserving constructions:

In Indexed Constraint Theory, both morphologically conditioned phonology and process morphology are handled by indexing a constraint or constraints to the morphological construction in question. For example, the Imperative and *-ai* plural constructions in Hausa could both be treated as affixes—[[ ] Ø] and [[ ] ai]—which are indexed to a high-ranking Markedness constraint requiring the surface tone pattern to be LH.

(41)   Tone=LH$_{imperative, \text{-}ai \text{ Plural}}$ » IDENT-Tone » Tone=LH

In both Cophonology and Indexed Constraint approaches, the method of imposing the LH tone melody is in principle entirely independent of whether or not an overt affix is present. Morphologically conditioned phonology and process morphology are handled by the same types of constraints. The only significant difference between the two is felt in theories of exponence which count the number of exponents of a morphological category; in such theories, constructions like Hausa *-ai* plurals would be classified as instances of multiple exponence, requiring a special statement. However, as noted already, such statements are needed anyway in cases of multiple overt affixation.

In contrast with Cophonology Theory and Indexed Constraint Theory, Level Ordering theories are forced by their architecture into the dichotomy between morphologically conditioned phonology and process morphology. Because the number of lexical levels in such theories is so small, ranging from 2 (in Stratal OT; Kiparsky 2000, 2008, 2010) to 4 or 5 (e.g. Kiparsky 1984; Mohanan 1986; Hargus 1988; Buckley 1994), it is impracticable to ascribe the particular phonology of a given process morphology construction to the level that the morphological process belongs to. In this chapter alone, in Hausa, for example, we have seen vowel shortening (in adverbs, (7)) and imposition of a LH tone melody (imperatives, (28)) as the sole markers of morphological constructions; in Level Ordering theory, this distinction would already consume two of the allotted strata, yet only a small fraction of Hausa constructions undergo either phonological alternation.

Levels in Level Ordering theories were designed to account for morphologically conditioned phonology which generalizes across morphological constructions, not for idiosyncratic alternations marking specific morphological categories, or for that matter, idiosyncratic morphologically conditioned phonology (as discussed in Chapter 2). Level Ordering theory is more a theory about higher-level generalizations in the phonology-morphology interface of a given language, or perhaps across languages, than it is a model of the entire phonology-morphology interface in any individual language. Level Ordering theory has called very interesting generalizations to the attention of researchers working on the phonology-morphology interface, highlighting, in particular, the phonological salience of stem-level subconstituents within words. But it is too blunt a knife to dissect the kinds of detail that make the phonology-morphology interface so compelling in individual languages, especially those with complex morphology.

4

Prosodic templates

Prosodic templates are morphological constructions, sometimes stem-forming and in other cases associated with derivational or inflectional morphological categories, which directly constrain the phonological shape of the derived stem. Templates have played a highly significant role in theories of phonology and morphology. Some of the most significant contributions to the literature on prosodic templates are McCarthy (1979, 1981), McCarthy and Prince (1990, 1995, 1996, 1999b), and Downing (2006).

The example of a prosodic template that comes first to the mind of most students of phonology and morphology is surely an entry in the Classical Arabic verb paradigm (McCarthy 1979, 1981). In Arabic, verb roots are purely consonantal in form; thus the root for 'write' is /ktb/, often represented as √ktb. All derived and inflected verb forms based on this root share these three consonants, but everything else about them, including their vowels and prosodic shape, is determined by the morphological category. For example, basic perfective verbs assume the prosodic shape [CV][CVC] (e.g. *katab* 'write'), while causatives take the form [CVC$_i$][C$_i$VC] (*kattab* 'make write') and reciprocals take the form [CVV][CVC] *(kaatab* 'correspond'). Connecting a long tradition of Arabic scholarship with the innovations of autosegmental phonology, McCarthy (1979) proposed that the causative, reciprocal, and other derivational verb categories are represented as segmentally empty templates, which guide the positioning of the consonants of verb roots. Templates also guide the positioning of vowels which constitute other morphemes in Arabic. For example, the perfective passive morpheme consists of the vowels /ui/. When combined with the root 'write' /ktb/ and the perfective template [CV][CVC], the verb *kutib* results.

A common sense distinction between templates, on the one hand, and other kinds of morphologically conditioned phonology or process morphology, on the other, is that templates are shape constraints, rather than processes. Flack (2007: 750) points to some Dinka data that usefully draw this distinction. In Dinka, the 3rd person singular agreement (1a) and "centrifugal" (signaling movement away) (1b) suffixes are two of several that increase root vowel length by one mora:

(1)   a. wèc + m → wè:c 'kick.3SG'   [Dinka]

          tèŋ + m → tè:ŋ 'dust.3SG'

          lè:r + m → lè::r 'roll.3SG'

          mì:t + m → mì::t 'pull.3SG'

      b. wèc + m → wé:c 'kick.CF'

          tèŋ + m → tê:ŋ 'dust.CF'

          lè:r + m → lê::r 'roll.CF'

          mì:t + m → mî::t 'pull.CF'

This is either morphologically conditioned phonology or process morphology, depending on how accompanying changes in tone or vowel quality are analyzed. Effects like this were discussed in Chapters 2 and 3 as vowel lengthening associated with a particular morphological construction.

By contrast, Dinka benefactives show templatic behavior. They are subject to the shape constraint that they must be bimoraic. This requirement can induce vowel lengthening in stems that would otherwise be monomoraic, as shown in (2a).

(2)   a. wèc → wé:c 'kick.BEN'

          tèŋ → tê:ŋ 'dust.BEN'

Most interestingly, as pointed out by Flack (2007: 753), the bimoraic template even prevents bimoraic benefactive stems from becoming trimoraic when they combine with the outer 3SG suffix, which normally adds a mora:

(3)

	gloss	root	+BENEFACTIVE	+3SG	+BENEFACTIVE, 3SG	
a.	'roll'	lè:r	lê:r			
	'pull'	mì:t	mî:t			
b.	'roll'	lè:r			lè::r	
	'pull'	mì:t			mí::t	
c.	'roll'	lè:r			lê:r	(*lê::r)
	'pull'	mì:t			mî:t	(*mî::t)

Foreshadowing the issue of interacting morphophonological requirements of different layers of morphology, to be discussed in Chapter 7, this Dinka example also illustrates the competition between two morphophonological requirements: bimoraicity (benefactive) and mora addition (3rd person singular). In this case, the benefactive wins.

From the perspective of phonology, templates have played an important role in illuminating the nature of phonological representations. In the late 1970s, McCarthy's seminal study of Arabic templates (1979, 1981) proved a need for the autonomous existence of the phonological representation of length. Subsequently, McCarthy and Prince (1996, 1999b) launched a new paradigm of work in Prosodic Morphology by showing that the phonological units of which templates tend to be composed are the universal prosodic units of mora, syllable, and foot. The Dinka benefactive template, for example, is a heavy (bimoraic) syllable. Recently, templates have moved to center stage once again as researchers (e.g. McCarthy et al. 2012) have begun to explore the question of whether templates are static representational phonological entities or the emergent effects of constraint interaction (e.g. McCarthy and Prince 1994b; Urbanczyk 2006; Downing 2006; McCarthy et al. 2012). Generalized Template Theory (e.g. Urbanczyk 1996, 1999, 2006; Downing 2006), discussed in section 4.4.3, is a particularly influential approach of the latter kind.

On the morphology side, templates have been cited as evidence that morphology is not strictly concatenative, a point we have already seen made, in a different way, in Chapter 3. Insofar as templates regulate the output shape of stems and words, they are a problem for simple implementations of the classical view that morphology consists of stringing morphemes together in a linear fashion (e.g. Hockett 1947; Matthews 1972). Considerable thought (see e.g. Anderson 1992: 58–9) has gone into the question of whether templates are items in grammar that constitute morphemes and can combine, additively, with other morphemes in a word, thus preserving the essence of Hockett's and Matthews's item-based approaches, or whether instead templates are simply extremely elaborate instances of morphologically conditioned phonology or process morphology.

We saw in Chapters 2 and 3 that morphologically conditioned phonology and phonologically realized morphology ("realizational" or "process" morphology) are closely related in their form and that it can be difficult to draw a line between the two. Templatic effects challenge this same line. When affixes impose templatic restrictions on the bases they attach to, it is tempting to classify the template as morphologically conditioned phonology; when the template is itself the realization of a particular morphological category, process morphology is the likelier identification. As discussed in sections 4.2–4.4, some templates can be described along a single phonological dimension, potentially merging with what would normally be called morphologically conditioned phonology, while others are multi-faceted, clearly rising to the status of templaticity. Finally, some templates are restricted to a small corner of the morphology of a language, exhibiting what in section 4.2 is called ISOLATED TEMPLATICITY, while others, discussed in sections 4.3 and 4.4, characterize large classes of morphological constructions. A comparative cross-linguistic survey of the proportion of constructions in a language that are templatic has not yet been carried out, and would be tricky to accomplish given the cline of templaticity to be described in this chapter.

Regardless of whether future psycholinguistic or typological research confirms or disconfirms their status as representational entities that could be classed with prefixes and suffixes as "morphemes," the study of templates sheds considerable light on the phonology-morphology interface. We begin with a tour of the phonological forms that templates have been observed to take.

4.1 Units of templatic form

Prosodic templates govern the shape of roots, stems, or words. Sometimes they function as a minimum, e.g. in Lardil, every word must be minimally bimoraic (section 4.4.1). Sometimes they function as a maximum, though this is less common, as in Tiene derivational stems (section 4.3.2). In the most dramatic cases, the fit between form and template must be exact, as in examples like Cupeño habilitatives (section 4.2.2), Guarani noise words (section 4.2.3), or Japanese hypocoristics (section 4.4.2).

The study of phonological templates in generative grammar got its start in the late 1970s when the framework of autosegmental phonology developed out of the need to separate the invariant CV skeletal structure of templates from the morpheme-specific segments fleshing them out in individual words in Semitic and other languages with templatic morphology (McCarthy 1979, 1981). This development revolutionized phonological theory, giving rise to autosegmental treatments not only of templates but also of tone and vowel harmony (see e.g. Clements 1976; Goldsmith 1976, 1979; Williams 1976; Leben 1978).

The theory of Prosodic Morphology was further developed in the late 1980s when McCarthy and Prince (in a 1986 manuscript published as McCarthy and Prince 1996, 1999b) showed convincingly that templates are described in terms of a small number of prosodic constituent types, rather than of CV skeletal units per se.

(4)   prosodic word
      foot
      syllable (heavy or unrestricted)
      mora

These are the units that describe the outputs of truncation, as seen in Chapters 2 and 3. Templates play a variety of other roles as well. Some constrain the minimal or maximal size of words, or supply precise instructions as to the shape of derived stems, as we will see in this chapter. Others determine the shape of reduplicants (Chapter 5).

Templaticity is particularly frequent in the domain of nicknames (hypocoristics, diminutives) or sound-symbolic vocabulary; truncation examples of this type were seen in Chapters 2 and 3, and other examples will be introduced in this chapter (e.g. section 4.2). However, many languages exhibit templatic constructions of other types in one corner of the grammar or other.

4.2 Isolated templaticity

We turn first to instances in which a single construction within a language imposes a prosodic shape requirement on its input or its output. Such cases are classified here as "isolated templaticity" because they are not part of a larger, systematic pattern of templaticity across a well-defined swath of the grammar.

4.2.1 English comparatives

In English comparatives and superlatives, templatic considerations affect the ability of adjectives to combine with comparative and superlative suffixes. Both comparative -er and superlative -est combine only with bases which are monosyllabic (5a) or whose second syllable is very short, e.g. consisting only of a syllabic consonant (5b). (There is some inter-speaker variation on this latter point.) Stems larger than those in (5a,b) cannot combine with the comparative and superlative suffixes (5c):

(5) a. σ

fine	finer	finest
sad	sadder	saddest
tall	taller	tallest
strange	stranger	strangest

b. σ + Ç

little	littler	littlest
common	commoner	commonest
crazy	crazier	craziest

c. σ σ⁺

vacant	*vacanter	*vacantest	(cf. empty, emptier, emptiest)
affable	*affabler	*affablest	(cf. nice, nicer, nicest)
gigantic	*giganticer	*giganticest	(cf. huge, huger, hugest)

Stems which do not conform to the templatic requirements of the comparative and superlative suffixation constructions instead form comparatives and superlatives by means of an alternative periphrastic construction, 'more ___' or 'most ___'. (See Chapter 9 for more discussion of this kind of phonologically driven "ineffability.")[1] This qualifies as a case of isolated templaticity because in general, English suffixes are not limited to monosyllabic bases; in general, suffixed English words are not limited to a disyllabic maximum.

4.2.2 Cupeño habilitatives

The Cupeño habilitative is another example of the imposition of a templatic requirement that is not found elsewhere in the language. In fact, the Cupeño habilitative can only be described in templatic terms. If the base is consonant-final, then its habilitative must have antepenultimate stress. However, stress does not move off of the syllable bearing it in the non habilitative input. In order to conform to the template, habilitatives which would otherwise be shorter than three syllables or whose input stress is on the penult or final syllable undergo reduplication and epenthesis in order for the stressed syllable to end up in antepenultimate position (Hill 1970; McCarthy 1979, 2000;

---

[1] Interestingly, English adjectives ending in -y are eligible to take -er and -est regardless of size, e.g. *slippery, slipperier, slipperiest* or *shadowy, shadowier, shadowiest*. The suffix–*y* is a special enabler of comparative and superlative. Hammond (1992) calls this effect "potentiation;" Fabb (1988) offers extensive discussion of this phenomenon within English morphology. Chapter 7 discusses the implications of potentiation for theories of Bracket Erasure and "inside access" to the morphological structures of bases of affixation.

McCarthy and Prince 1990; Crowhurst 1994). The data in (6) are from McCarthy 2000:

(6)   gloss   Plain stem   Habilitative   [Cupeño]

   a. 'leach acorns'   pácik   páčiʔik
      'be angry'   čáŋnəw   čáŋnəʔəw
      'joke'   čəkúkʷilʸ   čəkúkʷiʔilʸ

   b. 'husk'   čál   čáʔaʔal
      'see'   tə́w   tə́ʔəʔəw
      'hiccup'   həlʸə́p   həlʸə́ʔəʔəp
      'gather wood'   kəláw   kəláʔaʔaw

   c. 'sing enemy songs'   pínəʔwəx   pínəʔwəx
      'fall'   xáləyəw   xáləyəw

In (6a), whose nonhabilitative forms bear penultimate stress, a posttonic syllable is created via vowel reduplication and glottal stop epenthesis; the result is antepenultimate stress. In (6b), the inputs have final stress and so *two* posttonic syllables are created, again using vowel and glottal stop epenthesis. Crucial confirmation of templaticity comes from the forms in (6c), which, because they lexically exhibit antepenultimate stress, already meet the templatic requirements in the input. For these data, the templatic is already vacuously satisfied, and no change is needed. The habilitative and nonhabilitative forms are identical.[2]

Descriptively, the templatic part of the Cupeño habilitative does not straightforwardly match any of the prosodic units in (4). It is not a single mora or syllable. Whether it could be described as a single foot depends on the phonological theory or analysis being deployed. McCarthy and Prince (1990) propose a ternary foot, to which the portion of the base consisting of the stressed syllable through the last vowel is mapped to produce the habilitative.

Ternarity is a challenge for phonological theory generally, whether it is manifested in a ternary template (as in Cupeño, or in Gilbertese; Blevins and Harrison 1999) or in a stress system. Phonological theory emphasizes binary contrasts and binary branching constituents (see e.g. McCarthy and Prince 1996, 1999b). However, a minority of stress assignment systems are ternary, assigning stress to every third syllable.

---

[2] Bases which are vowel-final are exempt from the habilitative template, e.g. *séyki* 'gather seyily', which is unchanged in the habilitative (Hill 2005: 58). I am grateful to Erin Haynes for illuminating discussions of the Cupeño data.

For overviews, see e.g. Elenbaas and Kager (1999), Hayes (1995). One possibility that has been suggested for analyzing ternarity within the framework developed for primarily binary patterns is that ternary templates consist of a constituent "plus one." For example, Itô and Mester (2003) suggest that trimoraic loanword clippings in Japanese could be analyzed as a "loose minimal word":

(7) Loose minimal words in Japanese: $[[\mu\mu]_{Ft}\ \mu]_{Wd}$

'diamond'	daiyamoɴdo	→	daiya	$\sigma_{\mu\mu}\sigma_\mu$
'combination'	koubineesyon	→	koubi	$\sigma_{\mu\mu}\sigma_\mu$
'symposium'	siɴpoziumu	→	siɴpo	$\sigma_{\mu\mu}\sigma_\mu$
'Appendizitis' (< German)	appeɴdizitisu	→	appe	$\sigma_{\mu\mu}\sigma_\mu$
'basket'	basuketto	→	basuke	$\sigma_\mu\sigma_\mu\sigma_\mu$
'animation'	animeesyoɴ	→	anime	$\sigma_\mu\sigma_\mu\sigma_\mu$

According to Itô and Mester, these clippings are words which are minimally internally branching, consisting of a bimoraic foot (required of all derived words in Japanese) plus a light syllable. Analyses in this vein have been proposed for Cupeño as well. Crowhurst (1994) invokes two disyllabic feet in her analysis of Cupeño habilitatives. One (iambic) foot contains the stressed syllable; a second obligatory disyllabic post-tonic foot forces the stress into antepenultimate position. Similarly, McCarthy (2000) proposes that the tonic syllable must immediately precede a disyllabic foot.

This analytical variation for a straightforward ternary template fore-shadows a point we will make in more detail later, namely that what looks like a unitary template may be equally well, or arguably better, analyzed as the collective effect of a number of interacting phonological conditions.

4.2.3 Noise words in Guarani

The English and Cupeño examples are classically prosodic in that they involve syllable count and stress. But templates can also include segmental information; indeed, the Cupeño template in section 4.2.2 is imposed only on consonant-final bases, so itself has a minor segmental component. Guarani is the first of several such examples we will examine more closely. As described by Langdon (1994: 94–103), based on a single speaker, noise words in Guarani all have the shape CVrVrV. The three vowels are identical to one another, the medial consonants are both [r], and the initial consonant must be an obstruent or /w/; it cannot be instantiated by any (other) of the sonorant consonants in the Guarani inventory.

(8) piriri   'fire burning dry grass; crackle of new money'
    xiriri   'water coming out of faucet'
    perere   'chicken flapping wings; lumpy things in box'
    tarara   'chattering teeth; shivering; pecking'
    mbarara   'loud, deep; big drum; heavy books falling'
    pororo   'popcorn; sparks'
    wyryry   'crumpled paper; ferreting through box'
    sururu   'tight-fitting parts; forcing into tight slot'
    pãrãrã   'rocks in tin can'
    tõrõrõ   'monumental water fall'
    kĩrĩrĩ   'quietly'
    pỹrỹrỹ   'jumping, spinning top'
    pũrũrũ   'biting a ripe grape; cherry tomato; starched petticoat'

Noise words in Guarani are syntactically verbs, akin to English *rumble* or *reverberate*; they inflect and participate in derivational morphology like other verbs. They conform to Guarani phonotactics in having CV syllables and obeying nasal harmony, but their prosodic shape is much more restricted. In general, Guarani verbs that Langdon cites are not necessarily trisyllabic. They can be vowel-initial, and their vowels can differ (e.g. *puka* 'laugh', *hendu* 'hear', *wereko* 'to have', *purahei* 'sing', *ipota* 'want'; Langdon 1994: 100–101).

Clearly, noise verbs in Guarani conform to a highly restrictive template which is specific to this semantic class of verb. It is not uncommon to find templates of this kind characterizing ideophones or sound-symbolic classes of words; see e.g. Hinton et al. (1994) and Voeltz and Kilian-Hatz (2001) for useful surveys. As seen in Chapter 2, ideophones sometimes flout phonotactic generalizations which are otherwise imposed in a language; they can also, as seen here, be subject to special restrictions on their shape.

The Guarani example is particularly interesting because of its phonological complexity. Like the Cupeño habilitative template, the trisyllabic Guarani noise word template does not match a canonical prosodic unit within the set listed in (4). It is not a single mora or syllable, nor is it a canonical binary foot. And it has highly specific segmental components which are logically independent of one another.

4.2.4 Hausa V-X → N compounds

Pushing the envelope of what is standardly called templaticity is the set of phonological shape constraints associated with V(erb)-N(oun) compounding in Hausa. The template for this noun-forming construction is the following: the monosyllabic verb must be bimoraic, its tone must be L, and the final vowel of the noun must be short. Input verbs and nouns not meeting these requirements are adapted, via vowel lengthening, tone replacement, and vowel shortening (Newman 2000: 114, 116–17):

(9) a. /ʧǐ + fàːráː/ →[ʧìː-fàːrá] *cǐ fàra*   'eat-locust =type of bird'
     b. /bí + bángòː/→[bìː-bángò] *bì bangò* 'follow-wall = leakage
                                             from roof along wall;
                                             wall ivy'
     c. /gàː + rúwáː/→[gàː-rúwá] *gǎ ruwa* 'here_is-water = selling
                                             water in jerry cans'
                                                                    [Hausa]

This construction can be considered phonologically templatic because every output meets the same phonological description, regardless of whether or not an alternation has taken place to achieve it. What is constant is the shape, not the process. It is certainly a case of isolated templaticity; the template manifested in (9) is construction-specific. Short vowels, L tone, and monosyllabicity are not general concomitants of Hausa compounding constructions, of which there are many other types (Newman 2000). For example, Adj(ective)-N and N-N compounds preserve lexical vowel length, tone, and syllable count (Newman 2000: 115–19):

(10) Adj-N: báʄí-n + ʧíkìː   *baƙin cikî*   'black-belly = sad-
                                               ness, jealousy'
      N-N: sáːráː + súːkàː   *sārā-sūkà̀*   'slashing-stabbing
                                               = thuggery'
              ʧǐ-n + fúskàː   *cîn fuskà̀*   'eating-face =
                                               humiliation, insult'
      V-X: ʧǐ + káɾ̃-kà-mútù *ci-kaɾ̃-kà-mutù* 'eat-don't-you-die
                                               = tasteless food'

In the next sections we turn to templates which are more systematic and less isolated, within the context of the language containing them, than those seen in this section.

4.3 Systematic stem templaticity

Systematic templatic requirements hold across more than one construction in a language, rather than being specific to a particular affixation or compounding construction. Two such examples are provided in this section. Both involve verbal systems that provide a tightly restricted set of template shapes for stems in the verbal paradigm.

4.3.1 Root shape templaticity in Yowlumne

The templatic system of Yowlumne (Yokuts, Penutian; known in the literature as Yawelmani), is documented in Newman (1944) and has been amply discussed in the theoretical literature by Archangeli (1983, 1984, 1991); Noske (1985); Zoll (1993), among others. In Yowlumne, verb stem shapes are restricted to the three possibilities shown in (11):

(11) σ_μ (=CVC)
       $\sigma_{\mu\mu}$ (=CVVC)
       $\sigma_\mu\sigma_{\mu\mu}$ (=CVCVVC)

Roots in Yowlumne consist of one distinctive vowel and two or three consonants. Each root is lexically associated with one of the three templates in (11). Root vowel and consonants map to the root template in a predictable, left-to-right manner, modeled in autosegmental and prosodic phonology by Archangeli (1983, 1984, 1991: 125). For example, the root $\sqrt{\text{yawl}}$ is lexically associated with the $\sigma_{\mu\mu}$ template, to which its vowel /a/ and consonants /y,w,l/ map to produce the string *yawaal*.[3]

A root's lexical template characterizes the shape of the root when it combines with the kind of suffix that does not itself interfere with root shape. One such suffix is the aorist *-hin* (~ *-hun*), illustrated in (12) (Archangeli 1991: 247):

(12)

	Root	Template	Root + aorist /-hin/
a. 'shout'	$\sqrt{\text{caw}}$	σ_μ	**caw**-hin
'float'	$\sqrt{\text{hogn}}$	σ_μ	**hogin**-hin (< |hogn-hin|)
b. 'devour'	$\sqrt{\text{cum}}$	$\sigma_{\mu\mu}$	**c'om**-hun (< |c'oom-hin|)
'consent'	$\sqrt{\text{cupn}}$	$\sigma_{\mu\mu}$	**coopun**-hun (< |cuupun-hun|)

[3] Cited Yowlumne forms follow the transcription convention of Archangeli (1983, 1991), who in turn follows Newman (1944) except for using vowel doubling rather than a raised dot to indicate vowel length.

    c. 'become quiet' $\sqrt{\text{ni}}$　$\sigma_\mu\sigma_{\mu\mu}$　**ninee**-hin (< |ninii-hin|)

       'follow'　$\sqrt{\text{ywl}}$　$\sigma_\mu\sigma_{\mu\mu}$　**yawaal**-hin

Yowlumne is notorious for the phonological opacity that obscures templatic phonology. For example, long vowels shorten in closed syllables, which can obscure templatic vowel lengthening. Long high vowels shorten to mid, which is itself rendered opaque by long vowel shortening. Both effects are illustrated in *c'omhun* in (12b). The second forms in (12a,b) also exhibit epenthesis. For discussion of phonological opacity in Yowlumne, see e.g. Cole and Kisseberth (1997); McCarthy (1999, 2007).

    The reason for invoking templates to account for root shape in Yowlumne is largely due to the effects of affixation. A number of Yowlumne suffixes are also lexically associated with one of the three templates in (11). When a root combines with a template-selecting suffix, the root conforms to the template associated with the suffix, rather than to the template associated lexically with the root. Root templates emerge only when roots combine with non-templatic suffixes, as in (12). In (13), we see three different roots combining with the consequent adjunctive suffix, which imposes the iambic template. Each of the three roots is itself lexically associated with a distinct template. However, these lexical root templates are irrelevant in the consequent adjunctive: each root conforms perfectly to the demands of the iambic template associated with the affix. Forms in (13) are cited from Newman (1944: 163):

(13) a. $\sqrt{\text{tul}}$ **t'uloo**-ʔuy   lit 'burn-CONS.ADJ' (< |t'uloo-ʔuy|)
          (cf. lexical monomoraic root template, *t'ul*-)

      b. $\sqrt{\text{tan}}$ **tanaa**-ʔeːy   lit. 'go-CONS.ADJ' = 'footprint'
          (cf. lexical bimoraic root template, *taan*-)

      c. $\sqrt{\text{cuy}}$ **c'uyoo**-ʔoy-nu lit. 'urinate-CONS.ADJ-IND.OBJ'
                            (<|c'uyoo-ʔoy-nu|)
          (cf. lexical iambic root template, *c'uyoo*-)

    In (14), roots associated with three different lexical templates (11) combine with the desiderative affix -*hatin*, which imposes a moraic template. The roots all conform to the affix-associated template, surfacing as monomoraic with a single short vowel. Data from Newman (1944: 114):

(14) a. √linc'   linc'-atin   'speak-DESID'
                (cf. lexical monomoraic root template, *linc'-*)

      b. √wu?y   wu?y-atin   'go to sleep-DESID'
                (cf. lexical bimoraic root template, *woo?y-*)

      c. √li?   li?-hatin   'sink-DESID'
                (cf. lexical iambic root template, *li?ee-*)

The bimoraic template is imposed only by two suffixes, neither productive, but the pattern fits the expectation developed thus far. As seen in (15), regardless of root template, roots in combination with the continuative suffix -*'aa* assume a bimoraic shape, even when their lexical template is monomoraic (15a) or iambic (15b). Data from Newman (1944: 110):

(15) a. √linc   lenc'-aa   'speak-CONT' (< |liinc'-aa|)
                (cf. lexical monomoraic root template, *linc'-*)

      b. √hewt   hewt'-aa   'walk-DESID' (< |heewt'-aa|)
                (cf. lexical iambic root template, *hiweet-*)

Yowlumne is an interesting case for three reasons. One is the phonological opacity mentioned earlier. A second is the lexical association of templates with specific morphemes. A third is the conflict produced when a root and an affix in the same word are associated with conflicting templates which cannot both be satisfied. Such cases require a principle of conflict resolution. As seen already, the principle is simple: the affix template always wins. Chapter 7 deals more directly with the general situation of competing morphophonological generalizations within the same word. There we will see that sometimes the root "wins," sometimes the affix "wins," and sometimes the situation is more complex. Yowlumne also potentially bears on the Root-Affix Faithfulness Metaconstraint from Chapter 2, a hypothesis that preserving root structure is more important than preserving affix structure (McCarthy and Prince 1995). If Yowlumne templates are interpreted as pieces of lexical structure associated with root and with some affix morphemes, then the examples in (13)–(15) clearly contradict the RAFM. However, anticipating some of the discussion in section 4.4, it is also possible that the templatic effects in Yowlumne are emergent effects of morphophonological rules or constraints associated with particular morphological constructions. On such an approach, the RAFM is not necessarily applicable.

4.3.2 Tiene

A member of the Teke subgroup of Bantu, spoken in the Democratic Republic of Congo, Tiene (B.81) is subject to very strict restrictions on the forms that derived verb stems may assume (Ellington 1977; Hyman 2006). Tiene templates differ from those in Yowlumne in several ways. They are imposed not just on roots but on complex stems; they regulate not only prosodic size but also featural co-occurrence across the consonantal positions in the template.

Tiene exhibits typical Bantu verb structure (Hyman 2006). The root combines with (optional) derivational suffixes to form a subconstituent known as the D(erivational) Stem; this combines with a final inflectional suffix to form the complete I(nflectional) Stem, which in turn takes a number of inflectional prefixes.

Many Bantu languages place minimal or maximal size conditions on parts of the verb. For example, Ndebele imposes a disyllabic minimum on verbs as a whole, and, like many of its relatives, requires verb stem reduplicants to be exactly disyllabic (Downing 2001; Sibanda 2004; Hyman et al. 2009). Punu and Yaka limit the Inflectional Stem to four syllables; Koyo and Basaa limit it to three (Hyman 2008). Tiene goes even farther than these languages in imposing very tight templatic restrictions within the Dstem. These are summarized in (16):[4]

(16)   Restrictions on derived Dstems in Tiene
  a. Prosodic shape: bimoraic, either CVVC- or CVCVC-
  b. Place of articulation: in CVCVC- stems, C_2 must be coronal, C_3 must be grave (labial/velar)
  c. Nasality: in CVCVC- stems, C_2 and C_3 must agree in nasality

The size and place conditions (16a) and (16b) are the most actively templatic in that they can restrict morphological combination (a topic discussed in more detail in Chapter 9) by conditioning suppletive allomorph selection and affix placement. Condition (16c) is purely phonological, satisfied through phonological alternations in the feature [nasal]; see example (19) for illustration and discussion.

---

[4] Tiene also exhibits C, CV, and CVC Dstems, but these are monomorphemic. For discussion of constraints that apply to derived constituents only, see Chapter 8. The Definitive aspect construction in Tiene imposes a variant of the template described in (16) in which C_2 and C_3 are identical (Hyman 2006: 154; Ellington 1977: 93).

The effects of conditions (16a) and (16b) are illustrated in (17) by the Applicative and Causative suffixes. Both have coronal consonants: /l/ for Applicative, /s/ for Causative. When these combine with a mono-consonantal (CV) root, they are straightforwardly suffixed, as shown in (17a); the only effect of the template is to cause vowel lengthening in order to achieve bimoraicity (16a). But when these coronal suffixes combine with a CVC root, condition (16b) becomes relevant. If the root ends in a labial or velar, the templatic place of articulation requirements on C2 and C3 force the coronal Causative or Applicative affix to be infixed, with concomitant vowel epenthesis driven by templatic size considerations (17b). And if the CVC root ends in a coronal, neither infixation nor suffixation will satisfy the template. Instead a process of fusion, known as "imbrication" in the Bantu literature, takes place. The root-final consonant and the affixed coronal fuse into a single conson-ant (17c), with vowel lengthening as needed to achieve bimoraicity:

(17)   Coronal affixation in the Tiene Dstem: Causative /s/ (i) and Applicative /l/ (ii)

a.	i.	'eat'	lɛ	lee-s-ɛ	'feed'
		'fall'	vu	vuu-s-ɛ	'cause to fall'
	ii.	'throw, strike'	tá	tée-l-ɛ	'throw to/for'
		'wrap'	día	díi-l-ɛ	'wrap for'
b.	i.	'bathe'	yɔb-ɔ	yɔ-l-ɔb-ɔ	'bathe for'
		'reach'	bák-a	bá-l-ak-a	'reach for'
	ii.	'borrow'	suɔm-ɔ	sɔ-s-ɔb-ɔ	'lend'
		'hear'	yók-a	yólek-ɛ	'listen to'
c.	i.	'get thin'	taan-a	taa-s-a	'cause to get thin'
		'arrive'	pal-a	paa-s-a	'cause to arrive'
	ii.	'give birth'	bót-a	bóo-t-ɛ	'give birth for'
		'spread'	yal-a	yaa-l-a	'spread for'

Other suffixes exhibit both infixation and suppletive allomorphy in conforming to the Dstem template. For example, the stative suffix has two suppletive allomorphs, one with a velar cosonant /k/ and one with a coronal consonant /l/. As illustrated in (18a), coronal-final CVC roots select the velar allomorph, resulting in a derived stem that conforms to the template in (16b). CVC roots ending in a noncoronal consonant instead select—and infix—the coronal allomorph (18b), again produ-cing a template-conforming stem. In both cases, copy vowel epenthesis supplies the vowel needed to bring the stem into conformity with the template.

(18)   root   derived stem

a. ból-a   'break'   bóle-k-ɛ   'be broken' [/k/ suffix]
   kót-a   'tie'   kóte-k-ɛ   'be untied'
   yaat-a   'split'   yata-k-a   'be split'
   faas-a   'drive through' fasa-k-a   'be driven through'

b. kab-a   'divide'   ka-l-ab-a   'be divided'[/l/ infix]
   sook-ɛ   'put in'   so-l-ek-ɛ   'take out'
   nyak-a   'tear'   nya-l-ak-a 'be torn'

The lexicon of Tiene conspires to make it possible for a CVC root of any shape to have a template-conforming stative counterpart.

As mentioned earlier, the third Tiene templatic condition imposes nasal harmony between C_2 and C_3 of the derived stem template. This is accomplished by phonological alternations. The forms in (19a,b), derived by the stative (18a,b) suffix allomorphs, illustrate the application of nasal harmony to the affix. Suffixed /k/ and infixed /d/ nasalize in order to agree with a nasal root-final consonant. In the case of causative /s/, however, nasalization of the affix is not an option. Instead, the root oralizes (19c):

(19)   a. Suffixed stative /k/:
          vwuny-a 'mix'   vwunye-ŋ-ɛ 'be mixed'
       b. Infixed stative /d/:
          kam-a   'twist'   ka-n-am-a 'be turned over'
       c. Infixed causative /s/:
          dim-a   'become extinguished' di-s-eb-ɛ   'extinguish'

4.4 Pervasive templaticity

The term "pervasive templaticity" applies to cases in which the same template is imposed not on a single morphological construction, or just within verb stems as in Arabic, Yowlumne, or Tiene, but on so many unrelated constructions in the same language that it verges on having the status of a general stem or word template in the language. Known examples, including those discussed in this section, involve minimal word size.

4.4.1 Minimality in Lardil

Lardil, an influential case study in the early literature on Prosodic Morphology (McCarthy and Prince 1996, 1999b; Wilkinson 1988), is one of a number of languages that actively enforce a minimal size condition on content words. Both nouns and verbs in Lardil are subject to the requirement that they contain at least two moras, i.e. two short vowels or one long vowel. This condition is manifested in two ways: it can induce epenthesis in monomoraic words, and it can block an otherwise general apocope rule from applying to bimoraic words. This much-discussed Lardil pattern is documented in work by Hale (1973) and Klokeid (1976); significant treatments in the theoretical literature include Prince (1980), Wilkinson (1988), and McCarthy and Prince (1996, 1999b).

Example (20) illustrates epenthesis driven by the need to prosodically augment otherwise subminimal nouns (20a) and subminimal verbs (20b). The underlying form of these roots emerges under suffixation; suffixes in (20) are the accusative /-in/, on nominals, and the future /-uṛ/ and nonfuture /-in/, which can attach to nominals or verbs. The forms in (20c) show that augmentation does not apply to roots which are bimoraic or larger. These data are taken from Wilkinson (1988):

(20)

	Underlying	Plain	Suffixed	gloss	[Lardil]
a.	/wik/	wika	wik-in	'shade(-ACC)'	
	/wun/	wunta	wun-in	'rain(-ACC)'	
	/teř/	teřa	teř-in	'thigh(-NONFUT)'	
			teř-uṛ	'thigh-FUT'	
	/wik/	wika	wik-in	'shade(-NONFUT)'	
			wik-uṛ	'shade-FUT'	
b.	/peṯ/	peṯa	peṯ-uṛ	'bite(-FUT)'	
	/neṯ/	neṯa	neṯ-uṛ	'hit(-FUT)'	
c.	/peer/	peer	peerin	'ti-tree sp.(-NONFUT)'	
	/maan/	maan	maanin	'spear gen.(-NONFUT)'	
	/kentapal/	kentapal	kentapalin	'dugong(-NONFUT)'	

The same pervasive minimality condition blocks vowel apocope, which applies to unsuffixed nominals, i.e. those in the nominative case. Apocope (often termed "truncation" in the literature on Lardil) is shown applying normally to trisyllabic or longer forms in (21a):

(21) a. /yiliyili/   yiliyil   yiliyilin   'oyster'
         /yukarpa/   yukar   yukarpan   'husband'

      b. /parŋa/   parŋa   parŋan   'stone'
         /kela/   kela   kelan   'beach'

Apocope is blocked from applying to disyllabic forms in (21b), since its application would render these CVCV stems subminimal. While apocope itself is arguably morphologically conditioned (Blevins 1997), the minimality condition that blocks it is quite general in the language.

4.4.2 Minimality in Japanese

Like Lardil, Japanese enforces a bimoraic minimality condition through the lexicon. Detailed discussions of Japanese minimality can be found in Itô (1990) and Poser (1990), as well as in the many sources cited therein. In Japanese, a short vowel is one mora, a long vowel is two moras, and a coda consonant contributes one mora. The bimoraic foot can therefore take the three forms shown in (22):

(22) The bimoraic "foot":
      $[CV]_\sigma[CV]_\sigma$
      $[CVV]_\sigma$
      $[CVC]_\sigma$

As shown in a detailed study by Itô (1990), the bimoraic size requirement is imposed on a variety of morphologically derived stems: truncation (with or without concomitant affixation), compounding, loanword clipping. Example (23) illustrates the latter, which produces derived words of either one (23a) or two (23b,c) bimoraic feet:

(23) a. amachua   → ama   'amateur'   [Japanese]
          herikoputaa   → heri   'helicopter'
          terorizumu   → tero   'terrorism'
          chokoreeto   → choko   'chocolate'

      b. furasutoreeshoN   → furasuto   'frustration'
          asuparagasu   → asupara   'asparagus'
          iNtorodakushoN   → iNtoro   'introduction'

      c. waado purosessaa   → waa puro   'word processor'
          hebii metaru   → hebi meta   'heavy metal'
          rajio kasetto rekoodaa → raji kase 'radio cassette recorder'
          paasonaru koNpyuutaa → paso koN   'personal computer'
          jiiNzu paNtsu   → jii paN   'jeans pants'

Example (24) illustrates the imposition of a bimoraic stem template in tandem with the suffixation of /-tyan/, which form nicknames from proper girls' names. Names which are trimoraic or longer shorten (24a–c), and names which are monomoraic will lengthen to conform to the bimoraic template (24d) (Poser 1984):

(24)   a. akira   →   aki-tyan
           megumi   →   megu-tyan
           wa-sabu-roo   →   wasa-tyan

       b. syuusuke   →   syuu-tyan
           taizoo   →   tai-tyan
           kinsuke   →   kin-tyan

       c. midori   →   mii-tyan, mit-tyan, mido-tyan
           kiyoko   →   kii-tyan, kit-tyan, kiyo-tyan

       d. ti   →   tii-tyan

An interesting wrinkle in the Japanese case is that bimoraic minimality is not imposed on monomorphemic words in Japanese, some of which are monomoraic (e.g. *ki* 'tree', *e* 'picture', *no* 'field', *na* 'name', *su* 'vinegar'; Itô 1990: 218). Itô (1990) discusses this phenomenon at length; it is a species of derived environment restriction, the topic of Chapter 8.

Monomoraic CV roots do undergo vowel lengthening when suffixed by *-tyan*, as in (24), or when reduplicated or compounded. The following data from Poser (1990) and Itô (1990: 226) show lengthening induced by minimality requirements on base and copy in verbal stem reduplication (25a). As shown in (25b), lengthening is driven by minimality. Bases which are already bimoraic or larger in the input do not undergo vowel lengthening:

(25)   a. 'look'   mi   →   mii-mii   'while looking'
           'sleep' ne   →   nee-nee   'while dozing'
           'do'   sh(i)   →   shii-shii   'while doing'

       b. 'eat'   tabe   →   tabe-tabe   'while eating'
           'cry'   nak(i)   →   naki-naki   'while crying'
           'dance' odor(i) →   odori-odori   'while dancing'

Itô (1990: 226) reports a similar effect when CV number roots, e.g. *ni* '2', *shi* '4', *go* '5', *ku* '9', are compounded, e.g. as in reciting a telephone number. In summary, when a Japanese construction creates a new stem, it must meet the bimoraic minimality condition, a pervasive templatic constraint in the language.

4.5 The phonological analysis of templates

Templates have been modeled in phonological theory in three main ways. One method, which we may call DIRECT REPRESENTATIONAL, is due to McCarthy (1979, 1981) and McCarthy and Prince (1996, 1999b); see also McCarthy et al. (2012). This approach treats templates as pieces of representation, an empty skeletal frame into which the vowels and consonants of a given morpheme or stem or word must fit. While frameworks differ as to whether the representation consists of CV skeletal units (McCarthy 1979, 1981; Marantz 1982) or prosodic units (Steriade 1988; McCarthy and Prince 1990, 1996, 1999b), the main insight is the same: templates exist in the lexical representations of morphemes, and combine in a principled manner with the consonants and vowels that exist in the representations of those or other morphemes. In Yowlumne, for example, the lexical entry for the verb root meaning 'walk' consists of the prosodic template $\sigma_\mu \sigma_{\mu\mu}$ and the consonants /h,w,t/ and the vowel /i/. The lexical entry for the desiderative suffix, -'aa, consists of the suffix and the empty structure $\sigma_{\mu\mu}$, to which the root consonants and vowel associate.

A second approach, closely related to the first, treats each prosodic template as a single shape constraint on the output form of a stem or word. We can term this the DIRECT CONSTRAINT model. On this approach, Yowlumne would contain constraints to the effect "Root shape = $\sigma_\mu \sigma_{\mu\mu}$" and "Root shape = $\sigma_\mu \sigma_{\mu\mu}$." For each root and each templatic suffix, there would be a shape constraint lexically indexed to that specific morpheme, which would be applicable to any verb containing that morpheme. In Yowlumne, we saw that affix templates always take precedence over root templates. This could be modeled by a general constraint to the effect that all markedness constraints indexed to affixes outrank all markedness constraints indexed to roots (Zoll 1993). The DIRECT CONSTRAINT approach is consistent with frameworks that attribute all morpheme shape to morpheme-specific shape constraint. Hammond (1997), for example, suggests that instead of containing a lexical entry like /kæt/ for the lexeme CAT which specifies the input phonological shape of this root, the grammar instead contains a constraint "CAT = [kæt]" that specifies the output shape (Hammond 1997: 359). In their empirical predictions and overall insights, the DIRECT REPRESENTATIONAL and DIRECT CONSTRAINT approaches differ very little. Both treat template shape as essentially atomic, stipulated in the form of one constraint, or in one lexical representation.

Yet a third approach does not stipulate templatic shape outright at all, in representations or in morpheme-specific constraints. The EMERGENTIST approach derives templates from the interaction of general markedness constraints like FTBIN (feet must be binary at the moraic or syllabic level of analysis; Prince and Smolensky 1993[2004]) and *STRUC (which penalizes structure, favoring minimal forms). This approach derives from proposals by McCarthy and Prince (1994b), and has been further elaborated by Urbanczyk (2006) and Downing (2006) in Generalized Template Theory, discussed in section 4.5.3. The EMERGENTIST approach is applied by Hyman and Inkelas (1997) and Hyman (2006) to the Tiene data in section 4.3.2.

The EMERGENTIST approach has distinct advantages in dealing with templates that comprise both prosodic and segmental characteristics, as in Hausa (section 4.2.4), Yowlumne (4.3.1), and Tiene (4.3.2), and in dealing with templates showing contextual variation, as in Tiene, where the "template" does not assume a fixed shape but simply narrows down the class of possible stems. The EMERGENTIST approach essentially treats templates as an instance of morphologically conditioned phonology involving conditions on output size. We will examine two such analyses in the next two subsections.

4.5.1 Root templaticity in Sierra Miwok

The Sierra Miwok dialects are often characterized as exhibiting templatic morphology. Each verb root occurs in four different shapes ("First stem," "Second stem," etc.), illustrated in (26). These data are from Bye and Svenonius (2012), citing Freeland (1951), and represent the Central variety of Sierra Miwok (Freeland 1951; Freeland and Broadbent 1960).[5]

(26)

	First	Second	Third	Fourth	UR	
a.	tuyáaŋ-	tuyáŋŋ-	túyyaŋ-	túyŋa-	/tuyaŋ/	'jump'
b.	kóypa-	koyápp-	kóyyap-	kóypa-	/koypa/	'suck'
c.	hámme-	hamé??-	hámme?-	hám?e-	/hame/	'bury'
d.	lóot-	lótt-	lóttu?-	lót?u-	/lot/	'catch'

[Central Sierra Miwok]

---

[5] On the Northern dialect, see Callaghan (1987); on the Southern dialect, see Broadbent (1964).

The consonants and vowels of each root are lexical and not predictable. Stem shape is determined by the immediately following suffix in that suffixes select a particular stem type. However, the phonological form of the suffix does not correlate with the particular stem shape that is selected. For example, the 1+2 subject agreement suffix -ṭii selects for the First stem (yî̵lli̵-ṭii 'bite-1+2SUBJ'), while the negative habitual -wa꞉ selects for the Third stem (kállaŋ-wa꞉ 'dance-NEG.HAB.AG'). Both suffixes are -CVV in form. Overall, Sierra Miwok presents a superficially similar situation to what is found in Yowlumne.

The phonological templatic characteristics of the stem shapes are summarized in (27). All Second stems end in a geminate consonant, all Third stems have a medial geminate, and all Third and Fourth stems are disyllabic. Third and Fourth stems reverse the order of the root's final vowel and consonant. These fixed properties could readily be attributed to templates, listed in (27) from simplest to most detailed:

(27)   First stem   = CVCCV if root is vowel-final; CVCVVC if root is consonant-final and disyllabic, CVVC if root is consonant-final and monosyllabic.

Second stem = CVCC (imposed on last/only syllable of root; any preceding root syllables are unaffected)

Third stem   = CVC_iC_iVC, with C3 fleshed out by epenthetic [ʔ] in case of biconsonantal roots.

Fourth stem = CVCCV, with C3 fleshed out by epenthetic [ʔ] in case of biconsonantal roots.

Bye and Svenonius argue that none of these shape stipulations are necessary. Instead, they suggest, the specific templatic characteristics of the four Sierra Miwok verb stem shapes emerge from general properties of Sierra Miwok phonology and their interaction with stem-forming suffixes. Most of the variation in stem shape is at the right edge, involving the order of the final V and C or the length of the rightmost C.

According to Bye and Svenonius, First stems are formed from the root by suffixation of one of two suppletive allomorphs. V-final roots (like /hame/) form the First stem via infixation of a consonantal mora into the first syllable of the root (/hame/ + -μ_C- → ha<u>m</u>me). C-final roots (like /lot/) undergo suffixation of a vocalic mora (/lot/ + -μ_V- → lo<u>o</u>t).

Second stems are formed from the root by suffixing a consonantal mora. This mora is fleshed out by metathesis (/koypa/ + -μ_C- → kóya<u>pp</u>) or is realized as default [ʔ] (/hame/ + -μ_C- → hamé<u>ʔʔ</u>).

Third stems are formed by double affixation: suffixation of a consonant, and infixation of a consonantal mora into the first syllable. Monosyllabic roots must undergo vowel epenthesis in order to accommodate the affixed consonants, the second of which is fleshed out with default [ʔ]: /lot/+ -μ_C- + -C → lottuʔ. By contrast, disyllabic roots can absorb both the infix and the suffix without requiring epenthesis: /tuyaŋ/ + -μ_C- + -C → tuyyaŋ, /koypa/+ -μ_C- + -C → koyyap. The result is that Third stems are always disyllabic, a templatic property which on Bye and Svenonius's account emerges bottom-up from the lexicon rather than being stipulated top-down. For Bye and Svenonius, Fourth stems are formed by suffixing an empty V position to the Third stem which induces metathesis: /koyyap/ + V → *koypa*.

The stem-forming affixes are summarized in (28):

(28)

	Affix(es)	Example
First stem, V-final	-μ_C-	/hame/ → ha<u>mm</u>e
First stem, C-final	-μ_V-	/lot/ → lo<u>o</u>t
Second stem	-μC	/tuyaŋ/ → tuyá<u>nn</u>
		/koypa/ → kóya<u>pp</u>
		/hame/ → hamé<u>ʔʔ</u>
Third stem	-μ_C- + -C	/lot/ → lottuʔ
		/tuyaŋ/ → tu<u>yy</u>aŋ
		/koypa/ → ko<u>yy</u>ap
Fourth stem	-V	koyyap_Stem3 → koypa

The details of Bye and Svenonius's analysis are numerous and intricate. The takeaway point is, however, that it is possible to use a combination of affixation and morphologically conditioned phonology to derive apparently templatic shapes. The value of doing this lies in whether the phonological alternations required to convert inputs to the observed templatic shape are independently attested in the language, so that the rules or constraints involved already exist in the grammar of the language. If the phonological analysis required to convert an input to the output templatic shape is specific to that construction, then there is little insight to be gained by deconstructing a template into its component parts. In Sierra Miwok, the affixation + phonology analysis captures the generalization that most stem shape variation involves the right edge of the stem. In Tiene, as seen in the next section, a deconstruction of templates into a conspiracy of individual phonological constraints captures the relationship across coexisting templates in the same system.

4.5.2 Illustration of emergent templates: Tiene

Hyman and Inkelas (1997) develop an emergentist analysis of the Tiene templatic system (section 4.3.2) in which each component of the Dstem template in (16) is analyzed as a violable constraint. The constraints in (29) form the core of Hyman and Inkelas's analysis:

(29)   BIMORAIC MAX: A string contains no more than two vocalic moras
      BIMORAIC MIN: A string contains no fewer than two vocalic moras
      ONSET: A syllable must begin with a consonant
      FINALC: A string must end in a consonant

The two size constraints ensure that stems must have two V positions, while leaving the number of syllables unspecified; this allows for both monosyllabic and disyllabic DStems. ONSET and FINALC ensure that the only possible shapes are CVCVC and CVVC.[6] Hyman and Inkelas argue that deriving the template using constraints, rather than stipulating overall template shape in the form of a skeletal morpheme or as a single, complex constraint, has at least two advantages. First, the two Tiene derived Dstem templates (CVVC, CVCVC) are so similar that listing both in their entirety would miss generalizations (shared bimoraic size, shared final consonant) that the constraints in (29) capture. Second, both CVVC and CVCVC templates include components that are general throughout the grammar and need not be stipulated (e.g. the necessity for syllable onsets).

The segmental properties of DStems can also be specified by constraints. Hyman and Inkelas (1997) offer the three in (30). Several of these constraints refer to, and all apply to, what Hyman and Inkelas term the "trough," i.e. the Dstem minus its first syllable. This portion of the verb stem is a site for neutralization or restricted segments inventories in other Bantu languages as well (see e.g. Hyman 1998, on Yaka, and Hyman 2006, on languages more closely related to Tiene).

(30)   NADIR: An intervocalic C must be coronal
      OCP[Cor]:   No two adjacent coronals in the trough
      NASAL.HARMONY: Consonants in the trough must agree in nasality

---

[6] Note that these constraints, and this entire discussion, leave open the syllabification of the Dstem-final C. On the surface, it is always an onset, since it syllabifies with a following, obligatory, vowel-initial suffix. Within the Dstem, however, it is final. There is no overt evidence that it syllabifies as a coda.

Nᴀᴅɪʀ and OCP[Cor] collaborate to select velar suffix allomorphs for roots ending in a coronal, and select coronal suffix allomorphs when the stem ends in a noncoronal. They also force imbrication, fusing a coronal suffix (if no velar allomorph exists) with a root-final coronal consonant. Nᴀsᴀʟ.ʜᴀʀᴍᴏɴʏ has purely phonological effects, driving the nasalization and oralization of trough consonants, as illustrated earlier.

A virtue of capturing the featural conditions on the template by means of constraints is that the analysis can more elegantly capture the relationship between the Dstem template we have discussed so far and a variant which is applicable only in the Definitive Aspect. This morphological construction also creates CVCVC Dstems—but with the twist that C2 and C3 must be identical (Hyman 2006).

As shown in (31), biconsonantal (CVC) roots suffix a copy vowel and flesh out the C3 position with a consonant that is an exact copy of C2: /mat/ → *mat-at* (31a). The copy consonant brings the derived stem into conformity with the templatic size requirements. In (31b), we see root vowel shortening, also required by the size constraints: /maas/ → *mas-as*. CV roots, in (31c) add an *IVl* string which can be analyzed in several ways; one possibility is that the Definitive Aspect has an /-lV/ suppletive allomorph and undergoes consonant copy like the forms in (31a,b).

(31)   a. 'bathe'   yɔb-ɔ   yɔb-ɔb-ɔ   (yɔb-ɔ-b-ɔ)
           'go away'   mat-a   mat-at-a   (mat-a-t-a)
           'dance'   kén-a   kén-en-a   (kén-e-n-a)

       b. 'sweep'   kɔ́ɔ́m-ɔ   kɔ́m-ɔm-ɔ (kɔ́m-ɔ-m-ɔ)
           'cause to go away' maas-a   mas-as-a   (mas-a-s-a)

       c. 'fasten'   ka-a   ka-lal-a   (ka-l-a-l-a) [Tiene]
           'ripen'   bɛ-ɛ   bɛ-lɛl-ɛ   (bɛ-l-ɛ-l-ɛ)
           'crush'   tu-a (> twa) tú-lel-ɛ   (tú-l-e-l-ɛ)
           'hate'   sí-a   sí-lel-ɛ   (sí-l-e-l-ɛ)

Roots or Dstems which are CVCVC in shape, e.g. *kótob-* 'chase', cannot combine with either allomorph of the Definitive Aspect suffix (Hyman 2006: 154; Ellington 1977: 93), because such combinations would not obey the templatic size constraints.

The takeaway point from these data is that, while they conform like other Tiene Dstems to the size constraints, the Definitive Aspect stems violate the featural constraints in (30). C2 and C3 are identical, therefore agree in place; stems such as *mat-at-a* 'go away' violate OCP[Cor], while stems such as *yɔb-ɔb-ɔ* violate NADIR. While the size constraints in (29) describe all derived Tiene Dstems, those in (30) are outranked by the reduplicative constraints specific to the Definitive Aspect construction.

The approach taken by Hyman and Inkelas for Tiene, in which templates emerge from constraint interaction rather than being directly stipulated, is part of a general movement to derive templatic effects wherever possible. This approach has been applied not only to stem shape constraints, as in this chapter and in Bye and Svenonius (2012), but also to reduplication, as will be seen in Chapter 5 (see especially section 5.2.2 on A-templatic Reduplication).

4.5.3 *Generalized Template Theory and templatic size*

Moving beyond the individual language to generalizations across languages, Downing (2006) has called attention to an almost iconic relationship between morphological complexity and prosodic complexity. Downing develops "Morpheme-Based Generalized Template Theory," or MBT, according to which a branching morphological constituent, should, according to this principle, correspond to a branching (i.e. minimally binary) prosodic constituent.

In support of the constraint that complex stems must be minimally prosodically binary, Downing cites examples of disyllabic verb templates from Arabic and Hebrew, Sierra Miwok (section 4.5.1, though see Bye and Svenonius 2012 for counterarguments), and Javanese and Madurese. The bimoraic minimality condition imposed on morphologically complex stems in Japanese could also instantiate Downing's generalization. Here we present Downing's illustrative examples from Javanese and Madurese.

The "Active" nasal prefix in Javanese fuses with a stem-initial consonant in disyllabic roots (32a), but heads its own syllable when combining with monosyllabic roots (32b) (Downing 2006: 102, citing Uhrbach 1987: 233):

(32) a. cukur ɲukur   'shave someone'   [Javanese]
         bali   mbaleni 'return something'
         tulis nulis   'to write'
         dudut ndudut 'pull/interesting'
         sapu   ɲapu   'broom/to sweep'

b. cet   ŋəcet   '(to) print'
   bom   ŋəbom   '(to) bomb'
   dol   ŋədol   '(to) sell'
   tik   ŋətik   'typewrite/to type'
   bis   ŋəbis   '(to ride the) bus'

Downing points out that truncation itself sometimes violates the MBT, citing examples like Madurese vocative truncation (Downing 2006: 103, citing Stevens 1985: 83; Weeda 1987; McCarthy and Prince 1996, 1999b):

(33)

gloss	full	truncation	[Madurese]
'mother'	ibhu	bhu(ʔ)	
'one'	settoŋ	toŋ	
'yes'	enghi	ghi	

The MBT is, like the generalization that all templates correspond to one of the prosodic units in (4), defeasible, but expresses a strong cross-linguistic tendency about the form prosodic templates take.

Classic Generalized Template Theory (GTT; McCarthy and Prince 1994b, 1995; McCarthy 2000; Urbanczyk 2006, 2011) represents another step in the quest to capture cross-linguistic generalizations over templatic shape. In the Prosodic Morphology theory of the 1990s, the units of the prosodic hierarchy constrained representational templates, which had to be constructed from those units. In much the same way, Generalized Template Theory proposes to constrain templates by deriving them from two very basic types of constraints. In GTT, each template is classified as either an Affix or a Stem. These constituent types are associated universally with different prosodic shapes:

(34)   Affix = Syllable
        Stem = Foot

According to proposed universal constraints in GTT, the unmarked shape of an Affix is monosyllabic, while Stems are universally constrained to be prosodic words. Each Prosodic Word is universally constrained to contain a Foot, and each Foot is universally constrained to be binary at the moraic or syllabic level of analysis. In GTT, the prosodic binarity observed in the Tiene, Dinka, Arabic, Japanese, and Sierra Miwok templates is required by virtue of the classification of those templates as Stems. (To this, Downing 2006 adds the additional generalization that morphologically complex stems are disyllabic.)

Thus far in this chapter, all of the templates we have examined have been stems, which form the basis for affixation. However, templaticity is also found in reduplication, and here the tenets of GTT make an interesting prediction. In a survey of reduplication, Urbanczyk (2006) observes prosodic size differences across reduplicants which she suggests can be attributed to their classification as roots vs. affixes. This analysis was alluded to in Chapter 2 and will be discussed again in Chapter 5. Here we see a brief illustration from Lushootseed, as analyzed by Urbanczyk (2006) (see also Downing 2006). Urbanczyk assigns Affix status to the Diminutive, a CV reduplicative prefix, and Root status to the Distributive, a CVC reduplicative prefix. From Urbanczyk (2006), citing Bates et al. (1994):

(35)   Lushootseed reduplication
    a. Diminutives (reduplicant = type "Affix")
       'foot'   jə́səd   → ǰí-ǰəsəd   'little foot'
       'animal hide' s-kʷə́bšəd → s-kʷí-kʷəbšəd 'small hide'
    b. Distributives (reduplicant = type "Root")
       'foot'   jə́səd   → jə́s-jəsəd   'feet'
       'bear'   s-čə́txʷəd → s-čə́t-čətxʷəd 'bears'

As an Affix, a Diminutive reduplicant is constrained by GTT to assume a CV shape; as a Root, a Distributive reduplicant is constrained to be minimally bimoraic, i.e. CVC. The Diminutive is subject to vowel reduction (to [i], under most circumstances) (35a). By contrast, the Distributive vowel is a stressed schwa, which occurs only in roots (not in affixes). This asymmetry also follows from the Root/Affix distinction. By the Root-Affix Faithfulness Metaconstraint (McCarthy and Prince 1995) discussed in Chapter 2, this asymmetry follows from the classification of the Distributive and Diminutive as Root and Affix, respectively. Affixes are subject to phonological reduction from which root faithfulness protects roots.

GTT, including Downing's morphological complexity addition, constrains prosodic templates greatly, relative to the diversity of prosodic templates that can be imagined. The expectation is that templates will be bimoraic or disyllabic, for constituents classified as Stems, and that templates can be monomoraic for constituents classified as Affixes.

GTT does not lead us to expect the existence of ternary templates, as in Cupeño (6), Japanese (7), and Guarani (8); it is also ill-equipped to handle truncation of roots to CV syllables. The latter occurs in Zuni, applying to the first member of compounds (36a) and to stems combining with certain suffixes (36b) (McCarthy and Prince 1996, 1999b, citing Newman 1965):

(36) a. tukni   tu-mokʷkʷ'anne   'toe-shoe = stocking'
         melika   me-ʔoše   'Non-Indian-beːhungry = hobo'
      b. kʷ'alasi   kʷ'a-mme   'Crow'
         suski   su-mme   'coyote'

Despite these apparent counterexamples, it should be recalled that GTT is formulated within Optimality Theory, in which all constraints are in principle defeasible. The most important insight behind GTT is that templates are the result of constraint interaction, providing the theory with a means to model the language-internal and cross-linguistic variation seen in the templates discussed in this chapter.

4.6 Conclusion

We began this chapter with a definition of prosodic templates as phonological shape constraints on morphological constructions. The canonical case of a template would be a situation in which the output of a morphological construction assumes a fixed phonological output shape regardless of the phonological shape of its input. In such cases, the template could be—and has been—analyzed as a unit of prosodic representation that lacks segmental content of its own and is superimposed on morphological inputs, (re)defining their shape in a precise way. One of the clearest examples of this kind discussed in this chapter is nickname formation in Japanese, in which a long stem is truncated and a short stem is augmented so that the output stem is exactly bimoraic (section 4.4.2). However, most cases of templaticity discussed in this chapter deviate from the canon in at least one way. Some prosodic templates are only lower bounds on size (as in Lardil, section 4.4.1). Others are only upper bounds on size, as in English comparatives; section 4.2.1). Yet others characterize just part of a word, as in Cupeño habilitatives (section 4.2.2). And while the template observed in Guarani noise words has the rigid shape of a canonical template, the inputs to that construction do not exist independently, so evidence of overt conformity to a template is lacking. Finally, a great number of templates are complex, defined along a number of dimensions, with some elements more rigid than others. We saw examples of multicomponent templates in Hausa (section 4.2.4) and Tiene (4.3.2). These cases involve featural and segmental restriction; the notion of template as unit of prosodic representation is inadequate to describe them. Such cases motivate a different analysis of templates in which all of the aspects of templatic shape arise from the interaction of phonological constraints which apply to that construction. Such an approach is particularly appropriate for templates such as those in Tiene (section 4.3.2) or Sierra Miwok (section 4.5.1), which exhibit principled variation of a kind that is best captured in the grammar. We termed the grammatical approach to templaticity the EMERGENTIST view. On this view, templaticity is a special case of morphologically conditioned phonology or process morphology, and is best understood in the context of the phenomena discussed in Chapters 2 and 3.

5

Reduplication

Reduplication is the doubling of some part of a morphological constituent (root, stem, word) for some morphological purpose. Total reduplication reduplicates the entire constituent, as with plural formation in Indonesian (Western Malayo-Polynesian, Sundic): *kərá* 'monkey' → *kərá-kərá* 'monkeys' (Cohn 1989: 185). Partial reduplication duplicates some phonologically characterizable subpart, e.g. a maximal syllable, as in plural formation in Agta (Western Malayo-Polynesian, Northern Phillipines): *takki* 'leg' → *tak-takki* 'legs' (Marantz 1982: 439).

Reduplication has long been a topic of intense interest for morphological and phonological theory alike. From the morphological perspective, reduplication poses a challenge for item-based theories of morphology because of its process-like phonological character (see e.g. Anderson 1992: 59). From the phonological perspective, reduplication, along with other prosodic morphology like truncation and infixation, has trained a bright light on phonological representations, providing evidence outside phonology proper for constituents like the mora, syllable, and foot (see e.g. McCarthy and Prince 1996, 1999b). More recently, reduplication has been plumbed as a source of evidence for syntagmatic correspondence relationships among segments (e.g. McCarthy and Prince 1995, 1999a; Zuraw 2002). Reduplication is of interest in the study of morphological exponence, raising questions about the range of semantic and syntactic functions it is associated with (see Moravcsik 1978; Regier 1994; Kiyomi 1993, 1995). Reduplication also sheds light on the interleaving of phonology with morphology (the topic of Chapter 7).

5.1 Approaches to reduplication

Reduplication is at the same time a morphological and a phonological process. Theoretical approaches to, and typologically oriented surveys of, reduplication have focused to different degrees on these two sides to the phenomenon. It will be useful in our overview to distinguish two basic approaches to reduplication in the contemporary literature: **Phonological copying** and **Morphological doubling**. These approaches are distinguished in part by the differing interpretations they supply to the phonological identity effects accompanying—if not defining— reduplication, and the different ranges of effects they predict.

Phonological copying approaches, originating in the seminal work of Marantz (1982), McCarthy and Prince (1996, 1999b), and Steriade (1988), assume that the imperative to phonetically realize an abstract morpheme compels phonological copying from a base constituent. An early version of such a theory is depicted in (1). A reduplicant is a segmentally empty skeletal morpheme (here, a bimoraic syllable). The reduplicant derives its segmental content by means of copying from the base:

(1)   Reduplicant   +   Base   =   tak-takki

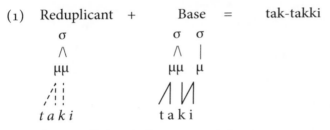

Copy and association

Most contemporary implementations of phonological copying theories take the approach in (1) as their starting point, though differ in the details of how copying is achieved. Serial Template Satisfaction (McCarthy et al. 2012) retains the item-based model of reduplicative templates but achieves copying through a constraint (Copy-X) rather than a rule-based process of copy and association. Base-Reduplicant Correspondence Theory (McCarthy and Prince 1995) goes farther, treating reduplicative templates as surface constraints on morpheme shape which are satisfied (sometimes imperfectly) through output correspondence between reduplicant and base. Some of the more salient empirical predictions of the constraint-based approaches, especially regarding base-reduplicant identity and the phonological reduction of reduplicants, will be discussed in sections 5.2 and 5.3.

The morphological doubling approach of Inkelas and Zoll (2005), sketched in more detail in sections 5.6 and 5.7, treats morphosemantic identity as basic. Phonological identity is a side-effect of inserting the same morpheme(s) twice, rather than an explicit imperative of the construction. Partial reduplication occurs when morphologically conditioned phonological truncation applies to one of the stems:

(2) Reduplication in Morphological Doubling Theory (Inkelas and Zoll 2005)

$$[\text{ tak-takki }]_{g([F])}$$

$$[\text{takki}]_{[Fi]} \qquad [\text{takki}]_{[Fi]}$$

Truncation   No truncation

Phonological copying theories were developed principally to account for phonological properties of reduplication, while Morphological Doubling Theory focuses more on morphological properties, while also addressing many of the same phonological generalizations.

Recent literature (Singh 2005; Yu 2005b; Inkelas 2008a) has suggested that phonological copying and morphological doubling may both be required, but in different, complementary contexts, a proposal to which we will return in section 5.4.

5.2 The phonology of reduplication

Any theory of reduplication must pay particular attention to the phonological form of reduplicants. This section surveys the major phonological components of reduplication, from prosodic shape (sections 5.2.1 and 5.2.2) to phonological reduction of reduplicants (section 5.2.3) to locality effects (sections 5.2.4 and 5.2.5). We begin with the prosodic shapes of reduplicants in partial reduplication.

5.2.1 Prosodic shape of reduplicant

Partial reduplication is the result of tension between the imperative to preserve base segments in the reduplicant and the imperative that the reduplicant should assume a particular prosodic shape: mora, syllable, foot, or prosodic word. This tension is observed whether the reduplicant is generated by phonologically copying base segments, as in phonological copying theories, or by morphologically supplying an independent double of the base and truncating it, as in Morphological Doubling Theory. We will focus here on the phonological considerations that affect reduplicant shape and relate the output form of the reduplicant to the morphological constituent that is its source.

In seminal articles, Moravcsik (1978) and Marantz (1982) observed that partial reduplication does not in general seem to duplicate an existing phonological constituent (e.g. syllable) of the base. Rather, partial reduplicants tend to have their own invariant overall shape, to which copied base segments are compelled to conform. In Mokilese (Oceanic), for example, partial reduplication, marking progressive aspect, always prefixes a bimoraic syllable to the base (Blevins 1996: 523, citing Harrison 1973, 1976):

(3) a. pɔdok   pɔd-pɔdok   'plant/planting'   [Mokilese]
         kasɔ   kas-kasɔ   'throw/throwing'
         nikid   nik-nikid   'save/saving'

     b. soorɔk soo-soorɔk 'tear/tearing'

     c. diar   dii-diar   'find/finding'
         wia   wii-wia   'do/doing'

In each case, the bimoraic monosyllabic reduplicant is fleshed out by copying segmental material from the base. However, the copied material does not itself necessarily constitute a bimoraic syllable in the base. In examples like (3a), the duplicated strings (e.g. [pɔd], [nik]) are split over two syllables in the base of reduplication ([pɔ.dok], [ni.kid]), but constitute a bimoraic syllable in the reduplicant. In examples like (3c), the reduplicant copies material which corresponds only to a mono-moraic CV in the base ([di], [wi]), lengthening the copied vowel in order to project two moras ([dii], [wii]). These data thus illustrate an important point made by Marantz (1982), namely that reduplication can copy either less than or more than the designated prosodic constituent from the base, as long as the segments that are copied can be reconfigured to form the desired shape.

Mokilese progressive reduplication also illustrates a second key generalization about partial reduplication, namely that what is invariant about reduplicant shape is prosodic, not skeletal or (usually) segmental. Early autosegmental approaches to reduplication, starting with Marantz (1982), proposed that reduplicant shape is characterized by CV units. However, pioneering work by McCarthy and Prince (1996, 1999b) and Steriade (1988) made clear that CV skeletal units are not the right level of generality; instead, reduplicants are more accurately and succinctly characterized in prosodic terms. Mokilese reduplicants can assume skeletally diverse shapes: CVC (3a) or CVV (3b,c). As seen in (4), vowel-initial bases in Mokilese give rise to yet a third reduplicant type, namely VCC:

(4) andip   and-andip   'spit/spitting'   [Mokilese]
     uruur   urr-uruur   'laugh/laughing'
     alu   all-alu   'walk/walking'

What unites the CVC, CVV, and VCC reduplicant shapes is the size
of the prosodic constituent added to the base as a result of reduplication. Each stem increases in size by exactly a bimoraic syllable.

The data in (4) illustrate a third key generalization about reduplicant
prosodic shape to which work in Optimality Theory has drawn particular attention, namely that while reduplication typically increases
prosodic size by a fixed amount, as is the case in (3) and (4), the
reduplicant itself is not always coextensive, in the output, with the
added prosodic constituent. This is clearly seen in the examples in
(4). The syllabification of *and-andip* is [an.d-an.dip], with the reduplicated string [and] split across two syllables; it is not *[and.-an.dip], in
which the reduplicant [and] is a surface syllable. This fact supplements
the observation made earlier that syllable reduplication does not necessarily copy existing syllables in the base; rather, it copies enough
material to make up a new syllable—and, as in cases like this, it can
copy even more than that if some of the copied material can fit into an
existing base syllable. The analysis given to [an.d-an.dip] by McCarthy
and Prince (1996, 1999b) is shown here:

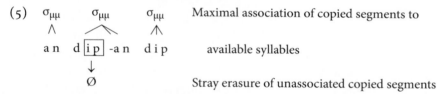

(5) $\sigma_{\mu\mu}$ $\sigma_{\mu\mu}$ $\sigma_{\mu\mu}$ Maximal association of copied segments to

     an d⌷ip⌷-an dip   available syllables

              ↓
              Ø   Stray erasure of unassociated copied segments

In Optimality Theory, patterns like those illustrated for Mokilese in
(3)–(4) have been taken as evidence that constraints on reduplicant
shape (e.g. REDUPLICANT = $\sigma_{\mu\mu}$) are minimally violable (Blevins 1996;
McCarthy and Prince 1994b, among many others).

The typology of shapes that reduplicants can be constrained to
assume has been a major topic of discussion in the literature.
McCarthy and Prince (1996, 1999b) contributed the central observation that the range of possible reduplicant shapes mirrors the range of
patterns that are found in truncation: both reduplicative and nonreduplicative truncation make use of the constituents in the prosodic
hierarchy, namely mora, syllable, foot, and prosodic word. The
examples from Tohono O'odham (Uto-Aztecan, Tepiman), Hausa,
and Manam (Oceanic) in (6) illustrate reduplicants of one mora (6a),

a bimoraic syllable (6b), and a bimoraic foot (6c), respectively. The Diyari (Pama-Nyungan) pattern in (6d) can be described either as a disyllabic foot or as a minimal prosodic word. The Acehnese pattern in (6e) can be described as maximal prosodic word reduplication, which amounts to the same thing as total reduplication, with no upper limit on the size of the reduplicant:

(6) a. Tohono O'Odham pluralizing reduplication: monomoraic syllable (Fitzgerald 2001: 942, 945)

'duck'	pado	→	pa-pado	'ducks'
'shawl'	tablo	→	ta-tablo	'shawls'
'cemetery'	siminǰul	→	si-siminǰul (→ sisminǰul)	'cemeteries'

  b. Hausa pluractional reduplication: bimoraic syllable (Newman 2000: 424)

| 'call' | kírá: | → | kík-kírá: | 'call (pluractional)' |
| 'beat' | búgà: | → | búb-búgà: | 'beat (pluractional)' |

  c. Manam reduplication forming adjectives, nouns and continuative verbs: bimoraic foot (Lichtenberk 1983; Buckley 1998)

'long'	salaga	→	salaga-laga
'knife'	moita	→	moita-ita
'ginger species'	ʔarai	→	ʔarai-rai
'go'	laʔo	→	laʔo-laʔo
'flying fox'	malaboŋ	→	malaboŋ-boŋ

  d. Diyari reduplication (multiple functions): minimal prosodic word (Poser 1990: 132, citing Austin 1981; see also McCarthy and Prince 1996, 1999b):

'woman'	wiḷa	→	wiḷa-wiḷa
'boy'	kanku	→	kanku-kanku
'to jump'	kuḷku	→	kuḷku-kuḷkuŋa
'bird species'	tjilpa	→	tjilpa-tjilparku
'catfish (pl.)'	ŋanka	→	ŋanka-ŋankaṇti

  e. Acehnese emphatic reduplication: maximal prosodic word (Durie 1985)

| 'drum' | tambô | → | tambô-tambô |
| 'mother' | ma | → | ma-ma |

In 'full copy' theories, e.g. Steriade (1988) and Morphological Doubling Theory (Inkelas and Zoll 2005), partial reduplication results from the truncation of one of the two copies in total reduplication. The question of what forms reduplicants can assume, therefore, reduces to the question of what truncation operations are possible in language. The Serial Template Satisfaction approach of McCarthy et al. (2012) takes an intermediate position, permitting both the copy of uninterrupted strings of segments and the copy of uninterrupted strings of syllables (and their segmental content).

In Base-Reduplicant Correspondence Theory (BRCT; McCarthy and Prince 1994b, 1995, 1999a), a theory of reduplication couched within Optimality Theory (Prince and Smolensky 1993, 2004), reduplicative templates are instantiated as constraints on the surface shape of reduplicants. The fact that constraints are violable permits BRCT to capture the potentially imperfect correspondence between a given reduplicant and the prosodic shape it is instantiating.

BRCT attributes reduplication to a phonological correspondence relation holding between two substrings in the output form of a word: the substring instantiating an abstract morpheme "RED", and the substring ("BASE") which is the output correspondent of the input. The RED-BASE correspondence is regulated by BR-Faithfulness constraints: MAX-BR (every element in BASE must have a correspondent in RED), DEP-BR (every element in RED must have a correspondent in BASE), and IDENT-BR (corresponding elements must be identical). If the BR-faithfulness constraints are completely satisfied, reduplication is total. If, however, a constraint on the shape of the reduplicant, e.g. RED=$\sigma_{\mu\mu}$, outranks MAX-BR, reduplication will be partial. This is illustrated in (7) with Mokilese data from (3):

(7)

	/RED-pɔdok/	RED=$\sigma_{\mu\mu}$	MAX-BR
a.	pɔdok-pɔdok	*!	
☞ b.	pɔd-pɔdok		* (ok)

A virtue of attributing reduplicant shape to constraints in a theory where constraints are ranked and violable is that the theory is capable of accounting for contextual variation in reduplicant shape and makeup. In Mokilese, for example, reduplication of vowel-initial bases copies not just the material needed to flesh out a bimoraic reduplicant syllable but also enough to provide an onset to the base-initial syllable. This is why *andip* reduplicates as *and-andip* instead of *an-andip* (4). This "overcopy" of [d], as shown by the analysis in (8), follows readily in BRCT, in which not only $\text{RED}=\sigma_{\mu\mu}$ but also syllable well-formedness constraints like ONSET ("a syllable must begin with a consonant") can determine how much material is copied. In (8a), the reduplicant is exactly bimoraic, but as its final consonant is a coda, the base-initial syllable and the reduplicant are both onsetless. In (8b), the reduplicant-final [n] provides the base with an onset, but leaves the reduplicant one mora below target. Candidate (8c) copies one segment more than will fit into the two moras projected from the reduplicant, but this is optimal because that extra copied segment, [d], provides the base-initial syllable with an onset, besting candidate (8a). The total reduplication candidate overcopies wildly without improving performance on the markedness constraints ONSET and $\text{RED}=\sigma_{\mu\mu}$ and loses to candidate (8c):

(8)

		RED-andip	ONSET	$\text{RED}=\sigma_{\mu\mu}$	FAITH-BR
	a.	an.-andip	**!		(dip)
	b.	a.n-andip	*	*!(-μ, +n)	(dip)
☞	c.	an.d-andip	*	*(+d)	(ip)
	d.	an.di.p-an.dip	*	*!**(+μ, +dip)	

More recent work on reduplication in Optimality Theory has embraced a movement towards deriving reduplicant shape instead of stipulating it with constraints like $\text{RED}=\sigma$. Under this umbrella fall the theories of Generalized Template Theory (McCarthy and Prince 1994b; Urbanczyk 1996; inter alia) and A-templatic Reduplication (Gafos 1998; Hendricks 1999).

Generalized Template Theory, discussed in Chapters 2 and 4, arose out of the desire to derive, rather than to stipulate, reduplicant shape. McCarthy and Prince (1994b) observed that, cross-linguistically, roots are often subject to foot-sized minimality constraints requiring them to be bimoraic or disyllabic, whereas affixes are often syllable-sized or smaller. Connecting this morphological observation to reduplication, McCarthy and Prince proposed that instead of stipulating reduplicant size constraints such as $\text{RED}=\sigma$ and $\text{RED}=\text{FOOT}$, it would be preferable to derive the size of an individual reduplicative morpheme from the classification of that morpheme as an Affix (thus smaller than or equal to a syllable) or a Root (thus larger than or equal to a binary foot). Downing (2006) observes that roots and affixes are not as uniform in prosodic size across languages as GTT presupposes, and proposes a revised version of GTT with a wider range of morphological categories—Affix, Root, Stem, Word—and a different mapping to phonological shape. Downing argues that reduplicative morphemes tend to assume the canonical shape in that language for the morphological category they correspond to, even when this shape is not one of the classic metrical categories. Recall from Chapter 4 the discussion of Lushootseed reduplication, in which the preposed Diminutive reduplicant is CV in shape (with a reduced vowel), while the preposed Distributive reduplicant is CVC in shape (with a full vowel):

(9) a. Diminutives (reduplicant = type "Affix")   [Lushootseed]
        'foot'   ǰásəd   → ǰí-ǰəsəd   'little foot'
        'animal hide' s-kʷə́bšəd   → s-kʷí-kʷəbšəd 'small hide'
     b. Distributives (reduplicant = type "Root")
        'foot'   ǰásəd   → ǰə́s-ǰəsəd   'feet'
        'bear'   s-čə́txʷəd   → s-čə́t-čətxʷəd   'bears'

Urbanczyk (2006) attributes the phonological shapes of the two types of reduplicant to their classification as Affix (constrained to be as small a syllable as possible) and Root (constrained to be minimally bimoraic).

The goal of GTT is to provide language-internal and cross-linguistic motivation for reduplicative templates. In general, however, the distinction between Root and Affix reduplication in this theory has been based on phonology, not morphology; prosodic shape aside, no semantic or distributional evidence supports classifying the Distributive in Lushootseed as a root.

5.2.2 A-templatic Reduplication

In contrast to templatic analyses in which an individual reduplicant is constrained to assume the shape of an affix, a root, a syllable, a foot, or some other representational unit, *A-templatic* Reduplication analyses have been given to cases of reduplication in which reduplicants are not directly subject to shape constraints and in which reduplicant form is simply a byproduct of constraints on stem shape. One example can be found in Temiar (Mon-Khmer, Aslian), in which continuative aspect is marked by consonant reduplication. Biconsonantal roots prefixally reduplicate both consonants (10a); triconsonantal roots exhibit infixing reduplication of their final consonant only (10b) (Gafos 1998: 517, citing Benjamin 1976):

(10) a. 'to call'   kɔɔw   →   kwkɔɔw   [Temiar]
          'to sit down'   gəl   →   glgəl
      b. 'to lie down'   slɔg   →   sglɔg
          'to ask a question' smaaɲ →   sɲmaaɲ

Gafos observes that the primary generalization is output stem shape (CC.CVC), which reduplication helps to achieve. A template is clearly involved, but the reduplicant itself is not fixed; the reduplicant is whatever size and in whatever place is needed to convert an input to a CC.CVC output. Hendricks (2001) develops a "compression" model for similar minimal reduplication effects in other languages in which reduplication appears to have the effect of slightly increasing stem size, but not by an amount equivalent to any of the familiar prosodic constituents (mora, syllable, foot).

5.2.3 Phonological reduction of reduplicants

Partial reduplication is prone to phonological reduction, in which segmental and prosodic structure is reduced, or neutralized, in the partial reduplicant. For example, Sanskrit intensive reduplication elim- inates onset clusters in the reduplicant (Steriade 1988: 105–8). Input stems in (11) are shown in their full grade form:

(11) 'cry out' krand   →   kan-i-krand   [Sanskrit]
      'fall'   bhranɛ   →   ban-i-bhranɛ   (→ baniːbhranɛ)
      'sleep'   svap   →   saː-svap-
      'sound'   dhvans   →   dan-i-dhvans- (→ daniːdhvans-)

A major achievement of approaches to reduplication within the BRCT framework is the ability to characterize and motivate the types of phonological reduction found in partial reduplication. Niepokuj (1991) and Steriade (1988), among others, were instrumental in draw- ing attention to the fact that partial reduplicants often exhibit structural simplification, e.g. restrictions on syllable shape or reduction of length contrasts, as well as segmental reduction, e.g. neutralization of segmental contrasts. The ability to capture both types of reduction is a cornerstone of Base-Reduplicant Correspondence Theory (BRCT; McCarthy and Prince 1995).

Steriade attributes the form of the prefixed reduplicants in (11) to a principle requiring reduplicants to exhibit the unmarked setting for the complex onset parameter, namely prohibition. This insight that reduplicants can have more stringent markedness restrictions than the bases they are derived from plays a key role in BRCT, in which reduplicant unmarkedness effects are analyzed as the emergence of general unmarkedness effects in the language which are normally subordinated to higher-ranking IO-faithfulness. In Sanskrit, complex onsets are not simplified in all syllable nuclei; MAX-IO protects onset clusters in bases and in unreduplicated words. However, by hypothesis, Sanskrit nonetheless shares *COMPLEX, the universal markedness constraint against complex onsets. If *COMPLEX outranks FAITH-BR, it will exert an effect in reduplicants. The reason it does not exert its effects everywhere is that it is outranked by FAITH-IO, which protects outputs that correspond to input stems:

(12)

	/RED-svap/	MAX-IO	*COMPLEX	MAX-BR
a.	svaː-svap		**!	
☞ b.	saː-svap		*	** (vp)
c.	saː-sap	*! (v)		* (p)

The "Emergence of the Unmarked" (TETU) scenario which results from the ranking FAITH-IO » PHONO-C » FAITH-BR plays out in many cases of reduplication (McCarthy and Prince 1994a). As Alderete et al. (1999) point out, TETU is one source of fixed segmentism in reduplication, the other being Melodic Overwriting, discussed later in the context of echo reduplication (section 5.6.4). As an example of TETU, Alderete et al. (1999: 328, 336–9), citing Akinlabi (1984) and Pulleyblank (1988), invoke the example of Yoruba gerundive reduplication, in which the vowel in the monomoraic prefixing reduplicant is always [i]:

(13)   'be warm, hot'   gbóná   →   gbí-gbóná   'warmth, heat'   [Yoruba]
       'be good'   dára   →   dí-dára   'goodness'
       'see'   jɛ   →   jí-jɛ   'act of seeing'

Alderete et al. (1999) analyze the fixed [i] vocalism in (13) as an emergent unmarkedness effect, pointing to convincing evidence that [i] is the unmarked vowel in the Yoruba inventory (Pulleyblank 1988, 2009), and observing that treating [i] as an affix or otherwise stipulating its quality would miss this essential generalization. Instead, Alderete et al. (1999) argue, reduplicative [i] is best modeled with the constraint ranking IDENT-IO » *{a,e,o,u}, IDENT-BR » *i.

Beyond capturing generalizations about unmarked segments, the TETU analysis of fixed segmentism also extends nicely to cases in which default segmentism is contextually conditioned. One example, from Lushootseed Diminutive reduplication (Bates et al. 1994; Urbanczyk 1996, cited in Alderete et al. 1999: 340), is also mentioned in Chapters 2 and 4. In Lushootseed (Central Salish), roots beginning with a single consonant and a short full vowel exhibit exact CV reduplication (14a). However, any other kind of root—one whose first syllable has an onset cluster, or a long vowel, or a schwa—exhibits *Ci* reduplication, where [i] is the default vowel used in case exact copy is not permitted (14b):

(14)   a. CV reduplication (roots beginning with [Lushootseed]
          CV, V = a short full vowel)
          'hand'   čáləs   → čá-čáləs   'little hand'
          'bad'   s-dukʷ   → s-dú-ʔ-dukʷ 'riffraff'

      b. Ci reduplication (roots beginning with Cə, CVː, CC)
          'run'   təláw-il   → tí-təlaw'-il 'jog'
          'knife'   s-dúːkʷ   → s-dí-duːkʷ 'small knife'
          'walking stick' c'kʷ'usəd → c'í-c'kʷ'usəd 'little walking stick'

According to Alderete et al., markedness constraints on syllable structure prevent the exact copying of anything but a CV sequence; inexact copying reverts to maximally unmarked structure, which for this position in the word is Ci.

TETU effects obtain almost exclusively in partial reduplication (see e.g. Steriade 1988; Niepokuj 1991; Urbanczyk 1996; Downing 2006). It is possible to imagine segmental TETU effects in total reduplication, but cases of this sort do not seem to occur. For example, one does not find total reduplication constructions in which all the vowels of one copy are replaced by schwa or [i] (e.g. hypothetical *sandroga → sandroga-sindrigi*); one does not find all complex onsets reduced to simple onsets (*sandroga-sandoga*), or all codas eliminated (*sandroga-sadroga*), just in one copy in total reduplication, even though reduction to schwa, simple onsets, and coda reduction are all hallmarks of partial reduplicants.

The behavior of CVC Distributive reduplication in Lushootseed (Urbanczyk 2006; Downing 2006) further illuminates this asymmetry. In the Distributive, the reduplicant vowel is an invariant, stressed schwa, which is more marked than [i] (15). Stressed schwa does not appear at all in affixes, for example. Data are from Urbanczyk (2006), citing Bates et al. (1994):

(15)   Lushootseed Distributives
    'foot'   ǰə́səd   →   ǰə́s-ǰəsəd   'feet'
    'bear'   s-čə́txʷəd   →   s-čə́t-čətxʷəd 'bears'

As discussed in Chapters 2 and 4, Urbanczyk (2006) analyzes the Distributive reduplicant as a Root with all the phonological privileges—stressed schwa, syllable coda contrasts—accorded to roots but not affixes. By contrast, the Diminutive is an Affix characterized by the smaller size and vowel inventory of affixes generally.

Whether or not this analysis is morphologically motivated, this example clearly shows the correlation between size (CVC vs. CV) and the degree to which marked structures are allowed. The prosodically smaller the reduplicant, the more prone it is to segmental reduction. This can be conjectured to follow from the diachronic hypothesis of Niepokuj (1991) that partial reduplication develops over time via the erosion of prosodic structure and segmental contrasts from the less prosodically salient of the two copies in total reduplication. As a result, the smallest partial reduplicants will be the oldest, and will show the most segmental neutralization. More research into the historical development of reduplication, and a more detailed cross-linguistic survey correlating prosodic size with amount of segmental neutralization, is clearly needed to test this hypothesis. One step in this direction has been taken recently by McCarthy et al. (2012), who survey foot-sized prefixing reduplication in Australian and Austronesian languages. They found that while omission of the final consonant of such reduplicants is common, omission of a medial coda is unattested. This finding is more suggestive of phonological erosion at the base-reduplicant boundary than of general, across-the-board unmarkedness in reduplicants.

5.2.4 Locality and nonlocality in reduplication

Turning from reduplicant size and shape to reduplicant positioning, we address the positioning in the word of partial reduplicants. Most cases of partial reduplication are local; these reduplicants are adjacent to the part of the base from which they draw their segmental substance. However, a small number of cases depart from this pattern, exhibiting "opposite-edge" reduplication. Examples are given in (16) from Madurese (Western Malayo-Polynesian, Sundic), in which opposite-edge prefixing reduplication encodes plurality (Steriade 1988, citing Stevens 1985), and from Koryak (Northern Chukotko-Kamchatkan), in which opposite-edge suffixing reduplication encodes absolute case (Riggle 2004, citing Bogoras 1969: 687–8):

(16)   Opposite-edge reduplication
    a. dus-garadus   'fast and sloppy'   [Madurese]
        waʔ-buwaʔ-(an) 'fruits'
        bit-abit   'finally'
        w̃ã-mõw̃ã   'faces'

    b. mɪtqa-mɪt   'oil'   [Koryak]
        kilka-kil   'shellfish'
        qanga-qan   'fire'

Based on the rarity of such patterns, Nelson (2003, 2005) argues that opposite-edge reduplication is not a real option in grammars, and that apparent cases always have another explanation. For Madurese, for example, Nelson offers an alternative analysis in which the construction is total reduplication with truncation of the first copy (e.g. *mõw̃ã-mõw̃ã → w̃ã-mõw̃ã*). In support of this account, Nelson observes that compounds undergo the same reduction: *tuzhuʔ* 'finger' + *ənpul* 'pink' → *zhuʔ-ənpul* 'pinky' (Nelson 2005: 141). In Morphological Doubling Theory, full copy with truncation is exactly the analysis that is given to all partial reduplication, not just in unusual cases (Inkelas and Zoll 2005):

(17)   Partial reduplication in Morphological Doubling Theory

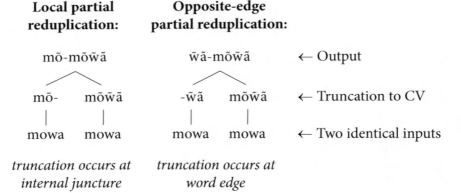

Local partial reduplication: **Opposite-edge partial reduplication:**

mõ-mõw̃ã   w̃ã-mõw̃ã   ← Output

mõ-   mõw̃ã   -w̃ã   mõw̃ã   ← Truncation to CV

mowa   mowa   mowa   mowa   ← Two identical inputs

truncation occurs at   *truncation occurs at*
internal juncture   *word edge*

The question for Morphological Doubling Theory would be why truncation occurs more often at the internal reduplication juncture, producing local reduplication, than it does at a word edge, resulting in opposite-edge reduplication.

For Chukchee, which resembles Koryak very closely, Nelson suggests that the source of opposite-edge reduplication is phonological, not morphological; opposite-edge reduplication is a phonological repair which protects the stem-final consonant from undergoing mutation. Reduplication is found in absolutive stems whose prosodic shape is one of the following: CVC, (C)VCV, (C)VCC, and (C)VCCV. Reduplication is never found in stems of other shapes, e.g. CVCVC, CVVCV, etc. According to Nelson (2005: 139–40), citing Krause (1980), "The shapes that do undergo the reduplication are 'uniquely those bases whose morpheme-final sequences would be predicted to undergo the word-final phonological mutations of final vowel reduction and/or schwa apocope and/or final epenthesis if left unaffixed' (Krause 1980:157)." Nonetheless, the process is uniquely associated with, and marks, the absolutive. Even if it is a phonological repair, it is morphologically conditioned to apply in all and only absolutive forms, which in most theories would put it squarely in the camp of morphology.

Opposite-edge reduplication is clearly unusual, cross-linguistically, but ruling it out altogether is probably premature without a better understanding of its historical origins. Reduplication creates new internal junctures, producing a derived environment at which phonological alternations are likely to take place. Erosion at the internal juncture is a plausible source of same-side partial reduplication. If, for example, partial reduplication arises from syncope of unstressed material in a form like hypothetical [mádi-mádi] → [mad-madi], then same-side reduplication is much likelier than opposite-side reduplication, which would require deletion of peripheral unstressed material: [madí-madí] → [dí-madí]. Peripheral deletion is certainly attested cross-linguistically; there is no reason to think it would never apply to the output of reduplication.

5.2.5 Internal reduplication

We turn in this section from adfixing reduplication—whether local or opposite-edge—to infixing, or internal, reduplication. An example of internal reduplication is given in (18), from Mangarayi (Yu 2007, citing Merlan 1982; see also Kurisu and Sanders 1999 for discussion):

(18) gurjag   g-**urj**-urjagji   'having a lot of lilies'   [Mangarayi]
      gabuji   g-**ab**-abuji   'old person'
      yirag   y-**ir**-irag   'father'
      waŋgij   w-**aŋg**-aŋgij   'child'
      jimgan   j-**im**-imgan   'knowledgeable one'

As for positioning within the word, internal reduplication is generally amenable to the same analysis as nonreduplicative infixes, discussed in greater detail in Chapter 6. For the purpose of illuminating properties specific to reduplicative infixes, it is important here to focus on two properties of reduplicative infixation: the locality effect and the "overcopying" effect.

5.2.5.1 Locality   Internal reduplication almost always copies adjacent material, as is the case in Mangarayi, where the reduplicative infix copies the immediately following substring of the base. The "opposite-edge" effects discussed in section 5.2.4 are even rarer in internal than in adfixing reduplication, if one is to judge on the basis of examples discussed in the literature on reduplication. One example of nonlocal internal reduplication has been discovered in Creek (Muskogean), in which plural adjectives are formed by suffixing a copy of the initial CV of the stem just before the stem-final consonant, which is the onset of the syllable headed by the adjectival ending [-iː]. The data in (19) are from Riggle (2004), who cites Haas (1977) and Martin and Mauldin (2000). Reduplicants are double-underlined:

(19) 'clean'   hasátkiː   hasat<u>hakí</u>ː   [Creek]
      'nasty, dirty, filthy'   likácwiː   likac<u>liwí</u>ː
      'soft'   lowáckiː   lowac<u>lokí</u>ː
      'sweet'   cámpiː   cam<u>capí</u>ː
      'torn up, mashed'   citákkiː   citak<u>cikí</u>ː
      'ugly, naughty'   holwakí   holwaː<u>hokí</u>ː

5.2.6 The "overcopying" effect, or exfixation

Many examples of apparent root reduplication may in fact be better analyzed as an outer layer of affixation which is phonologically infixing, looking 'inside' the base of reduplication to target an embedded prosodic constituent projected from the root. (On infixation more generally, see Chapter 6.) The argument for infixation in these cases comes for "overcopying" effects, where apparent root reduplication also copies segments from adjacent affixes which happen to syllabify, on the surface, with segments within the root. This phenomenon is termed "exfixation" in McCarthy and Prince (1995: 70). Subsequent discussions, from various points of view, can be found in Downing (1997b, 1998b, 1999b), Inkelas and Zoll (2005), and McCarthy et al. (2012).

A well-known example of exfixation is provided by Tagalog (Western Malayo-Polynesian), which exhibits CV root reduplication (e.g. Schachter and Otanes 1972). Reduplication is a concomitant of a number of Tagalog prefixes, including *maN-*, illustrated below in (21). As seen, reduplication roughly targets the first CV of the root. However, reduplication cannot completely straightforwardly simply be analyzed as the innermost layer of morphology, because it copies the effects of fusion between a (preceding) prefix-final consonant and a (following) root-initial segment. In (21a), the prefix-final and root-initial consonants fuse into one, which forms the onset of the CV substring that reduplicates. In (21b), the prefix-final consonant syllabifies with the root-initial vowel, constituting the CV substring that reduplicates.

McCarthy and Prince provide an exfixation and "backcopying" analysis in which the prefixed reduplicant fuses morphologically with a preceding prefix; the resulting CVC morpheme is required to phonologically match the base, resulting in the "backcopying" of the preceding prefix-final consonant to the base of affixation. Example (20), from McCarthy and Prince (1995: 61), illustrates graphically the fusion analysis. The diagram illustrates Samala (Ineseño Chumash), not Tagalog, but the logic is the same. The /s/ prefix fuses morphologically with the RED morpheme, resulting in a CVC reduplicative string which, through bidirectional correspondence, becomes identical to the first CVC of the following base:

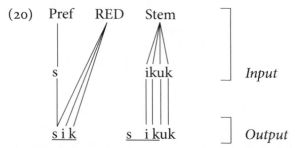

An alternative approach to exfixation effects treats them as morphologically regular (i.e. not requiring morphological fusion) but phonologically infixing. Booij and Lieber (1993), Fitzpatrick-Cole (1994),

Downing (1997b, 1998b, 1999b), and Inkelas and Zoll (2005) all build on Aronoff's earlier proposal that Tagalog exhibits head (root) reduplication by proposing that reduplication is an outer morphological process which targets an inner prosodic constituent, which we may call the Prosodic Root. This inner constituent corresponds closely but sometimes imperfectly to the morphological root. The Prosodic Root is demarcated with curly braces in (21). Data are taken from Inkelas and Zoll (2005), citing English (1986) and Schachter and Otanes (1972: 103):

(21)	root	maŋ -root	reduplication [Tagalog]
a.	bayan	ma{mayan}	mama{mayan}
	'town'	'to live or reside in a town'	'resident of a city or town'
b.	ibig	ma{ŋibig}	maŋi{ŋibig}
	'to be a suitor'	'beau, suitor, lover'	'love, fondness'

The mismatch between prosodic and morphological structure that is required to support this analysis of apparent exfixation is discussed in more detail in Chapter 10.

Additional support for the prosodic infixation analysis of Tagolog comes from variation in the location of reduplication. Rackowski (1999: 5) cites the variation depicted in (22), in which aspectual reduplication (underlined) can target any of the (bracketed) embedded subconstituents of the word. This general pattern is also discussed by Carrier (1979), among others.

(22)

Unreduplicated	...with contemplated aspect reduplication
ma-ka-pag-pa-hintay →	ma-[kaa-ka-pag-pa-hintay]
ABILITY-COMPLETE-TRANS-CAUSE-wait	ma-ka-paa-[pag-pa-hintay]
'be able to cause someone to wait'	ma-ka-pa-paa-[pag-hintay]
	ma-ka-pag-pa-hii-[hintay]

Variable order in Tagalog reduplication has been treated both in terms of dominance (hierarchical position) and precedence (simple linear ordering). Syntactic analyses of scrambling (Rackowski 1999) or lowering (Skinner 2008) manipulate the hierarchical position of reduplication in the word. Focusing instead on precedence, Ryan (2010) develops a maxent Harmonic Grammar (see e.g. Smolensky and Legendre 2006; Hayes and Wilson 2008) to weight constraints on prefix bigrams. Free ordering among prefixes, including reduplication, is modeled via equal weighting of the relevant bigrams. Combining hierarchical and precedence tactics, Condoravdi and Kiparsky (1998) develop an Optimality Theory analysis which attributes variable Tagalog reduplicant order to tension between Alignment constraints drawing the reduplicant to the root and Scope constraints compelling it to a high hierarchical position and forcing it towards the beginning of the word. Whichever approach is taken, the essential observation is that the reduplication process operates semantically on the entire word yet accesses enough internal structure to be able to infix to and copy the (Prosodic) root.

5.3 Phonological identity effects in reduplication

Phonological identity effects in reduplication are not surprising: whether it is analyzed as phonological copying or morphological doubling, in most cases the logical starting point in reduplication is two phonologically identical copies. In partial reduplication, identity is necessarily disrupted in terms of quantity, because the reduplicant must assume a fixed shape which is often smaller (or bigger) than the base. Identity can also be disrupted along the quality dimension, often in cases in which the reduplicant undergoes reduction while the base remains intact. Prosodic templaticity and reduction effects were discussed in sections 5.2.1 and 5.2.3, respectively. Base and reduplicant can diverge further if normal, word-level phonology applies to the output of reduplication, effecting changes such as assimilation or epenthesis at the base-reduplicant juncture (e.g. Hausa *tàm-tàmbáyà:* → *tàntàmbáyà:* ~*tàttàmbáyà:* 'ask (pluractional)'; Newman 2000: 425), or assigning word-level accent which happens to target a syllable which is in the base or the reduplicant (e.g. Chamorro *hugándo* 'play' → *hugágando* 'playing'; Topping 1973: 259).

5.3.1 Wilbur's Identity principle

Many researchers in reduplication have been struck by the impression that there is less phonological divergence between base and reduplicant than might be expected, given the general phonological alternations of the language. Wilbur (1973) terms this the "Identity Effect," pointing to cases in which an ordinary phonological alternation is either inhibited from applying if it would create divergence between base and reduplicant ("underapplication"), or applies even when not conditioned ("overapplication"), in order to keep base and reduplicant the same in some respect.

An example of underapplication occurs in Indonesian. As documented in Cohn (1989), Indonesian has alternating stress, with the rightmost stressed syllable exhibiting primary stress: *àmerikànisási* 'Americanization' (p. 170). Penultimate main stress assigned on a new cycle of affixation causes pre-existing stresses to delete under clash and otherwise to subordinate to secondary: *bìjaksána* 'wise' → *kə-bìjaksaná-an* 'NOM-wise-NOM = regulations' (p. 176). In compounds, the stress of the first member is subordinated to that of the second member: *polùsi udára* 'pollution' + 'air' = 'air pollution' (p. 188). In reduplication, however, stress subordination underapplies: *minúm-an* 'drink-NOM' reduplicates as *minúman-minúman* 'drinks' (p. 185). Significantly, if a reduplicated form is suffixed, it behaves exactly like a compound, with stress subordination applying normally: *[minùman-minumán]-ña* 'drinks-DEF = the drinks' (p. 185); cf. *anèka rágam* 'various' + 'way' = 'varied' (p. 188); *kə-[anèka-ragám]-an* 'NOM-varied-NOM = variety' (p. 189). Cohn and McCarthy (1998) analyze the stress in reduplication as underapplication of stress subordination, driven by reduplicant-base identity requirements. When a suffix is added, fusing prosodically into the base, the base and reduplicant no longer have the potential for total identity, and stress subordination can apply. But when stress subordination would be the only barrier to total identity, it underapplies.

An example of overapplication occurs in Dakota (Siouan; Shaw 1980: 344–5; see also Marantz 1982: 459), in which velars normally palatalize after /i/, and spirants voice intervocalically. Pluralizing CVC reduplication postfixes a copy of the CVC root, and in cases like the following, creates the context for "overapplication" of velar palatalization. In these examples, velar palatalization is conditioned transparently in the first copy of the root but not in the second:

(23)   wičhá-ki-**čax-čax**-ʔiyèya   'he made it for them quickly'
                      (root = /kax/)
     napé kí-**čos-čoz**-a   'he waved his hand to him'
                         (root = /kos/)

Underapplication and overapplication are opacity effects. The ability to capture them with the same mechanism that drives copying in the first place—an identity relation between base and reduplicant—is a cornerstone of BRCT.

5.3.2 *Reduplicative opacity in BRCT*

As seen in section 5.2.1, BRCT (McCarthy and Prince 1994b, 1995, 1999) attributes reduplication to a phonological correspondence relation holding between two substrings in the output form of a word: the substring instantiating an abstract morpheme "RED", and the substring ("BASE") which is the output correspondent of the input. The RED-BASE correspondence is regulated by faithfulness constraints: MAX-BR (every element in BASE must have a correspondent in RED), DEP-BR (every element in RED must have a correspondent in BASE), and IDENT-BR (corresponding elements must be identical). MAX-BR, DEP-BR, and IDENT-BR are counterparts of the input-output constraints (MAX-IO, DEP-IO, IDENT-IO) governing the correspondence between BASE and input.

(24)   RED   ⇔   BASE   Original ('Basic') model of BRCT

⇕

Input

In the original model of BRCT, there is no correspondence relation between RED and the input; RED is thus entirely dependent, for its substance, on BASE. (See McCarthy and Prince (1995) and Struijke (2000) for arguments that the input may in some cases directly influence RED, forcing a change in the architecture of BRCT.)

In BRCT, overapplication and underapplication result from high-ranking BR-Faithfulness constraints that mandate identity, causing the same alternation to apply to both BASE and RED even if it is only transparently conditioned in one of them, or preventing an alternation from applying because its effects would introduce a discrepancy between the copies. As an example of overapplication affecting RED, McCarthy and Prince (1995) cite the case of CVC reduplication in Madurese, a language which epenthesizes the glides ʔ, *w* between adjacent vowels. As seen in (25a,b), a glide epenthesized into the base will also appear in the (underlined) reduplicant, even when not intervocalic there. Overapplication of nasal harmony, normally conditioned only by a preceding nasal consonant, is also illustrated in the reduplicant in (25b). (Note the opposite-edge character of this reduplication (see section 5.2.4), an interesting wrinkle but orthogonal to the issue of overapplication.)

(25) a. /a–taña–a/   a-ñã̰ʔ-tañãʔã   'will ask often'   [Madurese]
      b. /moa/   w̃ã-mõw̃ã   'faces'

/Red-moa/	Max-BR	Onset	Dep-IO
☞ w̃ã-.mõ.w̃ã	** (mõ)		* (w)
ã̰-.mõ.w̃ã	***! (mõw̃)	*	* (w)
ã̰-.mõ.ã̰	** (mõ)	**!	

As an example of how Faith-BR can produce underapplication in Red, McCarthy and Prince (1995) cite the example, in (26), of š → č in Luiseño (Uto-Aztecan, Takic). In Luiseño, š and č are in complementary distribution: č occurs in onsets, and š in codas. McCarthy and Prince assume that š is underlying and converts to č when syllabified into the onset. In the forms in (26), reduplication postfixes a CCV copy of the CVCV root, setting up a situation in which the corresponding initial consonants of Base and Red occupy different syllable positions. If the š~č distributional pattern were enforced transparently, then in cases where the Base begins with č, Red should begin with š. However, this does not happen: Red begins with č, too, an underapplication in Red of the č~š constraints, in service of BR-identity. Base has a transparent č onset; Red has an opaque č coda. The Luiseño data in (26) are taken from Munro and Benson (1973: 18–19), who analyze the sibilant suffix as an absolutive marker which follows a (deleted) nominalizing suffix /-i/. The tableau is taken from McCarthy and Prince (1995):

(26) /čara/   'to tear'   ča.rá-č.ra-š   'torn'   *ča.rá-š.ra-š
      /čoka/   'to limp'   ča.ká-č.ka-š   'limping'   *ču.ká-š.ka-š
      /čaku-/ (unattested)   ča.kú-č.ku-š   'crest on   *ča.kú-š.ku-š
                                             roadrunner'

/ šaku-Red-š/	Ident-BR	*š-Onset	Ident-IO	*č
☞ ča.kú-č.ku-š			*	**
ča.kú-š.ku-š	*!		*	*
ša.kú-š.ku-š		*!		

BR-Faithfulness, like IDENT-BR in the tableau, is a symmetric constraint. It does not in itself privilege BASE and require RED to conform; it simply requires identity. As a result of this design feature of Optimality Theory constraints, BRCT predicts that BASE and RED are equally likely sites of identity-induced opacity. McCarthy and Prince cite several examples of overapplication and underapplication that have a "back-copying" character, in which BASE conforms to RED rather than the reverse. Such effects are difficult to describe in theories of reduplication without BR correspondence. To support backcopying, McCarthy and Prince cite examples in which external juncture effects are copied from RED to BASE, as in the Tagalog and Samala (Ineseño Chumash) over-application examples in (27). In both cases, a segmental interaction between a prefixal reduplicant and a preceding prefix is reflected in the base, even though it is not transparently conditioned there. The data and analyses in (27) are from McCarthy and Prince, citing Bloomfield (1933) on Tagalog, and Applegate (1976) and Mester (1986) on Samala:

(27) a. Tagalog: N-Ci $\rightarrow$ Ni

   paŋ-RED-putul $\rightarrow$ pa-<u>mu</u>-mutul   *pa-mu-putul

  b. Samala: C_i-ʔ $\rightarrow$ C_i'

   k-RED-ʔaniš $\rightarrow$ k'an-k'aniš   *k'an-ʔaniš

Stress and vowel length are not marked in the Tagalog example, following McCarthy and Prince (1995); typographical errors in the Samala forms have been corrected to conform to the data given in Applegate (1972, 1976).

5.3.3 Opacity as a cyclic effect

Interleaving between phonology and morphology (cyclicity, stratal effects) is a potential source of many opacity effects in reduplication, and constitutes an alternative to surface BR correspondence constraints in many cases. Cyclicity and interleaving are the focus of Chapter 7. Here we will focus only on cases in which phonology applies both to the input and to the output of reduplication.

For example, the "overapplication" of nasal harmony in Madurese reduplication, illustrated in (28), can be accounted for if nasal harmony applies to the stem prior to reduplication, which copies its effects. In this instance, "overapplication" of nasal harmony is simple input-output faithfulness:

(28) Stem cycle: /mowa/ → [mõw̃ã] [Madurese]
Reduplication cycle: [RED-mõw̃ã] → [w̃ã-mõw̃ã]

Inkelas and Zoll (2005) and Kiparsky (2010) have argued that most, if not all, cases of overapplication and underapplication yield to a cyclic account that obviates the backcopying power accorded to BRCT (see also McCarthy et al. 2012). As Inkelas and Zoll (2005) and Kiparsky (2010) observe, cyclicity is independently needed outside of reduplication. By contrast, bidirectional BR correspondence was introduced just to handle reduplicative opacity. If cyclicity turned out to be sufficient to handle opacity effects, bidirectional BR correspondence would be unnecessary.

The most celebrated example of backcopying does not yield to a cyclic analysis. McCarthy and Prince (1995) cite Onn's (1976) intriguing example of overapplication of nasal harmony in Johore Malay (Western Malayo-Polynesian, Sundic) (29). According to Onn, the rightward spread of nasality from consonants to vowels crosses the internal boundary in reduplication and is then reflected back into the first copy:

(29) hamɔ̃ hãmɔ̃-hãmɔ̃ 'germ/germs' [Johore Malay]
aŋãn aŋãn-aŋãn 'reverie/ambition'

As McCarthy and Prince argue, these data require the Identity constraints of BRCT, and cannot be handled cyclically.[1] Even if nasal harmony applies cyclically, before and after reduplication, it is only possible, on a cyclic analysis without Identity constraints, to derive

---

[1] Raimy (2000) analyzes Malay using his precedence-based approach to reduplication, in which a precedence loop is created between two points in a string; after linearization, the result is reduplication. In Malay, the loop goes from the last segment to the first, producing total reduplication. Nasal harmony applies after looping, following the precedence relations and producing the overapplication effect. This rule-ordered analysis is an alternative to both BRCT and cyclic approaches:

Input: $\# \to a \to ŋ \to a \to n \to \%$

Reduplication: $\# \to a \to ŋ \to a \to n \to \%$

Nasalization: $\# \to ã \to ŋ \to ã \to n \to \%$

Linearization: $\# ã_1 ŋ_1 ã_1 n_1 - ã_2 ŋ_2 ã_2 n_2 \%$

*hamɔ̃-hãmɔ̃, from reduplication of hamɔ̃ and assimilation of nasality across the internal boundary (hamɔ̃ → hamɔ̃ hamɔ̃ → hamɔ̃-hãmɔ̃).

While this case falls outside the descriptive capacity of cyclic accounts, the more restrictive predictions of cyclicity do capture a generalization pointed out by McCarthy and Prince (1995), Inkelas and Zoll (2005), and McCarthy et al. 2012. BRCT predicts possible opacity effects that appear not to occur, one example being the over-application of internal junctural effects in reduplication. For example, effects like *tami → tan-tani*, with overcopying of the assimilatory *m → n* alternation at the internal RED-BASE juncture, appear not to exist. These cannot be generated cyclically, a point in favor of cyclic approaches to opacity.

The competition between input-output (cyclic) and output-output (BRCT) correspondence-based accounts of reduplicative opacity continues to thrive; its resolution will depend in part on what types of opacity effects turn up in future investigations.

5.3.4 Templatic backcopying

McCarthy and Prince (1999) credit Philip Hamilton and René Kager with pointing out an interesting prediction of BRCT which influenced the course of research on reduplication, although it may not be correct. The so-called Hamilton-Kager prediction has to do with the possibility of backcopying a reduplicant's templatic restrictions to the base, in service of base-reduplicant identity. The result would be simultaneous reduplication and truncation, e.g. hypothetical *harpin → har-har* or *pin-pin*. For a time the pattern was thought not to occur (McCarthy and Prince 1999); a design feature of Generalized Template Theory (McCarthy and Prince 1994b; Urbanczyk 2006) was the inability to generate templatic backcopying. However, this pattern has since turned up in several languages. Inkelas and Zoll (2005) and Downing (2006) point out cases in several different languages in which a base word corresponds to a reduplicated, truncated counterpart, without the existence of independently truncated forms that would motivate an intermediate stage, or a third point in a triangle of related forms. For example, an informal survey of professional athletes reveals a number of $C_1V_2C_1V_2$ nicknames, for which it is implausible that the CV truncatum could ever have existed on its own: *Dietmar → Didi* (Dietmar Hamann, professional football (soccer) player), *Covelli → Coco* (Covelli Crisp, professional baseball player), *Thierry → Titi* (Thierry

Henry, professional football (soccer) player), *Lori* → *Lolo* (Lori Jones, track and field athlete), *Sisleide* → *Sisi* (Sisleide do Amor Lima, professional football (soccer) player), and *LeBron* → *Bron-Bron* (professional basketball player). One could argue that *Didi*, *Coco*, etc. were previously established nicknames that were assigned to *Dietmar* and *Covelli* on the basis of alliteration; however, *LeBron* is an uncommon name and the nickname *Bron-Bron* appears to have been created on the fly for this particular athlete.

Double truncation of this kind has been attested as an established grammatical construction in several languages. Perhaps the most striking comes from Guarijio (Uto-Aztecan, Tarahumaran) inceptive reduplication, which applies to verbs denoting iterated punctual events (Caballero 2007; data from Miller 1996: 65–6):

(30) | toní | 'to boil' | to-tó | 'to start boiling' [Guarijio] |
|------|-----------|--------|--------------------------------|
| sibá | 'to scratch' | si-sí | 'to start scratching' |
| čonó | 'to fry (INTR)' | čo-čó | 'to start frying' |
| nogá | 'to move' | no-nó | 'to start moving' |
| kusú | 'to sing (animals)' | ku-kú | 'to start singing' |
| suhku | 'to scratch body' | su-sú | 'to start scratching the body' |
| muhíba | 'to throw' | mu-mú | 'to start throwing' |

According to Caballero (2007: 278), "There is no independent process of truncation in the language, and the base is only shortened in this reduplicative construction." These Guarijio inceptives are thus structurally parallel to *Bron-Bron*, but without the wordplay dimension that can enter into nickname formation.

In considering the possibility of simultaneous truncation and reduplication, it is also worth making the connection to simultaneous truncation and affixation, which is quite common. A well-known example in the Optimality Theory literature is German nickname truncation + *i*-suffixation, exemplified by forms such as *Gabi* (< *Gabriele*), *Klinsi* (< *Klinsmann*), *Gorbi* (< *Gorbatschow*) (Itô and Mester 1997). The truncated bases of affixation in the German construction (*Gab-*, *Klins-*, *Gorb-*) do not exist as independent words, and violate phonotactic constraints on possible words; for example, they do not exhibit final consonant devoicing. Rather, these are bound, nonsurface stems generated as part of the overall construction, just like the truncata in Guarijio are generated as part of the reduplication construction.

Once the possibility of double truncation is acknowledged to exist (see e.g. McCarthy et al. 2012), a different question arises: why is it uncommon, if it is so easy for theories to generate? The answer to this question may be functional: truncation + reduplication removes a lot of lexical material from bases, and can therefore present recoverability problems. From this perspective, it is not surprising that our two examples have the properties that they do. Nicknames are notoriously exempt from recoverability concerns. In Guarijio, according to Caballero (2007) and Miller (1996), the class of verbs that undergoes abbreviated reduplication is tightly semantically restricted, therefore a small set, reducing the potential for neutralization. It would be surprising to see a productive construction applying to a large, open class of items (e.g. inflection, or nominalization) exhibit the extreme phonological curtailment seen in Guarijio inceptives. Nonetheless, this construction type seems to be possible in human language.

5.4 Phonological (compensatory) duplication

A challenge in developing theories of morphological reduplication is disentangling imposter cases of reduplication that may be purely phonological, instances of phonologically conditioned long-distance assimilation. In this section we will explore the boundary between morphological reduplication and phonological copying.

Yu (2005b) and Inkelas (2008a) discuss a number of cases of what Yu calls "compensatory reduplication" in which phonological considerations such as syllable well-formedness or the need to supply segments to a prosodic template can induce copying of single segments, substrings, or even syllabic constituents. For example, loanwords into Cantonese undergo syllable rhyme reduplication in order to break up a consonant-liquid onset cluster (Yu 2005b):

(31)   'break'   [pʰɪk̚lɪk]   [Cantonese]
        'clutch'   [kɪk̚lɪk̚tsi]
        'blood'   [pʌt̚lʌt̚]

Phonological copying theories such as BRCT could handle these phenomena using the same type of correspondence constraints used for morphological reduplication, except that the correspondence would be between output syllables instead of between Base and Red per se. In Cantonese, syllable structure considerations force epenthesis, but a high-ranking prohibition on epenthesizing default features forces the epenthetic segments to assimilate to, or correspond with, existing segments, mimicking the effects of morphological reduplication but without an abstract RED morpheme. Long-distance phonological assimilation, seen commonly in harmony systems, is at work in non-morphological reduplicative effects of the kind documented by Zuraw (2002: 396), e.g. *orangutan → orangutang, smorgasbord → smorgas-borg, persevere → perservere*, etc.

Taking this analysis one step farther, it is possible to attribute at least some cases previously analyzed as morphological reduplication to the phonology, as well. For example, monomoraic reduplications like the Yoruba gerundive (e.g. *gbóná → gbí-gbóná*) (see section 5.2.3) could be analyzed as prefixation of an underspecified vowel, which in turn triggers epenthesis of an underspecified onset consonant; both vowel and consonant acquire surface feature specifications through a combination of assimilation and default feature fill-in.

Yu (2005b) and Inkelas (2008a) find that phonological duplication and morphological reduplication have a number of distinct properties, including locality and size restrictions. These suggest a division in which phonological duplication is modeled like phonological assimilation (using correspondence constraints as in BRCT), whereas morphological reduplication is modeled like synonym compounding (using a theory like Morphological Doubling Theory).

Nonetheless, there exists a continuum of cases, both synchronic and diachronic, which straddles any line that can be drawn between phonological duplication (including lengthening and gemination) and partial morphological reduplication. A number of relevant cases arise with internal (infixing) reduplication and are discussed in more detail in section 3 of Chapter 6. Examining this issue more closely is likely to illuminate future theoretical models of reduplicative phenomena.

5.5 The morphology of reduplication

Reduplication can target the entire word, the root, or any subconstituent in between; it can even target individual affixes. For an example of this kind of variation within a language family, we can turn to the family of Bantu languages, in which verb reduplication is widespread. The schema in (32), based on work by Downing (e.g. 1995, 1997ab, 1998ab, 1999abc, 2000, 2001, 2006), Hyman (e.g. 1998, 2002, 2008, 2009), and others, shows an internal analysis of the verb which has been motivated in many Bantu languages, including the ones that will be illustrated here. Verb reduplication can target the whole verb, the macro-stem (stem plus preceding object marker), the inflectional stem (Stem), or the derivational stem (Dstem).

(32)   Verb
                            ⋀
              prefixes   inflectional stem (Stem)
                                    ⋀
        derivational stem (Dstem)   FV (=inflectional "Final Vowel")
                    ⋀
            root   derivational suffixes

In a study of the natural history of Bantu reduplication, Hyman (2009) identifies examples of reduplication at each level. The semantics of the constructions Hyman surveys are similar, indicating a common historical source. Ciyao (P.21; Ngunga 2000) manifests full Stem reduplication, including derivational suffixes (33a) and the final inflectional suffix (33b). By contrast, Ndebele (S.44; Sibanda 2004) reduplicates only the Dstem, excluding any suffix in the FV position (33c,d). In Kinyarwanda (N.61; Kimenyi 2002), only the root is reduplicable, as shown in (33e,f). Verb stems are shown, in all examples in (33), without inflectional or infinitival prefixes, as these do not undergo reduplication:

(33)   *Full stem reduplication (all suffixes)*   [Ciyao]
        a. telec-el-a   →   telec-el-a + telec-el-a
           'cook-APPL-FV'   'cook for someone frequently'
        b. dim-ile   →   dim-ile + dim-ile
           'cultivate-PERF'   'cultivated many times'
        Dstem reduplication (no inflectional suffixes)   [Ndebele]
        c. lim-el-a   →   lim-e + lim-el-a
           'cultivate-APPL-FV'   'cultivate for/at a little, here and there'
        d. lim-e   →   lim-a + lim-e   (*lim-e + lim-e)
           'cultivate-SUBJ'   'cultivate a little, here and there
                                   (subjunctive)'
        Root reduplication (no suffixes)   [Kinyarwanda]
        e. rim-w-a   →   rim-aa + rim-w-a (*rim-w-a + rim-w-a)
           'cultivate-PASS-FV'   'be cultivated several times'
        f. rim-ir-a   →   rim-aa + rim-ir-a (*rim-i + rim-ir-a)
           'cultivate-APPL-FV'   'cultivate for/at, here and there'

Reduplicants in all three of these languages, among others, are similar in another way: they must be minimally disyllabic. As will be discussed further (for Ndebele) in section 5.6.3, this requirement compels the use of a semantically empty dummy suffix (-*a* or -*aa*) which fleshes out the otherwise subminimal Ndebele and Kinyarwanda reduplicants in (33d–f).

In some languages, there is variation as to what portion of the word reduplicates. For example, Harley and Leyva (2009: 269, fns. 44, 46) report that in compound verbs in Hiaki (aka Yaqui; Uto-Aztecan), such as *nok-ii'aa* 'speak-want = want to speak', habitual/emphatic reduplication can target either member or both members:

(34) nok-ii'aa   speak-want   'want [someone] to speak' [Hiaki]
      no-nok-ii'aa   RED-speak-want   'want [someone] to **always** speak'
      nok-ii-ii'aa   speak-RED-want   '**always** want [someone] to speak'
      no-nok-ii-ii'aa RED-speak-RED-   '**always** want [someone] to
                       want   **always** speak'

As seen in (34), the constituent(s) which are reduplicated are those over which reduplication has semantic scope (glosses have been slightly modified from the original).

5.5.1 Root reduplication

The examples discussed from Hiaki, Ciyao, Ndebele, and Kinyarwanda are typical in that, no matter what the specific morphological and phonological conditions on reduplication may be, reduplication ends up copying at least a portion of the morphological root. This is probably no accident. As observed by Hyman (2009) and Hyman et al. (2009), partial reduplication tends cross-linguistically to occur on the opposite edge from the side of the root at which most affixation takes place in the language. Thus, while affixation tends cross-linguistically to be suffixing (e.g. Dryer 2011), reduplication tends to be prefixing (Rubino 2005, 2013). In the majority of Bantu languages, for example, as seen in (32), partial verb stem reduplication is almost exclusively prefixing, while stems themselves are otherwise internally exclusively suffixing, with the result that the copied material always includes some or all of the root.

Sometimes, however, even what looks like straight root reduplication will attract segments from a neighboring affix, as mentioned in section 5.2.6. This typically occurs under two conditions: pressures of minimality, and pressures of syllable well-formedness.

Minimality considerations pull prefixes into what would otherwise be straight root reduplication in Kinande and Emerillon. In Emerillon (Tupi-Guarani), preposed disyllabic "repeated action" reduplication targets the root (35a), but will recruit material from prefixes as needed to flesh out a monosyllabic reduplicant (35b) (Rose 2005: 353–9). In Kinande, (J.42; Mutaka and Hyman 1990: 77–80; Downing 1997a, 1999c, 2000; Hyman 2009), noun reduplication meaning "a real (noun)" or "a good example of a (noun)" normally targets only the root, not the noun class prefix (CL), as in (35c). But if a noun root is smaller than two syllables, the prefix is compelled to copy as well (35d):

(35) a. *o-dʒika-ŋ*   '3-kill-PL'   →   *o-dʒika-dʒika-ŋ* [Emerillon]
          o-eta   '3-cut'   →   *o-eta-eta*

      b. *o-ʔal-oŋ*   '3-fall-PL'   →   *oʔa-o-ʔal-oŋ*
          a-lo-wag   '1SG-CAUS.COM-go' → *a-lowa-lo-wag*

      c. *kʊ-gʊlʊ*   'CL-leg'   →   *kʊ-gʊlʊ-gʊlʊ*   [Kinande]
          mó-síka   'CL-girl'   →   *mó-síka-síka*

      d. *ri-bwɛ*   'CL-stone'   →   *ri-bwɛ-ri-bwɛ*
          ká-tɪ   'CL-stick'   →   *ká-tɪ-ká-tɪ*

      e. *ḿ-bʊlɪ*   'CL-goat'   →   *ḿ-bʊlɪ-m-bʊlɪ*

This is apparent "exfixation" (see section 5.2.6); the Kinande example is discussed by Downing (1997b, 1998b, 1999b) and Inkelas and Zoll (1995), among others.

Interestingly, as shown in (35e), a Kinande nasal class prefix will reduplicate along with a disyllabic root, even though the root by itself is of sufficient size. The Kinande pattern is thus best described as requiring a disyllabic reduplicant which contains the root and any preceding prefixes which can squeeze into the reduplicant in their entirety.[2]

Overcopying driven by syllable structure considerations is illustrated here by Eastern Kadazan, Javanese, and Samala (Ineseño Chumash). In Eastern Kadazan (Western Malayo-Polynesian, Borneo; Hurlbut 1998) and Javanese, affix consonants "overcopy" in order to provide onset or coda consonants for the reduplicated root, exemplifying a common cross-linguistic pattern discussed by Downing (1999b). In Eastern Kadazan, the first CV of the root is reduplicated, whether the root is

---

[2] Mutaka and Hyman (1990) also show that roots longer than two syllables typically do not reduplicate, and on the basis of all these facts posit a Morpheme Integrity Constraint preventing reduplicants from containing truncated versions of morphemes, whether prefixes or roots.

final, medial, or initial in the word (36a). (Roots are shown in boldface in underlying representation; reduplicants are underlined in surface forms.) If, however, the root is vowel-initial and preceded by a consonant-final prefix, the prefix-final consonant reduplicates along with the root-initial vowel (36b). (Note: "ng" = [ŋ], and "N" = a nasal which assimilates in place to a following consonant and otherwise surfaces as [ŋ].)

(36) a. Consonant-initial root   [E. Kadazan]
          /m-pi-ku-**bojo**/ 'AF-DU.REC-AUG-obey'   → miku<u>bo</u>bojo
          /pog-**baya**-an/ 'ASS.COL-ignore_someone-RF' → pog<u>ba</u>bayaan
          /**ruvang**-o-ko/ 'catch_an_illness-UF-YOU'   → <u>ru</u>ruvangoko

      b. Vowel-initial root
          /m-pi-siN-**alud**/   'AF-DU.REC-N.SER-   → misi<u>nga</u>ngalud
                                  paddle_a_boat'
          /soN-**onggom**/   'DIM-hold_in_hand'   → so<u>ngo</u>ngonggom

McCarthy and Prince (1995) analyze similar effects in Tagalog and Samala (Ineseño Chumash, extinct isolate of California) as exfixation and backcopying, in which material from other affixes fuses into the reduplicant and is then reflected back into the base under pressure of base-reduplicant identity; this type of analysis was discussed in section 5.2.6. Downing (1997b, 1998b, 1999b) and Inkelas and Zoll (2005) offer a different analysis of such cases, proposing that reduplication is infixing. On such an account, reduplication of the Eastern Kadazan type would copy the initial CV of the prosodic root, a constituent containing all of the segments of the root morpheme plus any segments that are syllabified together with those segments. Example (37a,b) illustrates this analysis for the type of data in (36). Morphological roots are again in boldface, while prosodic roots are demarcated with curly brackets:

(37) a. Prosodic root = Morphological root   [E. Kadazan]
          /m-pi-ku-{**bojo**}/ 'AF-DU.REC-AUG-obey' →   miku<u>bo</u>bojo

      b. Prosodic root > Morphological root
          /m-pi-si{N-**alud**}/ 'AF-DU.REC-N.SER-   →   misi<u>nga</u>ngalud
                                  paddle_a_boat'

      c. Prosodic root < Morphological root
          /i{**du**}-an-ku/   'run_away-RF-I'   →   i<u>du</u>duanku
          /in{**dad**}-an-po/   'wait-RF-N.COMP.M'   →   in<u>da</u>dadanpo

This type of analysis would work well for Kinande, illustrated earlier. For Eastern Kadazan, the infixation analysis is motivated particularly transparently by the data in (37c), in which the reduplicant infixes after the root-initial vowel. In this case, infixation is being motivated not only by overcopying but also by undercopying. As Downing (1997b, 1998b, 1999b) points out for other cases of this kind, this infixation pattern can be accounted for misalignment between morphological root and prosodic root, forced by the requirement that prosodic roots must be consonant-initial.

In Javanese, a case discussed in Inkelas and Zoll (2005), consonantal suffixes "overcopy" to provide a final coda to a reduplicant which otherwise is co-extensive with the morphological root. Root reduplication, which pluralizes nominals and, roughly, marks attenuation and/or repetition in verbs, is illustrated in (38a). Reduplication normally excludes affixes, as illustrated in (38b) and (38c). However, just in case a consonantal suffix follows a vowel-final root, it is included in the reduplication (38d–f), just as a preceding consonantal prefix may be included if it syllabifies into the root-initial syllable (38e,f)[3]. Data come from Horne (1961), Sumukti (1971), and Dudas (1976):

(38)   a. /medja/   medjɔ+medjɔ   [Javanese]
          'table'   'tables'

       b. /medja-ku/   medja+medja-ku
          'table-1SG.POSS' 'my tables'

       c. /don-an/   dun+dun-an
          'descend-NML'   'things which have been taken off or unloaded'

       d. /uni-an/   unɛ-n+unɛ-n
          'sound-NML'   'noise, saying'

---

[3] The behavior of consonantal prefixes is variable; Horne and Dudas present slightly different generalizations about when these prefixes reduplicate with a following root. The segmentation of simple causative -qake into bimorphemic -q-ake, following Inkelas and Zoll (2005), is based on the existence of two other causatives, the causative imperative -qnɔ and causative subjunctive -qnɛ, both of which also start with q. The segmentation of simple locative -ni into bimorphemic -n-i is based on the existence of two other locatives, the locative imperative -(n)ɔnɔ, and the Locative Subjunctive -(n)ane, both of which start with n. Inkelas and Zoll propose analyzing q and n as general causative and locative formatives, respectively. Note also, in (38), the interaction between suffix-triggering vowel alternations and reduplication; this has been discussed in the literature on Javanese reduplication. See e.g. McCarthy and Prince (1995); Inkelas and Zoll (2005). Transcription note: q = [ʔ]; dj = [dʑ]; ng = [ŋ]. t and d are dental; ṭ and ḍ are alveolar.

e. /tiba-q-ake/   tiba-q+tiba-q-ake
  'fall-CAUS-SIMPLE.CAUS'   'repeatedly drop'

f. /ng-ambu-n-i/   ng-ambɔ-n+ng-ambɔ-n-i
  'ACTIVE-odor-LOC-SIMPLE.LOC'

Morphologically sensitive reduplication often privileges the root, but this is not always the case. In Samala (Ineseño Chumash), reduplication targets the prosodic stem, which includes the root as well as any prefixes of the "cohering" type that incorporate into the Prosodic Stem. According to Applegate (1972, 1976), reduplication carries a repetitive, distributive, intensive, or continuative force; it appears to take wide semantic scope over the verb. Inkelas and Zoll (2005) analyze Samala much like Eastern Kadazan, with reduplication being a late process that targets the Prosodic Stem. Data in (39a–c) are from Applegate (1976: 281–2); (39d) is from Applegate (1972: 384). Roots are boldfaced and Prosodic Stems are demarcated with curly brackets in the inputs to reduplication, below; reduplicants are underlined in outputs:[4]

(39) a. k-{su-**pše?**}   → k<u>sup</u>supše?   [Samala]
  1SUBJ-CAUS-to_be_extinguished = 'I'm putting out a fire'

b. k-{su-**towič**}   → k<u>sut</u>sutowič
  1SUBJ-CAUS-? = 'I'm doing it fast'

c. s-{pil-**kowon**}   → sp<u>il</u>pilkowon
  'it is spilling'

d. k-{xu-ni-**yɨw**} (< /k-xul-ni-**yɨw**/)   → k<u>xun</u>xuniyɨw
  1SUBJ-?-TRANS-? = 'I am looking all over for it'

In some cases, reduplication copies affixes not just incidentally, as in Samala, but explicitly. The significance of these cases is discussed in Inkelas and Zoll (2005). According to Roberts (1987, 1991), to express iterative aspect in Amele (Trans New Guinea, Madang), "the whole stem is normally reduplicated if the verb does not have an object marker, otherwise the object marker is reduplicated either in place of or in addition to the reduplication of the verb stem" (Roberts 1991: 130–31). Data are from Roberts (1987: 252–4) and Roberts (1991: 131):

---

[4] Applegate (1972, 1976) does not provide interlinear glosses for every morpheme in every word; in (39), morpheme glosses are provided for those morphemes that are glossed in similar examples, and question marks stand in for the remainder.

(40) a. qu-qu   'hit' (iterative)   [Amele]
          ji-ji   'eat' (iterative)
          budu-budu-e?   'to thud repeatedly'
          g͡batan-g͡batan-e?   'split-INF' (iterative)

      b. hawa-du-du   'ignore-3s-3s' (iterative)
          gobil-du-du   'stir-3s-3s = stir and stir it'
          guduc-du-du   'run-3s-3s' (iterative)

      c. bala-bala-du-d-e? 'tear-3s-INF = to tear it repeatedly'

In Boumaa Fijian (Oceanic), stems formed by spontaneous or adversative prefixes mark plurality by reduplicating both the prefix and the root (Dixon 1988: 226):

(41) ta-lo'i   'bent'   ta-ta-lo'i-lo'i   'bent in many places'
      ca-lidi   'explode' ca-ca-lidi-lidi   'many things explode'
      'a-musu   'broken'   'a-'a-musu-musu   'broken in many places'
                                               [Boumaa Fijian]

The fact that the size of the reduplicants in (40) and (41) varies with the size of the morpheme being reduplicated suggests strongly that this is morpheme doubling, not phonological copying motivated by the need to flesh out an abstract, phonologically skeletal morpheme.

Harley and Leyva (2009) cite an interesting case of internal root reduplication in Hiaki, in which habitual reduplication appears to reach into N-V compounds to target the head V but semantically takes scope over the entire compound. Thus the verb *kuta-siute* 'stick-split = wood-splitting' reduplicates as *kuta-siu-siute* 'wood-splitting habitually'; *pan-hooa* 'bread-make = making bread' reduplicates as *pan-ho-hoa*; etc. Haugen (2009), like Aronoff (1988) before him, relates head reduplication to the phenomenon of head inflection, familiar from such English examples as *understand ~ understood* or *grandchild ~ grandchildren*.

An even more extreme case in which reduplication of an inner element can have semantic scope over a higher constituent comes from noun-noun compounds in Pima (Uto-Aztecan, Tepiman), in which either member, or both, can be reduplicated to effect pluralization, with no apparent difference in the meaning. According to Haugen (2009), citing Munro and Riggle (2004), speakers exhibit free variation according to whether the first member, the second member, or both reduplicate. Reduplicants are underlined:

(42)   a. 'ònk-'ús   [Pima]
          'salt-tree=tamarack'
          'ò-'onk-'ú-'us ~ 'ònk-'ú-'us ~ 'ò-'onk-'ú-'us
          'tamaracks'

       b. bàn-nód:adag
          'coyote-plant.type=peyote'
          bà-ban-nód:adag ~ bàn-<u>non</u>d:adag ~ bà-ban-<u>non</u>d:adag
          'peyote (pl.)'

This case can be instructively compared with the examples of Boumaa Fijian (41), in which both elements of an affixed stem must
reduplicate, and of Hiaki complex verb reduplication (34), in which
reduplication of either member of a compound is also possible, but
where the variation correlates tightly with meaning. The three-way
comparison shows that morphemes, or morphological subconstituents,
can be the direct target of reduplication processes whose contribution
to the syntax and semantics of the word is seemingly unrelated to
the meaning of the actual morpheme whose phonological material is
reduplicated.

5.5.2 Phrasal reduplication

Reduplication is normally characterized as a word-bounded process. It
performs derivational or inflectional functions; it can be interspersed
among other clearly lexical layers of morphology; it operates on lexical
inputs (roots, stems, words). It is normally studied in a morphology, if
not a phonology, class, and appears as a standard entry in morphology
textbooks.

    However, numerous studies have also documented reduplication at
the phrasal level (see e.g. Fitzpatrick-Cole 1994; Lidz 2001), and it
seems clear that while reduplication may be primarily a word-internal
phenomenon, it is equally possible for it to apply to syntactic structures.
For example, Emeneau (1955) reports that "echo" reduplication in
Kolami (section 5.6.4) can apply not only to words but also to phrases:
meˑkel toˑtev 'goat not' → *meˑkel toˑtev - giˑkel toˑtev* 'There are no goats
at all' (Emeneau 1955: 102). Lewis (1967: 237) reports compound and
phrasal echo reduplications in Turkish: *Ben adam [tarih hoca-sı-ymış]
[marih hocasıymış] anla-ma-m* 'I man [history teacher-POSS-EVID] [RED]
care-NEG-1SG = 'I don't care if he is [a history teacher or whatever].' Lidz
(2001) cites similar findings from Kannada (Southern Dravidian):

(43)   a. nannu [baagil-annu   much-id-e]   [giigilannu muchide]
           I-NOM [**door**-ACC   **close**-PST-1S]   [ECHO-REDUPLICANT]
           anta   heeLa-beeDa
           that   say-PROH

                                              [Kannada]
           'Don't say that I closed the door or did related activities.'

       b. pustav-annu [**meejin-a meele**] [**giijina meele**]   nooD-id-e
           book-ACC   [**table**-GEN **on**]   [ECHO-REDUPLICANT]   see-PST-1S
           'I saw the book on the table and in related places.'

Another interesting case of reduplication at the syntactic level is
found in Fongbe (Niger-Congo, Kwa). As discussed by Collins (1994)
and Lefebvre and Brousseau (2002: 505), and cited by Inkelas and Zoll
(2005) in support of the Morphological Doubling approach to reduplication, Fongbe verb doubling occurs in four syntactic constructions:
temporal adverbials (44a), causal adverbials (44b), factives (44c), and
predicate clefts (44d). In each case, an extra copy of the verb appears
initially in the verb phrase. The fronted copy is either identical to the
main verb or, for some speakers, truncated to its first syllable:

(44)   a. sísɔ́ ~ sí Kɔ́kú sísɔ́   tlóló   bɔ̀ xὲsí ɖì Bàyí [Fongbe]
           tremble Koku **tremble** as.soon.as and fear get Bayi
           'As soon as Koku trembled, Bayi got frightened'

       b. sísɔ́ ~ sí Kɔ́kú **sísɔ́**   útú   xὲsí ɖì Bàyí
           tremble Koku **tremble** cause fear get Bayi
           'Because Koku trembled, Bayi got frightened'

       c. sísɔ́ ~ sí ɖé-è   Bàyí **sísɔ́**,   ɔ́, vé   nú   mi
           tremble OP-RES Bayi **tremble**, DEF bother for me
           'The fact that Bayi trembled bothered me'

       d. sísɔ́ ~ sí wὲ, Kɔ́kú   **sísɔ́**
           tremble it.is Koku **tremble**
           'It is tremble that Koku did'

5.6 The morphological nature of reduplication

Many modular theories of morphology, including A-Morphous Morphology (Anderson 1992) and Distributed Morphology (Halle and Marantz
1993, 1994; Harley and Noyer 1999), segregate affixation, compounding,
and morphophonology in different components of the grammar. In such

theories, reduplication would lay claim to all three components. Reduplication sometimes resembles affixation (see e.g. Marantz 1982), at other times morphophonology, and at other times compounding in its form and integration with other morphological processes. These different faces of reduplication have motivated two basic theoretical models: phonological copying (Marantz 1982; Steriade 1988; McCarthy and Prince 1995, 1996, 1999b; Raimy 2000) and morphological doubling (Inkelas and Zoll 2005; Singh 2005). Phonological copying theories typically treat reduplication as the affixation of a segmentally null morpheme which must be fleshed out through the process of phonological copying of segments from the base of affixation. Morphological Doubling Theory, by contrast, treats reduplication as the insertion of two identical or semantically equivalent morphological constituents.

Both types of approach are descriptively rich enough that each has been fruitfully extended to virtually all types of reduplication. However, the two approaches do make different predictions in some key areas.

From a morphological point of view, the prototypical example of reduplication is as a stand-alone morphological process which serves as the sole marker of a morphological category. This description fits the Indonesian, Haiki, Samala, and Acehnese examples discussed in the previous sections, to name just a few. In this section we will focus on reduplication patterns which depart from this canonical morphological character; these patterns help to distinguish phonological vs. morphological approaches to reduplication.

We begin with cases in which reduplication is a concomitant of other morphological processes (section 5.6.1), and then move on to cases in which reduplication patterns more like compounding in that the reduplicant and base have distinct lexical bases (section 5.6.2) or in that the reduplicant is morphologically internally complex (sections 5.6.3, 5.6.4).

5.6.1 Reduplication as concomitant of affixation

Both full and partial reduplication are commonly found as part of a complex morphological construction which also features ordinary affixation. Such cases are of considerable interest to morphologists, as they disrupt the idealized one-to-one mapping between meaning and form (see e.g. Anderson 1992, ch. 3). In Roviana (Oceanic), for example, the derivation of instrumental or locational nouns from verbs is marked simultaneously by total reduplication and the nominalizing suffix *-ana; ha^mbo* 'sit' ~ *ha^mbo-ha^mbotu-ana* 'chair', *hake* 'perch' ~ *hake-hake-ana* 'chair', *hale* 'climb' ~ *hale-hale-ana* 'steps, stairs' (Corston-Oliver 2002: 469, 472). The reduplication co-occurring with *-ana* serves no distinct semantic function of its own. In Hausa, one class of nouns forms its plurals via CVC reduplication and suffixation of *-iː*, as in *gútsúrèː* 'small fragment', *gútsàttsárí* (< *gútsàr-tsár-íː*), *gáȓdàm* 'dispute, argument', *gáȓdàndámí* (<*gáȓdàm-dám-î*) (Newman 2000: 451).

In Ditidaht (Nitinaht; Southern Wakashan), about 40 suffixes trigger reduplication on the stems they attach to (Stonham 1994). For example, the "resemble" suffix triggers CV root reduplication:

(45) a. ƛ'ic-   'white'   [Ditidaht]
          ƛ'ic-ak   'white-DUR' = 'whiteness'
          ƛ'i-ƛ'ic-ak'uk   'RED-white-resembles' = 'flour'

      b. tuːχ-   'scare'
          tuːχ-apt   'scare-plant' = 'Spruce var.'
          tuː-tuːχ-ubq-ak'uk   'RED-scare-plant-resembles' = 'looks like a
                                   spruce tree (= juniper-leafed hair moss)'

      c. piːlaːq   'liver'
          piː-piːlaːq-k'uk   'RED-liver-resembles' = 'resembles liver
                                   (= yellow pond lily)'

In cases like these, reduplication can potentially be viewed as a morphophonological accompaniment to affixation, much like ablaut or other morphophonemic alternations which commonly apply to bases of affixation. Alternatively, reduplication that accompanies affixation can be analyzed in terms of what Aronoff (1994) and Blevins (2003) term "morphomic stems," i.e. semantically empty stem-forming constructions producing stems that certain affixes select for; this is the approach taken by Inkelas and Zoll (2005), who analyze reduplication in such examples as a semantically empty morphological process whose purpose is to form stems of a particular type. (For an overview of morphological types in the lexicon, see e.g. Riehemann 1998.) In Ditidaht, for example the "resembles" suffix selects for stems of the type formed by CV reduplication. Supporting evidence for a stem type analysis is that, as observed by Stonham, if two co-occurring suffixes both select for a reduplicated stem type, reduplication occurs only once (Stonham 1993: 49). Reduplication converts a root to a stem of the appropriate type, to which both affixes attach. This is true, however, only if the suffixes also create stems of that same morphological type. Stonham posits two morphological levels, or stem types, in Ditidaht. Reduplication can occur twice if triggered by affixes in both levels (p. 59).

In the examples discussed above, reduplication departs morphologically from canonical affixation in being an apparently semantically empty concomitant of an otherwise straightforward affixation process. In the next sections we look at other ways in which reduplication can depart from canonical affixation: reduplicants can consist of, or contain, morphemes not found in the apparent "base" of reduplication. We will look first at reduplication in which the reduplicant and base are synonyms or allomorphs of each other (section 5.6.2) and then at cases in which the reduplicant is morphologically complex and contains morphemes that the base does not (sections 5.6.3, 5.6.4). These examples tend to support the point of view that reduplication can consist of morphological doubling (Inkelas and Zoll 2005), instead of (or in addition to) phonological copying.

5.6.2 Synonym reduplication

Sye (Oceanic) reduplication illustrates the potential morphological independence of the two copies in reduplication. Here we build on the discussion in Inkelas and Zoll (2005), which is in turn based closely on the description and analysis of Crowley (1998, 2002). In Sye, most verb roots have two different forms, termed here for convenience Stem1 and Stem2. Examples can be seen in (46a). Many Stem1~Stem2 pairs exhibit a relatively transparent relationship, e.g. *aruvo~naruvo* 'sing', *owi~nowi* 'plant' (Crowley 1998: 81). In other cases, the relationship is opaque enough to motivate treating the allomorphy as suppletive. Examples include *owi~awi* 'leave', *ovoli~aompoli* 'turn it', *velom~ampelom* (singular imperative only) 'come'. Crowley likens such pairs to "strong verb alternations in Germanic languages" (Crowley 1998: 82)[5]. Each affixation construction selects for one of

---

[5] Building on the correspondences between stem alternants elucidated by Crowley (1998: 81–4), Frampton (2009) argues in favor of deriving the allomorphy using a combination of an *an-* prefix, which has two suppletive allomorphs and is subject to a number of lexically conditioned readjustment rules. The question of when to recognize allomorphy as suppletive and when to attribute it to phonology is notoriously difficult. The approach

the two stem shapes. (46b) illustrates the same root combining with two different prefixes, one of which calls for Stem1 (*arinova*) and the other of which calls for Stem2 (*narinova*). The point relevant to reduplication, made by Crowley, is that reduplication in morphological contexts calling for Stem1 yields two copies of Stem1, whereas reduplication in prefixing contexts that call for Stem2 surfaces as Stem2-Stem1. It is cases of this latter kind, illustrated in (46c), that support the idea that reduplication is drawing on the lexeme twice, rather than selecting it once and phonologically copying the segments of the chosen allomorph. Data come from Crowley 1998: 79, 84; 2002: 704:

(46) a.

Stem	Stem2	gloss	[Sye]
arinova	narinova	'provoke'	
omol	amol	'fall'	

b. etw-**arinova**-g   co-**narinowa**-nt
    2SG.IMP.NEG-**provoke$_1$**-1SG   3SG.FUT-**provoke$_2$**-1PL.INCL
    'Don't provoke me!'   '(S)he will provoke us.'

c. cw-**amol-omol**
    3.FUT-**fall$_2$-fall$_1$**
    'They will fall all over'

Another case of reduplication involving different allomorphs of the same morpheme occurs in Chechen (Nakh-Dagestanian, Nakh) which uses reduplication as one means of satisfying the syntactic requirements of a second position clitic (Conathan and Good 2000; see also Peterson 2001 and Good 2006 on the closely related language Ingush). As shown in (46), from Conathan and Good (2000: 50), chained clauses are marked by an enclitic particle '*a* (= IPA [ʔa]), which immediately precedes the inflected, phrase-final, main verb. The enclitic must be preceded by another element in the same clause. Two types of constituent may occur before the verb (and enclitic particle) in the clause: an object (47a), or a deictic proclitic or preverb (47b). If neither of these elements is present, then the obligatory pre-clitic position is filled by reduplicating the verb (47c):[6]

---

taken here is to treat allomorphy as suppletive unless the alternations that would derive it generalize beyond the morphemes in question; by that criterion, this allomorphy counts as suppletive.

[6] Note on practical orthography used here: right apostrophe = [ʔ]; 'c' = [ts]; 'ch' = [tʃ]; 'sh' = [ʃ]; 'zh' = [ʒ]; 'gh' = [ɣ]; 'kh' = [χ]. In glosses and verbs cited in isolation, "B" (47a), "D" (47b), and "V" (47c) refer to gender. Chechen has four noun genders; many verbs take gender prefixes which agree with the gender of the absolutive argument.

(47) a. Cickuo,   [ch'aara   ='a gina]$_{VP}$,   'i   bu'u   [Chechen]
          cat.ERG   [fish   =& see.PP]$_{VP}$ 3S.ABS B.eat.PRS
          'The cat, having seen a fish, eats it.'

      b. Aĥmada,   [kiekhat jaaz ='a dina]$_{VP}$,   zhejna dueshu
          Ahmad.ERG   [letter   write =& D.do.PP]$_{VP}$ book   D.read.PRS
          'Ahmad, having written a letter, reads a book.'

      c. Aĥmad,   [ʕa   ='a   ʕiina]$_{VP}$,   dʕa-vaghara
          Ahmad   [stay.INF$_{RED}$ =&   stay.PP]$_{VP}$ DX.-V.go.WP
          'Ahmad stayed (for a while) and left.'

The Chechen reduplicant occurs in infinitive form, while the main
verb is inflected. Inflected verbs require a different form of the verb
stem than that used in the infinitive; in some cases the stem allomorphy
is clearly suppletive, e.g. *Dala* 'to give' vs. *lwo* 'gives', or *Dagha* 'to go' vs.
Duedu 'goes'. As Conathan and Good (2000: 54) observe, the result is
that Chechen can exhibit suppletive allomorphy differences between
base and reduplicant (e.g. *Dagha 'a Duedu*, based on 'go').

Inkelas and Zoll (2005) draw a connection between the Chechen and
Sye cases, involving suppletive allomorphy, and synonym compounding constructions of the sort discussed by Singh (1982). As an example
of the latter, a construction in Modern Hindi pairs synonymous
adjectives, the first of native origin and the second of Perso-Arabic
origin, to give an overall meaning of "[noun] et cetera." Data are from
Singh 2005: 271:

(48) a. tan   badan   tan-badan [Hindi]
          'body' [+native] 'body' [-native] 'body, etc.'

      b. vivaah   shaadi   vivaah-shaadi
          'marriage' [+native] 'marriage' [-native] 'marriage, etc.'

Building on a related proposal by Singh (2005), Inkelas and Zoll
(2005) use constructions such as these to advocate for Morphological
Doubling Theory, in which reduplication is modeled by a construction
which calls for two semantically and syntactically equivalent subconstituents. In (49), the daughter nodes bear the same features, thus are
synonymous. The meaning of the construction as a whole is some
function of the meaning of the daughters; that function could be any
of the functions associated cross-linguistically with reduplication
(Moravcsik 1978; Regier 1994; Kiyomi 1995).

(49) A morphological doubling schema in Morphological Doubling
      Theory (Inkelas and Zoll 2005)

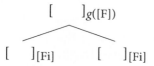

Because the equivalence between the daughters in (49) is defined over
the features that the daughters independently expone ([F$_i$]), morphological doubling could result either in the exact same morph being used
twice (50a), as in Indonesian pluralizing total reduplication, or in the co-
occurrence of different suppletive allomorphs or distinct but synonymous lexical items (50b), as in the Hindi "et cetera" construction:

(50)

a. Indonesian total reduplication construction

b. Synonym compounding in Hindi

Singh (2005) and Inkelas and Zoll (2005) observe that once total
reduplication and synonym constructions are connected under one
morphological analysis of synonym compounding, it also becomes
possible in the same formal model to relate both to compounding
constructions requiring different degrees of semantic similarity across
daughters, including part-whole and even antonym constructions. In
Acehnese, for example, Durie (1985: 40–44) documents a construction
which juxtaposes words of opposite meaning to yield a word whose
meaning encompasses both:

(51)   tuha-muda   'old and young'   [Acehnese]
        bloe-publoe   'buy and sell'
        uroe-malam   'day and night'
        beungöh-seupôt   'morning and evening'

Insofar as these constructions resemble, in their behavior, total
reduplication or synonym compounding, extending the schemas in

(50) to them is a useful ability. In the case of Acehnese, all three constructions—reduplication, synonym compounding, and antonym compounding—have the same stress pattern, a generalization which can be captured in an inheritance hierarchy (see e.g. Riehemann 2001), in which all three similar constructions inherit the same cophonology.

5.6.3 Morphologically complex reduplicants

Moving beyond synonym compounding, a different type of morphological independence between the two copies in reduplication is demonstrated by reduplicants which are morphologically complex, composed of elements not all of which are found in the apparent base of reduplication.

One way in which this can happen is when reduplicants contain semantically empty "filler" morphs. These have been the focus of several studies of Bantu reduplication by Downing (1998ab, 1999ab, 2000, 2006) and Hyman (Mutaka and Hyman 1990; Hyman and Mtenje 1999; Hyman et al. 2009), among others. The phenomenon in question is illustrated by the data in (52) from Ndebele (S.44, Zimbabwe; Sibanda 2004, Hyman et al. 2009). As discussed earlier in section 5.5 (see example (33)), the locus of verbal reduplication in Ndebele is the derivational stem, which consists of the root and derivational suffixes, but excludes the obligatory final inflectional suffix. Reduplicants are disyllabic and prefixed, as shown in (52). When the verb root itself is two syllables or longer, as in (52a), the reduplicant copies the first two open syllables of the stem. If the verb root is monosyllabic but combines with derivational suffixes such as applicative -el or causative -is, reduplication copies material from both, as in (52b). But reduplication cannot copy inflectional suffixes. When the derivational stem (root plus derivational suffixes) is only monosyllabic, as in (52c), the reduplicant recruits semantically empty -a to flesh out its obligatory disyllabic shape.[7] The suffix -a occurs on verb stems when one of the more contentful inflectional endings (e.g. subjunctive -e or

---

[7] Hyman et al. (2009) discuss a second empty morph, yi, which is used to augment reduplicants of stems formed from consonantal roots such as /dl-/ 'eat'. When reduplicated, stems like [dl-e] 'eat-SUBJUNCTIVE' or [dl-ile] 'eat-PERFECTIVE' recruit both -a and yi to the cause of reduplicant disyllabism, thus dl-a-yi-+dl-e or dl-a-yi+dl-ile. The facts in (52b) are more complex than reported here; see Hyman et al. (2009). Note also that all of the forms in (52) are provided in the infinitive, prefixed with uku-. However, the infinitive prefix is outside the scope of reduplication and can be ignored; for this reason it is parenthesized in the data in (52).

perfective *-ile*) is absent; it is the default filler of the obligatory inflectional suffix position. Because it has no meaning of its own, it is recruitable to flesh out subminimal reduplicants even of verb stems that end in one of the other inflectional suffixes:

(52)		stem	reduplicated stem	[Ndebele]
a.	'INF-taste-FV'	(uku-)nambith-a	(uku-)<u>nambi</u>+nambith-a	
	'INF-appear-FV'	(uku-)bonakel-a	(uku-)bona+bonakel-a	
b.	'INF-cultivate-APPL-FV'	(uku-)lim-el-a	(uku-)lim-e+lim-el-a	
	'INF-cultivate-CAUS-FV'	(uku-)lim-is-a	(uku-)lim-i+lim-is-a	
c.	'INF-cultivate-FV'	(uku-)lim-a	(uku-)<u>lim-a</u>+lim-a	
	'INF-cultivate-SUBJ'	(uku-)lim-e	(uku-)<u>lim-a</u>+lim-e	
	'INF-cultivate-PERF'	(uku-)lim-ile	(uku-)<u>lim-a</u>+lim-ile	
	'INF-send SUBJ'	(uku-)thum-e	(uku-)<u>thum-a</u>+thum-e	
	'INF-send-PERF'	(uku-)thum-ile	(uku-)<u>thum-a</u>+thum-ile	

Downing (2006) characterizes the morphologically complex reduplicants of Ndebele and several other Bantu languages as "canonical stems." The canonical verb stem in Bantu ends in the final vowel *a* and is minimally disyllabic; this is exactly the shape the reduplicant assumes when, because of various constraints on reduplication, it cannot copy the verb stem exactly. The ability of the reduplicant to assume the canonical morphological structure of verb stems even when that structure is not found in the apparent base of reduplication illustrates the potential morphological independence of reduplicant and base.

5.6.4 Echo reduplication and other types of morphologically fixed segmentism

A third scenario in which base and reduplicant can differ morphologically comes from so-called "echo reduplication", the term often applied to total reduplication constructions in which the beginning of the second copy is replaced by a fixed substring. Familiar English examples include the ironic or pejorative Yiddish-derived *fancy-schmancy, resolutions-schmesolutions*, in which the fixed substring [ʃm] stands in as the onset of the copy and replaces any existing initial consonant(s). Kolami (Central Dravidian) has an "et cetera" construction, exemplified by *maasur* 'men' → *maasur-giisur* 'men and the like' or *kota* 'bring it!' → *kota-gita* 'bring it if you want to' (Emeneau 1955), in which *gi* stands in for the initial (C)V of the copy.

Alderete et al. (1999) analyze the fixed material in echo reduplication as an affix which merges with the reduplicant into a constituent whose prosodic shape is determined by the reduplication construction; in most examples cited, this shape is determined by the base, since most examples involve total reduplication. The affix—*shm-* in English, *gi-* in Kolami—often supplements segmental material that would otherwise be expected to be copied, giving rise to the term "Melodic Overwriting" for the replacive affix found in echo reduplication (e.g. Yip 1992; McCarthy and Prince 1996, 1999b). In possessing an affix that the base lacks, reduplicants in Melodic Overwriting situations pattern with examples like Ndebele in which the reduplicant is morphologically complex, independently of the base.

Echo reduplication is very common cross-linguistically. It appears to be a contagious areal phenomenon, especially throughout South Asia, where pockets of it are found not just in Dravidian but also in Indo-Aryan, Tibeto-Burman, and Austro-Asiatic languages (see e.g. Abbi 1991; Keane 2001; Singh 2005). Further west, an echo reduplication pattern meaning "X and the like" is found in Turkish (Turkic), Armenian (Indo-European), and Abkhaz (Northwest Caucasian), languages from completely different families but spoken in the same general part of the world (see e.g. Johanson and Csato 1998; Vaux 1998). Turkish has a well-known "et cetera" construction involving *m-*: *ağaç* 'tree' → *ağaç-mağaç* 'trees and suchlike', *dergi* 'journal' → *dergi-mergi* 'journals and suchlike' (Lewis 1967: 237); a parallel construction is found in Armenian (*pətuʁ* 'fruit' → *pətuʁ-mətuʁ*; Vaux 1998: 246) and Abkhaz (*gaʒá-kʼ* 'fool' → *gaʒákʼ-maʒákʼ*, Vaux 1996, cited in Inkelas and Zoll 2005).

Echo reduplication is often subject to the requirement that the fixed substring not be identical to the substring that the copy would otherwise begin with. Yip (1992, 1998), invoking an anti-homophony constraint, relates this pattern to the dissimilation often required in poetic rhyme. Thus, for example, in Hindi the "et cetera" echo construction uses a replacive *v-*: *narendra* 'Narendra' (proper name) → *narendra-varendra* 'undesirables like Narendra' (Singh 2005: 266), *tras* 'grief' → *tras-vras* 'grief and the like' (Nevins 2005: 280). However, for stems that are already *v*-initial, *š* is used instead: *vakil* 'lawyer' → *vakil-šakil* 'lawyers and the like' (Nevins 2005: 280). In Kashmiri (Indic), *v*-replacement (*gagur* 'mouse ' → *gagur-vagur* 'mouse and the like', *poosh* 'flower' → *poosh-voosh* 'flower and the like') alternates with *p*-replacement: *vaan* 'shop' → *vaan paan*, *vwazul* 'red' → *vwazul pwazul* (Koul 2008). According to Lewis (1967), speakers cannot employ the Turkish *m*-construction when the input would begin with [m], and resort to a periphrastic alternative instead.

In habitual-repetitive total reduplication in Javanese (Western Malayo-Polynesian, Sundic), the two copies in reduplication must differ in the quality of their last vowel (Yip 1992, 1998). The basic pattern is for the last vowel in the first copy to be replaced with [a]: *eliŋ* 'remember' → *elaŋ-eliŋ* 'remember (habitual/repetitive)', *tuku* 'buy' → *tuka-tuku* 'buy (habitual/repetitive)'. If, however, that vowel would have been [a] anyway, then the last vowel in the second copy is replaced with [e]: *udan* 'rain' → *udan-uden* 'rain (habitual/repetitive)', *kumat* 'have a relapse' → *kumat-kumet* 'have a relapse (habitual/repetitive)'.

Analyzing echo reduplication as affixation, following Alderete et al. (1999), may not appear to cover cases like Javanese, in which the modification to the "echo" is not a segmentable affix. However, the insight that the "echo" in echo reduplication is morphologically complex still survives as long as one acknowledges the role of realizational processes like ablaut, mutation, and other phonological modifications in instantiating morphological constructions.

Some echo reduplication constructions ensure anti-homophony in a brute-force method, modifying *both* copies in distinct ways, as in the following data from Hua (Trans New Guinea, Eastern Highlands; Haiman 1980: 126) in which both copies undergo vowel replacement:

(53)   kveki   'crumple'   kveku kveke hu   'crumple'   [Hua]
       ebsgi   'twist'   ebsgu ebsge hu   'twist and turn'
       ftgegi   'coil'   ftgegu ftgege hu 'all coiled up'
       ha-vari 'grow tall' ha-varu ha-vare hu 'grow up'

While it might not be termed "echo" reduplication, the third logical subtype of reduplication+modification also exists, namely cases in which both copies are modified, but in the same way. This occurs in Siroi (Trans-New Guinea), where, like Javanese, Melodic Overwriting is internal. The medial consonant of the input stem is modified to [g] in both copies (Wells 1979: 37):

(54) a. tango maye   →   tango mage-mage   [Siroi]
         'man' 'good'
         'a mature man'   'mature men'

      b. tango sungo   →   tango sugo-sugo
         'man' 'big'
         'a ruler'   'rulers'

    c. tango kuen   →   tango kugen-kugen
       'man' 'tall'
      'a tall man'   'tall men'

Reduplication with Melodic Overwriting, including echo reduplication, is much more common in total reduplication than it is in partial reduplication; it is hard to find examples of partial echo reduplication that are comparable to the clear total reduplication cases in Kannada, Hindi, Kashmiri, Turkish, Javanese, and Siroi.

One clear case is documented in child language. As discussed in Inkelas (2003), between the ages of 2:5 and 4:6, child J, acquiring English, invented a language game involving reduplication. While the game evolved over time, in its first phase, the reduplicant was a disyllabic foot whose initial consonant was replaced with *b*: *towel-bowel, Minnesota-bota, stegosaurus-baurus, engineer-beer, helicopter-bopter*. For words whose reduplicated portion would already begin with *b*, J substituted *p* in its place: *ball-pall, Alabama-pama, alphabet-pet*. This pattern is very similar to that in Kannada, etc., except for being partial reduplication. However, clear cases like this are not easy to find in adult language.

One pattern of partial reduplication and Melodic Overwriting is clearly attested in a number of languages in the Micro-Altaic group (including Turkic, Mongolic, and Tungusic), as well as in various dialects of Armenian. The process in question intensifies adjectives and is marked by a preposed reduplicative syllable whose onset and nucleus are copied from the base but whose coda consonant is drawn from a small fixed set of consonants. Data from the Arabkir dialect of Armenian (Vaux 1998) and from the Tungusic language Oroqen (Li and Whaley 2000) are shown in (55). In Oroqen, in which the process only applies to color terms, the reduplicant copies a stem coda if there is one (55a), and otherwise inserts the fixed segment [b] (55b) (Li and Whaley 2000: 356). In Armenian, where a greater semantic range of adjectives participate, the reduplicant coda is [s] (55c) except before coronals, in which case it switches to [pʰ] (55d) (Vaux 1998: 243):

(55)   a. 'white' bagdarın bag-bagdarın 'very white,   [Oroqen]
                                          white as snow'

     b. 'yellow' ʃiŋarın ʃib-ʃiŋarın 'very yellow, golden yellow'
       'black' kara   kab-kara   'glossy black, very dark'

c. 'red'   karmir   kas-karmir   [Arabkir Armenian]
   'empty'   parap   pas-parap
   'violet'   moːr   moːs-moːr

d. 'black'   sev   sepʰ-sev
   'yellow'   deʁin   depʰ-deʁin

These cases aside, partial reduplication with fixed segmentism of the Melodic Overwriting type has not frequently been described. There are at least two plausible reasons why Melodic Overwriting in general, and echo reduplication in particular, are more common in total reduplication than in partial reduplication. One is the role of anti-homophony considerations. To the extent that anti-homophony is a motivating factor in the morphological modification of one of the two copies, this asymmetry makes sense: partial reduplication already intrinsically differentiates base and reduplicant, in most cases, removing the functional motivation for further modification.

Another reason that Melodic Overwriting has not been documented as often as an accompaniment to partial reduplication as it has for total reduplication is that there is an alternative analysis for many of the apparent partial reduplication cases. In Yoruba, for example, gerundive reduplication is marked with a CV prefix whose consonant is reduplicative but whose vowel is fixed as [í]: g͡bóná → g͡bí-g͡bóná, wɔ → wí-wɔ, etc. (see discussion of Yoruba around example (13)). This effect could be analyzed as partial reduplication with Melodic Overwriting by [í], but, as argued in Alderete et al. (1999), could also be analyzed as CV reduplication with reduction of the reduplicant vowel. This type of analysis, involving phonological copying and phonological reduction, is discussed in section 5.2.3, in the context of Base-Reduplicant Correspondence Theory.

Alternatively, the consonant copy which takes place in Yoruba *Cí* prefixation could be treated as epenthesis and assimilation, both independently motivated phonological phenomena which occur in nonreduplicative contexts; looked at from this angle, Yoruba might not be classified as reduplication proper at all. This is the approach Kim takes to a similar duplication phenomenon in the San Francisco del Mar dialect of Huave (isolate; Oaxaca, Mexico). As shown in (56a–c), the 1st person suffix, which surfaces in these data as a copy vowel followed by [s], copies the preceding stem vowel exactly, just as long as the palatality of the final stem vowel agrees with the frontness/backness of that vowel (Kim 2008: 143–88). If the conditions for vowel assimilation are not met, the vowel assimilates only to the preceding consonant, surfacing as [i] after a palatal (C^{pal}) or [a] after a plain consonant (C^{bk}), (56d,e).

(56) a. /t-a-mongbk-Vs/ →   t-a-mong-os   [Huave]
       CP-TV-pass-1   'I passed by'

      b. /a-xum^{bk}-Vj/   → a-xum-**uj**
         TV-find-3PL   'they find (it)'

      c. /t-a-j.chik^{pal}-Vs/ → t-a-j.chik-**is**   (→ [tachikius] due to later rule)
         CP-TV-jump-1   'I jumped'

      d. /t-a-j.mik^{bk}-Vs/ → t-a-j.mik-**as**   (→ [tamikas] due to later rule)
         CP-TV-descend-1   'I came down'

      e. /t-a-long^{pal}-Vs/ → t-a-long-**is**   (→ [talongius] due to later rule)
         CP-TV-hang-1   'I hung (it)'

Kim (2008) analyzes the copy vowel as epenthetic (pp. 143–88) and attributes its copy properties entirely to phonological assimilation; there is no need to formally classify the suffix as reduplicative, or invoke any special reduplicative apparatus, in this analysis.

In summary, fixed segmentism in reduplication is widespread. It can have its source in an affix which co-occurs with and supplants reduplicative material, a phenomenon that occurs commonly in total reduplication, or it can have its source in phonological reduction, which occurs commonly in partial reduplication. Fixed segmentism can also co-occur with phonological assimilation, giving the appearance of reduplication; whether such cases should be classified with other, more clearly morphologically reduplicative constructions remains an open question.

5.7 Conclusion

Reduplication has been and is likely to continue to be a phenomenon of enduring interest to morphologists and phonologists alike. It has a unique capacity to shed light on the internal structure of words, and it is a constant thorn in the side of reductionist theories which try to lump morphology with phonology or to lump morphology with syntax.

It is innovated readily in creoles and in the course of first language acquisition, and it is easily spread from one language to another. Of all of the elements in language games, reduplication is arguably the one that occurs most often in ordinary grammar as well. Reduplication is at the same time commonplace, occurring in virtually every language, and mysterious; its historical trajectory remains elusive. The study of reduplication has burgeoned in the last thirty years and is by no means exhausted; future decades are likely to turn up new typological discoveries as well as historical and psycholinguistic revelations about the nature of reduplication.

6

Infixation

Infixation is the situation in which an affix appears inside the base of affixation, rather than at one of its edges, the normal position for "adfixes," i.e. prefixes and suffixes. Infixation is generally viewed in theoretical treatments as being just like adfixation except that the affix is phonologically positioned within the stem instead of peripheral to it (see e.g. Moravcsik 1977, 2000; Marantz 1982; McCarthy and Prince 1993; Yu 2007). In Dakota (Siouan), for example, verbal agreement markers appear after the first CV of the stem (Yu 2007, citing Moravcsik 1977: 95–6 and Boas and Deloria 1941):

(1) manų   'steal'   ma-wa-nų   'I steal'   [Dakota]
    napca   'swallow'   na-wa-pca   'I swallow it'
    nawizi   'jealous'   na-wa-wizi   'I am jealous'

In Ulwa, construct-state (CNS) or agreement markers appear immediately following the first iambic foot in the stem. The data in (2a,b) are discussed by Yu 2007; the data in (2c) are discussed in McCarthy and Prince (1993), citing Hale and Lacayo Blanco (1989). All forms shown here are phonetic transcriptions taken directly from Green (1999):

(2) a. awa, awáː → awáː-ki   'silkgrass-CNS1' (61) [Ulwa]
       súru, surúː → surúː-kina   'log-CNS11' (61)

    b. áytak   → áy-mana-tak   'paper-CNS22' (65)
       aláːkuṃ   → aláː-ka-kuṃ   'Muscovy duck' (65)
       waráw̜wa   → waráw̜-kana-wa 'parrot sp.-CNS33' (65)

    c. súːlu   → súː-ma-lu   'dog-CNS2' (53, 65)
                      suː-ki-lu   'dog-CNS1' (67)
                      suː-ka-lu   'dog-CNS3' (84)
                      suː-kina-lu   'dog-CNS11' (65)

A standard description of the Dakota infixation case is that the agreement markers are prefixes which infix after the initial CV of the stem. A standard description of the Ulwa case is that the construct state/agreement markers are suffixes which attach directly to the first stressed syllable or stress foot, even if it is stem-internal. Describing infixes like those in Dakota as would-be prefixes and infixes like those in Ulwa would-be suffixes correctly predicts that in cases where the infixal pivot—the portion of the stem that is skipped over by the infix—is not present, the infix will appear as a regular prefix or suffix. This occurs in the Ulwa forms in (2a), in which the first iambic foot is also final in the stem. In this situation, the construct state marker appears as a suffix; there is no material between the first foot and the end of the word, and thus there is nothing for the infix to skip over.

The interest of infixation for the phonology-morphology interface lies in phonological generalizations about where in a word an infix can appear and about what, if anything, motivates infixation synchronically. Infixation has been considered one of the best examples of the influence of phonology on the linearization of morphemes, a topic which will be explored further in Chapter 9 (section 9.4).

6.1 What kinds of things can infix?

Infixes are found associated with a great variety of inflectional and derivational functions. This is of some interest; any association between infixation and certain types of grammatical or semantic functions would be relevant to theories of iconicity or other relations between form and function. In Chapter 5, we observed a tendency for reduplication to express iconic functions. Infixation, however, appears to be an arbitrary phonological alternative to adfixation.

Yu's (2007) survey of infixation draws on a database of 111 languages from 26 different phyla, including isolates. The 154 infixation patterns Yu documents include nominal inflection (plural, noun class/gender, construct state) and verbal inflection (agreement; agent or object focus; frequentative, intensive, durative, repetitive, continuative, and distributive aspect; perfectivity and completive aspect; present tense; realis and negative; pluractional; interrogative). Infixes can be derivational, as well. Yu's sample includes several instances of dimunitivizing and nominalizing infixes. Verbal infixes in the sample can affect argument structure (passivization, causativization, applicativization, (de)transitivization). Finally, many infixes are associated with language games and onomatopoeic or expressive language.

Infixes are almost exclusively dependent morphemes (affix, and occasionally clitics; see Harris 2000). It is rare, possibly nonexistent, outside of language play, to find infixation of roots, stems, or words inside other roots, stems, or words. One familiar example falls squarely in the domain of expressive language, namely the infixation of expletives before a stress foot in English (McCarthy 1982: 574–6, citing Siegel 1974 and Allen 1978; see also Yu 2007):

(3) Monòngahéla → Monònga-fuckin-héla
    fàntástic   → fàn-fuckin-tástic
    hándicàp   → hándi-bloody-càp
    kíndergàrten → kínder-goddam-gàrten

This productive construction admits a great variety of expletives; for example, an internet search on 7/23/10 turned up, for California, "Cali-liberal-fornia," "Cali-socialist-fornia," "Cali-friggin-fornia," "Cali-bloody-fornia," "Cali-god-damn-fornia," "Cali-kissmyass-fornia," "Cali-commie-fornia," among many other even less family-friendly examples. Expletive infixation is a common means of expressing frustration or disdain, although in some cases it can be used to express awe or admiration, e.g. "World-freakin' Champions!" (in reference to the San Francisco Giants in a blog post on 11/10/10).

An unusual example of root infixation occurs in Cantonese, in which the word *kwɐi* 'ghost' is infixed inside certain adjectives, conveying intensification (Yu 2007: 134, citing Matthews and Yip 1994: 43):

(4) lœntsœn 'clumsy' lœn-kwɐi-tsœn 'downright clumsy' [Cantonese]
    jʊksyn 'ugly'   jʊk-kwɐi-syn 'downright ugly'

The Cantonese words *mɐtkwɐi* and *mɛ*, meaning 'what', can also appear infixed, "to signify uncertainties the speaker might have about a word or a proposition" (Yu 2007: 134).

(5) a. jʊkˀsyn   'ugly'   jʊk-mɐtˀkwɐi-syn
    b. mɔlɔkˀkɔ   'Morocco'   mɔ-mɐtˀkwɐi-lɔkˀkɔ
                               ~ mɔlɔk-mɐtˀkwɐi-kɔ
    c. kilikulu   'gibberish' ki-mɛ-likulu
                               ~ kili-mɛ-kulu

These cases aside, however, the majority of reported cases of infixation involve elements that would unblinkingly be described as prefixes or suffixes if they were simply concatenated with the base of affixation, rather than being infixed into it. This is relevant to theories of the phonology-morphology interface, since it suggests that infixation is a property of individual affixes, rather than resulting from top-down principles of substring ordering in words. We will return to this observation in sections 6.4 and 6.5, which address the question of whether infixation is a phonological repair for phonotactic illformedness of morphologically complex constituents.

6.2 Location of infixes

Surveys of infixation from Ultan (1975) to Moravcsik (1977, 2000) to Yu (2007) have found a small and principled set of recurring phonological sites for segmental infixes. Infixes either occur next to a peripheral constituent (vowel, consonant, syllable) or, in lexical stress languages, next to a metrical prominence, e.g. the stressed syllable or the foot that carries primary word stress. Yu terms these "pivots"; a list appears in (6):

(6)   Edge pivots   Prominence pivots

First consonant	Stressed foot
First vowel	Stressed syllable
First syllable	Stressed vowel
Last syllable	
Last vowel	
Last consonant	

Not all of these potential pivots are distinguishable from each other in all cases—for example, in a language with rigid CV syllable structure, an infix that follows the first CV could be described as infixing after the first vowel or the first syllable.

Examples of infixes situated with regard to these pivots are presented in (7). These examples all consist of nonreduplicative infixes; as seen here, reduplicative infixes have a slightly different distribution:

(7)   Infix pivots exemplified
　　　 a. First consonant (after): Yurok (Algic; Garrett 2001, cited in
　　　　　 Yu 2007)

laːy-	'to pass'	l-eg-aːy
koʔmoy-	'to hear'	k-eg-oʔmoy-
tewomeł	'to be glad'	t-eg-ewomeł

b. First vowel (before): Chamorro (Malayo-Polynesian; Anderson 1992, Topping 1973, cited in Yu 2007: 89)

epanglo	'hunt crabs'	um-epanglo	'to look for crabs'
gupu	'to fly'	g-um-upu	'flew'
tristi	'sad'	tr-um-isti	'becomes sad'

c. Final syllable (before): Koasati verbal plurality (Muskogean; Kimball 1991, cited in Yu 2007: 108)

'to be hungry'	aká:non	aká-s-non
'to knock something away'	akopí:lin	akopí-s-lin
'to open the eyes'	maká:lin	maká-s-lin
'to be sexually attractive'	stipí:lan	stipí-s-lan

d. Stressed syllable (or stress foot): Ulwa construct state (Green 1999, cited in Yu 2007: 119)

sú:lu	sú:-ma-lu	'dog-CNS2'
alá:kuṃ	alá:-ka-kuṃ	'Muscovy duck-CNS3'
waráẉwa	waráẉ-kana-wa	'parrot sp.-CNS33'

According to Yu (2007), final consonant, final vowel, and initial syllable pivots are hard to identify. There are certainly cases that could be described in these terms, but they are difficult to disambiguate, often yielding equally well to other descriptions. For example, cases of infixation before the final consonant could, depending on the syllable structure of the language, also be analyzed as infixation after the final vowel. Similarly, cases of infixation after the first syllable could in languages with CV syllable structure be analyzed as infixation after the first vowel.

Yu (2007) makes the important observation that the pivots referenced in infixation belong to the set of elements that all words in the relevant language contain: edges and (in stress languages) culminative stress. By contrast, there is no evidence of infixation to syllables with particular tones, or to syllables containing particular types of segments (e.g. fricatives or ejectives) or to closed syllables. These are types of elements that some words may have but that are not universally guaranteed to be present in all words in the lexicon. Yu's generalization may be related to the fact that ineffability—the failure of an expected morphological combination to exist because of phonological reasons— is relatively uncommon. (Ineffability is discussed in Chapter 9.) An infix which selects for a phonological property possessed by only a minority of potential bases of affixation would have low utility in the grammar.

6.3 Internal (infixing) reduplication

Many infixes are reduplicative in nature. Reduplicative counterparts to
the segmentally invariant infixes seen above are given in (8). It is not
always easy to parse internal reduplication: which is the copy and
which is the original? In these examples, rather than setting off infixes
with hyphens, the relevant substring is underlined, allowing the reader
to keep an open mind as to which identical copy should be identified as
the infix:

(8)   Reduplicative infix pivots
   a. First consonant (before): Pangasinan plural marking (Malayo-
      Polynesian; Benton 1971, cited in Yu 2007: 81)
      kanáyon   <u>ka</u>kanáyon   'relatives'
      kúya   <u>ku</u>kúya   'older brother'
      amígo   a<u>mi</u>mígo   'friend'
      amíga   a<u>mi</u>míga   'female friend'
   b. First vowel (before): Kugu Nganhcara plural (Paman; Smith
      and Johnson 2000, cited in Yu 2007: 95)
      'stand'   thena   th<u>ene</u>na
      'child'   pukpe   p<u>uku</u>kpe
      'here-EMPH'   iiru-ma   <u>iirii</u>ruma
      'break'   ungpa   <u>ungku</u>ngpa
   c. Last vowel (after): Kamaiurá plural (Tupí-Guaraní; Everett and
      Seki 1985, cited in Yu 2007: 113)
      omotumuŋ   omo<u>tumu</u>tumuŋ   'he shook it repeatedly'
      ohuka   ohuka<u>huka</u>   'he kept on laughing'
   d. Final syllable (before): possibly Samala (=Ineseño Chumash;
      Chumashan; Applegate 1982, 1986, cited in Yu 2007: 110)
      ta<u>šu</u>šun   'to be fragrant'
      i<u>wa</u>wan   'to cut with a sawing motion'
      ox<u>yo</u>yon   'to be crazy'
      muc'uc'u?   'kind of very small bead'
      yux<u>wo</u>won   'to be high, tall'
   e. Stressed syllable: Ulwa distributive (Green 1999, cited in Yu
      2007: 119)
      'good-ADJ'   yám-ka   <u>ya</u>yám-ka
      'small-ADJ'   bisíː-ka   bi<u>sisíː</u>-ka
      'firm-ADJ'   burím-ka   bu<u>ri</u>rím-ka

As seen in (8), infixing reduplication occurs in most of the same locations as nonreduplicative infixation. The main asymmetry that Yu found in his cross-linguistic survey is that a number of reduplicative infixes, but few segmentally fixed infixes, unambiguously select a final vowel pivot.

Internal reduplication raises several questions which do not arise with fixed-segment infixes. One empirical question which arises with any type of reduplication (see Chapter 5) is what part of the base is copied: the preceding substring? The following substring? The beginning or end of the word? This issue is discussed further in section 6.3.1. A second, more analytical issue is whether a given instance of internal reduplication is morphologically mandated, or whether it is better analyzed as phonological assimilation. Particularly relevant to this question is the existence of hybrid infixes, which are partly fixed and partly reduplicative (section 6.3.2).

6.3.1 Locality in internal reduplication

While internal reduplication is unexceptional from the point of view of the location of the infix in the stem, it does appear to have one special property that sets it apart from adfixal reduplication. As mentioned in section 5.2.5.1, internal reduplication of syllable-sized units is almost always local, reduplicating base material which is adjacent to the location of the infix. The following examples illustrate this pattern:

(9) a. Mangarayi (Australian, Mangarayi; Yu 2007: 92, citing Merlan 1982 and Kurisu and Sanders 1999)
     gabuji   'old person'   ga<u>ba</u>buji
     yirag   'father'   yi<u>ri</u>rag
     jimgan   'knowledgeable one'   ji<u>mim</u>gan

     b. Chamorro (Topping 1973: 259, cited by Yu 2007: 122
     sága   'stay'   sá<u>sa</u>ga   'staying'
     hugándo   'play'   hugá<u>g</u>ando   'playing'

Internal reduplication rarely seems to show the long-distance or "opposite-edge" doubling that is occasionally found with adfixing reduplication (Chapter 5, section 5.3.4). Recall from Chapter 5 the following examples of opposite-edge reduplication from Madurese (10a) and Koryak (10b). In Madurese, opposite-edge prefixing reduplication encodes plurality (Steriade 1988, citing Stevens 1985); in Koryak, opposite-edge suffixing reduplication encodes absolute case (Riggle 2004, citing Bogoras 1969: 687–8):

(10) Opposite-edge reduplication
    a. dus-garadus   'fast and sloppy'   [Madurese]
       wa?-buwa?-(an) 'fruits'
       bit-abit   'finally'
       w̃ã-mõw̃ã   'faces'

    b. mɪtqa-mɪt   'oil'   [Koryak]
       kilka-kil   'shellfish'
       qanga-qan   'fire'

There are a few exceptions to the generalization that infixing reduplication is always local. A number of them involve single-segment copy. A few cases involve CV reduplication. The overarching generalization, based on cross-linguistic surveys conducted by Broselow and McCarthy (1983) and Yu (2007), is that long-distance internal reduplication always involves very short reduplicants. In Levantine Arabic intensifying reduplication, for example, a copy of the stem-initial consonant—a very short reduplicant—is infixed before the last stem vowel, converting CVCVC stems to CVC.CVC (Broselow and McCarthy 1983: 36, cited by Yu 2007: 117):

(11) barad bar-<u><u>b</u></u>-ad 'shaved unevenly'
      šaraħ šar-<u><u>š</u></u>-aħ 'criticized severely'
      ħalat ħal-<u><u>ħ</u></u>-at 'sheared unevenly'
      daħal daħ-<u><u>d</u></u>-al 'rolled gradually'

In Pima (Uto-Aztecan), plural reduplication infixes a copy of the initial consonant after the first vowel (Yu 2007: 161, citing Riggle 2006):

(12)

sg	pl	gloss
mavit	ma-<u><u>m</u></u>-vit	'lion'
koson	ko-<u><u>k</u></u>-son	'pack rat'
sipuk	si-<u><u>s</u></u>-puk	'cardinal'

In Creek (Muskogean), plural adjectives are formed by suffixing a copy of the initial CV of the stem just before the stem-final consonant, which is the onset of the syllable headed by the adjectival ending [-iː]. The data in (13) are from Riggle (2004), who cites Haas (1977) and Martin and Mauldin (2000). Reduplicants are double-underlined:

(13)

	Singular adjective	Plural adjective	[Creek]
'clean'	hasátk-iː	hasat-<u>ha</u>-k-íː	
'nasty, dirty, filthy'	likácw-iː	likac-<u>li</u>-w-íː	
'soft'	lowáck-iː	lowac-<u>lo</u>-k-íː	
'sweet'	cámp-iː	cam-<u>ca</u>-p-íː	
'torn up, mashed'	citákk-iː	citak-<u>ci</u>-k-íː	
'ugly, naughty'	holwak-íː	holwaː-<u>ho</u>-k-íː	

In all of these cases, the copied material is mora-sized or smaller (CV, C); only a single consonant and a single vowel are copied.

In Chapter 5 (section 5.4), an analytical distinction was drawn between reduplication, which is morphologically mandated and "compensatory duplication," Yu's (2005b) term for copying which is phonologically motivated, e.g. by the need to flesh out an empty or partially specified prosodic unit. Morphologically mandated reduplication is handled with morphological technology—a morpheme called "RED," or an analysis of morphological doubling—whereas phonologically motivated duplication is more plausibly analyzed as epenthesis (or affixation of an empty mora) and assimilation. In the case of very short reduplicants, it is possible to construct both types of analyses. This is relevant because of the generalization that nonlocal internal reduplication always consists of small (mora-sized or smaller) reduplicants. Such cases are accessible, if desired, to a phonological analysis of consonant or mora epenthesis and an assimilation process which anchors the epenthetic constituent not to a local counterpart but to a prominent one—the initial C or CV, in all of the cases in this section.

A possible source of nonlocal internal reduplication is the reduction of part of the reduplicant. Nakanai (Oceanic) presents a particularly interesting case of this kind (Broselow and McCarthy 1983; Carlson 1998). As seen in (14), Nakanai reduplication (which can mark a variety of verbal and nominal functions) duplicates a contracted version of the final two moras. The reduplicant is infixed before the string it copies. Reduplicant contraction always preserves the beginning and end of the base of reduplication, giving the appearance of nonlocality in (14b):

(14)   Nakanai (Broselow and McCarthy 1983: 59, citing Johnston 1980)

a. lolo   lo-lolo   'hearing'
   baa   ba-baa   'spaces'
   burulele buru-le-lele 'sliding on buttocks'
   bilau   bi-la-lau   'songs'

b. pati   pai-pati   'floating'
   gapu   gau-gapu   'beads'
   kedi   kei-kedi   'being careful'
   pita   pa-pita   'muddy'
   sile   se-sile   'tearing'
   valua   va-la-lua   'men'
   vokakea   voka-ka-kea   'white men'

Except for being infixing, Nakanai reduplication resembles cases like Temiar (Mon-Khmer, Aslian) and Ulu Muar Malay (Malayo-Polynesian), in which a prefixed reduplicant copies the beginning and end of the following stem. In the Temiar data in (15) (introduced earlier in Chapter 4), the copying is exact (15a); in Ulu Muar Malay (Hendon 1966; Kroeger 1990; Wee 1995), a copied final consonant is reduced to [ʔ] or a nasal, depending on its original sonority (15b) (Wee 1995: 222):

(15)   a. 'to call'   kɔɔw   →   kwkɔɔw   [Temiar]
       'to sit down'   gəl   →   glgəl
       'to lie down'   slɔg   →   sglɔg
       'to ask a question'   smaaɲ   →   sɲmaaɲ

     b. tariʔ   →   taʔ-tariʔ   'accordion'   [Ulu Muar Malay]
       sieʔ   →   siʔ-sieʔ   'is torn repeatedly'
       dayaŋ   →   dan-dayaŋ   'hand-maidens'
       tanam   →   bo-tan-tanam   'gardens regularly'

What seems so far to be rare or nonexistent is exact internal reduplication of a complex syllable or foot-sized constituent which is nonlocal to the reduplicant, e.g. *barital* → *ba-tal-rital*, *niktistra* → *nik-tra-tistra*, etc. This lends mild support to a phonological account of long-distance internal reduplication. Whether the data in examples (13)–(15) should be classified as morphological infixation or phonological duplication is not clear; the number of relevant cases is still small, and future research may be needed to decide this question.

6.3.2 Hybrid infixes

A number of cases of infixation are hybrid, containing some reduplicative material and some fixed material. This mixture is also found in adfixing reduplication, as discussed in Chapter 5 (section 5.6.4), where it goes under the name of "echo reduplication" or "Melodic Overwriting."

A clear example occurs in Huave. As documented by Kim (2008: 154–5), the passivizing infix *-rV-* is inserted before the stem-final consonant, with the result that a CVC root becomes CV-rV-C. The consonant of the infix is fixed as /r/, but the vowel copies the features of the preceding vowel:[1]

(16)

Root	+ passive infix	Example	gloss
-xeng	-xe-re-ng	a-xereng	'TV-raise.PASS = it is raised'
-xum	-xu-ru-m	t-a-xurum	'CP-TV-find.PASS = it was found'
-ndok	-ndo-ro-k	a-ndorok	'TV-fish.PASS = it is fished'

In the Tigre (South Semitic) frequentative, the formative -aː- is infixed before the final stem syllable; it is preceded by a copy of the penultimate stem consonant, producing a hybrid -Caː- infix (Rose 2003, cited in Yu 2007: 109):

(17) dənzəz- 'be numb' dənə-z-aː-zəz- 'be a little numb'
      gərf-aː 'whip'   ge-r-aː-rəf-aː   'whip a little'

Hybrid infixation presents some of the best examples of nonlocal internal reduplication attested in the literature. In Koasati punctual reduplication, the fixed formative óː is infixed before the stem-final syllable; its onset is a copy of the initial C of the stem (Yu 2007: 109, citing Kimball 1991):

(18) 'to be full'   alóːtkan   alot-l-óː-kan
      'to be angled' cofóknan   cofok-c-óː-nan
      'to be thin'   talásban   talas-t-óː-ban

This case, like those in section 6.3.1, is amenable to a phonological analysis, if desired: consonant epenthesis provides an onset to the fixed -óː affix, and the epenthetic consonant assimilates to a preceding strong (initial) consonant.

6.4 The P » M approach to infixation in Optimality Theory

A stimulating theory of infixation was introduced in the early 1990s, within the framework of Optimality Theory, by McCarthy and Prince (1993), who observed that many cases of infixation could be interpreted

---

[1] For a formally similar case from another dialect of Huave, involving indefinite actor focus, see Stairs and Hollenbach (1969), cited in Yu (2007: 117). In both cases, vowel feature copy sometimes fails and default vowel features are used instead; see Kim (2008) for extensive discussion.

as improving the prosodic structure of the derived word in comparison to the structure the word would have if the infixed element were instead adfixed. Infixation is a key motivator in McCarthy and Prince's proposal that at least some phonological constraints "P" can outrank morphological constraints "M," particularly those having to do with the edge-alignment of affixes.

The most convincing examples brought forth for this view, termed the "Phonological Readjustment" view in Yu 2007, involve syllable structure. McCarthy and Prince's original example concerns the agentive focus marker, -*um*-, in Tagalog, which precedes the initial vowel:[2]

(19)   aral   um-aral   'teach'
        sulat   s-um-ulat   'write'
        gradwet   gr-um-adwet   'graduate'

A similar example involving reduplicative infixation occurs in Timugon Murut (McCarthy and Prince 1993, citing Prentice 1971):

(20)   a. bulud   bu-bulud   'hill/ridge'
            limo   li-limo   'five/about five'
        b. abalan   a-ba-balan   'bathes/often bathes'
            ompodon   om-po-podon   'flatter/always flatter'

According to McCarthy and Prince, Tagalog -*um*- and the Timugon Murut syllable-sized reduplicant are prefixes, subject to an Alignment constraint aligning them with the left edge of the stem they create. That constraint competes with a phonological constraint which penalizes closed syllables. It is not possible to satisfy both constraints in the case of an input like *sulat*, which already contains one closed syllable and would have another if *um*- were prefixed. The optimal solution, according to McCarthy and Prince, is to infix *um*- after the first consonant. This solution keeps the number of closed syllables to a minimum, while also positioning *um*- as close to the beginning of the word as possible. The following Optimality-theoretic tableau models this analysis. The actual outcome, *s-um-ulat*, is one of three possibilities being considered, the other two being true prefixation (*um-sulat*, in (21a)) and true suffixation (*sulat-um*, in (21c)). In the manner of Optimality

---

[2] For discussion of this and related cases in Austronesian, see e.g. Crowhurst (1998) and Klein (2005). Klein observes that orthographically vowel-initial Tagalog words actually begin with [ʔ], in which case the forms in the first row of (19) are both consonant-initial. However, it is also quite possible to analyze initial [ʔ] as epenthetic, not present in the input to *um* affixation. See e.g. Crowhurst (1998) for discussion.

Theory, the output candidate which violates the higher ranked constraint (NoCoda) the least is declared the winner. Dots indicate syllable
boundaries:

(21)   VC infix: misaligned by one syllable onset, to optimize overall
       syllable structure

	/um, sulat/	NoCoda	Align-L(um, stem)
a.	um.-su.lat	**!	
☞ b.	s-u.m-u.lat	*	*
c.	su.la.t-um	*	**!***

The Tagalog -*um*- infix is VC in shape. McCarthy and Prince (1993)
observe that infixation sites are often closely connected to infix shape, in
the way that a syllable-optimizing P » M account would predict. Consider, for example, the Timugon Murut CV reduplicative infix, represented as Red$_\sigma$ in (22). Positioning this infix before the first consonant
optimizes syllable structure surrounding the infix (22b). By contrast, true
prefixation (22a) would produce vowel hiatus, as shown in the following
tableau:

(22)   CV infix: misaligned by one initial vowel (if any) to optimize
       syllable structure

	/Red$_\sigma$, abalan/	Onset	Align-L(Red$_\sigma$, stem)
a.	a.-a.ba.lan	**!	
☞ b.	a.-ba.-ba.lan	*	*
c.	a.ba.la.-la.-n	*	**!***

The ability to predict that CV and VC infixes will occur in complementary environments, i.e. will select complementary pivots, is a hallmark of the Optimality Theoretic P » M approach to infixation, in
which infixation results from the displacement of would-be adfixes in
order to optimize phonological structure.

6.4.1 Prosodic vs. segmental factors in optimizing displacement

By contrast to numerous examples like Tagalog or Timugon Murut in which infixation can be interpreted as improving syllable structure, very few examples have been found in which infixation can be construed as improving segmental phonotactics (see e.g. Yu 2007, chapter 6). This asymmetry raises interesting questions about the generality of the potential for "P" constraints to outrank morphological alignment.

We did see one case of segmentally conditioned infixation in Chapter 4, as part of the discussion of verb stem templaticity in Tiene (Bantu). Recall that in Tiene, the causative and applicative affixes, both coronal, are infixed into CVC roots ending in noncoronal consonants, in order to respect the requirement holding on CVCVC verb stems in Tiene that the medial consonant must be coronal and the final consonant must be noncoronal:

(23) a. Root + applicative /l/ + Final Vowel   [Tiene]
          'divide'   kab-a   kalab-a   'be divided'
          'tear'   nyak-a   nyalak-a   'be torn'
          'put in'   sook-ɛ   solek-ɛ   'take out'
      b. Root + causative /s/ + Final Vowel
          'become extinguished' dim-a   diseb-ɛ   'extinguish'
          'borrow'   suɔm-ɔ   sɔsɔb-ɔ   'lend'

The stative suffix also exhibits an infixal allomorph which is used under similar circumstances.

The Tiene case is unusual to begin with, because of its segmentally specified stem template. A case of segmentally conditioned infixation that does not have the templatic complication occurs in Kashaya (Pomoan). As demonstrated by Buckley (1997a), two of the suppletive allomorphs of the Kashaya Plural Act (pluractional) affix, namely *ta* and *t*, exhibit both suffixal and infixal variants. The other Plural Act suppletive allomorphs, VC in shape, are strictly suffixal. Which Plural Act allomorph occurs with a given root is lexically determined. However, whether an allomorph is suffixed or infixed is phonologically predictable and follows from a combination of prosodic and segmental factors.

Consider, in (24), the positioning of the allomorph *ta* in stems with which it combines. As Buckley shows, *ta* infixes when the stem ends in a noncoronal consonant (24a). Otherwise, it suffixes (24b):[3]

(24) a. 'feed'   bilaqʰam-   bilaqʰa-ta-m-   [Kashaya]
          'go to sleep'   simaːq-   sima-ta-q-
          'get lost'   duqaːc-   duqa-ta-c-

      b. 'fail (to do)'   dahqǫtol-   dahqǫtol-ta-
          'pick (berries)' duhluṇ-   duhluṇ-ta-

Buckley attributes this pattern to a coda condition constraint (CODA-COND, in (25)) against non-coronal coda consonants. This constraint would be violated if *ta* were suffixed to stems ending in non-coronal consonants (25a), since the stem-final non-coronal would be forced into coda position. Infixing *ta* before the last consonant is preferable (25b). Although the stem-final consonant, a noncoronal, appears to be in coda position in candidate (25b), Buckley explains that Plural Act stems are usually followed by vowel-initial suffixes, so that the stem-final consonants actually surface as onsets:[4]

(25)

	/simaːq-, -ta/	CODA-COND	ALIGN-R(at, STEM)
a.	simaq-ta-	*!	
☞ b.	sima-ta-q-		*
c.	ta-simaːq-		*!******

The VC allomorphs, -*at* and -*aq*, are always suffixed and never infixed (26).

---

[3] "c" is a palato-alveolar.

[4] Plural Act stems can sometimes be followed by consonant-initial suffixes, in which case the stem-final uvulars in (25) would surface as a coda. In such cases, the constraint against noncoronal codas could not distinguish candidates (25a), (25b), and (25c); all would tie with one violation, and the tableau would (incorrectly) predict straight suffixation. Buckley guards against this outcome by appealing to a principle of Paradigm Uniformity, which requires all Plural Act stems containing the same root and Plural Act allomorph to have the same surface shape, regardless of following context. Paradigm Uniformity is discussed in Chapter 11. Any Paradigm Uniformity analysis needs a way of identifying the key cell in the paradigm to which others must be faithful; in Kashaya, the key cell must be one in which a vowel-initial suffix follows the stem.

(26) 'dig (hole)'   dahal-   dahal-at
      'shake'   šuhweːn-   šuhweːn-at
      'prune (branch)'   diʔkol-   diʔkol-aq-

This pattern follows from the earlier analysis. The constraint against noncoronal codas is neutral with respect to whether a VC morph is suffixed or infixed to a VC-final stem. In fact, infixing a VC morph inside a final consonant would produce both vowel hiatus and a consonant cluster, neither of which is optimal.

Our third example of segmentally conditioned infixation occurs in the well-known case of Tagalog. (On similar patterns in related languages, see e.g. Crowhurst 1998). Schachter and Otanes (1972) observe that the Tagalog -um- infix is not observed to combine with m- or w- initial stems such as mahal 'expensive' or mura 'cheap'. In an experimental test of this generalization, Orgun and Sprouse (1999) confirmed that native speakers could insert -um- into novel borrowings from English (27a), but not if those words begin with m or w (27b):

(27) a. -um- infixation possible for loans: [Tagalog]
          keri   →   kumeri   'to carry'
          fejl   →   fumejl   'to fail'
          pejnt   →   pumejnt   'to paint'
          bejk   →   bumejk   'to bake'
      b. No -um- infixation for [m]- or [w]-initial loans
          meri   →   *mumeri   'to marry'
          mejk   →   *mumejk   'to make'
          walow   →   *wumalow   'to wallow'

The question of why infixation environments are more often prosodic than segmental is a compelling one for any displacement model of infixation. Interestingly, the same asymmetry obtains for phonologically conditioned suppletive allomorphy in general; see Chapter 9 and Paster (2006). Even further afield, studies of phonological sensitivity to part of speech also reveal a bias toward prosodic factors; see Chapter 2 and Smith (2011). Yu (2007, Chapter 5) suggests that the typology of infixation results from a combination of historical factors—e.g. metathesis, affix entrapment—and learning biases which favor maximally general phonological generalizations. Returning to Yu's intriguing observation that the pivots of infixation are sites that words in every language tend to possess, it may be that prosodic categories are generally more salient than segmental ones in the landscape of the grammaticalization of phonological conditions on morphological constituents.

6.5 A lexical approach to infixation

In the previous section we explored prosodic and segmental dimensions that are potentially optimized by infixing, rather than adfixing, affixes. However, not all cases of infixation transparently yield to optimization analyses of this kind. For example, infixation *to* a prominent position, like the main stressed syllable of a word, is not obviously optimizing; instead it must be stipulated, even in an Optimality-theoretic displacement model, by Alignment constraints. For example, McCarthy and Prince (1993: 2) propose an Alignment constraint stipulating that Ulwa infixes (seen earlier in (2)) must surface adjacent to the main stress foot in the word:

(28)   ALIGN([*ka*]_{Af}, L, Ft′, R): 'The affix *ka* follows, is a suffix to, the head foot'

Optimality Theory can easily model this type of affix, but its position does not follow from any general principles of improving prosodic structure.

The same is true of another type of infix, the kind which is displaced from the edge in a manner that is neutral with respect to the well-formedness of prosodic structure. McCarthy and Prince (1993) and Yu (2007) cite a number of examples of CV infixes which are infixed after the first CV of the word. Examples include the Dakota CV infixes in (1), to which Yu (2007: 30, 33) adds the cases of Hua and Budukh, among others:

(29)   a.   Hua negative infixation (Papuan; Haiman 1980)
           zgavo   zga-ʔa-vo   'not embrace'
           harupo   haru-ʔa-po   'not slip'

        b.   Budukh prohibitive infixation (Northeast Caucasian; Alekseev 1994)
           'to arrive'   yeči   →   ye-me-či
           'to be'   yɨxar   →   yɨ-mə-xər
           'to give'   yuc'u   →   yu-mo-c'u

McCarthy and Prince (1993) propose that such cases result from the interaction of two constraints: one positions the infix at a designated edge of the word, and the other requires the word to begin (or end) with material from the root. Ranked higher than affix edge-alignment, root edge-alignment can force an infix into the word by an amount that will not worsen overall syllable structure:

(30)

	/harupo, -ʔa/	ALIGN-R (ROOT,WORD)	ALIGN-R (ʔa,WORD)
a.	harupo-ʔa	*!*	
☞ b.	haru-ʔa-po		**
c.	ʔa-harupo		***!***

While all infixation may be describable in terms of constraint inter-action in Optimality Theory, only a subset of cases can truly be described as optimizing phonological well-formedness. Some of the cases of infixation seen thus far improve well-formedness over what would be achieved under straight adfixation, but others are a wash, with well-formedness being equivalent on both the actual infixation out-come and a hypothetical adfixation outcome.

6.5.1 Anti-optimizing infixation

As part of an extended argument in favor of accounting for all cases of infixation using lexically specific Alignment constraints, Yu (2007) documents a number of cases in which infixation actually makes phonological structure worse than it would be if the infix were instead prefixed or suffixed.

Consider, for example, the nominalizing *-ni-* infix in Leti (Malayo-Polynesian). This CV affix is positioned after the first consonant, producing marked consonant clusters and vowel sequences (Yu 2007: 28, citing Blevins 1999):

(31) kaati   'to carve'   k-ni-aati   'carving'   [Leti]
      polu   'to call'   p-ni-olu   'act of calling, call'
      kakri   'to cry'   k-ni-akri   'act of crying'
      kili   'to look   k-n-ili   'act of looking'

The [kn] and [ia] clusters in *k-ni-aati*, for example, would be avoided by simple adfixation (e.g. *ni-kaati*) or by infixation to a different position (e.g. *kaa-ni-ti*).

Yu (2007) concludes that cases of this kind should be handled using the same kind of lexical statements needed to account for the position-ing of CV infixes in Hua and Dakota. Building on the subcategorization proposals developed for infixation in Inkelas (1989), Yu states the lexical selectional conditions on infixes in terms of inviolable Alignment constraints. The constraint in (32), modified from Yu (2007: 77), positions the Leti affix *ni* immediately after the initial consonant of the word containing it:

(32)   ALIGN(*ni*, L, C₁, R)   (*inviolable*)

As Yu points out, this analysis of *ni* brings it formally into line with the type of infix that selects for a stressed syllable, as in Ulwa. In both examples, the infixes combine with stems possessing a certain structure and position themselves next to that structure. In Ulwa, it is a stressed syllable; in Leti, it is the leftmost consonant.

The ability to position an affix after the first consonant, regardless of the shape of the affix or the phonological structures that would result from infixation, raises the theory-internal question of whether it is necessary to have two different accounts for infix position: one, involving pivot-specific Alignment constraints as in (32), for arbitrary infix locations as needed in Leti or Ulwa, and another, involving only general Alignment constraints and a P » M ranking, for infix locations that can be interpreted as optimizing. As Yu points out, pivot-specific Alignment constraints can also account for the latter type of infix pattern. The *um* infix in Tagalog could equally well be described by a pivot-specific constraint locating it before the first vowel:

(33)   ALIGN(*um*, R, V₁, L)   (*inviolable*)

The main argument originally put forth for the P » M approach to infixation was its ability to correlate infix shape with infix location. However, as shown by data like Dakota, Hua, Budukh, and Leti, that correlation may not be as robust as initially thought.

6.6 Exfixation

"Exfixation" is the term used for reduplication which would be described as straightforward root or internal stem reduplication except that under certain phonological circumstances it pulls in segments from an adjacent affix in a layer of morphology external to the subconstituent apparently undergoing the reduplication operation. The phonological pressures invoked in exfixation analyses are typically syllable well-formedness or prosodic minimality. A case of exfixation in Tagalog was introduced in Chapter 5; the phenomenon is also discussed, in more detail, in Chapter 10.

In Kihehe (Bantu; Downing 1997b, 1998b, 1999b, citing Odden and Odden 1985), reduplication appears to target the (inflectional) verb stem, i.e. the root plus following suffixes. However, just in case the verb root (and therefore the stem) is vowel-initial, reduplication pulls in the preceding consonant-initial prefix as well (34b) (Downing 1997b: 92):

(34)   INF-root-FV = to [root]   [Kihehe]
   a. 'INF-ferment-FV'   kú-haát-a   kú-haata-haáta
      'INF-build-APPL-FV'   kú-ceeng-él-a kú-ceengela-ceengéla
      'INF-cough-FV'   kú-gohomól-a   kú-gohomola-gohomóla

   b. 'INF-pour-FV'   kw-íit-a   kw-íita-kw-iíta
      'INF-OM-pour-FV'   kú-lw-iít-a   kú-lw-iita-lw-iíta
      'INF-sing-FV'   kw-íimb-a   kw-íimba-kw-iíimba

If the morphological reduplication operation is ordered between stem-formation and object agreement prefixation, as in (35a), then the pattern in (34b) has to be analyzed an exfixation.

(35)   a. [INF [OM [RED [Stem]]]] exfixation analysis
       b. [RED [INF [OM [Stem]]]] infixation analysis

As discussed in Chapter 5, McCarthy and Prince (1995) assume the morphological analysis in (35a) and adopt the exfixation analysis, which they model with "back copying" in Base-Reduplicant Correspondence Theory. On McCarthy and Prince's account, the preceding INF prefix merges morphologically into a following RED prefix if the merger is needed for the syllabic well-formedness of the reduplicant. This occurs when the root is vowel-initial and the reduplicant would also be vowel-initial; incorporating the preceding CV INF prefix makes the reduplicant into a well-formed, consonant-initial syllable. The phonological structure of the resulting RED, including the segments acquired via the merger with the INF is then back copied to the base. McCarthy and Prince's analysis is schematized in (36), for the Kihehe forms in (34a,b). Multiple subscripts on the same morpheme, in (36b), indicate morphological merger:

(36)   a. Input: /ku$_i$-RED$_j$-[haat-a]$_k$/ (corresponds to (34a))
          Output: / ku$_i$-haata$_j$-haata$_k$/

       b. Input: /ku$_i$-RED$_j$-[it-a]$_k$/   (corresponds to (34b))
          Output: /kwiita$_{ij}$-kwiita$_k$/

Downing (1997b, 1998b, 1999b) and, subsequently, Inkelas and Zoll (2005) handle the bracketing paradox posed by Kihehe in a different manner: for them, this and other cases of exfixation are straightforward infixing reduplication, based on the morphological structure in (35b). The reduplicative construction is like Ulwa infixation in targeting an internal phonological structure as its pivot. But where Ulwa infixation targets a stressed syllable, Kihehe infixation targets an internal prosodic stem. On Downing's (1997b, 1998b, 1999b) analysis, the prosodic stem is based on, but is not identical to, the morphological stem of the word. It normally contains the root and following suffixes. But if it would be vowel-initial, it can also include a preceding prefix.

This analysis, applied to a verb with the morphological structure in (35b), is briefly sketched in (37). The verb in (37a) has a C-initial root; the verb in (37b) has a V-initial root. Curly brackets indicate the prosodic stem, which is the target of reduplication. The presumed morphological layering of the reduplicated verb is given on the right:

(37)   Prosodic stem   Output of reduplication

    a. kú-{haát-a}   kú-{haata}-{haáta]
    b. {kw-íit-a}   {kw-íita}-{kw-iíta}

The basic insight behind this analysis is the same as that of McCarthy and Prince, but replaces the concept of morphological merger with the concept of prosodic constituency. The latter type of structure, as well as its relevance for exfixation, is discussed in more detail in Chapter 10.

If correct, the analysis of exfixation is parallel to the analysis of infixation to a stressed syllable or foot; the category "Prosodic Root or Stem" is added to the list of internal reduplicative pivots, repeated in (38) with the addition in italics:

(38)   Potential pivots of phonological subcategorization (modified from (6))

Edge pivots	Prominence pivots
First consonant	Stressed foot
First vowel	Stressed syllable
First syllable	Stressed vowel
Last syllable	*Prosodic root or stem*
Last vowel	
Last consonant	

6.7 Edge-proximity in infixation

An important generalization about infixes that any theory of infixation must capture is their proximity to an edge. This is not true of infixes that are positioned next to the main stressed syllable or stress foot, but it is true of all other types of infixes. Infixes select for the first consonant in the stem, but not the second; they select for the final syllable, but not the penultimate syllable.

In Yu's approach, which supplies a pivot-specific Alignment constraint for every infix, edge proximity follows directly from the list of pivots that the theory makes available for Alignment constraints to reference: first/last vowel, first/last consonant, first/last syllable. According to Yu, this list is motivated by the universality of its elements.

An attractive quality of the displacement theory of infixation is that the edge proximity of infixes does not have to be stipulated. Infixes are misaligned in order to avoid a violation of phonological well-formedness; but because each infix is also associated with an edge-alignment constraint, displacement will be minimal.

A consequence of the P » M approach to infix displacement, however, is an unintended prediction of what Yu (2007) calls hyperinfixation. For example, consider what the ranking NoCoda » Align-L predicts for a hypothetical vocalic infix, -*u*-, depending on whether the base of affixation contains a closed syllable, and where in the stem that syllable is. Infixing *u* between adjacent consonants in the base can produce a stem with only open syllables. As shown, the P » M approach predicts the possibility that a prefix will infix arbitrarily far into a stem, even surfacing as a suffix, in order to avoid closed syllables. Some examples are given in (39):

(39)

CV.CV.CV.CV	u-CV.CV.CV.CV
CVC.CV.CV.CV	CV.C-**u**-.CV.CV.CV
CV.CVC.CV.CV	CV.CV.C-**u**-.CV.CV
CV.CVC.CVC.CV	CV.CV.C-**u**-.CVC.CV
CV.CV.CV.CVC	CV.CV.CV.CV.C-**u**
CV.CVC.CV.CVC	CV.CV.C-**u**-.CV.CVC

Such cases appear not to exist, a point emphasized by McCarthy (2003b: 94–100) in a paper designed to rid Optimality Theory of the gradiently violable Alignment constraints from which such predictions emanate. In their place, McCarthy suggests categorical constraints that stipulate the maximal distance from the edge of the word that any given infix is permitted to occur. This is similar to Yu's proposal to associate each infix with a constraint stipulating the pivot next to which it must occur.

Yu's (2007) pivot-specific inviolable Alignment constraints make an additional prediction, namely that an infix can fail to attach to a base if its conditions for infixation are not met. A case illustrating the value in making such predictions is Tagalog, seen earlier in (27). Recall that the infix *um* cannot combine with stems beginning with *m* or *w*. Postulating a high-ranking constraint against *mu* or *wu* sequences would correctly predict the ungrammaticality of forms like **m-um-eri*. However, it would also incorrectly predict the infixation of *um* beyond the first syllable, in order to avoid the ban on *m/wu* sequences:

(40)   Hyperinfixation: impossible in Tagalog

	/um, meri/	*m/wu	NoCoda	Align-L(um, stem)
a.	um-meri		*!	
b.	m-um-eri	*!		*
☞ c.	mer-um-i			***

Replacing Alignment with categorial constraints, following McCarthy (2003b), would correctly rule out hyperinfixation in this Tagalog example. A categorical constraint saying that *um* has to occur in the first syllable of the word would eliminate (40c). However, the analysis would still incorrectly predict either prefixation or regular infixation, depending on the relative ranking of **m/wu* and NoCoda:

(41)

	/um, meri/	Align-L(um, σ_1)	*m/wu	NoCoda
(☞) a.	um-meri			*!
(☞) b.	m-um-eri		*!	
c.	mer-um-i	*!		

The desired outcome in such cases is simple ungrammaticality, or ineffability, of the combination /um, meri/ (Orgun and Sprouse 1999; Zuraw and Lu 2009). *um* simply cannot combine with *m-* or *w*-initial stems. Orgun and Sprouse present a detailed analysis of how this can be accomplished, adjusting Optimality Theory so that it has a post-filter on derivations which rejects certain outcomes as ungrammatical.

A subcategorization analysis of the type suggested by Yu offers a simple account of the segmental conditions on *um* infixation. *um* is associated in its lexical entry with a subcategorization constraint requiring it to follow the first consonant. If the constraint cannot be satisfied by a given base, the lexical entry for *um* cannot enter into a morphological derivation with that base. We will return to the issue of lexical subcategorization, vs. grammatical optimization, in the context of suppletive allomorph selection in Chapter 9.

6.8 Conclusion

As discussed by Broselow and McCarthy (1983) and Yu (2007) (Ch. 6), infixation is often deployed in language play (e.g. Hausa *màimúnà* (name) → *máibàimúbùná*, *búːláːlàː 'whip'* → *bùgùdùlágádálàː*; Newman 2000: 297-298) suggesting that it is as salient to speakers as it is to linguists. Theoretical discussions of infixation patterns often include a statement to the effect that infixes are just like prefixes and suffixes, except that they are positioned inside the stem instead of adfixed to it. However, as seen in this chapter, the story is more complicated than this; infixes raise many interesting theoretical questions involving their substance, their positioning, and even their hierarchical ordering relative to other affixes in the same word. We turn in the next chapter to the importance of hierarchical ordering of affixes to the phonological interpretation of morphologically complex words. Infixes will play an important role in this next chapter, as well.

7

Interleaving: The phonological interpretation of morphologically complex words

This chapter discusses the phonological properties of morphologically complex words, i.e. those formed by more than one word-formation process. What we find in many such cases is clear evidence that phonology is sensitive to constituent structure in a way that can be captured through interleaving of phonology with morphology: the output of the phonological input-output mapping within a subconstituent is the input to the phonology of the larger constituent.

This chapter discusses both "cyclicity," in the strict sense of the same phonological alternation or constraint applying at each step of word formation, and "layering," in which phonology is imposed at each step of word formation, but the phonological mappings associated with the individual morphological constructions in question are not necessarily identical. Both types of interleaving share the essential property that phonology applies to nested subconstituents in a word from the inside out: the output of applying phonology to a daughter is the input to the application of phonology to its mother.

In this chapter we will touch on the main ideas behind several theoretical approaches to interleaving effects, many of which also surfaced in Chapters 2 and 3 in discussions of morphologically conditioned phonology and process morphology. These theories include Lexical Morphology and Phonology, Stratal Optimality Theory, Cophonology Theory, Indexed Constraint Theory, word and paradigm models, and Output-Output Correspondence theory. By its very nature, evidence of interleaving is likely to be evidence of morphologically conditioned phonology; there are therefore many points of contact, in terms of theory and phenomena, between this chapter and Chapter 2 of this book.

This chapter also connects to Chapter 11, in which some cross-word influences are explored. Some of these inter-word effects are hard to distinguish from cyclic effects, an issue which is postponed to Chapter 11.

7.1 Cyclicity

Although the term "cyclicity" is used somewhat variably in the literature, cyclicity proper is the situation in which the very same phonological alternation applies (or the very same constraint is imposed) at every step of the morphology, producing a result that would not obtain if the phonological alternation or constraint in question were imposed just once on the entire morphologically complex word. We may term this pattern "true cyclicity."

The minority of documented interleaving effects are truly cyclic. What has been observed far more commonly is the situation we may call "interleaving" or "layering," in which *some* phonological alternations potentially apply (or *some* constraints are enforced) at every step of the morphology, even if they are not the same ones. Layering will be discussed in section 7.2. In this section, however, we examine two examples of true cyclicity, involving syllabification and stress. These two phenomena dominate in the literature on true cyclicity, an observation due to Brame (1974: 58–9) and cited by McCarthy and Prince (1993: 43) in a discussion of cyclic effects.

7.1.1 Turkish syllabification

As an example of the cyclic application of syllabification, we turn first to Turkish, a language with fairly strict syllable structure (e.g. Clements and Keyser 1983). Turkish syllables may begin with V or C, but not CC; syllables rimes may consist of V, V:, VC, or, under limited conditions, V:C or VCC. The possible consonant clusters that may end a syllable are limited to a principled set (Clements and Sezer 1982). CC-final syllables occur only within roots. When the morphology would create a coda cluster, it is almost always broken by epenthesis. The argument for cyclic syllabification derives from the cyclic application of epenthesis.

In (1a), vowel epenthesis applies when consonantal suffixes attach to consonant-final roots. (The epenthetic vowel, double-underlined, is always high but otherwise follows the rules of vowel harmony, agreeing in backness and roundness with the preceding vowel; see e.g. Lewis 1967; Göksel and Kerslake 2005; etc.) These consonantal suffixes surface in their basic form, without epenthesis, when combining with vowel-final roots (1b):[1]

(1) a. i. /tʃaj/   tʃaj   'tea'   *çay* [Turkish]
              /tʃaj-m/   tʃajɯm   'tea-1SG.POSS'   *çayım*
              /tʃaj-n/   tʃajɯn   'tea-2SG.POSS'   *çayın*

          ii. /konuʃ/   konuʃ   'converse' (imperative)   *konuş*
              /konuʃ-r/   konuʃur   'converse-AORIST'   *konuşur*

      b. i. /kapɯ/   kapɯ   'door'   *kapı*
              /kapɯ-n/   kapɯn   'door-2SG.POSS'   *kapın*

          ii. /søjle   søjle   'say'   *söyle*
              /søjle-r/   søjler   'say-AORIST'   *söyler*

The evidence for cyclic application of epenthesis comes from roots which combine with two suffixes. Example (2a) illustrates consonant-final roots followed by a consonantal suffix which is in turn followed directly by another suffix. As seen, epenthesis applies between the root and consonantal suffix, even when the second suffix is vowel-initial (2a). These forms contrast with the ones in (2b), in which the same consonant-final roots are followed by a single CV suffix. Here, epenthesis does not apply between root and suffix:

(2) a. i. /tʃaj-m-E/   tʃajɯma   *tʃajma   *çayıma*
              'tea-1SG.POSS-DAT'

         ii. /el-n-I/   elini   *elni   *elini*
              'hand-2SG.POSS-ACC'

        iii. /konuʃ-r-m/   konuʃurum   *konuʃrum   *konuşurum*
              'converse-AOR-1SG'

      b. i. /tʃaj-dE/   tʃajda   *çayda*
              'village-LOC'

         ii. /konuʃ-tI/   konuʃtu   *konuştu*
              'converse-PAST'

The application of epenthesis in (2a) indicates that the first (consonantal) suffix triggers a cycle of syllabification in which the following

---

[1] Turkish data are presented in the literature in a variety of transcriptions, from orthographic to IPA and variant phonemicizations in between. To reduce confusion, Turkish data in this chapter will be presented in both IPA and orthography (always italicized). Underlying forms are given in IPA only, with the exception that underlying vowels whose quality is completely predictable from vowel harmony are represented in upper case, as is the tradition in generative analyses of Turkish.

suffix is not present. On the cycle on which it is attached, the consonantal suffix forms the coda of a syllable whose nucleus is the epenthetic vowel. On the subsequent cycle, the consonantal suffix resyllabifies to be the onset of the vowel at the beginning of the following suffix. If syllabification and epenthesis applied noncyclically, i.e. after the morphology had put the entire word together, the C suffix could syllabify directly as the onset of the V-initial suffix, eliminating the need to epenthesize a vowel between root and C suffix. Cyclic and noncyclic derivations of the form /tʃaj-m-E/ 'tea-1SG.POSS-DAT', from (2ai), are compared in (3):

(3)

	Cyclic	Noncyclic
Input to Cycle 1	/tʃaj/	/tʃaj-m-E/
Syllabification, Epenthesis, Vowel Harmony	[tʃaj]$_\sigma$	[tʃaj]$_\sigma$[ma]$_\sigma$
Input to Cycle 2	[tʃaj]$_\sigma$ + /m/	
Syllabification, Epenthesis, Vowel Harmony	[tʃa]$_\sigma$[jɯm]$_\sigma$	
Input to Cycle 3	[tʃa]$_\sigma$[jɯm]$_\sigma$ + /E/	
Syllabification, Epenthesis, Vowel Harmony	[tʃa]$_\sigma$[jɯ]$_\sigma$[ma]$_\sigma$	
Output	tʃajɯma çayıma	tʃajma çayma
	✓	💣*

Some roots in Turkish end in the same types of unsyllabifiable consonant clusters, e.g. /jn/, /lm/, that are broken by epenthesis in the examples given above. Interestingly, these roots do not undergo epenthesis if a vowel-initial suffix follows, as shown in (4):

(4)   Epenthesis into underlying root-final clusters *is* averted by vocalic suffixation:

a. 'film'	/film/	filim		*filim*
'film-ACC'	/film-I/	filmi	*filimi	*filmi*
b. 'forehead'	/aln/	alɯn		*alın*
'forehead-ACC'	/aln-I/	alnɯ	*alɯnɯ	*alnı*

These data suggest either that syllabification and epenthesis do not apply on the root cycle, contrary to what is indicated in (3), or that the final consonant is "extrametrical," i.e. outside the scope of syllabification, on the root cycle (e.g. Rice 1990; Inkelas and Orgun 1995). Either way, the root cycle is different from subsequent cycles in some manner.

The question of whether there is an initial cycle of syllabification and other phonological processes on monomorphemic roots, or whether the first cycle of phonology is triggered by the first morphological construction to combine with a root, has arisen in other languages as well. One generalization that has held up over the years is that morphologically bound roots do not undergo a cycle of phonology (Brame 1974; Inkelas 1989). But morphologically free roots, such as those in Turkish, are another matter; the evidence suggests that languages may differ in this respect (see e.g. Kiparsky 1982a). The question of an initial root cycle is related to the topic of nonderived environment blocking, discussed in Chapter 8.

7.1.2 Indonesian stress

The other phenomenon to display apparent true cyclicity in a number of cases is stress assignment. Analysis of stress systems displaying cyclicity include English and Russian (e.g. Chomsky and Halle 1968; Pesetsky 1979; Kiparsky 1982bc, 1985; Melvold 1986), Moses-Columbia Salish (Czaykowska-Higgins 1993), and Turkish (Inkelas and Orgun 2003), among many others.

We will examine here a case from Indonesian (Cohn 1989). Cohn's argument for cyclicity in Indonesian is based on the fact that a single set of stress rules can account for the stress of both monomorphemic and morphologically complex words, as long as it applies cyclically; however, the stress pattern of monomorphemic and complex words is different, showing that both types of words cannot be stressed, as wholes, by the same noncyclic rule.

As seen in (5) and earlier in Chapter 5, monomorphemic words exhibit the basic stress pattern (Cohn 1989: 170). The penultimate syllable receives main stress. The initial syllable receives secondary stress, as does every other syllable to the left of the penult, with the caveat that adjacent syllables may never both be stressed.

(5) σ́σ   cári   'search for'   [Indonesian]
               dúduk   'sit'
     σσ́σ   bicára   'speak'
               acárra   'plan'
     ὸσσ́σ   bìjaksána   'wise'
               màʃarákat   'society'
     ὸσσσ́σ   kòntinuási   'continuation'
               xàtulistíwa   'equator'
     ὸσὸσσ́σ   òtobìográfi   'autobiography'
               èrodìnamíka   'aerodynamics'
     ὸσσὸσσ́σ àmerikànisási 'Americanization'
               dèmilitèrisási 'demilitarization'

The ban on stress clash is a hallmark of the Indonesian stress system in
general, and is revealed in the stress of morphologically complex words
as well.

Suffixed words show a different pattern, attributable to the cyclic
application of the same pattern illustrated by monomorphemic words.
The only additional statements that are required involve the resolution of multiple stresses that arise from multiple cyclic applications
of penultimate stress assignment. On each new cycle of penultimate
stress assignment, input main stress is demoted to secondary stress. If
the newly assigned stress is adjacent to an input stress, creating stress
clash, the input stress is eliminated. This can lead to a different stress
pattern than is seen in monomorphemic words, as illustrated in (6).
(Prefixes do not participate in stress assignment and are parenthesized in the examples.) Complex forms whose stress pattern differs
from monomorphemic words with the same number of syllables are
bolded:

(6) | | no suffix | 1 suffix | 2 suffixes |
|---|---|---|---|
| a. | σσ́σ | σσ́-σ | σ-σ́-σ |
| | bicára | (mən-)carí-kan | (mən-)cat-kán-ña |
| b. | ὸσσ́σ | **σσσ́-σ** | ὸσ-σ́-σ |
| | bìjaksána | **(məm-)bicará-kan** | (mən-)càri-kán-ña |
| c. | ὸσσσ́σ | ὸσσσ́-σ | **σὸσ-σ́-σ** |
| | kòntinuási | (kə-)bìjaksaná-an | **(məm-)bicàra-kán-ña** |
| d. | ὸσὸσσ́σ | **ὸσσσσ́-σ** | ὸσὸσ-σ́-σ |
| | òtobìográfi | **kòntinuasí-ña** | (kə-)bìjaksàna-án-ña |

The example in (7) shows how the cyclic application of stress to the word *kontinuasi-ña* results in the correct surface pattern, while the noncyclic application of stress does not:

(7)

	Cyclic	Noncyclic
Input to Cycle 1	/kontinuasi/	/kontinuasi-ña/
Stress rules (Penultimate main stress; Initial secondary stress; leftward iteration of alternating secondary stress (unless prevented by Stress Clash)	kòntinuási	kòntinùasíña
Input to Cycle 2	kòntinuási + -ña	
Stress rule (as above)	kòntinuàsíña	
Word level: Destressing (deletion of first of two clashing stresses)	kòntinuasíña	
Output	kòntinuasíña	kòntinùasíña
	✓	💣

Cohn argues that Destressing, i.e. the deletion of stress from a syllable when followed by a stressed syllable, must be noncyclic. It must apply at the Word level in order to derive the correct outcome in words like *(kə-) bìjaksàna-án-ña*. Stress clash is created only through the cyclic application of stress assignment, and is what distinguishes morphologically complex from monomorphemic words. Each cycle inherits, as secondary stresses, any stress assigned on the previous cycle, and these remain unless removed at the end of the derivation by Destressing.[2]

7.1.3 Cyclic nasal harmony in Sundanese

As mentioned already, most cases of pure cyclicity in the literature are found in stress assignment and syllabification. However, cases of true cyclicity do also occur, if less frequently, in other domains. One

[2] A noncyclic analysis of Indonesian that makes use of Alignment constraints is offered in Cohn and McCarthy (1998).

well-known case involving the segmental process of nasal harmony occurs in Sundanese. Documented by Robins (1959) and Cohn (1992), and discussed for its significance to phonological theory by Anderson (1972), Stevens (1977), van der Hulst and Smith (1982), Cohn (1990), Benua (1997) among others, the Sundanese rule of nasal harmony propagates nasality from a nasal consonant rightward to all consecutive vowels. Glottal consonants (/h/ and /ʔ/) are transparent (8a), but all other consonants stop the rightward spread of nasality (8b).[3] Data are from Anderson 1972: 253–4:

(8) a. /maneh/   [mānẽh]   'you'
        /naian/   [nãĩãn]   'to get wet'
        /niis/   [nĩʔĩs]   'to take a holiday'
        /kumaha/   [kumãhã]   'how?'
        /bɤŋhar/   [bɤŋhār]   'to be rich'

     b. /mandi/   [mānᵈi]   'to bathe'
        /miasih/   [mĩʔãsih] 'to love'
        /ɲahokɤn/ [ɲãhōkɤn] 'to inform'
        /molohok/ [mōlohok] 'to stare'
        /marios/   [mārios]   'to examine'
        /maro/   [māro]   'to halve'

Evidence that nasal harmony applies cyclically comes from roots containing the infix /-aR/, which encodes plurality or distributivity. The consonant of the infix surfaces as [l] or [r] according to an independent rule of liquid dissimilation (see Cohn 1992 for discussion). Data from Cohn (1992: 200) and Anderson (1972: 254):

(9)
gloss	stem	plural
'messy'	kusut	k-ar-usut
'eat'	dahar	d-al-ahar
'little'	lɨtik	l-al-ɨtik
'visualized'	di-visualisasi-kɨn	di-v-ar-isualisasi-kɨn
'to run'	lɤmpan	l-al-ɤmpan
'to sleep'	sare	s-ar-are

As seen in example (10), nasal harmony appears to apply both before infixation, from a stem-initial nasal consonant to following vowels, as

---

[3] The transcriptions in examples (8)–(10) follow those of the authors cited; Anderson (1972) and Cohn (1992) differ slightly in their transcription of vowels, but this detail does not affect the argument about nasal harmony.

well as after infixation, such that the infix surfaces with a nasal vowel
when the stem begins with a nasal consonant. Data from Anderson
(1972: 255):

(10)

gloss	UR of root	stem	plural
'seek'	/moekɤn/	[mõẽkɤn]	[mãrõẽkɤn])
'say'	/naur/	[nãũr]	[nãlãũr]
'to cool oneself'	/niis/	[nĩʔĩs]	[nãrĩʔĩs]
'to know'	/ɲaho/	[ɲãhõ]	[ɲãrãhõ]
'to eat'	/dahar/	[dãhãr]	[(di)dãlãhãr]

Cyclic and noncyclic derivations of the plural of 'seek' are compared
in (11):

(11)

	Cyclic	Noncyclic
Input to Cycle 1	/moekɤn/	/m-aR-oekɤn/
Nasal harmony	[mõẽkɤn]	[mãroekɤn]
Input to Cycle 2	[m-aR-õẽkɤn]	
Nasal harmony	[mãrõẽkɤn]	
Output	[mãrõẽkɤn]	[mãroekɤn]
	✓	💣

Since the infix contains a consonant ([l] or [r]) that ordinarily blocks
nasal harmony, a straightforward way to account for nasal vowels
following the infix is to assume that nasal harmony applies both on
the root cycle and on the infixation cycle.[4]

7.1.4 Cyclic mutation in Cibemba causative stems

Another case of a cyclic segmental rule is found in Cibemba (Bantu;
M.42) (Hyman 1994, 2002; Hyman and Orgun 2005). In Cibemba and a
number of other Bantu languages, the causative suffix is a high front
vocoid which triggers palatalization or spirantization of a preceding
consonant (see discussion in Chapter 2). These effects, referred to in the

---

[4] A noncyclic analysis of Sundanese nasal harmony, using word-to-word output correspondence, is proposed by Benua (1997); see Chapter 11.

literature as "mutation," are illustrated in (12). The Cibemba verb stem consists of a root, potentially followed by derivational suffixes such as the causative, and an obligatory "Final Vowel" suffix, which in these examples is -*a*. Data from Hyman (2002):

(12)   Plain verb stem   Causative verb stem   [Cibemba]

leep-a	'be long'	leef-y-a	'lengthen'	< /leep-i̠-a/
lub-a	'be lost'	luf-y-a	'lose'	< /lub-i̠-a/
fiit-a	'be dark'	fiiš-y-a	'darken'	< /fiit-i̠-a/
cind-a	'dance'	cinš-y-a	'make dance'	< /cind-i̠-a/
lil-a	'cry'	liš-y-a	'make cry'	< /lil-i̠-a/
buuk-a	'get up (intr.)'	buuš-y-a	'get (s.o.) up'	< /buuk-i̠-a/
lúng-a	'hunt'	lúnš-y-a	'make hunt'	< /lúng-i̠-a/

Verbs in Cibemba can also be applicativized, by means of the suffix /-il/ (~ /-el/, by vowel harmony). As seen in (13), when a verb is both applicativized and causativized, the mutating effect of the causative is seen not only on the preceding applicative suffix but also on the root (Hyman 2002):

(13)

Applicative verb stem		Causative applicative verb stem	
leep-el-a	'be long for/at'	leef-eš-y-a	'lengthen for/at'
lub-il-a	'be lost for/at'	luf-iš-y-a	'lose for/at'
fiit-il-a	'be dark for/at'	fiiš-iš-y-a	'darken for/at'
cind-il-a	'dance for/at'	cinš-iš-y-a	'make dance for/at'
lil-il-a	'cry for/at'	liš-iš-y-a	'make cry for/at'
buuk-il-a	'get up (intr.) for/at'	buuš-iš-y-a	'get (s.o.) up for/at'
lúng-il-a	'hunt for/at'	lúnš-iš-y-a	'make hunt for/at'

The applicative suffix itself does not trigger mutation; the overapplication of mutation to the roots in causative applicatives is due, according to Hyman, to cyclicity. On Hyman's analysis, the causative suffix is attached first, and the applicative is infixed inside it. The extra-high vowel of the causative suffix triggers mutation on both cycles: first when it is attached directly to the root, and again when the applicative is infixed before it:

(14)   Cyclic vs. noncyclic derivations of *luf-iš-y-a* 'lose for/at'

	Cyclic	Noncyclic
Input to Cycle 1	/lub/	/lub-il-i̧-a/
Mutation	—	lubišya
Input to Cycle 2	lub + /-i̧/	
Mutation	lufi̧	
Input to Cycle 3	lufi̧ + /-il-/	
Mutation	lufiši̧	
Input to Cycle 4	lufiši̧-a	
Mutation	lufišya	
Output	lufišya	lubišya
	✓	💣

The noncyclic derivation of 'lose for/at', in (14), fails because the causative suffix is adjacent only to the applicative. Hyman shows that mutation is a strictly local process, failing to target consonants at a phonological distance. For example, root-initial consonants do not undergo mutation when a causative suffix follows the root. The only reason that multiple consonants are mutated is, according to Hyman, because the cyclic infixation analysis renders the causative suffix adjacent to two different morphemes, on different cycles. Hyman has argued elsewhere (2003) on morphological grounds that the morphological order of attachment of suffixes in the verb stems of a number of Bantu languages, including Cibemba, is Root-Causative-Applicative-Reciprocal-Passive. Infixation in Cibemba obscures the hierarchical order of attachment by reordering the applicative and causative morphs on the surface. (Similar cases from two other Bantu languages, namely Jita and Namwezi, are discussed in Chapter 11.)

7.2 Layering

We turn next to several cases of morphologically complex words showing evidence of layering, i.e. of the application of phonology as each layer of morphology is added. In these cases, however, the phonology associated with the different layers of morphology is not identical, distinguishing them from the pure cyclicity examples just seen. As discussed in Chapter 2, cases such as these can be modeled with cophonologies, phonological subgrammars associated with individual morphological constructions. The cases we examine in this section show layering: cophonologies apply to the subconstituents of a word created by the constructions with which they are associated, in the order in which those constructions combine.

7.2.1 Finnish

Kiparsky (2003) and Harrikari (2003) present consonant gradation in Finnish as an example of layering. Consonant Gradation (CG) is a weakening alternation that lenites singleton consonants (15a) and degeminates geminate consonants (15b) in the onset of a closed syllable. Data from Harrikari (2003) and Kiparsky (2003: 150):

(15) a. /katu-ssa/   ka.**dus**.ta   'street-ELATIVE'   (cf. katu 'street')
          /katu-mme/   ka.**dum**.me 'regret-1PL'
          /lupa-n/   lu.**van**   'permit-GEN.SG'   (cf. lupa 'permit')
          /valta-ssa/   val.**das**.sa   'power-INESSIVE'   (cf. valta 'power')
          /kaŋke-sta/   kaŋ.**ŋes**.ta 'pry bar-ELATIVE' (cf. kaŋki 'pry bar')
      b. /takki-n/   ta.**kin**   'coat-GEN.SG'   (cf. takki 'coat')
          /katto-lla/   ka.**tol**.la   'root-ADDESSIVE.SG' (cf. katto 'roof')

CG does not, however, apply before possessive suffixes (Harrikari 2003: 86–7):

(16) /katu-nsa/   ka.tun.sa   'street-3SG.POSS'   *ka.**dun**.sa
      /katu-mme/ ka.tum.me 'street-1PL.POSS'   *ka.**dum**.me
      /katu-nne/   ka.tun.ne   'street-1PL.POSS'   *ka.**dun**.ne

Kiparsky (2003) attributes the differential application of CG to its stem-level character. Case suffixes, illustrated in (15), form Stems, and fall in the domain of CG. Possessive suffixes, illustrated in (16), attach to Stems and form Words, thus falling outside the domain of CG.

   The argument for interleaving comes from instances of opacity, as in example (17). The final consonant of case endings deletes when immediately followed by a possessive suffix (a fact discussed in Chapter 9, in another context). CG applies to a stem-final syllable even if the triggering coda consonant is deleted in the environment of a following possessive suffix:

(17) a. /peruno-i-ten/   pe.ru.noi.den   'potato-PL-GEN'
      b. /peruno-i-ten-ni/ pe.ru.noi.de.ni 'potato-PL-GEN-1SG.POSS'

The layers of the interleaving analysis of (17b) are given in (18), with another possessed stem provided for comparison. The environment for CG is not present in any subconstituent of the comparison stem, /katu-ni/:

(18)   [[peruno-i-ten]_Stem-ni_Word] [katu-ni]
     Stem level: *-i-ten* suffixed, CG applies: CG not conditioned
                 pe.ru.noi.den   ka.tu
     Word level: *-ni* suffixed, obscuring   *-ni* suffixed
                 original environment
                 pe.ru.noi.de.ni   ka.tu.ni

CG applies only at the stem level. Subsequent Word-level morphology and phonology can render it opaque, as above. This is evidence of layering. Kiparsky (2000) argues that many instances of phonological derivational opacity—in which the trigger of an alternation is not present in the output form, or the trigger is present but the alternation fails to apply—result from layering of exactly this kind.

7.2.2 Hausa

In Chapter 2 we were introduced to the tone replacement properties of a number of morphological constructions in Hausa. The prediction, if phonology and morphology are interleaved, is that the phonological pattern associated with each morphological construction will apply to the stem formed by that construction. That pattern may in turn be altered by the phonological pattern associated with the next morphological construction to apply. In this section we will see that this prediction is borne out. When two (or more) morphological constructions in the same word are each associated with different phonological patterns, those patterns are imposed in the order in which the associated morphological constructions are combined.

Recall, from Chapter 2, that Hausa is a lexical tone language whose morphological constructions either preserve stem tone (comparable to the "recessive" morphology of Japanese, also discussed in Chapter 2) or replace it with a new tone melody (comparable to accent-deleting "dominant" morphology) (Newman 1986, 2000; Inkelas 1998b). As sketched in (19), whether or not a construction is dominant or recessive is independent of whether the construction is associated with an overt affix; for affixing constructions, the dominant/recessive parameter is also independent of the lexical tone pattern associated with the affix:

(19)   a. No affixation; tone replacement (imperative -LH)   [Hausa]
káːmàː   → kàːmáː   'catch (!)'
bíncìkéː   → bìncìkéː   'investigate (!)'
nánnéːmóː → nànnèːmóː 'seek repeatedly (!)' (< néːmóː 'seek')

b. No affixation, no tone replacement (Grade 2 verbal noun formation)
fànsáː   → fànsáː   'redeem/redeeming'
tàmbáyàː → tàmbáyàː 'ask/asking'

c. Overt affixation, tone replacement (various plural classes, ventive -óː)
máːlàm   → màːlàm-ái   'teacher-PL'   -LH
rìːgáː   → ríːg-únàː   'gown-PL'   -HL
tàmbáyà   → támbáy-óːyíː 'question-PL'   -H
gángàráː → gángár-óː   'roll_down-VENTIVE' -H

d. Overt suffixation, no tone replacement (various)
dáfàː   → dáfàː-wá   'cook-PPL'   -LH
gàjéːréː → gàjéːr-ìyáː 'short-FEM'   -LH
hùːláː   → hùːlâ-ř   'hat-DEF'   -L

As an illustration of how morphological constructions with different associated phonological patterns combine in a word, consider the example in (20). Here, a verb root, nèːmáː 'seek', combines with the dominant ventive suffix -óː, then undergoes pluractional reduplication, and is then converted, via zero-derivation, to an imperative. Both the ventive and the imperative constructions are dominant. The ventive imposes an all-H melody (e.g. 19c) (Newman 2000: 663). The imperative imposes a LH melody (e.g. 19a) (Newman 2000: 263–7). In (20), the ventive occurs hierarchically inside the imperative. Predictably in Hausa, the outermost dominant construction is the one whose pattern surfaces; in this case the outermost construction is the imperative, and consequently the whole word surfaces LH. (The imperative, a zero-derivation construction, is represented here by a null suffix, for purely graphical convenience.):

(20)

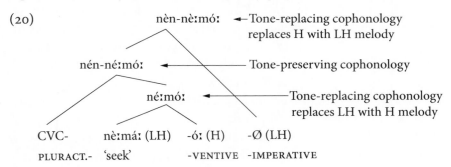

A second example from Hausa, in (21), illustrates a tone-replacing construction which is embedded within a tone-preserving construction. Here, a stem created by the dominant ventive construction is converted to a verbal noun through the suffixation of -ʼwáː, the recessive verbal noun-forming suffix. As predicted by interleaving, the tone-replacing effect of the ventive construction is limited to the ventive stem only; it does not alter the tone of affixes introduced by outer constructions, here the verbal noun-forming -ʼwáː, which is outside its scope:

(21)

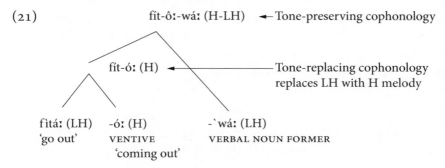

fít-ôː-wáː (H-LH) ← Tone-preserving cophonology

fít-óː (H) ← ————————— Tone-replacing cophonology
replaces LH with H melody

fìtáː (LH)   -óː (H)   -ʼwáː (LH)
'go out'   VENTIVE   VERBAL NOUN FORMER
                'coming out'

In sum, the way two cophonologies in the same word interact depends intrinsically on the hierarchical structure of the word. The outer construction has the last say.

7.2.3 Reduplication

In Tagalog and Ndebele, morphological constructions whose only phonological exponent is reduplication can be variably ordered with respect to other morphological constructions in the same word. The hierarchical order in which the constructions apply correlates with what phonological material gets reduplicated. If the reduplication layer is outside of a layer produced by affix X, then affix X is within the scope of reduplication; if the reduplication layer is inside the layer produced by affix X, then affix X does not undergo reduplication. This is an interleaving effect. We consider two cases, a relatively simpler one from Tagalog and a relatively more complicated one from Ndebele.

Tagalog is well known for its relatively free ordering of aspectual reduplication within the prefix complex. This morphological reorderability has phonological consequences. As shown in the data in (22) (from Rackowski 1999: 5), "contemplated" or imperfective aspectual prefixation is manifested via CVː reduplication of the root, or of any embedded prefixed stem in the word:

(22)

ma-ka-pag-pa-hintay   → ma-ka-pag-pa-**hii**-hintay
ABILITY-COMPLETE-TRANS-CAUSE-wait   ~ ma-ka-pag-**paa**-pa-hintay
'be able to cause someone to wait'   ~ ma-ka-**paa**-pag-pa-hintay
                                            ~ ma-**kaa**-ka-pag-pa-hintay
                                            *__maa__-ma-ka-pag-pa-hintay

This variability in what reduplicates is an interleaving issue. The relative order of reduplication with respect to other prefixes in Tagalog is variable; it is not random, as shown by Ryan (2010). However, the variation is morphological. The phonological variability in what reduplicates is due entirely to interleaving.

7.2.4 Ndebele reduplication

A second example of the interleaving of reduplication with other morphological processes comes from Ndebele, in which reduplication may target any subconstituent of the verb stem (Sibanda 2004; Hyman et al. 2009; Downing 2001, 2006). Reduplication in Ndebele, discussed also in Chapter 5, prefixes a CVCV reduplicant to the verb stem, which consists of a root followed by some number (possibly zero) of derivational suffixes and an obligatory inflectional suffix, known as the "Final Vowel" because most inflectional suffixes are of form -V. The CVCV reduplicant copies the first CVCV of the root, if it is that long. Otherwise, the reduplicant copies the entire root and then has two options for supplying the remainder of its obligatory CVCV shape. A reduplicant which is fleshed out by a CVC root may use the vowel [a], homophonous with the default Final Vowel suffix, to achieve CVCV shape. Alternatively, if the root is followed by a derivational suffix, the reduplicant also has the option of copying that vowel instead of using default [a]. From Hyman et al. 2009:

(23) a. nambith-a   nambi+nambith-a   'taste'
          thembuz-a   thembu+thembuz-a   'go from wife to wife'
      b. thum-a   thum-a+thum-a   'send'
          lim-a   lim-a+lim-a   'cultivate'
      c. lim-el-a   lim-a+lim-el-a   'cultivate for/at' (applicative -*el*)
                     lim-e+lim-el-a
      d. lim-is-a   lim-a-+lim-is-a   'make cultivate' (causative -*is*)
                     lim-i+lim-is-a

Downing (2006) characterizes CVC-*a* reduplicants as assuming the shape of the "canonical" verb stem. Reduplicants of this shape occur even when the stem itself ends in a different inflectional Final Vowel suffix. Final Vowel suffixes never reduplicate:

(24) a. lim-i   lim-a+lim-i   (negative -*i*)
                      *lim-i+lim-i

      b. lim-e   lim-a+lim-e   (subjunctive -*e*)
                      lim-e+lim-e

      c. lim-ile   lim-a+lim-ile   (perfective -*ile*)
                      *lim-i+lim-ile

As in Tagalog, the variable phonological form of the reduplicant can be attributed to the variable relative morphological order of the reduplication construction with respect to suffixation. Reduplication can target the root, or the root plus a derivational suffix (the "Derivational Stem" of Downing 1995 et seq.). Reduplication must, however, apply before Final Vowel suffixation. A table illustrating the potential morphological layers at which reduplication can take place is given in (25):

(25)

	optional reduplication	[[[lim]-is]-a] 'cultivate-CAUS-FV'	optional reduplication	[[lim]-e] 'cultivate-SUBJ'
Root Cycle	lim-a	lim-	lim-a	lim-
Derivational Suffix Cycle	lim-i	lim-is		
Final Vowel Cycle	—	lim-is-a	—	lim-e
	{lim-a, lim-i}	limisa	{lima-}	lime

A particularly interesting result of the optional interleaving of reduplication with derivational suffixation is illustrated by the passive suffix. The passive suffix takes the segmental form [w], but also is phonologically manifested by the palatalization it triggers on any preceding non-initial labial consonant in the stem:

(26) a. bal-a   'read'   bal-w-a   'be read'
          bik-a (H)   'announce'   bik-w-a   'be announced'
          phek-a   'cook'   phek-w-a   'be cooked'

      b. boph-a (H)   'tie'   botsh-w-a   'be tied'
          bumb-a (H)   'mold'   bunj-w-a   'be molded'
          thum-a (H)   'send'   thuny-w-a   'be sent'

As with the Causative suffix in Cibemba, discussed in section 7.1.4, the
Ndebele Passive suffix is subject to the strict Root-Causative-Applicative-
Reciprocal-Passive (CARP) template which governs linear affix order
(Hyman 2003). The Passive suffix is thus always linearly the last of the
derivational suffixes, immediately preceding the obligatory Final Vowel.
What is interesting from an interleaving perspective is that the Passive
has some freedom as to the relative hierarchical position it occupies
relative to other suffixes. As illustrated in (27), the Passive and Applicative can combine in either logical hierarchical order, yielding two different meanings, on the assumption that semantic scope and hierarchical
order are intimately correlated:

(27)

a. abantwana b-a-phek-el-w-a	ukudla	root appl pass
children they-PAST-cook-APPL-PASS	food	phek- -el- -w- 's.o. be cooked for sth.'
'The children were cooked food'		
b. ukudla kw-a-phek-el-w-a	abantwana	root pass appl
food it-PAST-cook-APPL-PASS	children	phek- -w- -el- 'sth. be cooked for s.o.'
'The food was cooked (for) the children'		

The Applicative and Passive must, however, occur in a fixed relative
linear order, meaning that when the Applicative suffix attaches
outside of the Passive, it must be infixed or interfixed in order to
conform to the CARP template (27b).[5] This analysis of Hyman

---

[5] The term "infixation" is generally used when the internal position of the affix is
described in phonological terms, e.g. "preceding the last syllable." The term "interfixation"
is used when the internal position is described in morphological terms, e.g. "preceding the
passive suffix." The internal positioning of the Applicative in (28) could be described either
way. Phonologists have tended to favor the phonological description whenever possible. See
Hyman and Orgun (2005) and Orgun (1996) for competing interfixation and infixation
analyses of the same affix in Cibemba.

(2003) may seem abstract, but Sibanda (2004) and Hyman et al. (2009) provide reduplication evidence in favor of it. As shown in (28), verb stem reduplication is sensitive to the hierarchical order of Passive and Applicative. The variable relative embedding of passive and applicative morphology correlates with variable reduplicability of the passive -*w*:

(28) a. Possible reduplications of the stem *phek-el-w-a* '(s.o.) be cooked for (s.t.)' (27a):
          phek-a+phek-el-w-a
          phek-e+phek-el-w-a

      b. Possible reduplications of the stem *phek-el-w-a* '(s.t.) be cooked for (s.o.)' (27b):
          phek-a+phek-el-w-a
          phek-e+phek-el-w-a
          phek-w-a+phek-el-w-a

The passive *w*, which fuses with the preceding consonant as an offglide, reduplicates only in stems in which it attaches hierarchically lower than the applicative and is adjacent to the root on its cycle of affixation. Derivations of the reduplicated verbs in (28a) and (28b) are shown in (29):

(29) Derivations of *phekelwa* and *phekelwa*, with reduplication as a possibility on any cycle

	optional reduplication	[[[[phek]APP] PASS]a] '(children) were cooked (food)'	optional reduplication	[[[[phek]PASS]APP]a] '(food) was cooked for (children)'
Cycle 1	pheka-	phek-	pheka-	phek-
Cycle 2	pheke-	phek-el-	phekwa-	phek-w-
Cycle 3	pheke-	phek-el-w-	pheke-	phek-el-w-
Cycle 4	pheke-	phek-el-w-a	pheke-	phek-el-w-a
Possible reduplicants	{pheka-, pheke-}	phekelwa	{pheka-, phekwa-, pheke-}	phekelwa

Clearly, if reduplication were not interleaved with suffixation and if it applied only at the word level, or for that matter at any given intermediate level, the variation in reduplication possibilities would not be attested.

7.3 Interleaving, morphological reorderability, and level ordering theory

Cases such as the ones already given, in which morphological constructions associated with characteristic phonological effects can combine in more than one order, are a test case for the differences between Level Ordering theory and Cophonology Theory. As discussed in Chapter 1, both are theories of the internal organization of morphologically conditioned phonology within a grammar.

Level Ordering theories include the theory of Lexical Morphology and Phonology (e.g., Kiparsky 1982bc, 1984, 1985; Mohanan 1986; Pulleyblank 1986) and Stratal Optimality Theory (Kiparsky 2000, 2008, 2010). These approaches assume that the morphological component of grammar consists of a small number of strictly ordered modules known as "levels" or "strata." Each module has its own characteristic morphological operations and phonological patterns. A given module is either cyclic or noncyclic, depending on the language.

Cophonology Theory (e.g. Orgun 1996; Anttila 2002; Inkelas and Zoll 2005) assumes a nonmodular approach to morphology in which each morphological operation is associated with its own phonological grammar (cophonology). Bochner's (1992) Lexical Relatedness Morphology, Booij's (2010) Construction Morphology, and Hippisley (1997) and Brown and Hippisley's (2012) Network Morphology can be classified under this rubric as well, though the latter three are better described as theories of process morphology than as theories of morphologically conditioned phonology. Cophonology Theory is explicitly a theory of both phenomena.

The claim of level ordering is one of the two main distinctions between Level Ordering theory and Cophonology Theory.

As discussed in Chapter 2, a level is that set of morphological constructions which are associated with the same phonological alternations and constraints. The claim of Level Ordering theory is that different levels are strictly ordered in the morphology:

(30)   Level Ordering theory
       Level 1 = innermost morphological constructions, associated with phonology 1
       Level 2 = next set of morphological constructions, associated with phonology 2
       Level 3 = next set of morphological constructions, associated with phonology 3
       etc.

A clear test of the Level Ordering claim is presented by cases of interleaving in which morphological constructions combine freely, and/or are potentially recursive. Cophonology Theory predicts that the cophonologies of the respective constructions apply in the flexible order in which the constructions combine, rather than being rigidly externally ordered.

By contrast, Level Ordering theory predicts that recursivity or re-orderability can happen only *within a level*, among constructions which share the same phonological mapping, giving rise to the kind of pure cyclicity seen in section 7.1. By imposing a fixed extrinsic order on levels, Level Ordering theory predicts that there should be no recursion or reorderability among morphological constructions which belong to different levels and thus are associated with different phonological mappings. Given two suffixes X and Y, each associated with a different phonological pattern, Level Ordering theory predicts the coexistence of both ordering scenarios in (31) to be impossible:

(31)   [[Root-X]-Y]   (phonology of X applies before phonology of Y)
      [[Root-Y]-X]   (phonology of Y applies before phonology of X)

A number of cases have been discovered which behave like (31) and thus violate the essential postulate of Level Ordering theory. Mohanan (1986), in one of the original expositions of Level Ordering theory, showed that Malayalam is a counterexample to fixed level ordering; Inkelas and Orgun (1998) present Turkish as another such example. We turn to these cases in the next two sections.

7.3.1 Malayalam

Perhaps the best known case of interleaving in a grammar with recursive morphology comes from Malayalam, one of two languages used to make the original case for Level Ordering theory. As analyzed by Mohanan (1982, 1986, 1995) and Mohanan and Mohanan (1984),

Malayalam has four levels or strata of morphology (Mohanan and Mohanan 1984: 581):

(32)   Stratum 1:   Derivation (negative, unproductive causative,
                                among others)
       Stratum 2:   Subcompounding, productive causative suffixation
       Stratum 3:   Cocompounding
       Stratum 4:   Inflection (case and tense)

Two of these strata are occupied by one construction each. Stratum 2 is the domain of Subcompounding (subordinate compounding), a noun-noun compounding process whose semantics follows a modifier +head pattern. Stratum 3 is the domain of Cocompounding (coordinate compounding), a noun-noun compounding process with coordination semantics. The two constructions are compared in (33) (adapted from Mohanan 1995: 49; stress, but not tone, is marked in the transcriptions):

(33)   Subcompound: [Malayalam]
       méeša-ppeṭṭi-kaḷə   'table-box-PL = table-boxes'
       Cocompound:
       méeša-péṭṭi-kaḷə   'table-box-PL = tables and boxes'

The reason that Mohanan assigns the two compounding constructions to different strata is that they differ quite markedly in their phonology. First, as discussed in Chapter 2 and discernible in (33), gemination applies to the initial consonant of the second member of a Subcompound, but does not apply within Cocompounds. Secondly, while the stress and tone assignment rules of Malayalam apply separately to the two members of a Cocompound, they apply to Subcompounds as a single unit. The stress rules of Malayalam are given in (34) (Mohanan 1986: 112):

(34)   Stress assignment (Stratum 2):
       a. Stress any syllable with a long vowel
       b. Stress the initial syllable unless a syllable with long vowel
          immediately follows
       c. Give main stress to the leftmost stressed syllable

Tone is also assigned on Stratum 2, and is sensitive to stress. According to Mohanan (1986: 115), a LH tone melody is assigned to every constituent formed by the morphology on Stratum 2. The L tone links to the syllable with main stress, while the H links to the final

syllable and spreads iteratively leftward onto secondary-stressed syllables. Example (35) illustrates the prosodic contrast between Subcompounds (35a) and Cocompounds (35b) (Mohanan 1995: 49):

(35) a. káaṭṭə-maṟam   'forest-tree'
         méeša-ppeṭṭi-kaḷə 'table-box-PL = table-boxes'

      b. áaṭə-máaaṭə-kaḷə   'goat-cow-PL = goats and cows'
         méeša-péṭṭi-kaḷə   'table-box-PL = tables and boxes'

Subcompounds and Cocompounds with more than two members
conform to the same pattern as binary compounds; the entire
Subcompound is a domain for stress and tone assignment, as is
each individual member of a longer Cocompound (Mohanan 1986:
116–17):

(36) a. Subcompounding

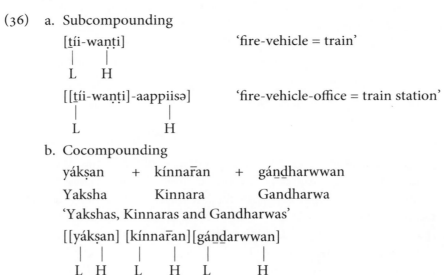

      b. Cocompounding

         yákṣan   +   kínnaṟan   +   gánḏharwwan

         Yaksha   Kinnara   Gandharwa

         'Yakshas, Kinnaras and Gandharwas'

The challenge that Malayalam poses for Level Ordering theory is that
Subcompounding and Cocompounding are not extrinsically ordered in
the way that level ordering predicts. Instead, either type of compound
can be embedded within the other. According to Mohanan (1995: 49),
"there is no morphological asymmetry between the two kinds of compounds: a co-compound can have a subcompound as one of its stems,
and a subcompound can have a co-compound as one of its stems..."
Example (37a) illustrates two Subcompounds embedded within a Cocompound, consistent with the predictions of the stratal ordering
model (Mohanan 1986: 111; transcriptions modified to match those

of Mohanan 1995). By contrast, (37b) illustrates a Cocompound embedded within a Subcompound, exactly the opposite scenario. (37c) illustrates Subcompounds embedded within a Cocompound which is in turn embedded in a Subcompound:

(37) a. moohanapatn̲iitaar̄akaan̲tanmaar̄ə (Mohanan 1986: 111)
          [[moohanan +   patn̲i]$_{Sub}$ + [t̲aar̄a + kaan̲tan]$_{Sub}$]$_{Co}$
          Mohanan   wife   Tara   husband
          'Mohanan's wife and Tara's husband'

      b. Cocompound within Subcompound (Mohanan 1995: 52)
          [[méeša + pétti]$_{Co}$ + kasáala]$_{Sub}$ -ka̲l
            table   box   chair   -PL
          'chairs made from tables and boxes'

      c. Subcompounds within Cocompound within Subcompound
          (Mohanan 1982: 50)
          maat̲rəsn̲eehapatn̲iwid̲weeṣawikaar̄aŋŋalə
          [[[maat̲r + sn̲eeham]$_{Sub}$ + [patn̲i + wid̲weeṣam]$_{Sub}$]$_{Co}$
            mother   love   wife   hatred
          + wikaar̄am]$_{Sub}$ -ka̲l
            emotion   -PL
          'the emotions of mother love and wife hatred'

To account for this free relative embedding of Subcompounding and Cocompounding, Mohanan proposes a "loop" between Strata 2 and 3. While effective in accounting for the free ordering possibilities between the two compounding types, the proposal clearly invalidates the claim that levels are strictly ordered.

In an attempt to preserve the strict ordering claim, several authors have proposed using prosodic structure to distinguish Subcompounds from Cocompounds, a move that would allow the two constructions to be collapsed in the same stratum. Sproat (1986) and Inkelas (1989) propose that Subcompounds consist of a single Prosodic Word, while the members of Cocompounds are Prosodic Words on their own. (This type of mismatch between prosodic constituency and morphological constituency is the focus of Chapter 10.) Stress and tone assignment is sensitive to the Prosodic Word (ω):[6]

---

[6] On this analysis, the suffix *-ka̲lə* may incorporate into the Prosodic Word on its stratum of attachment.

(38)　a. Subcompound: single Prosodic Word
　　　　　(káaṭṭə-maŕam)$_\omega$　'forest-tree'

　　　b. Cocompound: two Prosodic Words
　　　　　(áaṭə)$_\omega$-(máaaṭə)$_\omega$-kaḷə　'goat-cow-PL = goats and cows'

While this proposal accounts for the stress and tone asymmetries between the two types of compounds, Mohanan (1995) argues convincingly that it cannot account for the differential application of gemination in Subcompounds (see Chapters 2 and 10). Even if it could, there would still be a phonological difference between two constructions in the same level, which contradicts the principle of Level Ordering theory that constructions in the same level are subject to the same phonological patterns.

7.3.2 Turkish

Like Malayalam, Turkish exhibits free reorderability among a set of constructions each of which triggers a distinct phonological pattern. In the case of Turkish, the relevant pattern is stress assignment. (On Turkish stress, see e.g. Lees 1961; Lewis 1967; Underhill 1976; Underhill 1981; Kornfilt 1997; Kabak and Vogel 2001; Inkelas and Orgun 2003.)

The stress pattern that takes precedence, when two or more of these constructions co-occur within the same word, is always the innermost. The fact that the constructions can combine in multiple orders shows the effects of interleaving. The five stress patterns we will concern ourselves with in Turkish are the following:

(39)　Stress-neutral suffixation　derivational and inflectional suffixes
　　　　(no stress assigned):
　　　Pre stressing suffixation:　derivational and inflectional suffixes
　　　Sezer stress:　one zero-derivation place name-
　　　　　　　forming construction
　　　Compound stress:　two noun-noun compounding
　　　　　　　constructions
　　　Final stress:　word level

The first four of these are associated with specific morphological constructions. In Level Ordering theory, the four distinct phonological stress patterns would motivate four morphological levels. We will see, in the following discussion, that the "levels" in question are not strictly ordered; any of the four types of construction can combine with any of the others, in either order. What happens in such cases is what Cophonology Theory predicts. Stress is assigned in tandem with each individual construction, with the resulting "layering" effect in words containing multiple stress-assigning constructions.

7.3.2.1 Stress-neutral suffixation   In Turkish, every content word surfaces with exactly one stress, regardless of morphological complexity. The default position for stress in Turkish words is final. This pattern is exhibited in words containing morphemes none of which is lexically stressed, and which are subject to the word-level default final stress rule:

(40)   Final stress: words containing only "stress-neutral" morphemes

gloss	UR	surface (IPA)	orthography (+stress)
a. 'apple'	/elma/	el'ma	*elmá*
'apple-PL'	/elma-lEr/	elma'lar	*elma-lár*
'apple-PL-ABL'	/elma-lEr-dEn/	elmalar'dan	*elma-lar-dán*
b. 'eggplant'	/patlɯdʒan/	patlɯ'dʒan	*patlıcán*
'eggplant-1SG.POSS'	/patlɯdʒan-m/	patlɯdʒa'nɯm	*patlıcan-ím*
'eggplant-1SG.POSS-DAT'	/patlɯdʒan-m-a/	patlɯdʒanɯ'ma	*patlıcan-ım-á*
c. 'go'	/git/	'git	*gít*
'go-AOR'	/git-Er/	gi'der	*gid-ér*
'go-NEC'	/git-mElI/	gitme'li	*git-melí*
d. 'come'	/gel/	'gel	*gél*
'come-FUT'	/gel-EdʒEk/	gele'dʒek	*gel-ecék*
'come-FUT-PL'	/gel-EdʒEk-lEr/	geledʒek'ler	*gel-ecek-lér*
e. 'kick (n.)'	/tekme/	tek'me	*tekmé*
'kick-VBL (v.)'	/tekme-lE/	tekme'le	*tekme-lé*
'kick-VBL-PAST'	/tekme-lE-dI/	tekmele'di	*tekme-le-dí*

Lexically stressed roots and stressed suffixes override the default final stress rule. In a word containing one or more such morphemes, the leftmost (or innermost—as Turkish is exclusively suffixing, these two dimensions are largely conflated) prevails, and any stresses to the right are deleted. As shown in (41), stressed roots defy the default final stress rule, both in isolation and when combined with a suffix. By way of illustration, the stress-neutral dative suffix is used in this example, but any other neutral suffix would display the same behavior. Note that the set of lexically stressed roots varies somewhat across speakers:

(41)   Lexically stressed roots

gloss	Nominative		Dative (/-(j)E/)	
'blockade'	*ablúka*	ab'luka	*ablúkaya*	ab'luka-ja
'Europe'	*Avrúpa*	av'rupa	*Avrúpaya*	av'rupa-ja
'dried curd'	*tarhána*	tar'hana	*tarhánaja*	tar'hana-ja
(place name)	*Üskǘdar*	ys'kydar	*Üskǘdarja*	ys'kydar-a
(place name)	*Kastámonu*	kas'tamonu	*Kastámonuja*	kas'tamonu-ja
(place name)	*Érzincan*	'erzindʒan	*Érzincana*	'erzindʒan-a
'penalty kick'	*pénaltı*	'penaltu	*pénaltıya*	'penaltu-ja

Some suffixes are also lexically specified with stress. These also override the default final stress rule. Lexical stresses are indicated with acute accents in underlying representations:

(42)

Suffix	Example	gloss	cf. same root with neutral suffix	
/-Íjor/	*yap-íyor* ja'puɪjor	'do-PROG'	*yap-malí* japma'luɪ	'do-NEC'
	gid-íyor gi'dijor	'go-PROG'	*gid-ecék* gide'dʒek	'go-FUT'
/-ÉrEk/	*gid-érek* gi'derek	'go-by (=by going)'	*git-melí* gitme'li	'go-NEC'
	yap-árak ja'parak	'do-by (= by doing)'	*yap-acák* japa'dʒak	'do-FUT'
/-ÍndʒE/	*gel-ínce* ge'lindʒe	'go-when'	*gel-ecék* gele'dʒek	'come-FUT'
	yap-ínca ja'puɪndʒa	'do-when'	*yap-malí* japma'luɪ	'do-NEC'

These facts can easily be accommodated under the assumption that Turkish has a word-level, noncyclic stress rule, which applies only in the absence of input stress:

(43)   Assign final stress if no stress exists in the input (Word level)

It is possible for a word to contain more than one lexically stressed morpheme, either a root + stressed suffix (44a) or two stressed suffixes (44b). Examples, taken from Inkelas and Orgun (2003), are given in (44):

(44) a. Stressed root + stressed suffix
      i. ab'lukalajɯndʒa   *ablúkalayınca*
          /**ablúka**-la-**índʒE**/
          blockade-VBL-ADV
          'having blockaded'

      ii. mek'sikalɯlaʃɯjor   *Meksîkalılaşıyor*
          /**meksíka**-lI-lEş-**íjor**/
          Mexico-ASSOC-VBL-PROG
          'is becoming Mexican'

      b. Stressed suffix + stressed suffix
      i. ja'pɯverindʒe   *yapíverince*
          /jap-**íver**-**índʒE**/
          do-suddenly/easily-ADV
          'having suddenly/easily done'

      ii. bɯra'kɯvererek   *bırakívererek*
          /bırak-**íver**-**ÉrEk**/
          leave-suddenly/easily-ADV
          'by suddenly/easily leaving'

These facts can be accommodated with the following principle:

(45)   "Innermost Wins": Stress associated with a suffixation construction is deleted if the input stem already bears stress.

"Innermost Wins" can be argued to apply cyclically (see e.g. Barker 1989 for a proposal that Turkish stress is cyclic); however, the main evidence for interleaving comes from the interplay of the three other construction types which will now be introduced.

7.3.2.2 Prestressing suffixes   A number of suffixes in Turkish assign stress to the stem-final syllable (much like the pre-accenting Japanese suffixes discussed in Chapter 2). Prestressing suffixes are notated, in underlying form, with a circumflex to indicate that stress is assigned to the preceding syllable:

(46)

Prestressing suffix		gloss	cf. same root with neutral suffix	
/-^mE/	tekmelé-me	'kick-NEG'	tekmele-dí	'kick-PAST'
	tekme'leme		tekmele'di	
/-^mI/	arabá-mı	'car-INTERR'	araba-lár	'car-PL'
	ara'bamɯ		araba'lar	
/-^(j)lE/	patlıcán-la	'eggplant-INSTR/COM'	patlıcan-lár	'eggplant-PL'
	patlɯ'ʤanla		patlɯʤan'lar	
/-^(j)In/	tekmelé-yin	'kick-2PL.IMP'	tekmele-dí	'kick-PAST'
	tekme'lejin		tekmele'di	
/-^ʤE/	güzél-ce	'beautiful-ADV'	güzel-lík	'beautiful-NOM'
	gy'zelʤe		gyzel'lik	
/-^ʤE/	tat-lí-ca	'taste-with-MIT'	tat-lı-lík	'taste-with-NOM'
	tat'lɯʤa		tatlɯ'lɯk	
/-^lejin/	akşám-leyin	'evening-at'	akşam-lár	'evening-PL'
	ak'ʃamlejin		akʃam'lar	
/-^ʤEsInE/	hayván-casına	'animal-like'	hayvan-lár	'animal-PL'
	haj'vanʤasɯna		hajvan'lar	

The stress assigned by a prestressing suffix overrides the assignment of default Final stress at the word level (43), as expected. In words containing a stressed root and a prestressing suffix (47a), or a stressed suffix and a prestressing suffix (47b), or more than one prestressing suffix (47c), the stress assigned on the innermost constituent prevails, as shown in (47):

(47) a. Stressed root + prestressing suffix
        i. /pénaltɯ-^mI/[7] 'penaltumɯ (pénaltımı)
           penalty-INTERR 'is it a (soccer) penalty?'
       ii. /pendʒére-^(j)lE/ pen'dʒerejle (pencéreyle)
           window-COM 'with/by window'
   b. Stressed suffix + prestressing suffix
        i. /jap-ÉrEk-^mI/ ja'parakmɯ (yapárakmı)
           do-ADV-INTERR 'is it by doing?'

---

[7] The yes-no question marker /-^mI/ is written with a space preceding it in standard Turkish orthography. However, it behaves like other prestressing suffixes, and this orthographic quirk can be disregarded here.

ii. /jap-^mE-Íjor/   'japmɯjor (yápmıyor)
do-NEG-PROG   'he/she/it isn't doing (it)'

c. Two prestressing suffixes

i. /gel-^mE-^sIn/   'gelmesin (gélmesin)
come-NEG-3SG.IMP   'let him/her/it not come'

ii. /araba-^jlE-^mI/   ara'bajlamɯ (arabáylamı)
car-COM-INT   'by/with (a) car?'

At this point in the presentation, we have two types of suffixation construction: one associated with no stress assignment rule (40), and one associated with prestressing (46). The question for Level Ordering theory is this: do prestressing suffixes cluster in the word, either preceding or following the block of prestressing constructions, in the manner predicted by Level Ordering theory? The answer is no. As seen in (48), prestressing and stress-neutral suffixes can occur in either order:

(48)   a. Stress-neutral inside prestressing

i. /jaban-dʒI-^(j)Im/   jaban'dʒɯjɯm (yabancíyım)
wild-AGT-1SG.PRED   'I am a foreigner'

ii. /tekme-lE-^mE/   tek'meleme (tekméleme)
kick (n.)-VBL-NEG   'don't kick!'

iii. /tat-lI-^(j)dʒE/   tat'lɯdʒa (tatlíca)
taste-ASSOC-MIT   'sort of tasty'

b. Prestressing inside stress-neutral

i. /arap-^tʃE-dEn/   a'raptʃadan (arápçadan)
Arab-ADJ-ABL   'Arabic (ablative)'

ii. /bɯrak-^mE-dI/   bɯ'rakmadɯ (bırákmadı)
leave-NEG-PAST   'he/she/it didn't leave'

iii. /baʃka-sI-^(j)lE-(j)ken/   baʃka'sɯjlajken (başkasíylayken)
another-POSS-COM-WHEN   'when with someone else'

If stress-neutral (and stressed) suffixes are assigned to one level, and prestressing suffixes to another, based on whether or not stress assignment applies, then there must be a loop between the two levels in order to account for the data in (48):

(49)

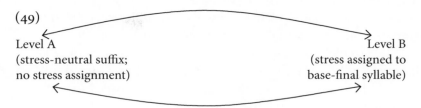

Level A   Level B
(stress-neutral suffix;   (stress assigned to
no stress assignment)   base-final syllable)

7.3.2.3 Sezer stems   The next construction, with its own stress properties, is a productive zero-derivation construction which converts a word
of virtually any part of speech to a place name (e.g. *Bebek* and *Kuzguncuk,*
areas within Istanbul, from *bebek* 'baby' and *kuzgun-cuk* 'raven-DIM'). The
construction, termed the "Sezer place name construction" in Inkelas and
Orgun (1998), is marked by a distinctive stress pattern first described
by Sezer (1981). The Sezer pattern places stress on the antepenultimate
syllable if the antepenult is heavy and the penultimate syllable is light
(monomoraic, i.e. CV in shape); otherwise, stress falls on the penultimate
syllable. Because of this stress pattern, many place names have stress in a
different location than the surface form of their word of origin:

(50)

	UR	As regular word (default final stress)	As place name (Sezer stress)
...σ$_\mu$σ́$_\mu$σ	/bak-adʒak/	baka'dʒak	ba'kadʒak
	'look-FUT'	*bakacák*	*Bakácak*
...σ$_\mu$σ́$_{\mu\mu}$σ	/kavak-lI/	kavak'lɯ	ka'vaklɯ
	'poplar-ASSOC'	*kavaklí*	*Kaváklı*
...σ$_{\mu\mu}$σ́$_{\mu\mu}$σ	/kuzgun-dʒIk/	kuzgun'dʒuk	kuz'gundʒuk
	'raven-DIM'	*kuzguncúk*	*Kuzgúncuk*
...σ́$_{\mu\mu}$σ$_\mu$σ	/sirke-dʒI/	sirke'dʒi	'sirkedʒi
	'vinegar-AGT'	*sirkecí*	*Sírkecí*

Sezer stress is a default pattern, like Final stress, in that it is overridden
by lexical stress on any of its input elements. As seen in (51), a lexically
stressed root keeps its stress even when converted to a place name; we will
see later (example (52)) that lexically stressed or prestressing suffixes are
also preserved when present in the input to Sezer place name formation.

(51)   Irregular lexical root stress in input blocks imposition of Sezer stress
    Af.ri.ka   'Africa'   **Áfrika*
    Av.rú.pa   'Europe'   **Ávrupa*
    Kas.tá.mo.nu   (place name)   **Kastamónu*
    Zón.gul.dak   (place name)   **Zongúldak*

This behavior is accounted for straightforwardly by INNERMOST WINS (45).

Because it is associated with a stress pattern different from that of stress-neutral or prestressing suffixes, a Level Ordering analysis would require the Sezer place name construction to occupy a distinct level, which we can call Level C. The question for a Level Ordering model of Turkish is: can Level C be strictly ordered with respect to the levels associated with stress-neutral and prestressing suffixes? The answer is no. As seen in (52), Sezer place name formation can be ordered before or after stress-neutral suffixation (52a-b) and prestressing suffixation (52c-d):

(52)   a. Neutral suffixes inside Sezer stem: Sezer pattern imposed on
            outer stem

[Kandíl-li]	(place name)	cf. *kandil-lí* 'oil lamp-ASSOC'
kan'dilli		kandil'li
[Ayrán-cɪ]	(place name)	cf. *ayran-cí* 'yogurt drink-AGT'
aj'randʒɯ		ajran'dʒɯ
[Kuzgún-cuk]	(place name)	cf. *kuzgun-cúk* 'raven-DIM'
kuz'gundʒuk		kuzgun'dʒuk

        b. Neutral suffixes outside Sezer stem: Sezer pattern prevails in
            inner stem

[Ménteşe]-cik	'Menteşe-DIM'	cf. *menteşe-cík* 'hinge-DIM'
'menteʃedʒik		menteʃe'dʒik
[Kandíl-li]-ye	'Kandilli-DAT'	cf. *kandil-li-yé* 'oil lamp-ASSOC-DAT'
kan'dillije		kandilli'je

        c. Prestressing suffixes inside Sezer stem: Prestressing pattern
            prevails (in inner stem)

[çam-lí-^ca]	(place name)	cf. *çam-lí-ca* 'pine-ASSOC-MIT'
tʃam'lɯdʒa		tʃam'lɯdʒa
[kan-lí-^ca]	(place name)	cf. *kanlíca* 'blood-ASSOC-MIT'
kan'lɯdʒa		kan'lɯdʒa

        d. Prestressing suffixes outside Sezer stem: Sezer pattern prevails
            (in inner stem)

[Ánkara]-^mɪ	'Ankara-INTERR'	cf. *arabá-^mɪ* 'car-INTERR'
'ankaramɯ		ara'bamɯ

[*Ánkara*]-*lı-laş-*^*mı-dı*   cf. *yaban-cu-láş-*^*mı-dı*
'ankaralʉlaʃmʉdʉ   jabandʒʉ'laʃmʉdʉ
'Ankara-ASSOC-VBL-NEG-PAST'   'foreign-AGT-ASSOC-VBL-NEG-PAST'

The fact that neutral suffixes can occur inside or outside the domain of Sezer stress, depending on which subconstituent of the word is converted to a place name, is evidence for interleaving. A derivation is provided in (53) for *Kandilliye*, which is the dative form of the place name *Kandilli* (< *kandil* 'candle' + ASSOCIATIVE -*li*). As seen, the internal place name *Kandilli* is assigned Sezer stress, which it preserves under subsequent dative suffixation:

(53)

Input to Cycle 1	/kandil/
<no cyclic stress rules>	kandil
Input to Cycle 2: suffixation of associative /-lI/	kandil + /-lI/
<no cyclic stress rules>	kandilli
Input to Cycle 3: conversion to place name	
Sezer stress rule applies	kan'dilli
Input to Cycle 4: suffixation of dative /-E/	kan'dilli + /-E/
<no cyclic stress rules>	kan'dillije
Word level: default Final stress rule blocked by pre-existing stress	—
Output	kan'dillije

In sum, stress-neutral suffixation, prestressing suffixation, and Sezer stem formation are not extrinsically ordered in the morphology of Turkish. The constructions can combine in all possible orders; when they do, the characteristic stress rules of each construction apply to the stems they create, in the order that the constructions are morphologically layered. A Level Ordering model of Turkish would have to have loops connecting every pair of levels:

(54)

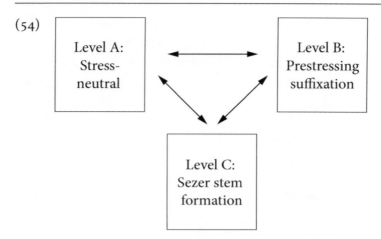

7.3.2.4 Compounding   The fourth relevant morphological construction is compounding. As discussed in Inkelas and Orgun (1998), there are two ways of forming compounds in Turkish: either straight concatenation, as shown in (55a), or by attaching a third person possessive suffix to the second constituent, as in (55b) (the "Izafet" construction; see e.g. Lewis 1967). The stress patterns of these two compound types are identical: the second member is stressless, and the first member receives the same stress it would exhibit if it were an independent word.

(55)   a.   Çengel+köy   [tʃenˈgelkøj]   'Çengel-village'
            Mehmet+bey   [mehˈmetbej]   'Mr. Mehmet'
            baş+bak-an   [ˈbaʃbakan]   'head-look-REL
                                                (=prime minister)'

            süt+beyaz   [ˈsytbejaz]   'milk-white'
       b.   bebek +   [beˈbekhastaːnesi]   'child-hospital-POSS =
            hastaːne-si   children's hospital'
            tarhana +   [tarˈhanatʃorbasɯ]   'dried_yogurt-soup-POSS
            çorba-sı   = dried_yogurt soup'
            meksika +   [mekˈsikafasuljesi] 'Mexico-bean-POSS =
            fasulye-si   Mexican jumping bean'

The following stress rule accounts for the stress pattern of compounds:

(56)   COMPOUND STRESS: delete input stress from the second member of a compound, and apply default Final stress to the first member

Because compounding is associated with a stress pattern different from that of the other three types of constructions discussed so far,

Level Ordering theory would require it to occupy its own unique level (D). And again, the question for Level Ordering theory is whether this level is strictly ordered with respect to any of the other three. The evidence shows that compounding is ordered freely with respect to neutral suffixation, prestressing suffixation, and Sezer stem formation. Illustrative examples are shown in (57):

(57) a. Compounds (square brackets) inside place names (curly brackets):

    i. *{[Saím+bey]-li}* 'Saimbeyli (place name, lit. 'Saim-Mr.-ASSOC')'
       sa'imbejli

    ii. *{[Áy+doğmuş]}* 'Aydoğmuş (place name, lit. 'moon-rise-EVID')'
        'ajdoːmuʃ

  b. Place names (curly brackets) inside compounds (square brackets):

    i. *[yürék+{Selanik}]* 'heart-Salonika = coward'
       jy'rekselaːnik   cf. se'laːnik *Selánik* 'Salonika (place name)'

    ii. *[{Kandíl-li}+cadde-si]* 'Kandilli street' (lit. 'oil_lamp-
                                          ASSOC-STRESS-3POSS')
        kan'dillidʒaddesi   cf. dʒadde'si *caddesí* 'street-3POSS'

  c. Compound (square brackets) inside prestressing suffix (bold):
     *{[Saím+bey]-^**di**}* 'Saim-Mr.-PAST = it was Mr. Saim'
     sa'imbejdi   cf. 'bej'di *beydí* 'Mr.-3POSS'

  d. Prestressing suffix (bold) inside compound (square brackets):
     *[unút-^**ma**+ben-i]* 'forget-NEG+1SG-ACC = forget-me-not'
     u'nutmabeni

  e. Compound (square brackets) inside stress-neutral suffix (bold):
     *[bebék-hastane]-**de*** 'child-hospital-DAT = children's hospital
                                          (DAT)'
     be'bekhastaːnede

  f. Stress-neutral suffix (bold) inside compound (square brackets):
     *[gün-é+bak-**an**]* 'sun-DAT+look-REL = sun-looker = sunflower'
     gy'nebakan

To account for these ordering facts, the four morphological levels of Turkish that Level Ordering theory would have to postulate thus far are freely ordered, necessitating the maximum looping possible:

(58)

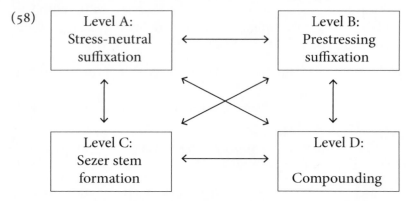

This situation is so far from what Level Ordering theory predicts that Inkelas and Orgun (1998) call it a case of *non*-level ordering. However, the interaction of the constructions with the four different stress assignment patterns in Turkish is exactly what is predicted in a cophonology model in which the phonology associated with a morphological construction applies in tandem with the construction, to the stem created by that construction.

Looking back earlier in this chapter, it is clear that the Hausa, Tagalog, and Ndebele cases discussed in sections 7.2.2 and 7.2.3 are also examples of interleaving that are not amenable to Level Ordering, but which should yield readily to accounts which incorporate layering, including Cophonology Theory and the recent Optimal Interleaving proposals of Wolf (2008).

7.4 Non-interleaving approaches to interleaving effects

The concept of cyclicity and interleaving has met with some resistance from researchers who favor a more surface-oriented approach to grammar, eschewing the abstractness of approaches in which the phonology applies to subconstituents of words, producing representations which are neither underlying nor surface. Two influential surface-oriented alternatives to cyclicity are Output-Output Correspondence theory, in which morphologically related words are grammatically constrained to be phonologically similar (e.g. Benua 1997; Ussishkin 1999; Steriade 2000; Downing 2005; Kenstowicz 2005), and Indexed Constraint Theory, which rejects cophonologies in favor of a single grammar containing morphologically specific phonological constraints.

Output-Output Correspondence theory is discussed in some detail in Chapter 11, as it crucially invokes the notion of the paradigm. In this section, we will focus instead on indexed constraints as an alternative to cophonologies.

7.4.1 Indexed Constraint Theory

Indexed Constraint Theory was developed within Optimality Theory as a way of capturing morphologically conditioned phonology without the use of cycles, levels, or cophonologies. Important works include McCarthy and Prince (1995), Smith (1997), Itô and Mester (1999), Pater (2000), and Alderete (2001a), among others. Indexed Constraint Theory posits a single fixed constraint ranking for the entire language; constraints within that fixed ranking are indexed to individual morphological contexts. In such approaches, constraints are potentially split into as many different indexed versions (e.g MAX-C$_{root}$, MAX-C$_{affix}$, MAX-C$_{BR}$, etc.) as are needed to describe morphologically conditioned phonology. The claim that there is one ranking for the entire language is the primary difference between Indexed Constraint Theory and Cophonology Theory, in which rules (in rule-based theories) or constraint rankings (in Optimality Theory) are associated with specific morphological constructions. A cophonology approach to morphologically conditioned phonology would posit a single set of (morphologically generic) constraints for a language but rank them differently for each distinct cophonology; an Indexed Constraint approach would, instead, split constraints into families whose members are indexed to particular morphological contexts.

In a comparison of the two approaches, Inkelas and Zoll (2007) construct analyses within each framework of some of the morphologically conditioned tone melody replacements in Hausa. Recall from section 7.2.2 that the Ventive construction deletes stem tone and imposes H tone on the entire ventive stem, whereas the Imperative construction deletes stem tone and imposes a LH melody. Thus a verb like *néːmàː* 'seek' takes the form *néːmóː* in the Ventive and *nèːmáː* in the Imperative. In Cophonology Theory, this tonal difference would be captured by ranking the constraints Tone=H, Tone=LH, and IDENT-tone differently in the cophonologies of the Ventive and the Imperative constructions:

(59) Ventive cophonology: Tone=H » Ident-tone » Tone=LH
       (this ranking is also used for other constructions, e.g. noun
       plural -o:Ci:)
       Imperative cophonology: Tone=LH » Ident-tone » Tone=H
       (this ranking is also used for other constructions, e.g. noun
       plural -ai)

The constraints in the analysis are fully general; it is only their rankings that are specific to particular morphological environments.

Indexed Constraint Theory would capture the distinction between the Ventive and Imperative by taking the general Tone=H and Tone=LH constraints and splitting them, as shown in (60), ranking the morphologically specific version(s) of each higher than Ident, and the fully general one low:

(60)   Tone=H$_{Ventive}$, Tone=LH$_{Imperative}$ » Ident-tone » Tone=H, Tone=LH

As Inkelas and Zoll observe, as long as constraints can be indexed not just to individual morphemes but (following Alderete 1999) to complex stems, Indexed Constraint Theory is capable of describing every individual morphologically conditioned phonological pattern that Cophonology Theory can describe. The difference between the two theories lies in their ability to account for morphologically complex words, i.e. for interleaving effects.

Inkelas and Zoll (2007: 148) note that the ranking in (60) "is not specific enough to predict the outcome in words containing both ventive and imperative morphology. In cophonology theory, the hierarchical structure of the word determines which cophonology applies to which subpart of the word, and in what logical order. But in indexed constraint theory, it is the highest ranked morphologically indexed constraint that determines the outcome—not the hierarchical structure of the word." Thus in order to know whether the tones of the root in a word like /[[[né:mà:]-o:]$_{Ventive}$]$_{Imper}$/ surface as H, as required by the ranking Tone=H$_{Ventive}$ » Ident-tone, or as LH, as required by the ranking Tone=LH$_{Imperative}$ » Ident-tone, it is necessary to rank Tone =H$_{Ventive}$ and Tone=LH$_{Imperative}$ relative to one another. If ranked as in (61a), the prediction is that imperative tone prevails over ventive tone, the correct outcome for the word in (61a). But if ranked as in (61b), the prediction is that ventive tone will prevail, no matter what outer tone-integrating suffixes are attached:

(61) a. Tone=LH$_{Imperative}$ »   [[[né:mà:] -o:]$_{Ventive}$]$_{Imper}$ →
          Tone=H$_{Ventive}$ [nè:mó:]

      b. Tone=H$_{Ventive}$ »   [[[né:mà:] -o:]$_{Ventive}$]$_{Imper}$ →
          Tone=LH$_{Imperative}$ *[né:mó:]

In short, Indexed Constraint Theory cannot connect the ranking between indexed constraints to the morphological layering of their respective morphological domains. Hausa does not allow the relative order of Ventive and Imperative formation to be reversed, but if it did, Indexed Constraint Theory would predict the same phonological outcome, regardless of layering, because of the fixed ranking of the indexed constraints. In a language like Turkish, where constructions with conflicting cophonologies can occur in either order, we have seen that the order of layering in a given word predicts the stress outcome. Interleaving is essential in such cases.

7.5 Bracket Erasure

An important question for any model of the morphology-phonology interface is whether phonological rules applying to one subconstituent can make reference to properties of embedded structure. The existence of juncture rules strongly suggests that the stem-affix or, in compounds, stem-stem boundary is available to phonological alternations operating on the cycle in which the juncture is created. However, there is little evidence to suggest that information about embedded junctures, i.e. granddaughter or niece constituents, is ever accessed. The figure in (62) is adapted from the discussion in Orgun and Inkelas (2002) of this question of "Bracket Erasure":

(62)

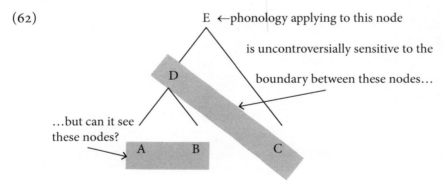

E ←phonology applying to this node

is uncontroversially sensitive to the

boundary between these nodes…

…but can it see these nodes?

Theoretical positions on Bracket Erasure vary. In the strictest approaches, phonology applying at node E, in (62), can never see nodes A and B. This is the approach taken by Chomsky and Halle (1968) and by Pesetsky (1979), who assume that internal morphological boundary symbols, or brackets, are "erased" at the end of each cycle of application of phonological rules. In the initial rollout of the theory of Lexical Morphology and Phonology, Kiparsky (1982b) proposes a weaker version of the Bracket Erasure principle in which internal brackets are erased only at the end of a morphological level. Among the facts motivating this weakening, Kiparsky cites the English construction converting nouns to verbs, e.g. *to pressure, to picture, to engineer, to reference,* all uncontroversially derived from the basic nouns *pressure, picture, engineer, reference.* The ubiquitous *to google* is a contemporary example. This conversion construction is inapplicable, Kiparsky observes, to nouns formed through level 2 suffixation: **to singer* (< *singer$_N$* < *sing$_V$*), **to freedom* (< *freedom$_N$* < *free$_{Adj}$*), **to championship* (<*championship$_N$* < *champion$_N$*). Kiparsky proposes that zero-derivation can apply only to unsuffixed bases:

(63)   *] X] Ø]

Citing evidence from stress neutrality, Kiparsky locates noun-to-verb conversion and suffixes like *-er, -dom, -ship* all at Level 2. In order for inputs like *singer, freedom, championship* to be ineligible for zero derivation, their internal structure must be visible. Therefore, Kiparsky argues, internal level 2 morphological boundaries must be visible to subsequent layers of level 2 morphology. By contrast, internal level 1 boundaries are *not* visible at level 2. Forms like *pressure, engineer, reference* all ostensibly are derived via level 1 suffixation (*press-ure, engin-eer, refer-ence*). These forms all undergo conversion without difficulty. Therefore, they must not violate the constraint in (63); therefore, it must be the case that internal brackets are erased at the end of level 1 so that derived level 1 outputs appear monomorphemic when scanned by level 2 morphology.

Another intermediate position between the strictest (cyclic Bracket Erasure) and the weakest (brackets always visible at all levels) is the Relativized Opacity Theorem (ROT) of Orgun and Inkelas (2002). According to this theorem, phonology and morphology have different degrees of access to internal morphological structure. With reference to the diagram in (62), phonology and morphology at node E can access daughter nodes D and C, and their boundary. Through a mechanism of type inheritance, the ROT also allows morphology access to the identities of morphological constructions contained in the daughter node D—but not directly to the boundary between A and B. Kiparsky's example of *pressure* → *pressure*$_V$ but *freedom* → **freedom*$_V$ is consistent with the ROT. The zero derivation construction has access to the information that *freedom* is derived by a level 2 construction, preventing its use.

The most permissive view of Bracket Erasure would grant phonology access to all morphological information, including boundaries, without restriction. This view is common in the Optimality Theory literature (e.g. McCarthy and Prince 1993). The question of Bracket Erasure and the relevance of morpheme boundaries has drawn little direct attention in Optimality Theory, and while many analyses allow phonological constraints to directly reference all embedded morphological structure, it is not always clear whether this follows from analytical necessity, from presentational convenience, or from the theoretical stance of many Optimality Theory practitioners that there are no cycles or levels, and that phonology interprets morphologically complex words as wholes.

Indexed Constraint Theory and Cophonology Theory differ from one another in their ability to accommodate principles of Bracket Erasure. Indexed Constraint Theory falls at the extreme in which all morphological structure is always visible; Cophonology Theory falls at the other extreme, in which only the boundary between the immediate daughters of a branching node can affect phonology.

In Indexed Constraint Theory, the presence of morphologically specific constraints in the single constraint ranking available for the language predicts that the effects of morphologically conditioned phonology are potentially global, rather than necessarily local. An indexed constraint can influence the phonology of morphological domains both smaller and larger than the one to which the constraint is indexed. A constraint referring to a deeply embedded morpheme could be ranked higher even than constraints referring to a word or phrase, producing rampant lexical and morphological exceptionality to word-level or phrasal phonological patterns. It is the apparent non-occurrence of precisely this type of phenomenon that prompted the original inclusion of Bracket Erasure principles in the theory of Lexical Morphology and Phonology. That Cophonology Theory derives the absence of such effects may this give it an explanatory advantage over Indexed Constraint Theory, which predicts them to occur.

So what is the evidence that phonology has what Shaw (2009) calls "inside access," or the ability to detect the derivedness, and internal morphological boundaries, of embedded constituents in morphologically complex words?

7.5.1 Access to internal roots and stems

Most of the compelling cases for the visibility of internal morphological constituent edges involve the root, or a stem. The root—and, specifically, the beginning of the root—is one of the elements typically identified in the literature as prominent. In Optimality Theory, it is one of the elements to which positional prominence constraints can refer (see e.g. Beckman 1997). We saw in Chapter 2 evidence that root faithfulness is often ranked higher than affix faithfulness. These facts may be all part of the same picture. Here, we will look at two examples in which the cophonology of a higher morphological layer makes explicit reference to a more deeply embedded morphological root or stem. Both are cases of accentuation in which accent (tone, in Tura; stress, in Musqueam) is attracted to the vicinity of the left edge of the root.

7.5.1.1 Tone assignment in Tura: evidence for internal stem visibility
Bantu languages are well known for patterns of tone assignment which target the verb stem, in some cases triggered by affixes outside the stem. Marlo (2008) presents a particularly elaborate case of this kind from the Bantu language Tura. Tense/aspect prefixes, themselves all inherently H-toned, are associated with patterns of H tone assignment which target specific positions in the stem. We will look at four of these in (64); numbering corresponds to that of Marlo (pp. 156–7). Pattern 4a (Remote Past, Remote Past Negative) assigns H to the first stem syllable (64a). Pattern 2b (Immediate Past Negative) assigns H to the second stem syllable (64b). Pattern 1a (Hesternal Perfective, Indefinite Future, Present) assigns H to the second stem syllable and spreads it all the way to the end of the stem (64c); Pattern 3b (Imperative singular) assigns H to the stem-final syllable (64d). The tense prefix triggering each stem tone pattern is underlined; stems are bracketed:

(64) a. Pattern 4a (illustrated with Remote Past prefix)   [Tura]
          β-aá-[téex-an-ir-a]   'they cooked for each other'
          y-á-mu-[líingeer-a]   'he watched him'
          y-ée-[tééx-er-a]   'he cooked for himself'

b. Pattern 2b (illustrated with Immediate Past Negative prefix)

sí-β-a-<u>xá</u>-[teex-án-ir-a] tá   'they did not just cook for each other'

sí-β-a-<u>xá</u>-mu-[liingéér-a] tá   'he did not just watch him'

sí-β-a-<u>xá</u>-ée-[liingéér-a] tá   'he did not just watch himself'

c. Pattern 1a (illustrated with Indefinite Future)

βa-<u>li</u>-[teex-ér-án-á]   'they will cook for each other'

a-<u>li</u>-mú-[liingéér-á]   'he will watch him'

a-<u>ly</u>-ee-[kaangúlúl-á]   'he will untie himself'

d. Pattern 3b (illustrated with Imperative singular)

[liingeer-á]   'watch!'

mu-[lííngeer-é]   'watch him!'

w-e-[káángulul-é]   'untie yourself!'

Tone assignment is clearly regulated by the location of stem boundaries, yet it is assigned by a prefix which is not always adjacent to the stem. In (64a–c), the triggering prefix is sometimes separated from the stem by another prefix, the 3sg object prefix *mu-* or the reflexive prefix *ee-*. These prefixes have no effect on the assignment of tone to the stem. Clearly, the left edge of the stem must be visible on the tense prefixation cycle in order for the various tense constructions to be able to assign tone in the correct location within the stem:

(65)

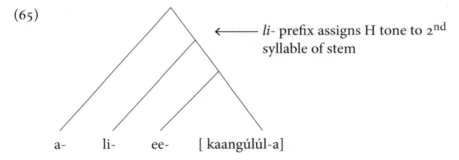

← —— *li-* prefix assigns H tone to 2nd syllable of stem

a-   li-   ee-   [kaangúlúl-a]

Similar effects, in which the left edge of the verb stem must be visible to tone assignment rules triggered in much larger domains, have been documented by Goldsmith (1992); Kidima (1990); Odden (1988, 1990, 1999); Hyman (1994); and many others. In a number of cases, researchers have suggested that the apparent visibility of internal constituents (roots or stems) to phonology applying in conjunction with outer layers of morphology is due not to the visibility of internal morphological boundaries per se but to prosodic structure. For example, on such accounts, the verb stem in Tura would map to a Prosodic Stem which, like syllable and foot structure, exists as a phonological structure and is accessible throughout the derivation. Analyses of this sort are best motivated when there is a demonstrable mismatch between morphological and prosodic constituency. Several such cases will be discussed in Chapter 10.

7.5.1.2 Musqueam stress assignment   Shaw (2009) argues that stress assignment in Musqueam (Salish; also known as *hən̓q̓əmin̓əm̓*) makes explicit reference to internally, potentially fairly deeply embedded, morphological boundaries. The essential morphological subconstituency that is relevant to Shaw's argument is given in (66). Every word contains a morphological root which, together with any suffixes, forms the MRoot domain. MRoots can combine with MStem-level reduplicative prefixes to form an MStem. MWord-level prefixes may also attach to MStems:

(66)   [$_{\text{MWord}}$ Nonreduplicative prefixes [$_{\text{MStem}}$ Reduplicative prefixes [$_{\text{MRoot}}$ Lexical root…]]]

According to Shaw (p. 244), "the salience of the internal MRoot edge is not eclipsed by prefixation within the two outer levels, contrary to what a theory assuming Bracket Erasure would predict."

Musqueam displays iterative trochaic stress foot assignment, as demonstrated by the words in (67), all of which are MRoot-initial. Disyllabic feet are the norm, as shown by the exhaustively parsed even-parity words in (67a) (p. 248); monosyllabic feet are constructed on a leftover syllable only if it contains a full vowel (67b) (p. 249). Leftover syllables with schwa vowels are left unfooted (67c) (p. 248):

(67)   a.   [Ɂəɫtən=aθən]   (Ɂə́ɫtə)(náθən)   [Musqueam]
              'eat=margin/edge = eat along the way'
              [ƛə[-l-]qt=əlʼ=eχən]   (ƛʼə́lqtə)(lʼéχən)
              'PL-long=connective=side = long arms'

        b.   [Ɂitət=ew̓txʷ]   (Ɂí.tə)(tów̓txʷ)
              'sleep-building = hotel'
              [k̓ʷin=əwinxʷ]   (k̓ʷə́.nə)(wíːnxʷ)
              'how.many=years = how many years'
              [ɫq̓ecəs=mat]   (ɫq̓ècəs)(mát)
              'five=bundles/kinds = five bundles of a kind'

c. [ʔənəxʷ-θət]   (ʔə́nəxʷ)θət
    'stop-REFL = stop oneself'
    [tey=əwəɬ]   (téyə)wəɬ
    'race=canoe/vessel = racing canoe'
    [k̓ʷec-ət-əs]   (k̓ʷécə)təs
    'see-T.TR-3TRSU = she/he saw him/her'

Musqueam stress is quantity-sensitive, to a point. If the initial syllable of the MRoot has a schwa but the second syllable has a full (heavy) vowel, footing will skip the initial syllable and start with the second, so that the full vowel can receive stress (p. 259). In the illustrative examples in (68), the initial MWord prefixes can be ignored, since MWord prefixes never participate in stress assignment. MRoots are demarcated by brackets:

(68)   tən-[səyə́m̓]   tən[sə(yə́m̓)
       'from the upper class'
       yə-xʷ-[k̓ʷəʔ=iqən̓]   yəxʷ[k̓ʷə(ʔíqən̓)
       'along-LOC-[ascend=belly] = belly up'

Foot-MRoot misalignment is limited to one syllable. An MRoot beginning with two schwa-vowelled syllables will, as in (67), foot those syllables.

While MWord prefixes have no effect on stress placement, MStem prefixes can be incorporated into feet. As Shaw demonstrates, the initial stress foot in a word may be misaligned from the left edge of the MRoot by at most one syllable, exactly when doing so enables the first foot to begin with a heavy (full vowel) syllable. This motivation can cause the first foot to occur one syllable before the left edge of the MRoot to include a prefix syllable with a full vowel. The examples in (69) involve reduplicative MStem prefixes: Plural (CVC-) and Progressive (CV-). Reduplicants have a full vowel if the root underlyingly has a full initial vowel (69a); otherwise, reduplicants have a schwa vowel (69b). As seen, prefixed reduplicants with a full vowel draw the stress foot one syllable leftward (69a), while those with schwa vowels do not (69b) (p. 262):

(69)   Words with MStem prefix: [Prefix [Root ...]_{MStem}]_{MRoot}
       Root UR   MRoot   Reduplicated MRoot

   a. MStem prefix with full vowel: misalignment with MRoot (left
       bracket shown)
       /p̓et̓ʼθ/   (p̓ət̓ʼθ)   (p̓é-[p̓ət̓ʼθ)   'sew (progressive)'
       /niw̓/   (níw̓-ət)   (ní-[n̓ə)w-ət   'advise him (prog.)'

/xakʷ/	(xá-k̓ʷ-ət)	(xá-[xə)k̓ʷ-ət	'bathe him (prog.)'
/k̓ʷaqʷ/	(k̓ʷáqʷ)	(k̓ʷáqʷ-[k̓ʷaqʷ])	'get hit (plural)'
/t'icəm/	(t'ícəm)	(t'íc-[t'ə)cəm	'swim (plural)'

b. MStem prefix with schwa vowel: no misalignment with MRoot

/t'pl'/	(t'ə́pəl')	t'ə-[(t'ə́pəl')	'play cards (prog.)'
/c̓q̓ʷ/	(c̓ə́q̓ʷ)	c̓ə-[(c̓ə́q̓ʷ)	'get pierced (prog.)'
		c̓ə́q̓ʷ-[(c̓ə́q̓ʷ)	'get pierced (plural)'
/pn/	(pə́n-ət)	pən-[(pə́n-ət)	'bury-TR (plural)'

Examples like those in (69a) are proof, according to Shaw, that stress footing operates within the MStem but is sensitive to the left edge of the MRoot. The fact that footing applies to material within the MStem domain, but refers to the internal MRoot domain, is, as Shaw argues, evidence against the invisibility of internal domain boundaries.

7.5.2 Root reduplication

A number of reduplication processes have been described as targeting the root morpheme in a complex word. In Chapters 5 and 6 it was suggested that at least some of these cases are really instances of infixing reduplication of the Prosodic Root, a constituent which is related to the morphological root but which is not isomorphic with it (see also Chapter 10). Insofar as prosodic structure is represented independently of morphological structure, the cases of apparent root or stem reduplication in Samala, Tagalog, Eastern Kadazan, and other languages are not true evidence that internal morphological structure is necessarily visible to outer morphological processes.

A particularly compelling example of root-seeking reduplication is presented in Stonham's (1994) analysis of Ditidaht (Nitinaht; South Wakashan). As Stonham shows, a number of suffixes in Ditidaht trigger reduplication and/or vowel lengthening in the root. In (70), roots are presented in square brackets and the affixes responsible for the reduplication are underlined. The forms in (70a–d) illustrate four different suffixes exerting reduplicative (and in some cases lengthening) effects on the roots they directly attach to; forms (70e–i) show that suffixes can intervene between the root and the (lengthening and) reduplication-triggering suffix (Stonham 1994: 41–55):

(70) a. i. [baλ]-aː   'tie-DUR = tied'
          ii. [baː-baλ]-'ad   'RED-tie-AT_THE_END = tied at the top'

      b. i. [ʔaλ]-iʔs   'two-ON_BEACH = two on the beach'
          ii. [ʔaː-ʔaλ]-iščχ   'two-IN_GROUP = two in a group'

      c. i. [hita]-quɫ   'LOC-AT_THE_FACE = face'
          ii. [hi-hiːta]-ʔačuɫ   'RED-LOC-AT_THE_FOOT = foot'

      d. i. [λ'ic]-ak   'white-DUR = whiteness'
          ii. [λ'i-λ'ic]-aƙuk   'RED-white-RESEMBLES = flour'

      e. i. [tuːχ]-apt   'scare-plant = Spruce var.'
          ii. [tuː-tuːχ]-ubq-   'RED-scare-plant-resembles = Juniper-
              aƙuk   leafed hair moss'

      f. [λ'uqʷ]-čiː-aːʔdɫ   'wide-PULL-ALONG_A_LONG_OBJECT = it
                                          was pulled along a long object'

          [λ'uː-λ'uqʷ]-aːʔdɫ-   'RED-wide-ALONG_A_LONG_OBJECT-VERY =
          aːp   (X's) legs are too big'

      g. [daʔuːk]-abaχsaː-s   'accompany-want-1SG.INDIC = I want to
                                          go along'

          [huː-hupʔ]-   'RED-help-want-tend_to = (X) is always
          abaχsaː-'eyk   wanting to help'

      h. [λ'iː-λ'iːdaqʷ]-   'RED-rubbery_skin-in layers-thing-
          aqs-ib-ƙuk   resembles = resembles whale's baleen =
                                          Dogtooth lichen'

      i. [č'i-č'it]-iyuːq-paɫ   'square'

These facts taken alone do not prove that a reduplication-triggering suffix needs direct access to the root. Without other prefixes to compete with, all a suffix would need to do is trigger prefixing reduplication of the base of affixation, regardless of its morphological complexity.

What suggests that the suffix is indeed targeting the root directly is the fact that when more than one reduplication-triggering suffix is present in a word, only one instance of reduplication takes place. In order for one suffix to know that another has "already" triggered reduplication, internal morpheme boundaries would appear to have to be visible (Stonham 1994: 49).

(71) [saː-saːtq]-'qsiɫ-aːp   '(X's) eyes were really itchy'

Stonham (2007: 120), citing Rose (1981: 341–2), presents similar facts from Nuuchahnulth (Nootka), which resembles its Wakashan relative in having bountiful suffix-triggered reduplication:

(72) a. [ƛ'uu-ƛ'uukʷ]-<u>anɬ</u>-<u>ap</u>   'RED-broad-AT_LEG-REALLY = 'his legs are really big'
      b. [puuc-puumaɬ]-<u>suɬ</u>-<u>ap</u>   'RED-itchy-AT_THE_EYE-VERY = he has really itchy eyes'
      c. [m̓aa-m̓aaɬ]-<u>'as</u>-<u>ap</u>   'RED-cold-AT_THE_WRIST-REALLY = he has really cold wrists'

Stonham shows that double reduplication is not ruled out across the board in either Ditidaht or Nuuchahnulth. On the contrary, reduplication which is *not* associated with particular suffixes, but which serves as the sole marker of a morphological category (e.g. distributive, plural) is permitted to co-occur with suffixal reduplication, leading to double reduplication. Ditidaht data (from Stonham 1994: 57) are given in (73a); Nuuchahnulth data (from Stonham 2007: 123) are given in (73b,c):

(73) a. ka-[ka-kawad]-ata<u>χ</u>
          DIST-RED-killer_whale-HUNT
          'hunt killer whales here and there'
      b. ʔi-[ʔi-ʔiš]-<u>č</u>-at-ee kʷan̓uxy̓ak
          PL-RED-chew_gum-ATTACHED TO-INAL-VOC urethra
          'you with your urethras fastened on with gum'
      c. hi-[hi-hiš]-cit-<u>sw̓anuʔ</u>-'aƛ-'at
          DIST-RED-BOTH-ON_SIDE-IN_ARMPIT-NOW-PASS
          'they grab them from both sides under the armpits'

Stonham provides a level ordering account in which reduplication processes are mutually exclusive within a level but may combine across levels. Suffix-triggered reduplication is restricted to level 1, and therefore may not iterate.

It would thus seem, as Stonham observes, that within a level, internal morpheme boundaries must remain visible. However, Stonham (1994: 52) argues even against this, offering a unification-inspired analysis of reduplication in which all that suffixes issue is the instruction to reduplicate. Multiple instructions unify, and are carried out only once, at the end of the level.

7.5.2.1 Morpheme Integrity in Kinande reduplication   Mutaka and Hyman (1990) argue that reduplication in Kinande must be directly sensitive to internal morphological boundaries because it respects a Morpheme Integrity Constraint. Verb reduplication in Kinande operates on the derivational stem, which consists of a root, some number (possibly zero) of derivational suffixes, and a final inflectional vowel (the "Final Vowel"). Reduplication is prefixation and disyllabic:

(74)   a. 'to bring'   e-ri-[twal-a]   e-ri-[twal-a]-[twal-a]   p. 86
        'let's beat'   tú-[húm-è]   tú-[húm-e]-[hum-è]   p. 93

Mutaka and Hyman's Morpheme Integrity Constraint, stated in (75) in abridged format, is evidenced by the behavior of stems which are longer than two syllables, either by virtue of being multiply suffixed or by virtue of containing a root which is larger than CVC.

(75)   Morpheme Integrity Constraint (abridged): If the whole of a morpheme cannot be successfully mapped into the bisyllabic reduplicative template, then none of the morpheme may be mapped.

As Mutaka and Hyman observe, reduplication copies either all of a morpheme or nothing. In (76a), copying the first two syllables of the stem would require splitting a morpheme. Instead the reduplicant copies just the CVC root and fleshes out the second syllable of the reduplicant with a default vowel, [a]. Evidence that this is a default vowel and not the -a which ends the complex stem *hum-ir-a* comes from the form in (76b), *hum-ir-e*. This stem ends in the subjunctive suffix -e, yet the reduplicant still assumes the shape *hum-a*:

(76)   a. 'to beat for'   e-ri-[hum-ir-a]   e-ri-[hum-a]-[hum-ir-a]   p. 92
                                         *e-ri-[hum-i]-[hum-ir-a]

        b. 'let's beat for'   tú-[húm-ir-è]   tú-[húm-a]-[hum-ir-è]   p. 94
                                         *tú-[húm-i]-[hum-ir-è]
                                         *tú-[húm-e]-[hum-ir-è]

Were it not for the reduplicated suffixed stems in (74), one might be tempted to analyze Kinande as having root reduplication, rather than stem reduplication. However, the forms in (77) argue against such an analysis. In (77a), a causative suffix is reduplicated along with the root and final vowel (Mutaka and Hyman 1990: 86); in (77b), an applicative suffix -er is reduplicated along with the preceding consonantal root and following final vowel (p. 92). Clearly, morphologically complex stems can reduplicate; the only condition is that the copied material be disyllabic and respect Morpheme Integrity:

(77)   a. 'to ask'   e-ri-[buɭ-y-a]   e-ri-[buɭ-y-a]-[buɭ-y-a]
       b. 'to grind for' e-ri-[sw-er-a]   e-ri-[sw-er-a]-[sw-er-a]

The fact that Kinande reduplication, which operates on stems, is sensitive to stem-internal morpheme boundaries is prima facie evidence that internal morphological structure must remain accessible to higher level processes. Kinande appears to be a clear counterexample to Bracket Erasure.

In fact, however, as Stonham (1994) foresaw, this conclusion is highly dependent on the theory of reduplication that is in use. In Chapter 5 we discussed the difference between phonological copying and morphological doubling approaches to reduplication. Morpheme Integrity is an obstacle to Bracket Erasure only on a phonological copying approach, in which the stem is fully constructed and then reduplicated. On a Morphological Doubling approach (see Chapter 5), the description of Kinande reduplication is quite different. Instead of building one stem (e.g. [hum-ir-a]), which is phonologically duplicated, the morphology constructs two stems (e.g. [hum-a], [hum-ir-a]), one of which ([hum-a]) meets the disyllabicity condition. The stems in any Morphological Doubling analysis are constrained to mean the same thing. If this constraint is outranked by the disyllabicity constraint on the first stem, the first stem will be prevented from including all of the morphemes that would make it semantically identical to the second stem. On such an approach, Morpheme Integrity translates into a local condition on how to fit morphemes into the prosodic template that characterizes the first stem. (On prosodic templates, see Chapter 4.)

7.5.2.2 Morphological access   Regardless of how strong the evidence is that phonology needs to access the internal structure of stems or words it applies to, there is also the question of whether morphology requires internal access. Although this question is somewhat beyond the scope of the present book, it does bear on the formulation or understanding of Bracket Erasure. Some of the most relevant phenonema are morphological selection for stems containing a particular affix, and affix metathesis or reordering.

7.5.3 Morphological selection for stem-internal affixes

In Tiene (Bantu), the "Final Vowel" in the indicative mood is /-a/ when it combines with monomorphemic stems (roots) and /-ɛ/ when it combines with morphologically complex (derived) stems (Hyman 2006; Ellington 1977). (/-ɛ/ assimilates to a preceding /ɔ/ or /a/, and /-a/ assimilates to a preceding /ɔ/, so only stems with the vowels /o/, /e/, and /u/ are shown here.)

(78)   [Root]-FV   [Root + Suffix/Infix]-FV   [Tiene]

   a. ból-a   'break'   ból-ek-ɛ   'be broken' (STATIVE)
   b. vwuny-a 'mix'   vwunyeŋ-ɛ   'be mixed' (STATIVE)
   c. yók-a   'hear'   yó-le-k-ɛ   'listen to' (APPLICATIVE)
   d. dum-a   'fun fast'   dun-em-ɛ   'run fast for'
                                               (APPLICATIVE)
   e. bót-a   'give birth'   bóot-ɛ   'give birth for'
                                               (APPLICATIVE)
   f. yóm-a   'become dry'   yó-se-b-ɛ   'make dry' (CAUSATIVE)
   g. lók-a   'vomit'   ló-se-k-ɛ   'cause to vomit'
                                               (CAUSATIVE)

A more elaborate version of this kind of sensitivity has been documented for English. In a study of English suffix combinatorics, Fabb proposes that the suffixes of English partition into four sets according to their sensitivity to the internal structure of the stem they attach to. Three of these sets are presented in (79):[8]

(79)   Types of suffix sensitivity to other morphemes in English (Fabb 1988)

Condition	Examples
Freely attach-ing suffixes	• *-able*, e.g. *manage-able, magnet-iz-able, indemn-ifi-able,* etc. • deverbal *-er*, e.g. *manag-er, magnetiz-er, indemn-ifi-er,* etc. • *-ness*, e.g. *happi-ness, sorrow-ful-ness, penni-less-ness,* etc.

---

[8] The fourth set, Fabb's "problematic" affixes, are all suffixes each of which can follow roots or any of a small set of suffixes; they illustrate the same kind of sensitivity as Set 2, just on a larger scale.

Suffixes which never attach to an already suf-fixed word	• denominal *-ful,* e.g. *sorrowful* • deverbal *-hood,* e.g. *motherhood* • deadjectival *-ify,* e.g. *solemnify* • *-ment,* e.g. *entrapment* • adjective-forming *-y,* e.g. *shadowy* (etc.)

Suffixes which attach outside one specific suffix only	• Noun-forming *-ary* may only follow *-ion,*
	  e.g. *revolutionary* (n.)
	• *-ic* may only follow *-ist,* e.g. *modernistic*
	• deadjectival *-y* may follow only *-ent,* e.g.
	  residency
	(etc.)

Orgun (1996) has argued that this type of sensitivity can be accounted for by appealing to stem type, rather than by referring directly to internal morpheme boundaries. The Tiene suffix /-ɛ/ needs to know only that the stem it attaches to is of the type "derived"; it does not need to know where the internal boundary is. The English suffix *-y* needs to know that the stem it attaches to is the type formed by the *-ent* construction, but it does not need to access the boundary between root and *-ent.* There is a large literature on stem type; see e.g. Carpenter (1992); Aronoff (1994); Koenig and Jurafsky (1995); Riehemann (1998, 2001), among many others.

Phenomena which would provide more convincing evidence of morphological access to internal morpheme boundaries would be interfixation or morpheme metathesis. It is not easy to prove that these phenomena occur; the evidence in any given case must be meticulously developed. One potential case of interfixation has been mentioned already in this chapter, namely the interfixation of the Cibemba applicative inside the causative suffix, *-i.* This case is discussed in Orgun (1996) and Hyman and Orgun (2005), who analyze the interfixation as simple infixation inside a stem-final superhigh vocoid. The case is ambiguous between interfixation and infixation.

Affix ordering is a promising area in which to look for evidence bearing on the question of whether morphological operations have access to the internal structures of the stems they operate on. (For a recent overview of affix ordering, see Rice 2011.) However, affix-ordering is a difficult question to talk about in a theory-neutral way. The question of how to analyze affix combinatorics is answered very differently in different theories of morphology. Some, like A-Morphous Morphology (Anderson 1992) and other realizational models (e.g. Stump 2001), posit no internal structure at all, and treat affix order as a matter of rule ordering rather than as the linear sequencing of morphs. Others, like Distributed Morphology (e.g. Harley and Noyer 1999), make much more internal structure available.

8

Morphologically derived environment effects

It has been widely observed that phonological alternations which are triggered in derived environments may fail to apply when the same phonological environment occurs in nonderived environments. This is especially true of phonological patterns which potentially neutralize phonological contrasts. The definition of what constitutes a morphologically derived environment is tricky. In the best-known type of example, the trigger and target of a phonological alternation fall on opposite sides of a morpheme boundary. Phonologically derived environments are those which exist only by virtue of the application of another phonological alternation. Alternations which are conditioned in either of these two ways are often referred to as "derived environment effects;" the non-application of such alternations morpheme-internally is known as "non derived environment blocking" (NDEB). This chapter will sample the range of morphologically derived environment effects and explore the variety of theoretical approaches taken to them over the past decades. The diversity of approaches is striking, as is the limited scope of each approach. The chapter concludes with a discussion of whether derived environment effects really constitute an internally uniform and distinct natural class of phenomena, or whether the so-called derived environment condition simply amounts to an acknowledgment that, as seen in Chapter 2, many lexical phonological patterns are morphologically conditioned.

8.1 A common type of morphologically derived environment effect

Many discussions of morphologically derived environment effects start with the classic and much-discussed example of Finnish Assibilation, an alternation by which underlying /t/ neutralizes to /s/ before the vowel /i/ (e.g. Keyser and Kiparsky 1984; Kiparsky 1993). Assibilation converts underlying /t/ to /s/ before /i/. It applies to /t-i/ sequences that are heteromorphemic (1a,b), but not to those wholly contained within a root (1b,c).

(1)   a. /halut-i/   → halusi   'want-3P.SG.PRET'   [Finnish]
         /halut-a/   → haluta   'want-INF'

      b. /tilat + i/ → tilasi   'order-3P.SG.PRET'   (*silasi)
         /tilat-a/   → tilata   'order-INF'   (*silata)

      c. /æiti/   → æiti   'mother'   (*æisi)

The Finnish Assibilation pattern has numerous direct parallels in other languages. In Polish, palatalization of /k/ to [č], /x/ to [š], and /g/ to [ž] occurs when the target consonant and triggering /front/ vowel are separated by a morpheme boundary (2a), but not when target and trigger both belong to the same morpheme (2b) (Łubowicz 2002). As shown in (2c), the same word can contain both a protected tautomorphemic sequence as well as a derived sequence that undergoes palatalization:

(2)   a. 'to step'   kro[k]-i-ć   → kro[č]-i-ć   [Polish]
         'to frighten'   stra[x]-i-ć   → stra[š]-i-ć
         'to weigh'   va[g]-i-ć   → va[ž]-i-ć

      b. 'kefir'   [ke]f'ir
         'jelly'   [k'i]śel
         'agent'   a[ge]nt
         'plaster'   [g'i]ps
         'chemist'   [xe]m'ik
         'hygienist'   [x'i]g'jeńistka

      c. 'chemist-DIM'   [xe]m'i[k]-ek   → [xe]mi'[č-e]k

In Hausa, coronal obstruents, including /t/, palatalize before front vowels across the stem-suffix boundary (3a), but not within morphemes (3b) (Newman 2000):

(3)   a. 'steal'   [sáːt-àː]   [Hausa]
         'steal' (before noun object)   [sàːtʃ-í]
         'steal' (before pronoun object)   [sàːtʃ-éː]

      b. 'street'   [tíːtiì]

The recurrence of this general pattern in so many languages has inspired attempts to capture it in the form of a single principle. Proposals for what exactly this principle might be vary widely. This is due partly to differing views as to the synchronic motivation of the effects, and partly because of differing understandings of the basic generalization. What kinds of phonological patterns are affected? What environments count as "derived?" How general is the condition cross-linguistically, or for that matter within any given language?

8.2 Which phonological patterns are subject to morphologically derived environment effects?

The parade example of a morphologically derived environment is that in which the trigger and target belong to different morphemes, and in which the relevant alternation neutralizes a phonemic contrast. This is the case for the Finnish, Polish, and Hausa examples given already: the alternation in question applies to a consonant only when the triggering vowel belongs to the following morpheme. It is the basis for McCarthy's (2003a: 21) definition of a morphologically derived environment effect:

(4) Morphologically derived environment effect: "a process that takes place only when its conditions are crucially met by virtue of material from two different morphemes."

This definition, and the examples in section 8.1, are the type of examples that traditional derived environment constraints and principles refer to (e.g. Kean 1974; Mascaró 1976; Kiparsky 1982b, 1985; Halle and Mohanan 1985; Kaisse and Shaw 1985; Pulleyblank 1986; Rubach and Booij 1990). Mascaró's (1976) original Strict Cycle Condition (SCC) connects derived environment effects with cyclic rules, i.e. those associated with the morphological production of derived or inflected words. Noncyclic rules, including those enforcing absolute patterns throughout the language, are exempt:[1]

---

[1] The full definition also includes phonologically derived environments: "A representation ϕ is derived w.r.t. rule R in cycle j iff ϕ meets the structural analysis of R by virtue of a combination of morphemes introduced in cycle j or the application of a phonological rule in cycle j." Phonologically derived environment effects will be discussed in section 8.3.

(5) Strict Cycle Condition (statement from Kiparsky 1982b:4):
    a. Cyclic rules apply in derived environments.
    b. *Definition:* A representation φ is derived w.r.t. rule R in cycle j
        iff φ meets the structural analysis of R by virtue of a combin-
        ation of morphemes introduced in cycle j.

Kiparsky (1985) amends the SCC so that it applies only to structure-changing rules, i.e. those potentially neutralizing lexical contrasts. This restriction exempts purely structure-building rules, such as syllabification, which applies to derived and nonderived words alike. "Strict Cycle" conditions constitute an important component of the theory of Lexical Morphology and Phonology (e.g. Kiparsky 1982b, 1985).

In subsequent sections, we will explore several schools of thought about why derived environment effects exist, and examine attempts to move beyond the condition in (5) in the pursuit of a deeper understanding of derived environment effects.

8.2.1 The Alternation Condition, or the role of lexical contrast

One school of thought attributes morphological derived environment effects to lexical contrast preservation. This approach goes back to Kiparsky's (1968) Alternation Condition. Later abandoned by Kiparsky (1982b) in favor of the Strict Cycle condition, the Alternation Condition captures the generalization that a given morpheme will undergo a neutralizing phonological alternation only if that morpheme appears both in contexts in which the alternation is applicable and in contexts in which the alternation is not applicable. The latter type of context is necessary in order for the underlying form of the morpheme to be recoverable by the learner. Two statements of the Alternation Condition, just prior to its being abandoned in favor of the Strict Cycle Condition, are given in (6), from Kiparsky (1982b: 148, 152):

(6) Obligatory neutralization rules cannot apply to all occurrences of
    a morpheme (*Alternation Condition*)

    or

    Obligatory neutralization rules apply only in derived environ-
    ments (*Revised Alternation Condition*)

Applied to Finnish Assibilation, it is easy to see conceptually that the Alternation Condition rules out the application of Assibilation within a root like *tilat*; since Assibilation is conditioned by a *ti* sequence, it would apply to the initial *ti* of every occurrence of *tilat*, violating the

Alternation Condition. The final *t* of *tilat*, by contrast, sometimes occurs in an Assibilation context and sometimes does not. As a consequence it may alternate between *t* and *s* without obscuring the lexical contrast between stem-final /t/ and /s/. Applying Assibilation to the heteromorphemic *t-i* sequence in /*tilat-i*/ is consistent with the Alternation Condition.

The Alternation Condition was ahead of its time, ill-suited for the rule-ordering phonological framework that was in use from the 1960s through the 1980s. However, recent developments in Optimality Theory make it possible to imagine implementing the insights behind the Alternation Condition in a more suitable framework.

For example, as will be discussed at greater length in Chapter 11, several proposals in Optimality Theory appeal to anti-homophony constraints to keep words distinct within an inflectional or derivational paradigm. Similar constraints could be appealed to in order to prevent potential lexical neutralization within a lexicon. Paradigmatic anti-homophony constraints in Optimality Theory involve not just input-output faithfulness and markedness for an individual word, but also the phonological relationships among words in a paradigm (e.g. McCarthy 2005; Downing 2005). Paradigmatic anti-homophony constraints have been invoked to account for cases in which an expected phonological alternation would merge two different suffixes, rendering the words they would form homophonous.

In Finnish, applying Assibilation to the initial *ti* in *tilat*- would merge /tilat-/ with hypothetical stem /silat-/. It does not matter to this argument whether the stem /silat/ actually exists; its potential existence could be enough, in this type of approach, to block the realization of input /tilat-/ as [silat]. The table in (7) shows roughly how lexeme merger would be computed, with hypothetical inputs /tilat/ and /silat/, in two representative morphological contexts, before the suffixes /-i/ and /-a/. If the Assibilation constraint *ti is satisfied completely, as in candidate paradigm set (7a), the paradigms for /tilat-/ and /tilas-/ merge. This is also true of candidate paradigm set (7c), in which only tautomorphemic /ti/ becomes [si]. The choice thus comes down to candidate paradigm set (7b), in which all /ti/s surface intact, and candidate paradigm set (7d), in which only heteromorphemic /ti/ is converted to [si]. The latter does a better job of satisfying the ban on *ti, and wins the competition.

(7)

	Input lexemes	Possible morphological contexts and constraint satisfaction			
	/tilat/, /silat/	/-i/	/-a/	Distinct paradigms	*ti
	a) all /ti/→[si]	[silasi], [silasi]	[silata], [silata]	*!	
	b) no /ti/→[si]	[tilati], [silati]	[tilata], [silata]		***!*
	c) tautomorphemic /ti/→[si]	[silati], [silati]	[silata], [silata]	*!	**
☞	d) heteromorphemic /t-i/→[si]	[tilasi], [silasi]	[tilata], [silata]		**

In sum, implementing the idea behind the Alternation Condition requires reference to the entire derivational and inflectional paradigm of every root in the language. The global paradigm distinctiveness constraint is violated only if two stems would merge phonologically in every word in which they could be used. Optimality Theory makes it possible to state the paradigm distinctiveness constraint that would be needed. But evaluating it is unwieldy in practice, especially in languages with rich recursive morphology in which the number of words that could contain a given stem is extremely large and potentially unbounded. Such a theory would need to trim the set of words that would have to be considered in a principled way.

8.2.2 Comparative Markedness

A more tractable approach to the problem of derived environment effects in Optimality Theory has been offered in the form of Comparative Markedness, a proposal introduced by McCarthy (2003a) in which markedness constraints can distinguish between structures which are present in the input ('old markedness') and structures which are present only in the output ('new markedness'). In this theory, derived environment effects are a result of ranking the ban on new markedness high, and the ban on old markedness low, with faithfulness to the relevant structure ranked between new and old markedness. This ranking ensures that old marked structures will be preserved, while new ones will not be created.

With some involvement of paradigmatic constraints, Comparative Markedness can be extended to derived environment effects of the type discussed in section 8.1. As an illustration, McCarthy discusses an example from Korean which is structurally parallel to those in section 8.1. McCarthy (2003a) cites Ahn (1988). The data in (8) come from Cho (2009: 466).

(8)   a. Palatalization across derivational suffixes   [Korean]

mat-i	→	maci	'eldest-NML = eldest son'
kut-i	→	kuci	'be_firm-ADV = firmly'
put^h-i	→	puc^{h}i	'adhere-CAUS = to affix'
hɛ tot-i	→	hɛ toci	'sun rise-NML = sunrise'
mut-hi	→	muc^{h}i	'bury-PASS = to be buried'

      b. Across inflectional suffixes

pat^h-i	→	pac^{h}i	'field-NOM= field'
kyət^h-i	→	kyəc^{h}i	'side-NOM = side'
pat^h-ita	→	pac^{h}ita	'field-COP = to be the field'

      c. Inapplicable morpheme-internally

əti	'where'
titi-ta	'to tread'
t^{h}i	'blemish'
nɨt^{h}i-namu	'zelkova tree'

McCarthy's insight into derived environment effects is that a structure in an affixed word is targeted for repair only if it is "new," i.e. not present in the output form of the unaffixed base of that word. In Korean, the relevant structure is Ci (where "C" is a coronal obstruent). The morphologically derived form /mat-i/ contains /ti/, which is able to be repaired (to [ji]) because it does not occur as [ti] in the faithful output candidate of the base /mat/. By contrast, the /ti/ sequence in /mati/ does surface as [ti] in the fully faithful output candidate, and qualifies as an "old" markedness violation.

McCarthy proposes a constraint family PAL which bans [ti] (or [t^{h}i]) strings; appropriately ranked above consonantal faithfulness constraints, PAL induces palatalization. PAL has at least three members. IO-$_N$PAL penalizes output [ti] sequences which are not present in the fully faithful candidate (i.e. "new" markedness). IO-$_O$PAL penalizes output [ti] sequences which *are* present in the fully faithful candidate (FFC) (i.e. "old" markedness). And finally, OO-$_N$PAL penalizes output [ti] sequences which are not present in the output of the unaffixed base of a derived word ("new" by virtue of morphology).[2] Of course, OO-$_N$PAL is relevant only to derived words. As seen here, when OO-$_N$PAL is the only PAL constraint to rank above IDENT, [ti] will surface intact when internal to a root, but will be forced to change to [si] otherwise. Two tableaux are presented in (9): one (in (9a)) for /pat^h/, so that the output of the base of affixation is known, and one (in (9b)) for /pat^h-i/, the derived form in question:

(9)

a.	/pat^h/	OO-$_N$PAL	IDENT	IO-$_O$PAL
☞ (FFC)	pat^h			
	pac^h		*!	
b.	/pat^h-i/	OO-$_N$PAL	IDENT	IO-$_O$PAL
(FFC)	pat^hi	*!		*
☞	pac^hi		*	

By contrast, a monomorphemic input like /mati/ (10), which has no related simple form, cannot violate OO-$_N$PAL. There is no related form with respect to which the output [ti] sequence in [mati] could be considered "new," and hence OO-$_N$PAL is not relevant in this case. Instead, IDENT holds sway and prevents palatalization from occurring:

(10)

	/mati/	OO-$_N$PAL	IDENT	IO-$_O$PAL
☞ (FFC)	mati			*
	maji		*!	

---

[2] A drawback of this proposal is that morphologically bound roots also exhibit non-derived environment blocking, even though bound roots are not able to surface unaffixed as words and therefore have no isolation output form for OO-$_N$Pal to refer to. While the root /pat^h/ in example (9) is a noun, which can surface unaffixed as a word in Korean, (8a) shows that exactly the same derived environment pattern is observed by Korean verb roots, all of which are morphologically bound.

The essential insight behind Comparative Markedness has points of contact with the "neighborhood preservation" insight of Itô and Mester (1996) and the sequential faithfulness proposal of Burzio (1997), who proposed that some derived environment effects could be due to a markedness constraint which is inhibited by faithfulness to input sequences instantiating the relevant structure. Only "new" sequences, i.e. those created by the morphology (or phonology) and not present in the input, escape sequential faithfulness. For these types of account to work, it is necessary to assume, as is common in Optimality Theory, that stems and affixes are not linearized in the input. A conceptually closely related proposal is that of Cho (1998), who proposes that grammatical constraints faithfully preserve input transitions between input segments (see also Bradley 2002). Segments which surface adjacent across a morpheme boundary do not have input transitions to be faithful to, on the assumption that stems and affixes are linearized only in the output. For Korean, Cho (1998) proposes a constraint (OVERLAP) requiring gestural overlap. When the gestures for /t/ and a following /i/ overlap, the release of /t/ is affricated, causing palatalization. OVERLAP is blocked by transitional faithfulness, which applies only to tautomorphemic /ti/ sequences.

Slightly farther afield but still related is the proposal of Łubowicz (2002), who proposes to conjoin markedness and faithfulness constraints so that markedness constraints will apply only if the environment is new, in the sense that the morphology creates an environment to which faithfulness constraints are not applicable. What unites all of these approaches is the insight that there is more lexical information to be faithful to within morphemes than across morpheme boundaries.

8.3 Phonologically derived environment effects

An asset of Comparative Markedness is its ability to extend to phonologically derived environment effects, which have been thought to be linked to morphologically derived environment effects. A phonologically derived environment effect is one in which some component of an alternation—either the target or some component of the triggering environment—must be derived, i.e. nonidentical to its input form. As an example of a phonologically derived environment effect, McCarthy (2003a) cites the epenthesis of glottal stop in Makassarese. This case is illustrated in (11a), where [ʔ] is epenthesized at the end of vowel-final words—but only in case the final vowel is itself epenthetic. [ʔ] is *not* epenthesized following underlying vowels (11b):

(11)   a.   /rantas/   rántasaʔ   'dirty'   [Makassarese]
             /teʔter/   téttereʔ   'quick'
             /jamal/   jámalaʔ   'naughty'
        b.   /lompo/   lómpo   (*lómpoʔ)   'big'

The motivation for vowel epenthesis in (11a) is the restriction in Makassarese against word-final consonants other than [ʔ]. The words in (11a) thus undergo epenthesis of both a vowel and [ʔ].

Łubowicz (2002), citing Rubach (1984), identifies another instance of a phonologically derived environment, in Polish (Łubowicz 2002: 244). As seen already, the phonological rule of First Velar Palatalization applies at morpheme boundaries. Łubowicz argues that palatalization interacts with another process, Spirantization, which applies only to derived palatals. Stem-final /g/ is converted by Palatalization to [ǰ], which Spirantization then turns into [ž], producing alternations like those in (12a). However, as shown in (12b), *underlying* stem-final /ǰ/ does not undergo Spirantization. Łubowicz attributes this to a condition on Spirantization that it apply only in phonologically derived environments, i.e. only to palatals which are derived but not underlying:[3]

(12)

a.	Palatalization and Spirantization of underlying /g/:		
	'to weigh'	/va[g]+i+ć/	(→ va[ǰ]+i+ć)	→ [va[ʒ]+i+ć]
	'pole (dim.)'	dron[g]+ ĭk +ɨ	(→ dron[ǰ]+ek)	→ drõw̃[ž]+ek
	'snow-storm'	śńe[g]+ĭc+a	(→śńe[ǰ]+ic+a)	→ śńe[ž]+ic+a
b.	No Spirantization of underlying /ǰ/:		
	'bridge (dim.)'	briǰ[ǰ]+ ĭk+ɨ		→ briǰ[ǰ]+ek
	'jam'	[ǰ]em+ɨ		→ [ǰ]em

Kiparsky (1982b, 1993) points to Assibilation in Finnish as at least one example of a derived environment alternation that can be triggered

---

[3] The data for 'weigh', based on Hall (2006: 806), correct an apparent typographical error in Łubowicz (2002).

by either type of derived environment. Assibilation is triggered not just by the underlying *i* vowel of a suffix, as seen earlier in (1), but also by *i* vowels that result from word-final raising of underlying *e*:

(13)   Word-final raising of /e/ to /i/ triggers Assibilation in Finnish
       /vete/ 'water' → |veti| → [vesi]

The final [i] in [vesi] is tautomorphemic with the preceding [t], but is eligible to trigger Assibilation by virtue of being *phonologically* derived.

Comparative Markedness handles these cases with ease; in fact, the analysis is much simpler than that given to morphologically derived environment effects, which require paradigmatic output-output constraints. McCarthy's Comparative Markedness analysis of Makassarese provides a straightforward illustration. Recall from (11) that in Makassarese, words ending in derived (epenthetic) vowels are subject to final consonant epenthesis, while words ending in underlying vowels are not. On McCarthy's analysis, the restriction of [ʔ] epenthesis to phonological derived environments results from the ranking of old markedness over new markedness. ₙFINAL-C is violated by word-final vowels which are "new," i.e. not present in the fully faithful candidate (FFC). ₒFINAL-C is violated by word-final vowels which are "old." In example (14), the input /rantas/ ends in a buccal consonant and must undergo vowel epenthesis; this is effected by markedness and faithfulness constraints ranked higher than ₙFINAL-C. What is relevant is that the epenthetic vowel is "new," relative to the FFC, and thus triggers a violation of ₙFINAL-C:

(14)

	/rantas/	*(constraints banning stem-final buccal consonants and consonant deletion, metathesis, etc.)*	ₙFINAL-C	DEP	ₒFINAL-C
(FFC)	rantas	*!			
	rantasa		*!		
☞	rantasa?			*	

By contrast, a vowel-final input does not violate ₙFINAL-C and, therefore, does not trigger consonant epenthesis:

(15)

	/lompo/	(constraints banning stem-final buccal consonants, consonant deletion, etc.)	$_N$FINAL-C	DEP	$_O$FINAL-C
☞ (FFC)	lompo				*
	lompo?			*!	

The ability of Comparative Markedness to unify morphologically and phonologically derived environment effects is promising, and in its analysis of morphologically derived environments in particular, Comparative Markedness clearly makes contact with the insight behind the Alternation Condition.

8.4 A broader range of morphologically derived environment effects

In this section we turn to a set of examples for which the Strict Cycle Condition and Comparative Markedness cannot readily account, for the reason that they involve phonological patterns which are prosodic and non-structure-changing, and because they cannot be described in terms of morpheme boundaries. Nonetheless, they share with more classic examples the property that the phonological pattern in question takes effect in morphologically derived words but not in monomorphemic ones. In this sense they belong in the range of phenomena for which a theory of morphologically derived environments should account. After a brief tour of the examples, we will proceed to a discussion of their theoretical significance.

8.4.1 Tohono O'odham

Fitzgerald (1997) and Yu (2000) call attention to a nonderived environment blocking (NDEB) effect in Tohono O'odham in which stress applies differentially to morphologically complex and monomorphemic words. In Tohono O'odham, main stress is assigned to the initial syllable. Secondary stress occurs on every other following syllable. The NDEB effect is observed only in words with an odd number of syllables (odd-parity words). *Nonderived*, i.e. monomorphemic, words prohibit final stress, and thus prohibit secondary stress from being assigned finally:

(16)   Nonderived words   [Tohono O'odham]
       kí: 'house'
       pí:ba   'pipe'
       ʔásugal   'sugar'
       pákoʔòla   'Pascola dancer'

By contrast, derived words permit final secondary stress. As seen in
(17), stress falls on the final syllable of odd-parity words and on the
penultimate syllable of even-parity words, as predicted by the basic
stress rule of the language, plus the provision that final stress is
permitted in morphologically complex words. This pattern cannot be
attributed to inherent stress on suffixes. Suffix syllables are stressed if
they fall into odd-numbered syllable positions, and not otherwise.
Furthermore, (reduplicative) prefixation (17b) induces final stress
exactly when the resulting word is odd-parity (Fitzgerald 2001: 943–6):

(17)   a. Suffixation
          ʔásugàl-t   'to make sugar'   (odd parity)
          hím-ad   'will be walking'   (even parity)
          číkpan-dàm   'worker'   (odd parity)
          músigò-dag   'to be good at being a   (even parity)
                              musician'
          pímiàndo-màd   'adding pepper'   (odd parity)

       b. Reduplication
          tó-toñ   'ants'   (even parity)
          pí-pibà   'pipes'   (odd parity)
          mú-msigò   'musicians'   (< músigo 'musician')
          sí-sminǰùl   'cemeteries'   (< síminǰul 'cemetery')
          pá-pkoʔòla   'Pascola dancers'   (even parity)

       c. Suffixation and reduplication
          hí:-him-àd   'will be walking, pl.'   (odd parity)
          hí-hidòḍ-a   'the cooking, pl.'   (even parity)
          há-haiwàñ-ga-kàm   'ones having cattle'   (odd parity)

The placement of stress on a final syllable in the odd-parity forms in
(17) is not directly conditioned by a nearby morpheme boundary; this
is shown most straightforwardly by prefixed forms like *pí-pibà* (17b), in
which the stressed final syllable is tautomorphemic with the preceding
syllable. Rather, as both Fitzgerald and Yu emphasize, it is the fact of

morphological complexity that renders a stem or word eligible to receive final stress.

8.4.2 Turkish minimality

Another sticky complication for the standard definition of "morphologically derived environment" in (4) is presented by Inkelas and Orgun (1995), in an analysis of prosodic minimality effects in Turkish. As initially observed by Itô and Hankamer (1989), Turkish imposes a disyllabic minimality condition on morphologically complex words. Monomoraic words are immune from the condition, as seen in (18a). However, derived words are subject to it. Turkish possesses several consonantal suffixes, including the 1st and 2nd person possessive suffixes (/-m/, /-n/) and the passive suffix (/-n/). In combination with CV roots, these suffixes would produce monosyllabic words. Both Itô and Hankamer (1989) and Inkelas and Orgun (1995) found that speakers reject such words as ungrammatical (18b,c):[4]

(18)   Turkish minimality (Itô and Hankamer 1989, Inkelas and Orgun 1995)

   a. *do* 'note *do*'   *ham*   'unripe'
      be 'letter *b*'   *yen*   'alight (!)'
      ye 'eat (!)'   *ok*   'arrow'
      de 'say (!)'

   b. **do-m* 'note *do*-1SG.POSS'   cf.   *araba-m*   'car-1SG.POSS'
      *be-n 'letter *b*-2SG.POSS'   cf.   *elma-n*   'apple-2SG.POSS'

   c. **de-n* 'say-PASS = be said (!)'   cf.   *anla-n* 'understand-PASS'
      *ye-n 'eat-PASS = be eaten (!)'   cf.   *çine-n* 'chew-PASS'

Some of the starred morpheme combinations in (18b,c) can be used as stems of longer words, e.g. *de-n-ecek* 'say-PASS-FUT= will be said', *ye-n-miş* 'eat-PASS-EVID = was apparently eaten' (Orgun and Inkelas 1995: 772). As words, however, they are rejected as subminimal. Their ungrammaticality is due entirely to their phonological size, as shown by the semantically parallel polysyllabic forms to their right in (18b,c).[5]

---

[4] Vowel length in some of the nominal roots in (18b) varies across speakers (see Inkelas and Orgun 1995). Short vowels are depicted here, but speakers with long vowels in these roots also reject the monosyllabic suffixed forms.

[5] The nominal forms in (18b) cannot, according to Inkelas and Orgun (1995), be rescued by further suffixation. This suggests that the disyllabic size condition is actually a condition on stems, rather than words. See section 8.6.1.

In this case, the environment in which the minimal size constraint applies does contain a morpheme boundary. However, this case differs from the examples in section 8.1 in not conforming easily to the definition in (4). First, there is not a clear phonological process involved; the issue is whether or not a word is grammatical, not whether or not an alternation applies. Second, there is not a clear sense in which the environment for the imposition of the minimal size constraint is crucially provided by two morphemes. In contrast to the /t-i/ sequence in Finnish /halut-i/, which Assibilates to [si], the monosyllabicity of /do-m/ is equally true of its base, /do/. Only if the Turkish minimal size condition is redescribed as a condition holding only on CVC words does /do-m/ crucially meet the condition by virtue of being morphologically derived, in contrast to a CVC monosyllable like /ham/.

8.4.3 Japanese minimality

Japanese resembles Turkish in that it has been described as imposing a bimoraic minimal size condition in derived environments. As observed by Itô (1990) (and discussed in Chapter 4), Japanese has a number of monomoraic (CV) roots which can be used, intact, as roots (19a). However, when short roots are used in compounding constructions (19b–d), the result is bimoraic. Truncation also results in minimally bimoraic stems (19e,f), supporting the status of the bimoraic stem as canonical in the language:

(19)   a. *su* 'vinegar', *na* 'name', *no* 'field', *ka* 'mosquito', *te* 'hand', *ha* 'tooth', etc.
   b. Telephone numbers: *ni* '2', *go* '5', etc.; but *nii-goo-*... '54...'
   c. Weekday compounds: /ka-do/ → *kaa-doo* 'Tuesday-Saturday'; cf. *ka-yoobi* 'Tuesday', *do-yoobi* 'Saturday'
   d. Verb root reduplication: *ne* 'sleep'→ *nee-nee* 'while sleeping'; cf. *tabe* 'eat' → *tabe-tabe* 'while eating'
   e. Shortening of loanwords: *herikoputaa* → *heri* 'helicopter', *amachua* → *ama* 'amateur'
   f. Compound abbreviations: *waado purosessaa* → *waa puro* 'word processor'

Itô (1990: 219) characterizes these facts as morphologically derived environment effects: "[T]he minimal bimoraic template in Japanese is enforced on *derived* forms only, not on *underived* forms. Truncated hypocoristics and abbreviated loanwords are *derived* from their base forms, and hence must satisfy the minimality requirement of the language."

8.4.4 Interim summary

The three examples just discussed pose challenges to a Comparative Markedness approach. In Turkish, the constraint at issue is a ban on monosyllabic words (say, DISYLL). A Comparative Markedness of Turkish analysis parallel to that offered for Korean would invoke OO-$_N$DISYLL, expressing the idea that "old" monosyllabicity can be tolerated but "new" monosyllabicity cannot.

According to McCarthy's definition of "new" OO markedness, OO-$_N$-DISYLL would be violated if the locus of violation—a monosyllabic word—is not present in the output of the unaffixed base. It is true that [fam], as the potential output of input /fa-m/, is not present in [fa], the output of its base, /fa/. However, both [fa] and [fam] are monosyllabic words, and in that sense both violate the simple markedness constraint DISYLL equally. Affixation of /-m/ does nothing to change the syllable count of /fa/; the monosyllabicity of [fam] is not "new" in that sense.

It may be possible to define OO-$_N$DISYLL in such a way that [fam] would violate it, and successfully extend Comparative Markedness to Turkish minimality.

However, Tohono O'odham poses an even more challenging problem for Comparative Markedness. The data in (16) require that in monomorphemic words, the constraint compelling binarity (FTBIN) outranks the requirement that syllables be footed (PARSE), with the effect that final odd syllables are left unfooted:

(20)

	/musigo/	FTBIN	PARSE
☞	(músi)go		*
	(músi)(gò)	*!	

Unexpectedly, derived words with an odd number of syllables, as in (17), require the final odd syllable to be footed with a degenerate foot, in violation of FT-BIN. Either these degenerate feet or the unfooted syllables in nonderived odd-parity words must be the marked structures on which a Comparative Markedness analysis would have to rest.

If degenerate feet are the marked structure in question, then the relevant constraints would be OO-$_N$FTBIN ("Assign a violation to a degenerate foot which is not present in the output form of the unaffixed base of the word") and IO-$_N$FTBIN ("Assign a violation to a degenerate foot on a syllable which lacks a degenerate foot in the input"). OO-$_N$FTBIN and IO-$_N$FTBIN would be violated by a suffix with a degenerate foot, since the suffix (and therefore its foot) is not present in the unaffixed base of the word. But these constraints are not helpful, since suffixes *do* acquire degenerate feet in odd-parity words:

(21)   *Suffixed odd-parity word*
       Unaffixed base: (číkpan)

	/čikpan-dam/	IO-$_N$FTBIN	PARSE	IO-$_O$FTBIN	OO-$_N$FTBIN
💣*	(číkpan)dam		*		
(☞)	(číkpan)(dàm)	*!		*	*

OO-$_O$FTBIN ("Assign a violation to a degenerate foot which is present in the output form of the unaffixed base of the word") is not relevant here; since nonderived words do not possess degenerate feet (see (20)).

Perhaps the marked structure in question is the unfooted final syllable, not the footed final syllable. In that case, it would be nonderived words that possess marked structure. PARSE would be split into several constraints: OO-$_O$PARSE would penalize unparsed syllables that are present (and unparsed) in the unaffixed base, while OO-$_N$PARSE would penalize "new" unparsed syllables, i.e. syllables which are present but footed in the unaffixed base, such that their lack of parsing in the affixed word would be considered "new." As seen in (22)–(24), suffixation and prefixing reduplication can cause "new" parsing violations by assigning a different footing than that found in the unreduplicated base:

(22)   *Reduplicated odd-parity base, with syncope*
       Unaffixed base: (músi)go

	/RED-musigo/	OO-$_O$PARSE	OO-$_N$PARSE	FTBIN	IO-$_N$PARSE
	(mú-msi)go	*!			* go
☞	(mú-msi)(gò)			* (gò)	

(23) *Suffixed odd-parity base, even-parity output*
Unaffixed base: (músi)go

	/músigo-dag/	OO-$_O$PARSE	OO-$_N$PARSE	FTBIN	IO-$_N$PARSE
☞	(músi)(gò-dag)				
	(músi)go-(dàg)	*! go		* (dàg)	* go
	(músi)(gò)-dag		*! dag	* (gò)	* dag
	(músi)go-dag	*! go	* dag		** go, dag
	(músi)(gò)-(dàg)			*!* (gò),(dàg)	

(24) *Reduplicated even-parity base, odd-parity output*
Unaffixed base: (píba)

	/RED-piba/	OO-$_O$-PARSE	OO-$_N$PARSE	FTBIN	IO-$_N$PARSE
	(pí-pi)ba		*! ba		* ba
☞	(pí-pi)(bà)			* (bà)	

While successful so far, this analysis fails in the case of simple suffixation to an even-parity base. Because suffixes are, by definition, not present in the output of the unaffixed base, Output-Output (OO) constraints comparing affixed and unaffixed forms of the same base are blind to the metrical properties of suffixes. As seen in (25), the outcome of suffix footing is therefore decided by FTBIN and IO-$_N$PARSE, which, as seen earlier in (20), leave final odd-parity syllables unfooted:

(25)   *Suffixed even-parity base, odd-parity output*
       Unaffixed base: (číkpan)

	/číkpan-dam/	OO-$_O$PARSE	OO-$_N$PARSE	FTBIN	IO-$_N$PARSE
☞*	(číkpan)dam				*
(☞)	(číkpan)(dàm)			*! (dàm)	

It might be possible, by using additional constraints or considering additional constraint interactions, to get Comparative Markedness to work in these cases, but the insight behind Comparative Markedness is much less transparently applicable here than in the cases of segmental alternations at the stem-suffix boundary, as in Korean.

In addition, by generating morphologically derived environment effects through output-output faithfulness to the outputs of unaffixed stems, Comparative Markedness requires that the unaffixed stem be able to surface as a word, which is not always possible in languages that require all stems to be inflected, or which possess bound roots (see footnote 2).[6]

In sum, the effects in section 8.4 are derived environment effects in the sense that they apply only to morphologically complex words, a property they share with the derived environment effects in section 8.1. However, standard definitions of derived environment effects, and the principles designed to capture that type of derived environment effect into phonological theory, capture only the type in section 8.1.

8.5 Cophonological approaches to NDEB effects

A number of derived environment effects emerge directly from the architecture of Cophonology Theory without requiring a dedicated

---

[6] By the same logic that suffixes in Tohono O'odham are exempt from OO constraints on 'old' vs. 'new' markedness in stems, Comparative Markedness predicts that affix-internal phonotactics could be identical to the phonotactics of unaffixed bases; nonderived environment blocking is thus predicted to occur within affixes as well as within roots. Finnish, for example, could have a suffix *-ti*, which (lke root-internal *-ti*) flouts Assibilation; Korean could have a suffix *–mati* which (like root-internal *ati*) violates Palatalization; Turkish could have a suffix *-aka* which, like root internal VGV, defies Velar Deletion. To my knowledge this prediction has not been systematically tested, so its correctness is unknown.

principle of the kind in (5). This is a virtue insofar as Cophonology Theory can account for some of the cases that Comparative Markedness and the Strict Cycle Condition cannot. However, the insight offered by Cophonology Theory is very different, raising the question of whether a single insight, or theoretical approach, can unify all morphologically derived environment effects.

As seen in Chapter 2, Cophonology Theory associates a cophonology with each individual morphological construction. With regard to any phonological pattern P, the word-building morphological constructions within a language can be separated logically into two subsets: those associated with cophonologies which enforce P (call this subset M_P), and those associated with cophonologies which do not enforce P (call this subset $M_{\neg P}$). Words not containing any of the morphological constructions in M_P will never be subject to pattern P. This gives rise to a prediction in Cophonology Theory: nonderived words often evade patterns imposed within complex words. No principle or constraint ranking in the grammar is needed to achieve this NDEB result.

Precisely this kind of cophonology analysis has been given in the literature for the type of effects discussed in section 8.4, as we will now see.

8.5.1 Turkish minimality

The immunity of monomorphemic roots to the disyllabic minimal size condition observed to hold (for some speakers) in Turkish is due, according to Inkelas and Orgun (1995), to the fact that disyllabic minimality is associated with a subset of suffixation constructions. According to Inkelas and Orgun, who divide Turkish suffixation constructions into four ordered morphological levels, the constructions crucially imposing disyllabic minimality are those at levels 2 and 3. Inkelas and Orgun, working in the general Level Ordering framework of Lexical Morphology and Phonology (e.g. Kiparsky 1982b, 1985; Mohanan 1986), use the term "level skipping" to refer to the fact that monomorphemic roots do not show the effects of the disyllabic size condition, imposed only in levels 2 and 3; roots not undergoing morphology at levels 2 and 3 simply skip those levels altogether.

In Cophonology Theory, level skipping does not have to be stipulated; the prediction that a word is not subject to phonological effects that are morphologically tied to suffixes not appearing in that word falls out automatically from the structure of the theory. The basic analysis is sketched below, with Inkelas and Orgun's levels 2 and 3 recast as "Stem" phonology:

(26)

root	Stem-level affixation	Word construction	
	(cophonology imposes disyllabic minimality)	(cophonology does not impose minimality)	
/elma/	[elma-m]$_{Stem}$	[el'mam]$_{Word}$	'my apple'
/fa/	*[fa-m]$_{Stem}$	N/A	(intended: 'my note *fa*')
/fa/	N/A	['fa]$_{Word}$	'note *fa*'

Roots and (derived) Stems both must be licensed by the Word construction in order to enter the syntax as words. Like each suffixation construction, the Word construction is associated with a cophonology. Applying to monomorphemic roots and derived stems alike, the Word cophonology assigns default final stress and ensures that words are properly syllabified.

8.5.2 Tohono O'odham stress

A cophonological account is offered by Yu (2000) for the derived environment effects on secondary stress assignment in Tohono O'odham discussed in section 8.4.4. Yu proposes that word-formation constructions (prefixation, suffixation, truncation) are associated with cophonologies permitting final secondary stress, whereas the Word-level construction is associated with a cophonology that does not assign final secondary stress. As a result, monomorphemic roots—which undergo only the Word cophonology—are subject to nonfinality, but derived words are not.

(27)

root	Affixation constructions	Word construction	
	(cophonology assigns secondary stress to all non-initial odd-parity syllables)	(cophonology will not assign final stress, though will preserve input stress even if final)	
ʔasugal	N/A	[ʔásugal]	'sugar'
ʔasugal	[ʔásugàl-t]	(input stress preserved, no change)	'to make' sugar'
piba	[pí-pibà]	(input stress preserved, no change)	'pipes'

An alternative account of Tohono O'odham is offered by Fitzgerald (1997, 2001, 2002), who proposes a Morpheme-to-Stress Principle (MSP) (Fitzgerald 2001: 950) that requires each morpheme to contribute (at least) one stressed mora to the representation. This principle permits a monomorphemic trisyllabic word like *ʔasugal* to surface with only one stress but requires a bimorphemic trisyllabic word like *pi-piba* to have two stresses. The cophonological and the MSP approaches share the insight that morphological and phonological complexity go together. The advantage of the cophonological approach is that this correlation follows from the basic architecture of the theory, rather than requiring the addition of a new constraint.

The cophonological account does not, however, offer much direct insight into the examples of derived environment effects in section 8.1. Consider, for example, the Finnish form /tilat-i/ → *tilasi (*silasi)*. Clearly, Assibilation either applies to stems formed by the suffix *-i* or is a general rule applying to all words; one of those statements must be true, in order for the alternation to apply to /tilat-i/. But in either case, a cophonological account cannot, absent an additional principle, explain why the tautomorphemic /ti/ does not also undergo Assibilation. Cophonologies may account for some derived environment effects, but an additional principle is still needed to account for others.

8.5.3 Interim summary

Comparative Markedness works well for some morphologically derived environment effects, while cophonological interactions capture others. But thus far, no single theoretical construct has been shown to apply insightfully to all cases of morphologically derived environment effects.

Perhaps more significantly, neither Comparative Markedness nor cophonological approaches predict nonderived environment blocking as a necessity. Both can describe it, but both are also equally capable of describing situations in which it does not hold. For example, embedded in the broader context of Optimality Theory, Comparative Markedness is capable of describing "anti-Polish." Recall from (2) that in real Polish, velars palatalize before front vowels only in derived environments. The initial velar in *[x]em'ik* 'chemist' is protected, but the stem-final velar palatalizes before a front vowel: *[x]em'ik + ek → [x]emi'[č]-ek*. This follows, as shown in (28), from the same ranking that generated the Korean derived environment effects back in (9) and (10):

(28)

a.	/xem'ik/	OO-_NPal	Ident -IO	_OPal
☞	xem'ik	(N/A)		*
	šem'ik	(N/A)	*!	

b.	/xem'ik ek/ (cf. [xem'ik])		Ident -IO	_OPal
	šem'ikek	*!	*	*
	šem'iček		*!*	
	xem'ikek	*!		**!
☞	xem'iček			*

Demoting Ident-IO and adding OO-_NPal will produce Anti-Polish, in which palatalization applies only stem-internally and not at the stem-suffix boundary. In (29a), _OPal >> Ident-IO ensures palatalization on the stem cycle. In (29b), Ident-OO ensures that stems are preserved intact under suffixation, protecting stem-final /k/ and resulting in the failure of stem-final palatalization.

(29)

a.	/xem'ik/	IDENT-OO	OO-$_N$PAL	$_O$PAL	IDENT-IO
	xem'ik	(N/A)	(N/A)	*!	
☞	šem'ik	(N/A)	(N/A)		*

b.	/xem'ik ek/ (cf. [šem'ik])	IDENT-OO	OO-$_N$PAL	$_O$PAL	IDENT-IO
☞	šem'ikek		*		*
	šem'ič=	*!			**
	xem'ikek	*!	*	*	
	xem'ič=k	*!*	*	*	*

Cophonology Theory generates the same prediction. It would, for example, be completely possible in Cophonology Theory to generate anti-Tohono O'odham, in which root-final odd-numbered syllables receive secondary stress, but none is assigned to the final syllables of derived stems. This pattern would ensue if Tohono O'odham had a root cophonology assigning final stress, but suffix- and word-level co-phonologies did not do so. On such an analysis, root-final odd-syllable stress would be "grandfathered" into words that otherwise do not exhibit morpheme-final stress.

Phonological restrictions holding only in roots but not in derived words are a common occurrence. The fact that theories of nonderived environment blocking can predict them is therefore a virtue. Viewed in context, NDEB is just one type of morphologically conditioned phonology.

8.6 Is NDEB a valid cross-linguistic generalization?

We have by now seen an impressive variety of approaches devoted to capturing the generalization that some if not all lexical phonological patterns—particularly, those which are contrast-neutralizing—are blocked from applying in nonderived environments. But the phenomena are diverse, and no single approach posited thus far seems to work for all of them.

A reasonable conclusion in the face of this situation would be that further effort is required to isolate exactly the right principle that will capture the morphologically derived environment generalization.

However, an alternative approach is to wonder if the diversity of proposed solutions reflects the fact that the putative morphologically derived environment generalization is not, in fact, real.

Past theoretical approaches to NDEB effects have assembled a variety of examples of derived environment effects in different languages, assuming that each is representative of the phonological grammar of its language and seeking a broad principle to account for all of them. However, several recent studies that look more deeply into a range of morphological constructions in a single language lead to questions about the robustness or accuracy of the derived environment generalization. We examine findings from Turkish, Japanese, and Finnish in the following sections.

8.6.1 Turkish minimality revisited

Recall from (18) the derived environment effect in Turkish in which monomorphemic words may be monosyllabic but derived monosyllables are rejected as ungrammatical. The example illustrating this principle for verbs used the consonantal passive suffix -*n*, repeated in (30b). However, as noted by Itô and Hankamer (1989) and Inkelas and Orgun (1995), the consonantal aorist suffix -*r* attaches to these same CV roots without problem (30c):

(30) a. de   'say!'   [Turkish]
          ye   'eat!'

      b. *de-n* 'say-PASS = be said (!)'   cf. *anla-n* 'understand-PASS'
          ye-n 'eat-PASS = be eaten (!)'   cf. *çine-n* 'chew-PASS'

      c. de-r   'eat-AOR = says'
          ye-r   'eat-AOR = eats'

Thus the Turkish minimality condition is morphologically restricted, rather than holding in all morphologically derived environments in the language.

8.6.2 Japanese minimality revisited

As discussed in Chapter 3 and section 8.4.3 of the present chapter, Itô (1990) characterizes the bimoraic minimal size condition in Japanese as a property of morphologically derived stems, rather than as a condition holding on all words. The reason for this is not only the existence of monomoraic monomorphemic words, but also the details of the morphological conditioning of the bimoraic size condition.

As shown here, bimoraicity is imposed on the bases to which the diminutive -chaN attaches, even though the derived stem (with -chaN) would be at least bimoraic in any case (31a) (Itô 1990:214). However, bimoraicity is not imposed on the CV bases of affixation in (31b), in which morphemes corresponding to the days of each week are suffixed with a morpheme meaning 'day'. The same morphemes do undergo vowel lengthening in (31c), when compounded with each other (repeated from (19); Itô 1990: 225):

(31) a. *mariko* (girl's name) → *mari-chaN ~ riko-chaN ~ mako-*
       chaN ~ maa-chaN

   b. *nichi-yoobi*   'Sunday'
      getsu-yoobi   'Monday'
      ka-yoobi   'Tuesday'
      sui-yoobi   'Wednesday'
      moku-yoobi   'Thursday'
      kiN-yoobi   'Friday'
      do-yoobi   'Saturday'

   c. *kaa-moku*   'TuTh'
      getsu-kaa   'MoTu'
      kaa-doo   'TuSa'

Itô proposes a morphological distinction in Japanese between roots and stems. Stems are subject to a bimoraic minimal size requirement, but roots are not. Morphological constructions differ as to whether their inputs can be bare roots (as in (31b) or whether they are stems (as in (31a) and (31c)). In (32), from Itô 1990 (p. 227), -chaN suffixation requires a base which is a Stem, subject to the bimoraic ('F' for foot) requirement. In (32b), a constructed example, a suffixed monomoraic root undergoes suffixation directly; to account for the lack of lengthening, it is necessary to assume that the -*yoobi* suffix attaches to roots, not stems:

(32)   a.

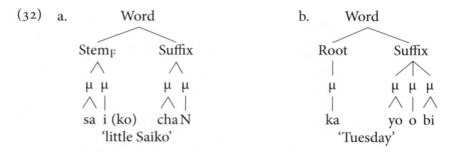

Most constructions discussed by Itô are of the type in (32a), which require the base of affixation (or the members of compounds) to be stems, but not all are. Thus the sensitivity of the bimoraic size condition is not to derived environments in general, but to the derived category Stem, in particular.

8.6.3 Finnish (Anttila 2006)

Finnish Assibilation, the parade example of an NDEB effect, turns out to be both morphologically *and* lexically conditioned in ways that go beyond the simple clarity of any derived environment generalization. As Anttila (2006) observes, citing Karlsson (1983: 343), Assibilation applies before some /i/-initial suffixes and not before others:

(33)   a. Suffixes triggering Assibilation   [Finnish]
           /vuote-i-nA/   → vuosina   'year-PLURAL-ESS'
           /huuta-i-vAt-kO/   → huusivatko 'shout-PAST-3P.PL-
                                             QUE'
           /uute-impA-nA/   → uusimpana   'new-SUPERLATIVE-
                                             ESS'

       b. Suffixes not triggering Assibilation
           /lentä-ime-n/   → lentimen   'fly-INST-GEN'
           /tunte-isi/   → tuntisi   'feel-COND'

       c. Suffix that optionally triggers Assibilation
           /vete+inen/ →   vesinen ~   'water-ADJ =
                             vetinen   watery'

Anttila, building on earlier observations by Karlsson, proposes a Stratal OT analysis in which Assibilation applies in derived environments at the Stem level. However, this is not the whole story. While all the suffixes that normally trigger Assibilation are Stem-level, some of those which do not trigger Assibilation also belong to this level, based on other evidence Anttila marshals for the Stem category. Furthermore, the adjective-forming /-inen/ triggers Assibilation only optionally. And finally, as Anttila points out, there is considerable lexical variation. Some of this Anttila convincingly attributes to metrical size: in verbs, "the longer the stem, the more common Assibilation" (p. 905). However, in nouns, length is not a predictor of Assibilation. Rather, Assibilation applies to a small class of e-final nouns (34a) but otherwise is not applicable to nouns at all (34b) (Anttila 2006: 912):

(34) a. /vete-i-nä/   vesinä   'water-PL-ESS'
          /vuote-i-na/   vuosina   'year-PL-ESS'
          /tuhante-i-na/   tuhansina   'thousand-PL-ESS'

      b. /sota-i-na/   sotina   'war-PL-ESS'
          /vuota-i-na/   vuotina   'skin-PL-ESS'
          /varastoi-nti-i-en/ varastointien   'store-ing-PL-GEN'
          /egypti-i-en/   Egyptien   'Egypt-PL-GEN'

In sum, while Assibilation appears restricted to morphologically derived environments, it does not apply in all morphologically derived environments, even within the Stem domain where it appears most active. Once the Assibilation environments are stipulated, the derived environment condition becomes, at best, a redundant necessary condition; it is not sufficient to predict Assibilation.

8.7 Derived environment effects: a distinct phenomenon, or just morphologically conditioned phonology?

The discussion of Turkish, Japanese, and Finnish in section 8.6 suggests that at least some apparent derived environment effects are morphologically conditioned beyond simple reference to morphological derivedness. In Turkish, for example, it is not the case that a general principle rules out all derived monosyllables; it depends upon the morphological construction involved. This observation raises the question of how general morphologically derived environment effects truly are. Thus far, we have looked at several hand-picked examples of derived environment effects, and another set of hand-picked counterexamples in the same languages. How are we to interpret these contradictory examples? The only way to know for sure the extent to which the derived environment generalization is real is to explore deeply within languages. Section 8.8 offers exactly that, for one alternation, namely velar deletion in Turkish. Ideally, of course, one would explore all of the morphophonemic alternations in a given language, but that is beyond the scope of this chapter.

8.8 Case study: Turkish velar deletion

Turkish velar deletion is simultaneously a textbook example of, and a puzzling counterexample to, any general statement of the derived environment condition.

Like the three alternations discussed in section 8.1, Turkish velar deletion applies at the stem-suffix juncture, deleting stem-final /k/ and /g/ that are rendered intervocalic by the addition of a suffix (e.g. Lewis 1967: 10–11; Zimmer and Abbott 1978; Sezer 1981; Göksel and Kerslake 2005: 14–17):[7]

(35)

	(nominative)	Dative /-A/	Genitive /-In/
/bebek/ 'baby'	[be.bek] *bebek*	[be.be.e] *bebeğe*	[be.be.in] *bebeğin*
/katalog/ 'catalog'	[ka.ta.log] *katalog*	[ka.ta.lo.a] *kataloğa*	[ka.ta.lo.un] *kataloğun*
/matematik/ 'mathematics'	[ma.te.ma.tik] *matematik*	[ma.te.ma.ti.e] *matematiğe*	[ma.te.ma.ti.in] *matematiğin*

Deleted velars are represented in the orthography as "ğ". In some dialects they are pronounced as velar glides.[8] Data reported here reflect the

---

[7] As noted by Sezer (1981) and confirmed experimentally by Zimmer and Abbott (1978), velar deletion does *not* apply when the preceding vowel is long (e.g. /meraːk/ 'curiosity'; *meraːk-a* (dative), not **meraː-a*).

[8] Even in standard Istanbul Turkish, "ğ" is sometimes reported to manifest as a weak labial glide between round vowels or as a weak palatal glide between front vowels (e.g. Lewis 1967: 5; Göksel and Kerslake 2005: 8). These glides are arguably excrescent, the expected phonetic transitions between vowels rendered adjacent by velar deletion, as in *diğer* [dier] 'other'.

variety of Turkish represented in TELL (Turkish Electronic Living Lexicon), in which the velars are phonologically and phonetically deleted.[9] This is the pattern reported by Lewis (1967), Zimmer and Abbott (1978), and Sezer (1981), as well.

Velar deletion applies to stem-final consonants when rendered intervocalic by suffixation, as in (35), but not to consonants which are intervocalic within a root morpheme, as in (36):

(36) 'lawyer'   *avukat*   /avukat/   [a.vu.kat]
     'motion'   *hareket*   /hareket/   [ha.re.ket]
     'railway car' *vagon*   /vagon/   [va.gon]
     'insurance'   *sigorta*   /sigorta/   [si.gor.ta]

Examples with medial and final velars illustrate the condition most clearly: the stem-final velar deletes in the derived VGV environment, but the tautomorphemic VGV sequence is unaffected:

(37) 'street'   /sokak/   [sokak]
     'street-ACC' /sokak-I/   [so.ka.ɯ]
     'street-DAT' /sokak-E/   [so.ka.a]

Although Turkish velar deletion appears to be a classic morphologically derived environment effect, closer inspection shows that no matter how "derived environment" conditioning is defined, Turkish velar deletion does not actually meet its description. The alternation turns out to be highly morphologically and phonologically conditioned. The fact that environments in which the rule does apply are derived is a side effect of its other morphological and phonological conditioning, not the explanatory factor.

8.8.1 The part of speech condition

Turkish velar deletion is morphologically general in the sense that it applies to native and loan vocabulary (Zimmer and Abbott 1978) and to monomorphemic and complex stems alike. As seen here, velar deletion applies regularly to velars at the ends of monomorphemic

---

[9] Except where otherwise noted, Turkish data cited in this paper come from TELL (Turkish Electronic Living Lexicon; <http://linguistics.berkeley.edu/TELL>). Larry Hyman, Aylin Küntay, Anne Pycha, Eser Taylan, and Bengisu Rona contributed helpful discussion of the Turkish facts discussed in this section, which is based in part on Inkelas (2012).

(38a) and complex stems (38b), with one systematic exception: it does not apply to verb roots (38c).

(38)

	UR		cf.	
a.	/bebek-A/	[be.be.e]	/bebek/	[be.bek]
	'baby-DAT'			
	/arkeolog-I/	[ar.ke.o.lo.u]	/arkeolog/	[ar.ke.o.log]
	'archeologist-ACC'			
b.	/gel-AdʒAk-A/	[ge.le.dʒe.e]	/gel-AdʒAk /	[ge.le.dʒek]
	'come-FUT-DAT'			
	/git-TIk-I/	[git.ti.i]	/git-TIk/	[git.tik]
	'go-REL-ACC'			
	/anla-mAk-A/	[an.la.ma.a]	/anla-mAk/	[an.la.mak]
	'understand-INF-DAT'			
	/badem-CIk-I/	[ba.dem.dʒi.i]	/badem-CIk/	[ba.dem.dʒik]
	'almond-DIM-ACC = tonsil (acc.)'			
c.	/gerek-Ijor/ 'be necessary-PROGRESSIVE'	[ge.re.ki.jor]	*[ge.re.i.jor]	
	/bɯrak-r/ 'drop out-AORIST'	[bɯ.rakɯ.jor]	*[bɯ.ra.ɯ.jor]	
	/birik-en/ 'gather-REL'	[bi.ri.ken]	*[bi.ri.en]	
	/gerek-AdʒAk/ 'be necessary-FUT'	[ge.re.ke.dʒek]	*[ge.re.e.dʒek]	

Standard descriptions of Turkish velar deletion state that it applies to substantives only. This statement is consistent with the data in (38b) if the /k/-final suffixes in (38b) are assumed to produce nominal forms;

this is a reasonable assumption given that infinitival and participial forms inflect like nouns, despite their verbal semantics. From a synchronic perspective, the part of speech restriction is arbitrary. Both noun and verb roots combine with vowel-initial endings; both permit the full inventory of consonants and vowels; both exhibit a range of monosyllabic to polysyllabic size and permit both open and closed syllables. Verb roots are on average much shorter than noun roots, due in large part to the many polysyllabic nominal loans, and exhibit almost no long vowels or geminate consonants, but these statistical differences cannot account for minimal pairs like *gerek* 'need (n.)' and *gerek* 'be necessary (v.)':

(39)

Nominal	gerek	'need'
	gere-i	'need-ACC'
	gere-e	'need-DAT'
	gere-in	'need-2SG.POSS'
Verb	gerek-mek	'be_necessary-INF'
	gerek-ir	'be_necessary-AOR'
	gerek-ijor	'be_necessary-PROG'
	gerek-en	'be_necessary-REL'

8.8.2 Suffix-initial velars

While velar deletion applies in the / ... VK-V ... / environment, it does not apply in the / ... V-KV/ environment, even though both environments are morphologically derived. In each case, the VKV environment for velar deletion is heteromorphemic. However, the / ... V-KV/ environment—a velar-initial suffix combining with a vowel-final base—never triggers velar deletion. Turkish has a number of velar-initial suffixes, varying in productivity. Some, like -(y)ken 'while being', exhibit a palatal glide-initial allomorph when combining with vowel-final bases, e.g. *öğrenci* 'student', *öğrenci-yken* 'while a student'. Others combine directly with vowel-final bases, creating a V-KV environment. These never undergo velar deletion. Three of the quite productive *k-* and *g*-initial suffixes are illustrated in (40). (The suffix glossed as -GON combines with numbers and forms polygon names.)

(40)

-gen	altıgen	/altɯ-gen/ 'six-GON' = 'hexagon'	[al.tɯ.gen]
	yedigen	/jedi-gen/ 'seven-GON' = 'septagon'	[je.di.gen]
-gil-ler	baklagiller	/bakla-gil-lAr/ 'beans-GRP-PL' = 'pulses'	[bak.la.gil.ler]
	amcasıgiller	/amca-sI-gil-lAr/ 'uncle-3POSS-GRP-PL' = 'his/her uncle & family'	[am.dʒa.sɯ.gil.ler]
-ki	seneki	/sene-ki/ 'year-REL' = 'this year's'	[se.ne.ki]
	adadaki	/ada-DA-ki/ 'island-LOC-REL' = 'the one on the island'	[a.da.da.ki]

8.8.3 Lexical exceptions

There are some lexical exceptions to stem-final velar deletion; these vary somewhat by speaker. According to Zimmer and Abbott (1978), most exceptions are loanwords, but not all loanwords are exceptions. Loans from Persian or Arabic (e.g. *mahrek, mahreki* 'orbit(-ACC)', p. 36) are more likely to resist velar deletion than are loans from European languages, which tend to be adapted to the rule (e.g. *kartotek, kartoteği* 'card catalogue(-ACC)', p. 37). Zimmer and Abbott also note a tendency for younger speakers to apply velar deletion to loans more regularly than older speakers. In the TELL database, about 90% of velar final nominal stems exhibit velar deletion, which is comparable to the rate at which speakers applied the rule in an experimental study by Zimmer and Abbott. The following forms are drawn from the 100 or so lexical exceptions that exist in the TELL database, representing just one speaker. Considerable variation across the population is expected with these forms:

(41)

orthography	(Nominative)	Accusative (/-I/)	gloss
antartik	antartik	antartiki	'Antarctic'
lâik	laik	laiki	'secular'
orak	orak	orakɯ	'sickle'
patolog	patolog	patologu	'pathologist'
salacak	saladʒak	saladʒakɯ	'slab for corpse'
Selanik	selaːnik	selaːniki	'Salonika'
sinagog	sinagog	sinagogu	'synagogue'
sitreptokok	sitreptokok	sitreptokoku	'streptococcus'

In conclusion, when we take into account the part of speech condition, the fact that suffix-initial velars are immune, and the existence of lexical exceptions, it is clear that while being in a morphologically derived environment may be necessary for an intervocalic velar to undergo velar deletion, it is not sufficient.

8.8.4 Phonologically derived environments

Turkish exhibits high vowel epenthesis to break up consonant clusters which cannot be syllabified (see e.g. Lewis 1967: 9–10; Göksel and Kerslake 2005: 18; Hankamer 2011; Taylan 2011). Vowel epenthesis can create the environment for velar deletion.

Final consonant clusters that cannot occur as codas are broken by epenthesis when no vowel-initial suffix is available with which the stem-final consonant can syllabify (see e.g. Clements and Sezer 1982):

(42)

UR	(Nominative)	Locative (/-DA/)	Accusative (/-I/)	gloss
/nesr/	[ne.sir]	[ne.sir.de]	[nes.ri]	'prose'
/film/	[fi.lim]	[fi.lim.de]	[fil.mi]	'film'
/keʃf/	[ke.ʃif]	[ke.ʃif.te]	[keʃ.fi]	'exploration'
/kutB/	[ku.tup]	[ku.tup.ta]	[kut.bu]	'pole'

The vowel-zero alternation must be analyzed as epenthesis, in order to capture distinctions like that between *koyun* 'sheep' and *koyun* 'bosom'. The former has a fixed CVCVC structure, while the latter is underlyingly CVCC, with epenthesis:

(43)

	(Nominative)	Accusative	gloss
/kojn/	[ko.jun] *koyun*	[koj.nu] *koynu*	'bosom'
/kojun/	[ko.jun] *koyun*	[ko.ju.nu] *koyunu*	'sheep'

The relevance of epenthesis is that it can produce new VKV environments. Whether velar deletion applies in these is a test of whether the phonologically derived environment condition is applicable to Turkish velar deletion. The answer is mixed: epenthetic vowels trigger velar deletion when epenthesis itself applies in a morphologically derived environment, but not when epenthesis splits up consonants belonging to the same root.

As seen in (44), epenthesis into root consonant clusters does not trigger velar deletion, even though the resulting intervocalic environment for the velar is derived, not underlying:[10]

(44)

UR	(Nominative)	Locative (/-DA/)	Accusative (/-I/)	gloss
/akl/	[a.kɯl]	[a.kɯl.da]	[ak.lɯ]	'intelligence'
	akıl	*akılda*	*aklı*	
/aks/	[a.kis]	[a.kis.te]	[ak.si]	'reflection'
	akis	*akiste*	*aksi*	
/fikr/	[fi.kir]	[fi.kir.de]	[fik.ri]	'idea'
	fikir	*fikirde*	*fikri*	
/hükm/	[hy.kym]	[hy.kym.de]	[hyk.my]	'judgment'
	hüküm	*hükümde*	*hükmü*	

[10] Some of the epenthetic vowels in (44) are disharmonic (front, even though the stem-final vowel is back). Normally, epenthetic vowels harmonize with the preceding vowel. Some roots, however, trigger suffix disharmony. As noted by Lewis (1967: 19–20) and Clements and Sezer (1982), inter alia, some Turkish roots, mainly loans from Arabic and Persian, exceptionally take front vowel harmony on suffixes even though the root vowels are all back. Examples include *saat* 'hour', *saat-i* 'hour-ACC', *mentol* 'menthol', *mentol-ü* 'menthol-ACC', as well as the disharmonic examples in (44). Whatever triggers disharmony on suffixes also affects the quality of epenthetic vowels.

By contrast, epenthesis *does* trigger velar deletion when it applies as a result of the suffixation of consonantal suffixes to consonant-final stems, as seen in (45):

(45)

UR	(Nominative)	1sg.possessive (/-m/)	Accusative (/-I/)	gloss
/bebek/	[be.bek]	[be.be.im]	[be.be.i]	'baby'
	bebek	*bebeğim*	*bebeği*	
/inek/	[i.nek]	[i.ne.im]	[i.ne.i]	'cow'
	inek	*ineğim*	*ineği*	
/sokak/	[so.kak]	[so.ka.ɯm]	[so.ka.ɯ]	'street'
	sokak	*sokağım*	*sokağı*	
/bak-adʒak/	[ba.ka.dʒak]	[ba.ka.dʒa.ɯm]	[ba.ka.dʒa.ɯ]	'look-FUTURE'
	bakacak	*bakacağım*	*bakacağı*	
/gel-me-dik/	[gel.me.dik]	[gel.me.di.im]	[gel.me.di.i]	'come-NEG-PPL'
	gelmedik	*gelmediğim*	*gelmediği*	

In a form like /bebek-m/ 'my baby', a rule ordering account would posit the following derivation:

(46)   /bebek-m/
    Epenthesis   bebekim
    Velar deletion   bebeim

The interaction of epenthesis and velar deletion produces a situation of notable twofold derivational opacity: velar deletion eliminates the environment for epenthesis, rendering epenthesis opaque on the surface (over-application), and velar deletion produces the environment that normally would trigger glide epenthesis (underapplication). What is important for our purposes here, however, is that the same vowel epenthesis process triggers velar deletion when the target consonant is absolutely stem-final (45) but not when the target velar is root-internal (44). This suggests that the condition of being a phonologically derived environment is not sufficient to trigger velar deletion.

One possible explanation for the inapplicability of velar deletion in the root-internal epenthesis environments in (44) is that the target velar follows the first root vowel. In addition, velar deletion is subject to a very robust condition that the participating stem be polysyllabic (Lewis 1967: 10–11; Zimmer and Abbott 1978; Sezer 1981; Inkelas and Orgun 1995; Göksel and Kerslake 2005: 16). Deletion is the norm for polysyllabic roots but the exception for CVC roots:

(47)

gloss		(Nominative)	Dative (/-A/)	1sg.possessive (/-m/)
'root'	/køk/	[køk]	[kø.ke]	[kø.kym]
		kök	köke	köküm
'affix'	/ek/	[ek]	[e.ke]	[e.kim]
		ek	eke	ekim
'arrow'	/ok/	[ok]	[o.ka]	[o.kɯm]
		ok	oka	okɯm
'league'	/lig/	[lig]	[li.ge]	[li.gim]
		lig	lige	ligim
'fugue'	/fyg/	[fyg]	[fy.ge]	[fy.gym]
		füg	füge	fügüm

Only two CVC roots (çok 'a lot', gök 'sky') undergo velar deletion (çoğ-u 'a lot-ACC', göğ-ü 'sky-ACC').[11]

Thus Turkish phonology and morphology conspire to produce the situation in which phonology could, in a morphologically *nonderived* environment, produce a phonologically derived environment; in this situation, velar deletion is not triggered. The phonologically derived

---

[11] Interestingly, CVC monosyllabic roots are also systematic exceptions to plosive voicing alternations (e.g. *sahip, sahib-e* 'owner-(-DAT), but *ip, ip-e* 'string(-dat))' (see e.g. Lewis 1967: 11; Göksel and Kerslake 2005: 10; Inkelas and Orgun 1995). As expected, the monosyllable-final, nondeleting velars in (47) do not show voicing alternations. It may be that whatever exempts velars at the ends of monosyllabic CVC roots from undergoing velar deletion (and voicing alternations) may be protecting these internal velars as well. Plosives rendered intervocalic by epenthesis into /CVCC/ roots also do not show voicing alternations; a typical example is /metn/ → *metin ~ metn-i* 'text(-DAT)'. See Inkelas and Orgun (1995: 780–90) for discussion.

environment condition is neither necessary nor sufficient for the application of velar deletion.

8.9 Morphologically derived environment effects in the context of morphologically conditioned phonology

A close inspection of velar deletion in Turkish shows that there is little evidence to support the intuition that neutralization alternations should apply in derived environments but not in nonderived environments. In Turkish, all of the environments in which velar deletion applies are morphologically derived, but velar deletion does not apply in all morphologically derived environments. Some of the environments are phonologically derived, but velar deletion does not apply in all phonologically derived environments. The derived environment condition both undergenerates and overgenerates predictions of velar deletion applicability; it is simply not a useful principle in this case:

(48) Conclusions re velar deletion

1.	Is morphological derivedness necessary, for velar deletion to apply?	Yes
2.	Is phonological derivedness necessary?	No
3.	Is morphological derivedness sufficient?	No
4.	Is phonological derivedness sufficient?	No

This case study generates a broad question: is there *any* phonological pattern whose morphological conditioning can be captured perfectly by the generalization that the environment must be morphologically derived, or is it always the case that highly specific morphological conditioning is required (in addition)? Given that highly specific morphological conditioning is necessary, is a general statement like the Derived Environment Condition actually needed?

The result of this study, and indeed the consensus emerging from many past attempts to formalize derived environment effects (e.g. Kiparsky 1993; Inkelas 2000; McCarthy 2003a; Anttila 2009) is that morphological "derived environment effects" are not a unitary phenomenon. Instead, they seem to emerge from a combination of interacting factors, rather than requiring a single principle. Anttila (2009) concludes that derived environment effects in Finnish cannot be tied to specific alternations, but are the emergent effects of markedness and root faithfulness interactions in grammar.[12]

Perhaps the most interesting question to arise from revisiting standard examples such as those in section 8.1, which seemed so successfully to be accounted for by Comparative Markedness, is why so many derived environment effects arise at the stem-suffix boundary. Why are effects at the prefix-stem boundary not as commonly found? Further research is needed to explore whether this asymmetry is true only of the literature on derived environment effects or whether it is a fact about language. Łubowicz (2002) has suggested that the preponderance of derived environment effects at the stem-suffix boundary may have to do with resyllabification of stem-final consonants. The change forced by resyllabification in stem-final phonology catalyzes, on this view, other changes in its immediate vicinity. The locality of derived environment effects, as well as their generality, is an issue that should inspire many future investigations.

---

[12] Phonologically derived environment conditioning has also proved elusive to pin down as a general condition in languages. In Finnish, for example, word-final raising of /e/ to [i], a phonological alternation, creates a derived environment for Assibilation: /vete/ 'water' → |veti| → [vesi]. But it is not the case that just any phonologically derived /ti/ sequence is subject to Assibilation. Consonant gradation, which degeminates inter-sonorant voiceless plosives in closed syllables, can convert /...tti.../ strings to /...ti.../, meeting the structural description for Assibilation. However, examples like ott-i-n → otin (*osin) 'take-PAST' show that Assibilation is not triggered in this environment (Anttila 2006: 896). Miller (1975), Anderson (1969), and Kiparsky (1984, 1993) discuss similarly problematic cases from West Greenlandic and Icelandic, respectively; see Inkelas (2012) for discussion.

9

When phonology interferes with morphology

This chapter discusses cases in which morphological constructions are prevented from combining with certain bases, or from combining with each other in the expected manner, because of phonological conditions that the combinations would violate. In previous chapters we have seen cases in which the phonological shape of morphological constructions is affected by phonological shape conditions; Chapter 3, on prosodic templates, provided the most dramatic examples of this phenomenon. In almost all of those cases, morphological combination succeeded; the only issue was the phonological shape of the product.

In this chapter we will focus instead on cases in which phonological considerations directly interfere with morphology. These situations are described in Optimality Theoretic terms as instantiating the P » M ranking, in which a phonological consideration outranks a morphological consideration (e.g. McCarthy and Prince 1993). As a warm-up, we will start (in section 9.1) with cases of suppletive allomorphy in which two allomorphs are in complementary distribution, with their distribution regulated (to some degree) by the phonology. We will then move on (in section 9.2) to cases in which affixation or some other morphological construction is prevented from combining with a stem for phonological reasons, creating a morphological gap. The chapter then turns (in sections 9.3 and 9.4) to a discussion of two phenomena which suggest the phonological interference of phonology into morphology, but whose interpretation is somewhat controversial: the Repeated Morph Constraint and phonologically conditioned affix ordering.

9.1 Suppletive allomorphy

Suppletive allomorphy is familiar to every beginning morphology student as the situation in which a given morphological category has two or more exponents which cannot be derived from a common form but must be stored separately. Suppletive allomorphy enters the realm of the morphology-phonology interface when the choice between or among suppletive allomorphs is phonologically determined. This is very common. In Turkish, for example, the causative suffix has two regular suppletive allomorphs, -t and -DIr. Allomorph -t combines with polysyllabic bases ending in a vowel, /l/, or /r/ (1a), while -DIr occurs in the complement set of environments (1b) (see e.g. Lewis 1967; İz et al. 1992; Kornfilt 1997; Göksel and Kerslake 2005):

(1)

		Root	Causative		[Turkish]
a.	'understand'	anla	anla-t	'teach'	
	'fly'	esne	esne-t	'stretch'	
	'extract'	tʃukar	tʃukar-t	'cause to remove'	
	'ascend'	jyksel	jyksel-t	'raise'	
b.	'eat'	je	je-dir	'make eat, feed'	
	'be twisted'	bur	bur-dur	'twist'	
	'take'	al	al-dɯr	'make take'	
	'leave'	bɯrak	bɯrak-tɯr	'make leave'	
	'be present'	bulun	bulun-dur	'make be present, have ready'	

9.1.1 Phonologically optimizing allomorphy

In a number of cases of phonologically conditioned suppletive allomorphy, the distribution of suppletive allomorphs appears to resonate with phonological patterns in the language, suggesting that the phonological grammar could be responsible for handling the distribution of suppletive allomorphs (Mester 1994; Kager 1996; Carstairs-McCarthy 1998; Bonet et al. 2007; see Paster 2006 and Wolf 2008 for overview and discussion). A particularly clear example of this occurs in Modern Western (Istanbul) Armenian, in which the definite suffix takes the shape -n following vowel-final nouns (2a) and -ə following consonant-final nouns (2b); Vaux 1998: 252.[1]

---

[1] Vaux (1998: 252) analyzes the definite suffix as underlyingly /-n/ and attributes the schwa allomorph to rules of epenthesis and consonant deletion; however, as the n~ə alternation is specific to the definite, most researchers would probably classify this as suppletive allomorphy. Ambiguity of this kind highlights a potential turf war between morphologically conditioned phonology (Chapter 2) and suppletive allomophy.

(2)   gloss   Plain   Definite   [Istanbul Armenian]

   a. 'tongue'   lezu   lezu-n
     'cat'   gadu   gadu-n
     'wine'   kini   kini-n

   b. 'chair'   atorr   atorr-ə
     'book'   kirk   kirk-ə
     'piece'   hat   hat-ə

Similar effects are familiar from Korean, in which several suffixes exhibit V- and C-initial suppletive allomorphs which occur after C- and V-final stems, respectively. Thus, the nominative, accusative and topic-marked forms of *param* 'wind' are *param-i*, *param-ɨl*, and *param-ɨn*, vs. the corresponding forms of *pori* 'barley': *pori-ka*, *pori-rɨl*, *pori-nɨn* (Paster 2006: 67, citing Odden 1993: 133).

The distribution of allomorphs in cases like these makes eminent phonological sense. From any phonological point of view, a consonant will syllabify better with a preceding vowel (to whose syllable it supplies a coda consonant) than with a preceding consonant; coda *Cn* clusters are not allowed in Armenian. Furthermore, a vowel will syllabify better with a preceding consonant (which will form the onset of the syllable it heads) than with a preceding vowel; VV hiatus, while tolerated in some languages, is never a preferred structure. In Optimality Theory the distribution of the Armenian *-n* and *-ə* allomorphs is easy to characterize. The lexicon makes both available; the grammar, via a set of constraints abbreviated in (3) as "SYLLABLE STRUCTURE," assesses the options and chooses the one which is phonologically preferable:

(3)

/kirk/, {/-n/, /-ə/}	SYLLABLE STRUCTURE
/kirk-n/	*!
/kirk-ə/	✓

In a broad cross-linguistic survey of suppletive allomorphy, Paster (2006) uncovers a continuum of cases: some suppletive allomorphy (especially cases conditioned by syllable or metrical structure) is easy to characterize as phonologically optimizing, while other cases of allo-morphy seem arbitrary or even non-optimizing. Wolf (2008) and Embick (2010) also survey this field, with Wolf emphasizing cases in which the distribution of suppletive allomorphs is phonologically rational, and Embick emphasizing cases in which the opposite is true.

The Turkish causative allomorphy in (1) is described as arbitrary by Bonet et al. (2007: 904). However, Paster observes that even this case may have some phonological virtues. The stems taking /t/ all end in syllables with which /t/ can syllabify; adding /-t/ to these stems, rather than /-dIr/, minimizes the number of syllables in the word, on oft-cited cross-linguistic desideratum; see e.g. Prince and Smolensky 1993, 2004 on the family of *STRUC constraints, which favor words with less phonological structure. The fact that monosyllabic bases all select /-dIr/ could be attributed to a disyllabic minimality condition, of which Turkish shows evidence in other sectors of the grammar; see Chapter 8, section 8.5.1, and section 9.2.2. However, it is more difficult to explain why polysyllabic stems ending in /n/ or /s/ do not take the /-t/ allomorph. Turkish permits /rt/, /lt/, /nt/, and /st/ syllable codas (e.g. Clements and Sezer 1982), yet only /r/- and /l/-final stems take Causative /-t/.

In such cases, it may be necessary on a phonological optimization account to stipulate (following e.g. Kager 1996; Bonet 2004; Mascaró 2007; Wolf 2008) that one suppletive allomorph is morphologically preferred over another. The other allomorphs are used only in order to avoid a highly specific phonological problem that the morphologically preferred allomorph would cause.

In the case of Turkish causatives, the morphological preference would be for /-t/, but it would be outranked by two phonological constraints: a ban on monosyllables, and a requirement that coda /t/ be preceded by a segment whose sonority is equal to or greater than that of a liquid. This requirement is weak generally in Turkish, but is ranked higher than the morphological preference for the /t/-allomorph of the causative.

9.1.2 Phonologically non-optimizing allomorphy

Some cases are especially poor fits for a model of phonological optimization. Consider, for example, the case of Haitian Creole, in which a particular determiner takes the form -a following vowels and -la following consonants (Paster 2006: 86, citing Hall 1953: 32, via Klein 2003):

(4) panié-a   'the basket'
     trou-a   'the hole'
     pitit-la   'the child'
     madãm-lã   'the house'

This distribution is exactly opposite that seen in Armenian (2); instead of privileging open (CV) syllables, it creates VV hiatus and CC clusters. Yet, overall the syllable structures of these languages are similar. If one allomorphic distribution makes sense in terms of universal syllable structure preferences, the other cannot. Of course, conditions other than syllable structure may be at play; Paul Kiparsky has suggested (p.c.) that the allomorph /-la/ serves the function of ensuring perfect alignment between syllable boundaries and morpheme boundaries. If /-a/ were to attach to the consonant-final bases in (4b), a syllable would straddle segments from two different morphemes: [pi. ti.t-a]. On this view, /-a/ would be the preferred allomorph, but /-la/ would be used in order not to violate stem-syllable edge alignment.

9.1.3 Syllable-counting allomorphy

Many cases of suppletive allomorphy in Paster's survey are syllable-counting. Such cases are also the subject of a study by Kager (1996). In a number of syllable-counting situations, the distribution of allomorphs serves the purposes of enabling the resulting word to be exhaustively metrically footed, in a manner that could not be accomplished with the opposite distribution of allomorphs. Consider, for example, Estonian partitive plural allomorphy, cited by Kager as motivating the phonological regulation of allomorph distribution.[2] Whether the partitive plural takes the form *-it* or *-sit* depends on whether the base has an odd or even number of syllables, respectively. Kager analyzes the allomorphy in terms of optimal metrical parsing, as seen in (5):

(5)

#stem σ's	Partitive plural	Metrical footing		[Estonian]
1	ma-it	(má-i)t	*(má-.si)t	*light stressed σ*
2	häda-sit	(hǎ.da)-.sit	*(hǎ.da-i)t	*heavy unstressed σ*
3	paraja-it	(pára)(jà-i)t	*(pára)(jà.si)t	*light stressed σ*
4	atmirali-sit	(át.mi)(rà.li)sit	*(át.mi).(rà.li-i)t	*heavy unstressed σ*

---

[2] The genitive plural and partitive singular also show metrically sensitive allomorphy. Not included in (5) are stems with heavy syllables; these behave predictably but require a more subtle generalization involving moras, and have been omitted here for simplicity's sake.

Feet in Estonian are binary (disyllabic or bimoraic) trochees, and stressed syllables are ideally heavy (CVV or larger). The reason the suffix -*it* has a different distribution from the suffix -*sit* is that -*it* can syllabify with a preceding open syllable, whereas -*sit* must always start its own syllable. When -*it* syllabifies leftward, a heavy syllable is created. This is optimal if the syllable is in position to be stressed, as it is in odd-parity words; it is suboptimal if the syllable is in position to be unstressed, as in even-parity words.

As Paster points out, however, there are cases of syllable-counting allomorphy which are not as easily rationalized as Estonian. Consider the case of noun pluralization in Istanbul Armenian (Vaux 1998: 31, 2003: 104), marked via two suffixes, -*er* and -*ner*. The suffix -*er* attaches to monosyllabic nouns (6a), while -*ner* attaches to polysyllabic nouns (6b):

(6)   gloss   Singular Plural   [Istanbul Armenian]

a. 'horse'   tsʰi   tsʰi-er
   'rock'   kʰɑɾ   kʰɑɾ-er
   'battle'   rɑzm   rɑzm-er
   'brother-in-law'   dɑkʰɾ   dɑkʰɾ-er

b. 'beard'   moɾukʰ   moɾukʰ-neɾ
   'child'   jeɾeχɑ   jeɾeχɑ-neɾ

None of the usual parameters of optimization—syllable structure, metrical footing, syllable/morpheme alignment, prosodic size—can explain why -*er* is favored following monosyllables.

For apparently arbitrary phonologically conditioned allomorphy of this kind, lexical subcategorization is one common approach (e.g. Kiparsky 1982; Inkelas 1989; Booij 2002; Paster 2006). In the lexical entry for the Armenian plural, for example, one or both allomorphs is listed with a selectional frame listing the number of syllables that the base of affixation is required to have, e.g.:

(7)   [[σ] er]
        elsewhere [[ ] neɾ]

This lexicalist approach is taken by Vaux (1998: 104).[3] The alternative approach is to associate particular suppletive allomorphs with gram-matical constraints on their surface phonological environments. This

---

[3] Vaux states the allomorph contexts in terms of a Vocabulary Insertion rule, which is equivalent to a selectional frame in a lexical entry.

constraint-based approach is advocated by Wolf (2008), in a discussion of the well-known case of arbitrary syllable-counting allomorphy in Dyirbal (Dixon 1972, discussed in McCarthy and Prince 1990, 1993; Bonet 2004; Bye 2007, among others). The Dyirbal case is not unlike Armenian plural marking: the Dyirbal ergative takes the form *-ŋku* when the base is disyllabic (8a), but *-ku* when the base is longer (8b):

(8) a. jaṛa-ŋku 'man-ERG' [Dyirbal]
b. jamani-ku 'rainbow-ERG'
palakara-ku 'they-ERG'

Wolf decomposes *-ŋku* into two morphemes, *-ŋ* and *-ku*, such that what needs to be accounted for on his account is the conditions under which *-ŋ* occurs (p. 92). Wolf proposes a surface Alignment constraint essentially requiring *-ŋ* to follow a word-initial disyllabic foot. This condition can only be met by disyllabic stems (8a); elsewhere, *-ku* occurs on its own, without *-ŋ* (8b).

9.1.4 Opaquely conditioned allomorphy

An interesting challenge arises for an approach which uses output constraints to regulate suppletive allomorphy, whether of the unambiguously phonologically optimizing kind (as in Estonian or the Armenian definite article), or the more arbitrary kind (as in the Haitian Creole determiner, the Armenian plural, and the Dyirbal ergative). As Paster (2006) observes, there are cases in which seemingly phonologically optimizing suppletive allomorphy is opaque, conditioned by input factors which are obscured in the output by phonological alternations affecting the derived stem. In such cases, input conditioning is necessary even though the distribution of allomorphs makes phonological sense.

One case discussed by Paster is Turkish possessive allomorphy. The 3rd person possessive suffix has two suppletive allomorphs: /-I/, used after consonant-final stems (9a), and /-sI/, used after vowel final stems (9b) (Lewis 1967; see also Paster 2006: 99):

(9)

	gloss	noun	3SG.POSS	[Turkish]
a.	'house'	ev	ev-i	
	'school'	okul	okul-u	
b.	'mother'	anne	anne-si	
	'pleasant smell'	burdʒu	burdʒu-su	

At first glance, this distribution is identical to other phonologically reasonable allomorphic distributions discussed earlier; CV syllable structure is preserved wherever possible. This very sensible distribution is rendered opaque, however, when intervocalic velar deletion applies to a suffixed stem. In Turkish, as seen in Chapter 8, stem-final velars delete when rendered intervocalic by suffixation. While deletion has some morphological exceptions, it applies very regularly to inflected nouns, as seen in (10a) where the triggers are the dative and accusative case endings. The 3rd person singular possessive suffix /-I/ is also a trigger of velar deletion, as seen in (10b). But this produces a paradox: the suffix /-I/ selects for consonant-final stems, but by conditioning the rule of velar deletion, ends up following a vowel, which is the surface environment in which /-sI/ is expected instead:

(10)   a.

gloss	UR	Nominative	Dative /-E/	Accusative /-I/
'cow'	/inek/	[i.nek]	[i.ne.e]	[in.e.i]
'squash'	/kabak/	[ka.bak]	[ka.ba.a]	[ka.ba.ɯ]

b.

gloss	UR	3SG.POSS	
'cow'	/inek/	[i.ne.i]	*[i.nek.si], *[i.ne.si]
'squash'	/kabak/	[ka.ba.ɯ]	*[ka.bak.sɯ], *[ka.ba.sɯ]

A surface optimization approach, given the choice between [i.ne.-i] and [i.nek.-si], would almost certainly be expected to pick [inek-si] (or even [ine-si]). CC clusters across morpheme boundaries, as would occur in [inek-si], are commonplace in Turkish and never repaired by deletion or epenthesis, whereas VV clusters across morpheme boundaries are tolerated nowhere else in the language. Thus Paster analyzes this case not as output optimization but purely as input selection.

In one very interesting case of opaque allomorph selection in Polish, Łubowicz (2007) cites phonological contrast preservation as the motivation for the choice between suppletive allomorphs. The locative is marked either by -e or -u. Like other front suffix-initial vowels in Polish, -e triggers palatalization of a stem-final coronal consonant (11a). Exactly those stems whose final consonant is underlyingly palatal take -u instead (11b) (Łubowicz 2007: 231):

(11)

		Nominative	Locative	[Polish]
a.	'letter'	lis[t]	o liś[ć]-e	
	'troublemaker'	łobu[z]	o łobu[ź]-e	
b.	'leaf'	liś[ć]	o liś[ć]-u	
	'butterfly sp.'	pa[ź]	o pa[ź]-u	

Łubowicz attributes the selection of the suppletive -*u* locative allomorph to contrast preservation. Exactly when -*e*, the preferred allomorph, would merge the contrast between underlyingly plain and underlying palatal root-final coronal consonants, -*u* is selected instead. It is important to note that the contrast being preserved here is a phonological one. While 'letter' and 'leaf' form a minimal pair, the same distribution of -*e* and -*u* is found with roots that are independently distinct in other ways, e.g. *łobu[z]* (nominative), *o łobu[ź]-e* (locative) 'troublemaker', but *pa[ź]* (nominative), *o pa[ź]-u* (locative) 'type of butterfly'. For readers interested in anti-homophony effects, this case can be instructively compared to the otherwise similar case in Chapter 11 of suffixal anti-homophony in neuter nouns in Bulgarian, discussed by Crosswhite (1997), in which anti-homophony constraints block segmental neutralization only when two actual wordforms would be rendered homophonous as a result.

9.2 Phonologically conditioned morphological gaps (ineffability)

In some cases a word-formation construction, such as affixation, reduplication, or truncation, can apply only if phonological conditions on input or output are met. A number of such cases are discussed by Orgun and Sprouse (1999), Carstairs-McCarthy (1998), Raffelsiefen (2004), Rice (2005), among others. Some of these cases resemble what we have seen for suppletive allomorphy, in that individual affixes are restricted to such specific phonological environments that if the input (or output) stem does not meet those conditions, affixation fails (section 9.2.1). Others resemble the template phenomena discussed in Chapter 3, in that the phonological conditions on output shape are prosodic (section 9.2.2). The key difference between these restrictions and templatic morphology is that the conditions discussed in this section function as output filters, rejecting words which do not conform to them, rather than templates to which words are able and required to adapt.

In case of suppletive allomorphy, it is common for one allomorph to be the elsewhere case, available if conditions making possible the use of the other are not met. But when there is no such fall-back option, the word simply cannot be formed, resulting in a paradigm gap. Alternative morphological or syntactic strategies must be used to express the meaning that the underivable word would have contributed.

9.2.1 Phonological selectional requirements on affixation

Individual affixes often impose phonological requirements on bases of affixation; bases not meeting these requirements cannot combine with the affix. An often-cited example in English is the comparative suffix *-er*, which is productive but combines only with bases which are monosyllabic (12a), or which are disyllabic by virtue of a very small final second syllable (12b) (see e.g. Poser 1992):

(12)   a. green   greener
          huge   huger
          light   lighter
          fair   fairer

       b. common   commoner
          subtle   subtler

       c. orange   *oranger   (cf. more orange)
          pedantic   *pedanticer   (cf. more pedantic)
          brilliant   *brillianter (cf. more brilliant)
          divine   *diviner   (cf. more divine)
          sublime   *sublimer   (cf. more sublime)
          honest   *honester   (cf. more honest)
          difficult   *difficulter (cf. more difficult)

Adjectives which, due to the strict selectional requirement on the comparative suffix, cannot form morphological comparatives instead default to the periphrastic comparative construction, 'more ___', as seen in (12c).[4]

9.2.2 Phonological output conditions

The distinction between input sensitivity and output sensitivity is not always clearly demarcated, but the examples in this section are plausibly analyzed in terms of the well-formedness of potential outputs. Several of these cases are discussed in papers in Rice and Blaho (2009), a recent survey of ineffability effects.

Zuraw and Lu (2009) document a range of responses within Western Malayo-Polynesian—indeed, within Austronesian more generally—to a constraint against *labial...labial* sequences that would be generated

---

[4] One finds some comparatives like those in (12c), e.g. *sublimer* and *honester*, in occasional use, but they are not standard forms, and are dwarfed in usage statistics by their phrasal counterparts, e.g. *more sublime* and *more honest*.

by infixation of -*um*-. (These cases were also discussed in Chapter 6.) In some languages in the family, the constraint is satisfied by fusing the labial consonant of the infix with that of the base. In Timugon Murut, inputs like *gajo* show -*um*- infixation (→ *g-um-ajo*), while labial-initial inputs such as *patoj* show fusion (→ *m-atoj*). In other languages, the stem-initial consonant becomes velar to avoid the *labial...labial* sequence. In Limos Kalinga, inputs such as *datoŋ* 'come' show regular -*um*- infixation, while labial-initial inputs such as *pija* 'good' show dissimilation: *k-um-ija* (Zuraw and Lu 2009: 209). In Tagalog, neither repair strategy is used, and a morphological gap results. Infixation is prohibited outright when the undesirable *labial....labial* sequence would result (Schachter and Otanes 1972; Orgun and Sprouse 1999; Zuraw and Lu 2009: 199). The prohibition with *m* is exceptionless, according to English's (1986) dictionary of Tagalog; two *w*-initial words take –*um*-, but otherwise the pattern occurs with *w* too. Orgun and Sprouse found support for this lexical pattern in an experimental study in which subjects willingly infixed -*um*- into novel words except those beginning with *m* and *w*:

(13)   Tagalog -*um*- infixation

Stem-initial consonant	Stem	Actor focus, infinitive/past	gloss
t	takot	t-um-akot	'frighten'
d	damaj	d-um-amaj	'sympathize'
s	sulat	s-um-ulat	'write'
n	nipis	n-um-ipis	'become thin'
l	lipat	l-um-ipat	'move'
k	kanta	k-um-anta	'sing'
g	gawaʔ	g-um-awaʔ	'make'
ŋ	ŋitiʔ	ŋ-um-itiʔ	'smile'
h	hiɲiʔ	h-um-iɲiʔ	'ask for'
p	pili	p-um-ili	'choose'
b	bukas	b-um-ukas	'open'

9.2.2.1 Norwegian imperatives   Rice (2005) discusses a case of imperative formation in Norwegian which, for some speakers, results in paradigm gaps. According to Rice, imperatives are identical in form to the underlying stem, while infinitives suffix a schwa to consonant-final stems. Consonant-final stems, as in (14a), thus display an alternation in shape between imperative and infinitive, while for vowel-final stems, as in (14b), the two word forms are segmentally identical. The phonological problem for imperatives arises in the case of stems ending underlyingly in unsyllabifiable coda clusters, as in (14c). In such cases, the bare stem imperative would be phonologically ill-formed:

(14)		gloss	Infinitive	Imperative	[Norwegian]
	a.	'eat'	å spise	spis	
		'talk'	å snakke	snakk	
		'lift'	å løfte	løft	
	b.	'pray'	å be	be	
		'take'	å ta	ta	
		'turn'	å snu	snu	
	c.	'open'	å åpne	— (*åpn)	
		'paddle'	å padle	— (*padl)	
		'bike'	å sykle	— (*sykl)	

Rice reports that some speakers repair the problem phonologically by devoicing the final sonorant, while others simply recruit the infinitive form for use as the imperative. Still other speakers experience a genuine paradigm gap in these cases, and resort to periphrasis to express the intended meaning.

9.2.2.2 Turkish prosodic minimality   Turkish enforces a disyllabic minimal size condition on suffixed words (also discussed in Chapter 8; Itô and Hankamer 1989; Inkelas and Orgun 1995). While most Turkish root-suffix combinations are easily disyllabic by virtue of each morpheme containing at least a syllable, the condition can be detected in the event that a CV root combines with a C suffix. CV roots are illustrated in (15a); -C suffixes are illustrated combining with polysyllabic V-final roots in (15b). The ungrammatical combinations are presented in (15c):

(15) a. je   'eat'   [Turkish]
          de   'say'
          do   'musical note *do*'   ([doː], for some speakers)
          be   'alphabetic letter *b*'   ([beː], for some speakers)

      b. søjle-n   'speak-PASS = be spoken'
          araba-m   'car-1SG.POSS'
          anne-n   'mother-2SG.POSS'

      c. *do-m   'note *do*-1SG.POSS'   (*[doː-m])
          *be-n   'letter *b*-2SG.POSS'   (*[beː-m])
          *de-n   'say-PASS = be said (!)'

      d. solʲ-ym   'note *sol*-1SG.POSS'
          a-be-dʒe-n 'your alphabet-2SG.POSS' cf. a-be-dʒe lit. 'a-b-c' =
          'alphabet'
          gør-yl   'see-PASS = be seen (!)'

The ungrammaticality of the words in (15c) is unrelated to their
semantic content, as illustrated by the semantically comparable but
phonologically larger combinations in (15d), which are grammatical.
The best analysis of these facts is to assume an output disyllabic
minimal size constraint on Turkish stems. Note that an input size
condition would not (as neatly) capture the facts. Consonantal suffixes
can combine with monosyllabic bases as long as they are consonant-
final; the reason is that in such cases epenthesis applies to break up the
resulting consonant cluster, rendering the output disyllabic:

(16) a. /ev/   ev   'house'
          /ev-m/   ev̲i̲m   'house-1SG.POSS'
          /ev-n/   ev̲i̲n   'house-2SG.POSS'

      b. /al/   al   'take'
          /al-n/   al̲ṵṵn   'take-PASS'

Another paradigm gap induced by an output condition on phonological size is Kinande, in which a disyllabic size condition on reduplicants interacts with the Morpheme Integrity Constraint to render stems
longer than two syllables unreduplicable (Chapter 7, section 7.5.2.1).

9.2.2.3 Finnish case and possessive suffixes   Kiparsky (2003) presents, as an instance of a phonologically induced morphological gap,
a case from Finnish in which consonantal case endings are omitted
before possessive suffixes, due to an output constraint that stems must
end in vowels (p. 146):

(17)   Stem Constraint (Finnish): stems must end in -V

The Stem Constraint applies to stems that are suffixed but not to those which surface unsuffixed as words.[5] Kiparsky (2003: 148) cites several phenomena triggered by the Stem Constraint. For example, loan nouns that end in coronal consonants are phonologically permissible words, as illustrated by the noun *nailon* 'nylon' (18a). However, in order to receive case endings, which attach to stems, such items are adapted to the required V-final stem shape by means of a stem-final -*i* (18b–d):

(18)   a. nailon   'nylon (NOM.SG.)'   [Finnish]
       b. nailoni̲-n   'nylon (GEN.SG.)'
       c. nailoni̲-ssa 'nylon (INESS.SG.)'
       d. nailoni̲-a   'nylon (PRT.SG.)' (*nailon-ta; cf. laidun-ta 'pasture
                                       (PRT.SG.)')

As Kiparsky observes, there is no general process of *i*-epenthesis in Finnish; this is a stem-forming strategy compelled by the Stem Constraint. The fact that stems are adapted to conform to the Stem Constraint shows that it is an output condition.

The relevance of the Stem Constraint to phonologically conditioned morphological gaps is shown by nouns which combine both with case suffixes and with possessive suffixes (to be seen in (20)). In Finnish, possessive suffixes attach outside case suffixes. Kiparsky argues, assuming a Stratal Optimality Theory framework (see Chapters 2 and 7), that case suffixes attach to Stems and form new Stems, while possessive suffixes attach to Stems but form Words:

(19)   [[[Noun]Stem -Case]Stem-Possessive]Word

Because case endings produce Stems, they are subject to the Stem Condition. Some case suffixes (e.g. Inessive singular /-ssA/ and Partitive singular /-A/, in 18c,d) end in vowels; others (e.g. genitive singular /-n/, in 18b) end in consonants. When a Possessive suffix attaches outside a case-marked noun, one of three things must happen. If the suffix is syllable-sized or larger, such as the Genitive plural -*ten* or Illative -*seen*, it loses its final consonant so as to provide a vowel-final Stem for the possessive suffix to attach to (20a) (p. 150). A case suffix which is monoconsonantal may not co-occur with a following Possessive suffix. In some instances this prohibition causes the case ending to be omitted.

---

[5] This is an example of a derived environment constraint; see Chapter 8.

This is true of the Genitive/Accusative -*n* or Nominative/Accusative plural -*t* in (20b). In these forms the Possessive endings attach directly to the bare stem. As a result, forms ending in possessive suffixes, as in (20biii), are ambiguous: Nominative singular, Nominative or Accusative plural, Accusative or Genitive singular (p. 151):

(20) a. Phonological deletion of final C of case suffix, preceding possessive suffix

      i. /huonee-seen/   → huoneeseen 'room-ILL.SG'
         /huonee-seen-si/ → huoneeseesi 'room-ILL.SG.-2SG.POSS'

      ii. /saare-i-ten/   → saarien   'island-PL-GEN'
         /saare-i-ten-si/ → saariesi   'island-PL-GEN-2SG.POSS.'

    b. Morphological omission of consonantal case suffix, preceding possessive suffix

      i.   /hattu-i-hin-ni/ → hattuihini 'hat-PL-ILL.PL-1SG.POSS'
      ii.   /hattu/   → hattu   'hat' (NOM.SG.)
      iii. /hattu-n/   → hatun   'hat-ACC/GEN.SG'
          /hattu-t/   → hatut   'hat-NOM/ACC.PL'
          /hattu-si/   → hattusi   'hat-2SG.POSS' (NOM.SG.)
                          ~ 'hat-2SG.POSS' (ACC/GEN.SG)
                          ~ 'hat-2SG.POSS' (NOM/ACC.PL)

The third option, ineffability, is associated with Instructive (instrumental) -*n*. When this consonantal case ending would precede a Possessive suffix, a phonologically motivated paradigm gap ensues (21b). The morphology cannot produce a possessed Instructive. Unlike the forms in (20biii), (21a) is not ambiguous:

(21) a. /pitkä-i-n   askele-i-n/   → pitkin askelin
        long-PL-INSTR   step-PL-INSTR   'with long steps'

    b. */pitkä-i-n   askele-i-n-si/   → (no output)
        long-PL-INSTR   step-PL-INSTR-2SG.POSS   Intended: 'with your
                                      long steps'

Instead, a different suffix (the Comitative -*ne*) is recruited in lieu of Instrumental case preceding Possessive suffixes (p. 152):

(22) /pitkä-i-ne   askele-i-ne-en/   → pitkine askelineen
     long-PL-COM   step-PL-COM-3SG.POSS   'with his long steps'

In the case of the paradigm gap created by the Stem Constraint in (21b), the morphology supplies an alternative, just as the syntax supplies an alternative in the case of English comparatives in (12c).

9.2.3 Ineffability in morphological context

Albright (2003, 2009) has made the important observation that many
apparent cases of phonologically conditioned ineffability also involve
morphological conditioning, calling into question the degree to which
the phonology of the language predicts the gap to occur. This is true of
most of the examples discussed in this chapter.

Consider, again, the case of Norwegian (Rice 2005), in which verb
stems ending in clusters of rising sonority, e.g. obstruent-resonant (OR)
clusters, cannot be used in the imperative (23c):

(23)		Imperative (root)	Infinitive (å + root (+ ə))	root gloss
a.	V-final stems	snu	å snu	turn
		ta	å ta	take
		be	å be	pray
b.	C-final stems	spis	å spise	eat
		snakk	å snakke	talk
		løft	å løfte	lift
c.	OR-final stems	*åpn	å åpne	open
		*padl	å padle	paddle
		*sylk	å sykle	bike

Infinitives formed from these same stems are unproblematic because
of the schwa desinence which permits the stem-final consonant cluster
to be split across two syllables.

What makes this more than a simple case of phonological ill-
formedness blocking a morphological derivation is the fact that Norwegian does have a strategy for splitting unsyllabifiable consonant
clusters. Nouns ending in clusters of rising sonority split them with
epenthetic schwa, e.g. /adl/ 'nobility', pronounced in isolation as [adəl].
As observed by Rice (2005), some roots can be used either as nouns or
as verbs. Those ending in clusters of rising sonority undergo epenthesis
when used unaffixed as nouns but are ungrammatical as bare (imperative) verbs[6]:

---

[6] Following Rice (2005), data are given in Norwegian orthography.

(24)

		As noun	As verb	gloss
a.	/skriv/	skriv	skriv	'document'/ 'write!'
	/kost/	kost	kost	'broom'/'sweep!'
	/dans/	dans	dans	'dance'/'dance!'
b.	/sykl/	sykkel	*sykl	'bicycle'/'bicycle!' (cf. *sykl-ist* 'cyclist')
	/hindr/	hinder	*hindr	?? /'hinder!'
	/ordn/	orden	*ordn	?? /'arrange!'

Rice (2005) and McCarthy and Wolf (2009) offer theoretical accounts of the missing imperatives in the verbal paradigm. Rice's proposal, drawing on McCarthy's (2007) Optimality Theoretic approach to paradigm well-formedness, is that every morphological category corresponds to a constraint, MAX{category}, requiring its expression in the paradigm. Among the paradigm constraints in Norwegian are MAX{infinitive} and MAX{imperative}. MAX{infinitive} is ranked highly, but MAX{imperative} is ranked below phonological constraints banning epenthesis and rising-sonority clusters. The result is a violation of MAX{imperative}, i.e. a morphological gap. The tableau in (25) is modified from Rice (2005). SONSEQ is the constraint banning codas of rising sonority; FAITH penalizes all of the possible phonological repairs to such sequences. The input consists of (partial) nominal and verbal paradigms of the root *sykl* 'cycle':

(25)

	sykl (N.SG., N.PL., V.INF., V.IMP.)	MAX{V.INF.}, MAX{N.SG},MAX{N.PL}	SONSEQ	FAITH	MAX{IMP.}
a.	sykl (N.SG.) sykl-er (N.PL.) sykl-e (V.INF.) sykl (V.IMP.)		*! *		
b.	sykk͟el (N.SG.) sykl-er (N.PL.) sykl-e (V.INF.) sykl (V.IMP.)		 *!	*	
c.	sykk͟el (N.SG.) sykl-er (N.PL.) sykl-e (V.INF.) sykk͟el (V.IMP.)			* *!	
☞ d.	sykkel (N.SG.) sykl-er (N.PL.) sykl-e (V.INF.) ———			*	*

It is, of course, not uncommon to find morphological conditioning of phonological effects, as was discussed in Chapter 1. What is noteworthy is that morphological conditioning seems to characterize so many cases of apparently phonologically motivated ineffability. In Turkish, as noted, the disyllabic minimality condition applies to words morphologically derived through the suffixation of 1st person singular possessive -*m* (26a), 2nd person singular possessive -*n* (26b), and passive -*n* (26c), but not to the (two) CV roots which combine with aorist -*r* (Hankamer and Itô 1989; Inkelas and Orgun 1995) (26d):

(26) a. /solʲ-m/   solʲ-ym   'note *sol*-1SG.POSS'
          /do-m/   *do-m   'note *do*-1SG.POSS'

      b. /solʲ-n/   solʲ-yn   'note *sol*-2SG.POSS'
          /do-n/   *do-n   'note *do*-2SG.POSS'

      c. /søjle-n/   søjle-n   'speak-PASS = be spoken'
          /de-n/   *de-n   'say-PASS = be said'

      d. /søjle-r/   søjler   'speak-AOR = speaks'
          /de-r/   der   'say-AOR = says'
          /je-r/   jer   'do-AOR = does'

Finnish also exhibits morphologically conditioned phonological ineffability; the vowel-final condition compelling gaps in (21) pertains only to some subconstituents of words—those termed "Stems" by Kiparsky (2003)—and not to others.

The morphologically conditioned examples discussed in this section dramatically illustrate a general point about ineffability that can be made, if more subtly, even for the examples in section 9.2: the phonological problem that is apparently insurmountable in the ineffability examples is not typically a very serious one. In many cases the language either tolerates the same phonological structure in other contexts or exhibits, elsewhere, the very phonological alternations that could repair the phonologically illicit form.

For example, the ungrammatical monosyllabicity of derived monosyllables in Turkish stands in contrast with completely acceptable monosyllabicity for nonderived monosyllables. (This "Derived Environment Effect" is discussed in Chapter 8.) Moreover, the expected monosyllabicity of forms like /do-m/ 'note *do*-1SG.POSS' could easily be repaired, e.g. to [domu] or [dojum], using the very regular independent processes of vowel epenthesis and palatal glide epenthesis that Turkish uses to repair consonant clusters and vowel hiatus (/ok-m/ → [okum]

'arrow-1SG.POSS', /elma-A/ → [elmaja] 'apple-DAT'). It is not generally the case that phonological ineffability results from phonological problems so severe that the language cannot recover from them.

9.2.4 Ineffability in lexical contrast: The role of determinacy

Albright (2009) has argued that in at least some cases, ineffability is due not to a phonological problem with the nonexistent form, but instead to an indeterminacy in the system that prevents speakers from settling decisively on a particular phonological output. Phonological indecision, rather than ill-formedness, is at play. This insight potentially sheds light on the highly specific morphological conditioning in many examples of ineffability.

Consider, for example, the case of Russian 1st person singular verb inflection, famously discussed by Halle (1973: 7). Around 100 verbs which end in /t, d, s, z/, fail to exhibit a 1st person singular inflected form. Examples are given in (27), from Albright (2009). Halle says the gaps in the 1st person singular are essentially unpredictable. Possible phonological explanations include the palatalizing alternations that would result—yet other forms undergo these, e.g. *šutít'* 'jest (infinitive)', *šuču* 'jest-1SG'—or the homophony that would result—yet homophony is often tolerated, e.g. *vožu* 'I lead', *vožu* 'I cart' (Halle 1973: 7):

(27)

Infinitive	1sg (expected)	gloss
mutít'	*muču	'stir up'
pob'edít'	*pob'ežu	'beat'
dubásit'	*dubašu	'batter'
lázit'	*lažu	'climb'

Albright (2009) observes that several factors single out coronal-final second conjugation 1st person singular verbs in Russian. First, Albright notes that "the 1sg is the least predictive of all forms in the paradigm: it does not clearly reveal the conjugation class of the verb, it suffers from neutralizations caused by [palatalization], and it frequently differs from the remaining forms in the location of stress." In a study of second conjugation verbs based on a comprehensive dictionary and 40 million word corpus, Albright found that coronal-final verbs are more prone to stress alternation than, for example, labial-final verbs are. Albright also observed that many inflected verbs in the second conjugation are only infrequently attested. The factors of underrepresentation and phonological alternation contribute, according to Albright, to uncertainty about the surface form of coronal-final second conjugation verbs, and, therefore, to the observed lexical gaps.

9.3 Haplology effects

In an influential article, Menn and MacWhinney (1984) claimed it to be generally, if not universally, true that sequences of homophonous morph(eme)s are prohibited. The Repeated Morph Constraint (RMC) is a prima facie case of phonology interfering with morphology. Published overviews of the prohibition on morph repetition include, besides Menn and MacWhinney, Stemberger (1981) and Ackema and Neeleman (2005). In most cases, these effects occur with suffixes. Menn and MacWhinney cite a handful of examples of prefix repetition avoidance, but they are in the distinct minority.

A well-known example occurs in English, where the possessive ending /-z/ is not added to—or at least not realized on—words ending in the homophonous plural suffix /-z/ (Stemberger 1981; Menn and MacWhinney 1984; see also Halpern 1992). As (28a,b) show, the plural and possessive suffixes in English are homophonous. (28c) shows that forms in which both suffixes surface are ungrammatical. The prohibition on /-z-z/ is not a purely phonological or purely semantic issue. Irregular plurals take the possessive (28d) and so do words ending in strings homophonous with allomorphs of the plural (i.e. [(ɨ)z] or [s]) (28e):

(28)   a. *Singular + possessive:*
         tiger's   [tajgɚz]
         flea's   [flijz]
         porpoise's   [poɹpəsɨz]

       b. *Regular plural*
         tigers   [tajgɚz]
         fleas   [flijz]
         porpoises   [poɹpəsɨz]

       c. *Regular plural + possessive:*
         tigers'   [tajgɚz]   (*tigers's   [tajgɚzɨz])
         fleas'   [flijz]   (*fleas's   [flijzɨz])
         porpoises' [poɹpəsɨz] (*porpoises's [poɹpəsɨzɨz])

d. *Irregular plural + possessive:*
The bartender filled the women's water glasses

e. *Singulars or irregular plurals ending in /s,z,ɨz/ + possessive: OK*
The zookeeper filled the fox's water dish
The zookeeper filled the mice's water bottles

The phenomenon illustrated in (28c) is classified as a case of haplology, or deletion of one of two identical adjacent suffixes which the
morphology has contributed, because the word in question is capable of
being used in the morphosyntactic context that normally would call for
both plural and possessive suffixes. Morphologically, [tajgɚz] can fill in
either for 'singular tiger, possessive' or 'plural tiger, possessive':

(29) The zookeeper filled the [tajgɚz] water dish

Orthography serves to disambiguate *tiger's* (one tiger, possessive),
tigers (two tigers, not possessive) and *tigers'* (more than one tiger,
possessive) in English, but pronunciation does not.

In other cases the RMC can also cause a paradigm gap, a situation
Menn and MacWhinney call *avoidance*. In such cases, a periphrastic
alternative is used instead. One example cited by Menn and MacWhinney is the English adverbial *-ly* ending, which cannot combine with
those adjectives already ending in *-ly*:

(30) adjective adverb

a. quick   quick-ly
   slow   slow-ly
   happy   happi-ly
   grudging   grudging-ly

b. manly   *manli-ly
   heavenly   *heavenli-ly
   studly   *studli-ly

Speakers vary in their judgments of forms like those in (30b), but there
are certainly many speakers for whom they are ungrammatical. (There
are also dialects of English in which adjectives can be used, unaffixed, as
adverbs, e.g. *She ran quick* instead of *She ran quickly*; in these dialects, the
question of double *-ly* suffixation is simply irrelevant.)

The ban on *-ly-ly* creates a lexical gap. In a context where the
adverbial form of *heaven-ly-ly* would be called for, it must be approxi-
mated by a phrase like *in a heavenly manner*.

9.3.1 Suppletive allomorphy

In some instances where the morphology has the potential to string together adjacent homophonous morphs, suppletive morphology is available to come to the rescue. Menn and MacWhinney cite a number of cases of suppletive allomorphy in which the distribution of allomorphs conspires to avoid RMC violations. One well-studied case is Turkish, which, as shown earlier in example (1), has two suppletive allomorphs of the causative: /-t/ and /-DIr/ (see e.g. Lewis 1967; Göksel and Kerslake 2005). The two allomorphs are conditioned in complementary environments. As it happens, /-t/ attaches to stems of the phonological type that /-DIr/ creates, and vice versa. Turkish permits at least two layers of causative morphology in the same word (see Key 2013 for arguments that causative iteration is strictly bounded). The result of the conditions on allomorphy is that in words with more than one causative, the two morphs occur in alternating sequence:

(31)   a. *öldürt*   [Turkish]
         øl-dyr-t
         'die-CAUS-CAUS = have someone killed'

       b. *okuttur*
          oku-t-tur
          'read-CAUS-CAUS = make someone (e.g. a teacher) cause someone to read'

9.3.2 RMC in morphological context

The RMC is clearly not universal, even within a language. There exist many unperturbed sequences of homophonous morphs. In English, for example, there is a third suffixal element which is homophonous with the plural and possessive suffixes, namely the reduced form of the auxiliary *is*. This syllabifies with and assimilates to a preceding word in exactly the same way that the plural and possessive suffixes do:

(32)   tigers   [tajgə-z]   'tiger-PL'   e.g. *the tigers are hungry*
       tiger's   [tajgə-z]   'tiger-POSS'   e.g. *the tiger's dish is empty*
       tiger's   [tajgə-z]   'tiger-3SG.AUX'   e.g. *the tiger's about to pounce*

However, the auxiliary combines safely with plural and possessive forms: *One of the tigers's getting ready to pounce* (-PL-AUX), or *Ask Andie if you can take her car, 'cause Dave's's completely out of gas* (-POSS-AUX).

Menn and MacWhinney cite many examples of this kind from a variety of languages, concluding that the RMC is a "weak universal" (p. 529).

The RMC's status as a weak universal constraint is weakened further by the fact that suppletion and lexical gaps occur even when morph repetition is not an issue. This point can be made clearly with an example which Menn and MacWhinney cite as supporting the RMC. In Turkish, the 3rd person possessive suffix, whose suppletive allomorphs are /-I/ and /-sI/, is not only used to encode 3rd person singular possession (33b) but also serves as a marker of a very product-ive compounding construction (33c). As seen in (33d), it is semantic-ally possible for a compound to be possessed, but it is not possible to add a 3rd possessive suffix to a compound that already ends in a 3rd possessive suffix. As a result, forms like those in (33c) are ambiguous for whether or not they are possessed:

(33) a. aile   'family'
         araba   'car'

      b. aile-si   'his/her/its family'
         araba-sɯ   'his/her/its car'

      c. aile araba-sɯ   'family car' or 'his/her/its family car'

      d. *aile araba-sɯ-sɯ

If this were the end of the story, it would be a straightforward example of the RMC. But as so often happens in the phonology-morphology interface (and as is undoubtedly, unfortunately, probably true of many of the examples taken at face value in this book), there is more to the story. It turns out that *no* possessive suffix may be attached directly to a compound ending in /-sI/; instead, the inner /-sI/ is omitted in the event that a compound is possessed:

(34) a. aile araba-m   'my family car'   *aile araba-sɯ-m
      b. aile araba-n   'your (sg.) family car' *aile araba-sɯ-n
      c. aile araba-mɯz 'our family car'   *aile araba-sɯ-mɯz

Other suffixes that attach to nouns also cause the omission of /-sI/ when attaching to compounds, e.g. 'associative' /-lI/ and 'occupational' or 'agentive' /-CI/:

(35) a. aile araba-lɯ   *aile araba-sɯ-lɯ
         'endowed with a family car'
         ʧodʒuk kitap-lɯ   *ʧodʒuk kitab-ɯ-lɯ
         'child-book-ASSOC = with children's book'

      b. ʧodʒuk kitap-ʧɯ   *ʧodʒuk kitab-ɯ-dʒɯ
         'child book-AGT = children's book author'

Thus there is an entire class of suffixes with which compounding marking /-sI/ cannot co-occur; one of these (/-sI/ itself) is homophonous with /-sI/, but the others are not. Given this situation, how, then, are we to know whether affix co-occurrence restrictions between homophonous affixes are a distinct subtype of affix co-occurrence restrictions generally, or just an arbitrary subset that does not require its own distinct explanation? Further research is required in this area, but answers are likely to be of two types. One is statistical: if homophonous affix pairs form a larger than expected subset of the class of morpheme pairs that cannot occur next to each other in any given language (or in some pool of languages that is surveyed), the RMC would be supported, though this task would be hard to accomplish given current data. A second possible answer would be to show that the lexical gaps or lexical ambiguities resulting from RMC effects pattern differently from those resulting from other, more arbitrary morpheme co-occurrence restrictions.

9.3.3 Implications of the RMC for a theory of the phonology-morphology interface

Since it affects word shape and can create morphological paradigm gaps, the RMC would seem to be a clear case of phonology interfering with morphology. The RMC is also a prima facie counterexample to Bracket Erasure, discussed in Chapter 6, which is an integrity or locality principle to the effect that morphological constructions do not have access to the internal morphological structure of the bases they combine with. Clearly, in order to distinguish the suffixed plural *sock-s* from the irregular plural *feet* and from the [s]-final singular noun *fox*, the possessive construction has to know that only one of these nouns ends in a plural suffix.

9.3.4 A continuum of phonological similarity

In fact, however, the morpho phonological nature of the RMC is not as clear-cut as the examples mentioned may make it seem. A number of cases cited by Stemberger (1981) and by Menn and MacWhinney (1984) do not meet the standard of "sequences of identical morphs," either in underlying or surface phonological representation. Many simply involve a high degree of phonological similarity between the suffix in question and the edge of the stem. For example, the suffix *-ly* fails to attach not only to adjectives derived via the suffix *-ly*, but also to monomorphemic bases which just happen to end in a [li] syllable (Menn and MacWhinney 1984: 524):

(36)　ugly　　*ugli-ly　　*ug
　　　comely　*comeli-ly　*come　(as noun)
　　　surly　　*surli-ly　　*sur

Plag (1998) discusses an array of cases like the following, from English (also discussed by Raffelsiefen 1996, 2004). The English verbalizing suffix *-ize* requires the omission of the final VC of its base of affixation, just in case the final syllable of the stem has identical onset and coda consonants and is the second of two consecutive unstressed syllables (data from Plag 1998; Raffelsiefen 2004) (37a). Otherwise, no truncation takes place (37b):

(37)　a.　*-ize* triggers VC truncation
　　　　émphasis　emphas-ize　　*emphasis-ize　　*[v̆sv̆s]
　　　　féminine　femin-ize　　　*feminin-ize　　*[v̆nv̆n]
　　　　mínimum　minim-ize　　　*minimum-ize　　*[v̆mv̆m]
　　　　metáthesis　metathes-ize　*metathesis-ize　*[v̆sv̆s]

　　　b.　*-ize* doesn't trigger VC truncation
　　　　féderal　　federal-ize　　*feder-ize　　[v̆rv̆l]
　　　　vítamin　　vitamin-ize　　*vitam-ize　　[v̆mv̆n]
　　　　repúblican　republican-ize　*republic-ize　[v̆kv̆n]
　　　　pýramid　　pyramid-ize　　*pyram-ize　　[v̆mv̆d]

Note that while Plag analyzes the data in (37a) as instances of phonological truncation, Raffelsiefen analyzes them in terms of affixation directly to a bound stem, e.g. *emphas-* + *-ize* = *emphasize*. Both accounts appeal to the same essential phonological constraint as the triggering factor. Whether this is phonological truncation or affix omission, it is clearly not an instance of the RMC per se, as the triggering suffix *-ize* is not homophonous with the omitted material. Instead, it is a case of the avoidance of identical consonants straddling an unstressed vowel, a situation which is well known in phonological circles as a common environment for syncope (see e.g. Odden 1988 on "anti-anti-gemination" effects, as well as chapter 7 of Blevins 2004).

In conclusion, the status of the RMC continues to be interesting and controversial. Whether RMC effects should be attributed to purely phonological anti-identity effects that particular morphological constructions are sensitive to, or whether RMC effects are morphological in nature, remains unresolved. Menn and MacWhinney's (1984) interpretation of the RMC is that it is an effect of "affix checking," the process whereby speakers and listeners scan a word to see whether it contains the expected surface form of the affix they are looking for. Haplology effects arise, according to Menn and MacWhinney, when the same phonological substring does double duty, satisfying the "checking" procedure for two different affixes. Importing this insight into a generative theory of word formation suggests that at least some affixational constructions may be better seen as templatic constraints on output, in line with realizational approaches to morphology discussed in Chapter 2. For example, the English plural and possessive suffixes might both be implemented as output constraints requiring the stem they combine with to end in a sibilant. The story is not that simple by any means, but further study of RMC effects may shed light on the nature of affixation constructions.

9.4 Morphological order

Some cases have been described in which phonology constrains or determines ordering effects in morphology. Such cases have been handled in Optimality Theory by the general P » M schema proposed by McCarthy and Prince (1993) in which phonological considerations ('P') outrank morphological considerations, e.g. affix ordering ('M').

The most commonly documented influence of phonological considerations on the linearization of morphemes is infixation, which is generally described as being just like affixation except that the affix is phonologically positioned within the stem instead of peripheral to it (see e.g. Moravcsik 1977, 2000; McCarthy and Prince 1993; Yu 2007). The interest of infixation for the phonology-morphology interface lies in phonological generalizations about where in a word an infix can appear and about what, if anything, motivates infixation synchronically.

As laid out in Chapter 6, the positioning of infixes falls into two subtypes: infixes which are internally positioned adjacent to a prominent constituent (the primary-stressed syllable or the (prosodic) root), and infixes which are positioned adjacent to the leftmost or rightmost phonological element of a given type (e.g. the first/last vowel). It has been hypothesized that infix placement reflects the prioritization of phonology over morphology. However, as also discussed in Chapter 6, doubt has been cast on this interpretation; there are a number of counterexamples in which the placement of an infix conflicts with where its optimal position would be, were phonological considerations ranked topmost.

Because infixation is dealt with in Chapter 6, we will say no more about it here, focusing instead on three other scenarios in which it can be argued that P » M is in force. The first is coordinate compounding, in which the order of elements should not matter semantically and is sometimes determined phonologically. The next is mobile affixes, in which the realization of a given affix as a prefix vs. a suffix appears to be phonologically determined. Finally, we will examine the evidence for affix metathesis or phonologically determined affix ordering.

9.4.1 Coordinate compounding

A number of cases have been described in which phonology constrains the linear order of morphemes. Mortensen (2006) presents examples in which the constituents of coordinate compounds are ordered according to their phonological properties, principally vowel quality and tone. In one dramatic case from Jingpho, which Mortensen draws from Dai (1990a b) and Dai and Xu (1992), the order of elements in compounds with coordinate semantics follows from the height of the tonic (root) vowels: the stem with the higher vowel always precedes the stem with the lower vowel. The chart in (38) illustrates the possible sequences:

(38) Coordinate compound sequencing possibilities in Jingpho

V1 \ V2	i	u	e	o	a
i	✓	✓	✓	✓	✓
u	✓	✓	✓	✓	✓
e			✓	✓	✓
o			✓	✓	✓
a					✓

Several examples cited by Mortensen (2006: 223–4) are given in (39):

(39) **high < high**
   a. kɔ́khûm   +   ŋkjin
      pumpkin   cucumber
      'melons and gourds (as a class)'

   high < mid
   b. tìp + sep
      press   exploit
      'exploit'

   high < low
   c. ʧî + khaì
      grandfather grandmother
      'maternal grandparents'

   mid < mid
   d. nèn + tsɔ̰̀
      low   high
      'height'

   mid < low
   e. ləko + kə̀tá?
      foot   hand
      'hands and feet'

   low < low
   f. sài + ʃàn
      blood   flesh
      'flesh and blood; kind'

Mortensen documents many such compounding cases, mainly involving vowel quality and/or tone, in which the order of elements follows a scale, sometimes phonetically understandable (as in this case of vowel height) and sometimes not, when historical changes have obscured the original phonetic or phonological basis for the scale.

Parallel examples are found even in English, as Mortensen observes (2006: 176, 187–90), both in the limited set of echo-reduplications like tip-top, sing-song, and flip-flop, but also in the broader class of what Malkiel (1959) terms "irreversible binomials": *hither and yon, spick and span,* etc. However, in English, phonological factors are only part of the story; their influence is statistical rather than the primary force in ordering generalizations (see e.g. Benor and Levy (2006) and the discussion by Mortensen).

9.4.2 Mobile affixes

Several compelling cases exist of "mobile" affixes, which vary freely between prefixal and suffixal attachment. These unusual cases are relevant to the phonology-morphology interface inasmuch as phonological considerations are the deciding factors. Cases of this kind have been documented in Afar (Fulmer 1991) and two dialects of Huave (Noyer 1994; Kim 2008).

In the San Francisco del Mar dialect of Huave, the subordinate marker *m*, stative marker *n*, completive marker *t* and 1st person marker *s* attach as prefixes to vowel-initial bases (40a) but as suffixes to consonant-initial bases (40b) (Kim 2008: 269, 276–7, 332, 338–9):

(40) a. m-[u-ty]   'SB-TV-eat = (that) s/he eats'
          n-[a-kants]   'ST-TV-red = red'
          t-[a-rang]   'CP-TV-do'
          s-[a-xijp]   '1-TV-bathe'

      b. [mojk-o]-m   'face.down-V-SB = (that) s/he lies face down'
          [pal-a]-n   'close-V-ST = closed'
          [wit-io]-t   'rise-V-CP'
          [wit-io-t-u]-s 'rise-V-CP-ITR-1'

      c. [ñ-u-kwal]-as 'ST-TV-child-1 = I am pregnant'
          [t-a-rang]-as 'CP-TV-do-1 = I did it'

When the base is consonant-initial and consonant-final (40c), phonological considerations are neutralized, since epenthesis would be required in either event. In such cases, suffixation and [a]-epenthesis emerge as the preferred option.

In the examples in (40a), the base-initial vowel whose presence is responsible for the prefixation of mobile affixes is, in each case, a theme vowel. Whether theme vowels are prefixed, as in (40a), or suffixed, as in (40b), is a lexical property of roots, generally predictable from the verb's valence. However, the prefix/suffix status of mobile affixes is not itself directly related to this lexical distinction. As Kim (2008) shows, the position of a mobile affix can vary even when the root is held constant (41a) vs. (41b), (41c) vs. (41d), (41e) vs. (41f); what matters is the phonological makeup of the initial element in the base of affixation, which could be the root or a variety of prefixes of different kinds (p. 339). The morpheme whose initial segment determines mobile affix placement is underlined in (41). (Brackets demarcate the base of affixation; see Kim (2008) for extensive discussion of the hierarchical structure of the Huave verb.)

(41)   Prefixed mobile affix   Suffixed mobile affix
     a. t-[e̲-chut-u-r]   b. [chut-u]-t
        CP-2̲-sit-V-2I   sit̲-CP
        'you sat'   's/he sat'
     c. s-[a̲-rang]   d. [t̲-a-rang]-as
        1=T̲V̲-do   CP̲-TV-do-1
        'I do'   'I did (it)'
     e. i-m-[e̲-pajk-a-r]   f. i-[[pajk̲-a]-m]
        FT-SB-2-face.up-V-2I   FT-face.up̲-V-SB
        'you'll lie face up'   'I lie face up'

As proposed by Kim (2008) and, for similar facts in San Mateo Huave, by Noyer (1994), such cases can be modeled in Optimality Theory by the general schema proposed by McCarthy and Prince (1993) in which phonological considerations ('P') outrank morphological considerations, e.g. affix ordering ('M'). In Huave, according to Kim, mobile affixes are preferentially suffixing (the 'M' condition), but will prefix if suffixation would produce consonant clusters that would require epenthesis (the 'P' condition) (Kim 2008: 340-41). That is, if suffixation would incur excess phonological cost, prefixation is resorted to instead. This is illustrated in (42) with the subordinate marker m:

(42)   Base of affixation: [a-rang]   'TV-do'
       Suffixed outcome: *[a-rang]-Vm   /gm/ cluster phonologically
                                            ill-formed; would require
                                            epenthesis to repair
       Prefixed outcome: m-[a-rant]   Phonologically well-formed

In cases where both prefixation and suffixation options would require epenthesis, suffixation is preferred, as illustrated in (43) with 1st person s (Kim 2008: 276, 340, 342).

(43)   Base of affixation: [t-a-rang]   'CP-TV-do = did (it)'
       Suffixed outcome: [t-a-rang]-as   /gs/ cluster phonologically
                                            ill-formed; requires epen-
                                            thesis to repair
       Prefixed outcome: *sV-[t-a-rang]   /st/ cluster phonologically
                                            ill-formed; would require
                                            epenthesis to repair

9.4.3 Local affix ordering

The Huave case just discussed illustrates the ability of phonology to determine the location of attachment of an affix on its cycle of attachment. In this sense, Huave mobile affixes pattern with infixes in theories in which infixation is regarded as phonologically optimizing (Chapter 6), and with cases of suppletive allomorphy whose distribution appear to be determined by the grammar (this chapter, section 9.1). What all of these cases have in common is that, within a given "step" or "layer" of morphology, the linear outcome of morphological combination is determined (to some degree) by phonological considerations.

An even more dramatic case of P » M would be a situation in which the actual morphological structure of a word—the hierarchical structure reflecting the relative order in which co-occurring affixes attach to a base—is affected by phonological considerations. Such cases are not easy to find. One example of local reordering, described as affix "metathesis" by Hargus and Tuttle (1997) (see also Hargus 2007: 383–4), occurs in Witsuwit'en. As in other Athapaskan languages, the negative prefix *s-* in Witsuwit'en normally linearly precedes "tense" (a category which, in Hargus and Tuttle's analysis, also includes aspect) in the verb. Illustrative examples are provided in (44a). However, the negative prefix will switch positions with a tense prefix if by doing so it can surface as the coda of a syllable (44b) (p. 207). The vertical bar indicates the boundary between prefixes and stem:

(44)   a. s_{NEG} < TENSE PREFIX   (basic order; s_{NEG} in onset, preceding vocalic tense prefix)

    i. /we#c'-<u>s-ɛ</u>-xw|.../   [wec'ə<u>sɛ</u>xwʔɛnʔ]   *[wec'ə<u>ɛs</u>xwʔɛnʔ]
        we#UNSP.OBJ-<u>NEG-PROG</u>-2PL.SUBJ 'you (pl.) don't see anything'

    ii. /we#<u>s-ə</u>-xw|.../   [we<u>sə</u>xwtl'et]   *[we<u>əs</u>xwtl'et]
        we#<u>NEG-OPT</u>-2PL.SUBJ 'you (pl.) aren't farting'

   b. TENSE PREFIX < s_{NEG} (s_{NEG} in syllable coda, following vocalic tense prefix)

    i. /we#c'-<u>ɛ-s</u>-|.../   [wec'<u>ɛs</u>|ʔɛnʔ]   *[wec'<u>sɛ</u>|ʔɛnʔ]
        we#UNSP_OBJ-<u>PROG-NEG</u>   's/he doesn't see anything'

    ii. /we#ts'-<u>ə-s</u>-|.../   [wets'<u>əs</u>|tl'et]   *[wets'<u>sə</u>|tl'et]
        we#1PL.SUBJ-<u>IMPF-NEG</u>   'we're not farting'

Hargus and Tuttle develop an analysis in which the imperative for the negative prefix /s_{NEG}-/ to occupy coda position outweighs the morphological imperative for /s$_{NEG}$-/ to precede tense prefixes. In the examples in (44b), the phonological imperative is satisfied, and the morphological imperative is (minimally) violated. In (44a), however, satisfying the phonological imperative is not possible, since metathesizing /s$_{NEG}$-/ and the vocalic tense prefix would create an ill-formed phonological sequence. In these cases, therefore, the morphological imperative is obeyed, and /s$_{NEG}$-/ occupies its normal position preceding tense.

9.4.4 Global affix ordering: Pulaar

One case that comes suggestively close to illustrating a global phonological principle that determines affix ordering is that of Pulaar, discussed by Arnott (1970) and Paster (2005). In a study of the Gombe dialect of Pulaar, Arnott (1970) observed that a dozen C or CV suffixes in the same general "zone" of the word occur in a phonologically determined order: suffixes with 't' precede suffixes with 'd', which precede suffixes with 'n', which precede suffixes with 'r' (Paster 2005: 164):

(45)   a. 'o jaɓ-<u>t-id-ir</u>-an-ii   yam depte 'e   semmbe[7] [G. Pulaar]
           3SG take-INT-COM-MOD- 1SG books with force
               DAT-PAST
           'He snatched all my books from me by brute force'

       b. 'o yam-ɗ-<u>it-in-ir</u>-ii   mo lekki   gokki kesi
           3SG$_i$ healthy-DEN-<u>REP-CAU-MOD</u>-PAST 3SG$_j$ medicine other new
           'He$_i$ cured him$_j$ with some new medicine'

       c. 'o   maɓɓ-<u>it-id</u>-ii   jolɗe   fuu
           3SG   close-<u>REV-COM</u>-PAST doors   all
           'He opened all the doors'

Paster (2005) discusses a similar "TDNR" template involving a half dozen suffixes in the Fuuta Tooro dialect. In a careful study of affix combinatorics conducted with a native speaker consultant, Paster finds that the order of affixes in Fuuta Tooro Pulaar largely conforms to semantic ordering principles of the kind articulated by Bybee (1985) and Rice (2000). Paster examines nine pairs of TDNR affixes which can co-occur. Of the nine pairs, four or five were found to vary in their ordering, with scope-related meaning differences. These include {Separative (T), Comprehensive (D)}, {Repetitive (T), Comprehensive

---

[7] CAU = causative, COM = comprehensive, DAT = dative, DEN = denominative, INT = intensive, MOD = modal, REP = repetitive, REV = reversive.

(D)}, {Modal (R), Comprehensive (D)} and {Repetitive (T), Causative (N)}. The latter pair is illustrated in (46) (pp. 176–177):

(46)   a. o   jaŋŋg-<u>in-it</u>-ii   kam   [Fuuta Tooro Pulaar]
        3SG learn-CAU-REP-PAST   1SG
        'he taught me again' (he taught me before)
        [[he taught me] again]

    b. o   jaŋŋg-<u>it-in</u>-ii   kam
        3SG learn-REP-CAU-PAST   1SG
        'he made me learn again' (before, I learned voluntarily)
        [he made me [learn again]]

Four pairs occur only in a fixed order. In two cases, this order does not contradict semantics or syntactic ordering principles. As with the separative and causative in (47), only one scopal relationship is pragmatically felicitous (Paster 2005: 175):

(47)   o   udd-it-in-ii   kam baafal ŋgal (*o udd-in-it-ii kam)
      3SG close-SEP-CAU-PAST 1SG door   det.
      'he made me open the door'

In another case {Repetitive, Modal}, order is fixed, regardless of the relative scope of the affixes (p. 178):

(48)   a. o   udd-it-ir-ii   baafal ŋgal sawru wodndu
                                  (*o udd-ir-it-ii)
        3SG close-REP-MOD-PAST door   det. stick   different
        'he closed the door again with a different stick'

    b. mi   udd-it-ir-ii   baafal ŋgal sawru (*mi udd-ir-it-ii)
        1SG close-REP-MOD-PAST door   det. stick
        'I closed the door with a stick again' (the same stick)

Paster concludes that there is no case in which the phonological TDNR template contravenes an ordering that one might otherwise expect on morphological grounds, and thus no clear evidence that phonology is interfering with morphology.

Paster also observes that the TDNR template, in which consonant sonority increases from left to right, is not particularly compelling as a phonological well-formedness condition to begin with, since on the surface, vowels typically separate the consonants which correspond to the elements of the template. Sonority-based ordering of consonant sequences is well known within syllables and across syllable boundaries, but these consonants are not adjacent. In sum, Paster concludes, the

Pulaar pattern is significant for coming closer than any other example
to being a case of phonologically driven affix sequencing—but still not
fully meeting that description.

9.4.5 Summary

In general, the extent to which phonology has been shown to affect the
ordering of morphological operations is fairly limited. Witsuwit'en
stands out as an exception to the generalization that the great bulk of
affix ordering is determined by the morphology, not by the phonology.
As a thought experiment, let us examine a very simple example from
Turkish, a language in which affix ordering is quite rigid, modulo the
potential for recursion in derivational morphology. The morphological rigidity of suffix order is phonologically non-optimizing in some
very obvious ways. Consider, for example, the interaction of the "occupational" suffix /-CI/ and case endings, e.g. the dative /-E/. Both can
attach directly to roots; as we will see, they can also combine with each
other. (In (49), orthographic representations are shown in italics;
otherwise, representations are in IPA.)

(49) a. "occupational" /-CI/   [Turkish]
          bilet   bilet   'ticket'   *biletçi*   bilet-ʧi   'ticket-seller'
          sigorta sigorta 'insurance' *sigortacı* sigorta-ʤɯ 'insurance
                                                                  underwriter'

      b. Dative /-E/
          bilet   bilet   'ticket'   *bilete*   bilet-e   'ticket-DAT'

The issue is phonological alternations that are required to repair
phonologically ill-formed sequences arising from suffixation, alternations which could be avoided if the morphology simply attached
suffixes in a different order.

Turkish epenthesizes vowels to break up unsyllabifiable consonant
clusters, and epenthesizes glides to break up vowel-vowel sequences.
Thus we find alternations like these:

(50)

gloss	UR	Occupational	(orthography)	Dative	(orthography)
a. 'film'	/film/	filim-ʤi	*filimci*	film-e	*filme*
'name'	/ism/	isim-ʤi	*isimci*	ism-e	*isme*
'clique'	/hizb/	hizip-ʧi	*hizipçi*	hizb-e	*hizbe*
b. 'appetizer'	/meze/	meze-ʤi	*mezeci*	meze-je	*mezeye*
'insurance'	/sigorta/	sigorta-ʤɯ	*sigortacı*	sigorta-ja	*sigortaya*

Forms like those in (51) illustrate how morphological reordering could optimize phonology. When /-CI/ and /-E/ co-occur, affix order is fixed. /-CI/, as a derivational suffix, always precedes case:

(51)   a. /film-CI-E/   *filimciye*   fil[i]mdʒi[j]e   epenthetic [i], [j]

b. */film-E-CI/   *filmeci*   *filmedʒi   no epenthesis

c. /meze-CI-E/   *mezeciye*   mezedʒi[j]e   epenthetic [j]

d. */meze-E-CI/   *mezeyeci*   *meze[j]edʒi   epenthetic [j]

In the attested outcome of /film-CI-E/ 'filmmaker (dative)' (51a), two epenthesis operations are required to bring the syllable structure of the resulting word into conformity with Turkish requirements. By contrast, the alternative affix ordering in which Dative /-E/ precedes Occupational /-CI/ (51b) would produce perfectly well-formed syllables with no need for epenthesis. But *filmeci* is completely impossible in Turkish; phonological considerations do not trump morphological constraints on relative affix order. This simple example of what does not occur does not prove anything by itself, but it is highly representative. It is simply not the case that affixes are freely reordered so as to optimize the phonology of individual words. The exceptions, like Huave, prove the rule.

9.5 Conclusion

The survey of existing and hypothetical P » M effects suggests that while it is possible for a language user to formulate a grammar in which a phonological constraint outweighs the morphological factors determining affix order, this is quite rare. Further research is needed to determine whether the reasons for this are historical, certain reanalysis possibilities being statistically unlikely to arise or be learned, or synchronic, with certain patterns falling outside of the scope of what universal grammar can describe.

10

Nonparallelism between phonological and morphological structure

In the preceding chapters of this book, we have seen many instances in which phonological patterns are imposed on morphological subconstituents of words. This was the particular focus in Chapter 7, on interleaving effects between phonology and morphology, and was in evidence in all of the other chapters as well. Insofar as the domains of lexical phonological patterns are coextensive with morphological subconstituents like root, stem, and word, phonology provides strong evidence about the internal branching morphological structure of a complex word.

However, on certain occasions there are clear structural mismatches in which phonological domains are not identified with morphological subconstituents. In some cases the phonological domain—often termed for convenience "Prosodic Root," or "Prosodic Stem," or "Prosodic Word"—is a subportion of a word (see e.g. Booij 1984; Sproat 1986; Inkelas 1989; Booij and Lieber 1993, among many others). This occurs most notably in the following situations:

(1) • Compounding, in which each constituent of the compound forms a separate phonological domain, vs. compounding in which the entire compound forms a single phonological domain. (This possibility was alluded to in Chapter 7, in the discussion of Malayalam stratum ordering.)

 • Noncohering affixes, which form a separate phonological domain from the stem they attach to, vs. cohering affixes, which form a unitary phonological domain with the base of affixation.

 • Prosodic Roots or Prosodic Stems which incorporate some material from outer affixes in order to be phonologically well-formed. (Cases of this were seen in Chapter 5, on reduplication, and Chapter 6, on infixation.)

These kinds of mismatches, in which phonology diagnoses a structure different from morphology, have sometimes been called "bracketing paradoxes" (e.g. Aronoff 1988; Cohn 1989).

Bracketing paradoxes are not limited to word-internal structure. There is also strong evidence that word-sized prosodic domains can include material outside of the morphological or lexical word, without being matched perfectly to existing syntactic constituents. Clitics are perhaps the most obvious example of this. It has been widely argued that clitics are phonologically defective syntactic terminal elements which must join with another (nonclitic) syntactic terminal element to form a single prosodic word (e.g. Inkelas 1989; Halpern 1992; Booij 1996; see also Zwicky and Pullum 1983; Kaisse 1985; Klavans 1985). Sometimes, as emphasized by Klavans (1985), the clitic combines phonologically with a constituent to which it is not syntactically related, as in this Serbo-Croatian example adapted from Browne (1974: 41), with glosses supplied by Anderson (1992: 203):

(2) Taj=mi=je   pesnik napisao knjigu   [Serbo-Croatian]
     That=ME=PAST   poet   wrote   book
     'That poet wrote me a book'

The famous second-position clitics of Serbo-Croatian can either follow the entire subject NP or, as in (2), the first (nonclitic) word in that NP. Zec and Inkelas (1990) propose that the clitics incorporate into the preceding Prosodic Word. The syntactic constituency of examples like these may be unclear, but it is unlikely that anyone would seriously propose that the dative object and the auxiliary verb are syntactically sister to the determiner of the subject NP.

The focus of this chapter will be not on clitics but on word-internal prosodic mismatches of the kind identified in (1). We begin with a brief tour of the prosodic hierarchy.

10.1 The prosodic hierarchy

In the 1980s, a focus on mismatches between phonological rule domains and morphological or syntactic constituency gave rise to a theory of autonomous prosodic structure which is related to but not isomorphic with morphological and syntactic structure. Several constituents occupy the "prosodic hierarchy" that is involved. A common version of the hierarchy, due to Selkirk 1978, 1986; Nespor and Vogel 1986; and Hayes 1989, is shown in (3):

(3)

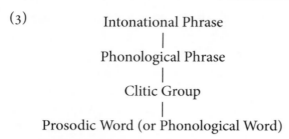

Intonational Phrase
|
Phonological Phrase
|
Clitic Group
|
Prosodic Word (or Phonological Word)

Most of these constituents are relevant only to sentence-level phonology; a large literature, including the articles collected in Inkelas and Zec (1990) and the recent overview by Selkirk (2011), discusses the relationship of these constituents to syntactic structure, including cliticization. There is also a lively literature on whether prosodic word structure can be recursive; see Peperkamp (1996); Itô and Mester (2003); Kabak and Revithiadou (2009); Selkirk 2011, among others.

The question of how the Prosodic Hierarchy should be extended down into the word level has been answered in two ways. One answer, offered by e.g. Nespor and Vogel (1986), Selkirk (1986, 2011), and McCarthy and Prince (1996, 1999b), is that the hierarchy bottoms out in the concrete metrical constituents of foot and syllable (4a). The other answer, put forward by Inkelas 1989, is that the Prosodic Word dominates more abstract constituents, Prosodic Stem and Prosodic Root, which function like the higher constituents, as formal rule domains (4b):

(4)   a.   b.

Prosodic Word   Prosodic Word
| |
Foot   Prosodic Stem
| |
Syllable   Prosodic Root

In practice, the literature on word-internal phonological domains has tended to avoid identifying the precise constituent involved, using general terms like "prosodic word" or simply "prosodic domain." That will largely be the case in the examples discussed here as well. It is the rare example that provides enough different kinds of mismatches between phonological domains and morphologixal constituents to be able to identify a Prosodic Root (different from a morphological root), a Prosodic Stem (different from a morphological stem), *and* a Prosodic Word in the same language.

10.2 Compounding: One prosodic domain or two?

The literature on the phonology of compounding constructions has often drawn attention to a distinction between compounds that behave phonologically like one word and those that behave phonologically like two words. For example, Nespor and Vogel (1986) propose that while Greek compounds form a single prosodic word and thereby receive one stress, e.g. *kúkla* 'doll' + *spíti* 'house' → [*kuklóspito*]$_\omega$ 'doll's house' (p. 112), the members of Hungarian compounds form separate prosodic words and retain their own lexical stresses: [könyv]$_\omega$[tár]$_\omega$ 'book collection' (p. 123).

10.2.1 Indonesian

In a detailed study of Indonesian, Cohn (1989) documents a stress difference between two constructions that concatenate stems: head-modifier compounds impose stress reduction on one member (5a) (p. 188), suggesting that they are competing for prominence within a single phonological word, while total reduplication constructions maintain two equal stresses (5b) (p. 184).

(5) a. polùsi udára   'pollution-air = air pollution'   [Indonesian]
          tùkaŋ cát   'artisan-print = printer'
          bòm átom   'bomb-atom = atom bomb'
          lùar nəgərí   'outside-country = abroad'

     b. waníta-waníta   'woman-woman = women'
         màʃarákat-màʃarákat   'society-society = societies'
         hák-hák   'right-right = rights'
         kərá-kərá   'monkey-monkey = monkeys'

Cohn attributes this stress difference to a prosodic differential: total reduplication consists of two prosodic domains, which Cohn terms "Clitic Groups," while compounding produces one (p. 201). The Main Stress Rule, which is responsible for subordinating all but the final stress to secondary stress, applies within the Clitic Group:

(6) { { polùsi }$_\omega$ { udára }$_\omega$ }$_{CG}$
     { { waníta }$_\omega$ }$_{CG}$ { { waníta }$_\omega$ }$_{CG}$

The fact that reduplication forms two Clitic Groups rather than one could potentially be seen as a reduplicative identity effect (see Cohn and McCarthy 1998, and Chapter 5). As Cohn shows, adding a suffix to a reduplicated structure causes it to be mapped into a single Clitic Group, resulting in stress subordination. The minimal pair in (7) is adapted from Cohn (1989: 202–3):

(7) a. { { kərá }$_\omega$ }$_{CG}$ {{ kərá }$_\omega$ }$_{CG}$ 'monkey-monkey= monkeys'
     b. { { kərá }$_\omega$ { kərá }$_\omega$ -ña}$_{CG}$ 'monkey-monkey-DEF = the monkeys'

Cohn and McCarthy (1998) assume that even suffixed reduplicated words, as in (7b), form two Clitic Groups, and that stress subordination applies regardless. On their account, suffixation introduces an asymmetry between base and reduplicant which makes it impossible for the two constituents to be identical. Once segment identity is unachievable by suffixation, Cohn and McCarthy reason, there is nothing to be gained by maintaining stress identity in violation of the more general constraint in the language against two main stresses in the same word. Cohn and McCarthy's account does not depend on Clitic Group parsing to distinguish between words with stress subordination and words without. This is made possible by the fact that Cohn and McCarthy assume a non-interleaving account in which phonological constraints have global access to the morphological structure of the entire word, rather than being constrained to applying only within prosodic domains.

10.2.2 Japanese

Itô and Mester (1996) invoke a distinction in Japanese, similar to that invoked by Cohn for Indonesian, in which Japanese stem-stem compounds form one Prosodic Word domain, and word-word compounds form two domains.

The evidence illustrating this asymmetry is presented in (8). Within Sino-Japanese stem-stem compounds, an initial member ending in /t/ will undergo assimilation, or what is termed "Contraction" in the literature, to a following obstruent (8a). However, when a stem-stem compound is itself compounded with another stem-stem compound into an [[A B] [C D]] structure (8b) (Itô and Mester 1996: 34–5), Contraction does not apply across the B] [C boundary:

(8)   Contraction   No contraction [Japanese]

a. *[AB] compounds: Contraction applies at the AB juncture*
   'different seat'   bes-seki   *betu-seki
   'annexed table',   bep-pyoo   *betu-hyoo
   'schedule'
   'lead-pen', 'pencil'   em-pitu   *eN-hitu
   'opposite start', 'rebel'   ham-patu   *haN-hatu
   'separate building'   bek-kaN   *betu-kaN
   'separate distribution'   bep-pai   *betu-hai

b. *[[AB][CD]] compounds: Contraction applies at AB, CD junctures but
   not at B][C juncture*
   'special building superintendent'   [toku-betu]-[kan-tyoo]
   'special delivery'   [toku-betu]-[hai-tatu]

Itô and Mester (1996: 34–9) propose that Contraction applies
within the Prosodic Word, and that Sino-Japanese compounding
combines two stems, or feet, into a single Prosodic Word. When
two compounds, each consisting of a Prosodic Word, are themselves
compounded together, the bipartite Prosodic Word structure remains
intact.

What is particularly interesting is the situation in which a stem-stem
compound is compounded with a single stem into an [[A B] C] or [A [B
C]] branching structure. As seen in (9), Contraction applies within the
inner stem-stem compound, but not between the single stem and its
compound sister:

(9)   a. [[A B] C] compound: Contraction applies at AB juncture but
          not at B]C juncture
          'special (assigned)'   *[toku-bes]-seki   [toku-betu]-seki
          seat'
          '10,000 year pen',   *[man-nem]-pitu   [man-neN]-hitu
          'fountain pen'

      b. [A [B C]] compound: Contraction applies at BC juncture but
          not at A [B juncture
          'separate transcription'   *bep-[pyoo-ki]   betu-[hyoo-ki]
          'new invention'   *sim-[patu-mei]   siN-[hatu-mei]

Within the framework of their prosodic analysis, Itô and Mester
propose that when a single Sino-Japanese stem is compounded with an

existing compound, it does not incorporate into that Prosodic Word, and instead forms its own. Because of the resulting Prosodic Word boundary, Contraction cannot apply across the boundary between an internal Sino-Japanese compound and another constituent.

The prosodic structure of the compounds illustrated in (8a,b) and (9a,b) are summarized here:

(10)

Structure	gloss	example	Contraction?
a. [A B]	'different seat'	{bes-seki}$_\omega$	yes
b. [[A B] C]	'special (assigned) seat'	{toku-betu}$_\omega$ {seki}$_\omega$	no
c. [A [B C]]	'separate transcription'	{betu}$_\omega$ {hyoo-ki}$_\omega$	no
d. [[A B][C D]]	'special delivery'	{toku-betu}$_\omega$ {hai-tatu}$_\omega$	no

The "type-shifting" of an individual stem to Prosodic Word status in the 3-member compounds in (10b,c) is forced by Itô and Mester's (p. 38) "Prosodic Homogeneity Principle:"

(11)   Prosodic Homogeneity: Compound members must be of equal prosodic rank

A similar principle is proposed by Han (1994) for compounding in Korean.

10.2.3 Malayalam

A set of facts that are at least superficially parallel to those in Indonesian and Japanese can be found in Malayalam, whose two compounding constructions were discussed in Chapter 7. In Malayalam, Subcompounds, with head-modifier semantics, form a single domain for accentuation, whereas Cocompounds, with coordination semantics, form separate domains for accentuation (Mohanan 1982, 1986, 1995). Malayalam compounds figured in a discussion of phonology-morphology interleaving in Chapter 7; they are one of the case studies that inspired the theory of stratum ordering. A minimal pair illustrating the contrast between Subcompounds and Cocompounds is given in (12), adapted from Mohanan 1995: 43, 49). Stress is marked with an acute accent. Tone, not marked in the source, has been added to these examples in accordance with the general principles elucidated by

Mohanan (1995: 51): Low tone (L) falls on the syllable with primary stress, while High tone (H) falls on the final syllable of the domain:

(12)   [Malayalam]

Subcompound: [méeša-ppetti]-kaḷə 'table-box-PL = tables-boxes'
                      L   H

Cocompound: [méeša-petti]-kaḷə 'table-box-PL = tables and boxes'
                    L H   L H

Subcompound: [káattə-maṟam]   'forest-tree = forest tree'
                       L   H

Cocompound: [áatə-máatə]-kaḷə   'goat-cow-PL = goats and cows'
                     L H L   H

As was briefly mentioned in Chapter 7, Sproat (1986) proposes that the difference between the two types of compounds in Malayalam can be captured by analyzing Subcompounds as one Prosodic Word and Cocompounds as two Prosodic Words (see also Inkelas 1989). On this account, stress and tone assignment would not have to be sensitive to morphological level but would simply apply automatically within a Prosodic Word. Only the mapping between morphological and Prosodic Word structure would be sensitive to construction type:

(13)   a. Subcompound: single Prosodic Word
          {méeša-ppetti}$_\omega$-kaḷə   'table-boxes'
          {káattə-maṟam}$_\omega$ 'forest-tree'

       b. Cocompound: two Prosodic Words
          {méeša}$_\omega$-{ppétti}$_\omega$-kaḷə   'tables and boxes'
          {áatə}$_\omega$-{máatə}$_\omega$-kaḷə   'goat-cow-PL = goats and cows'

By complicating the representations with this new layer of structure, Sproat and Inkelas argue, the grammar can be simplified by locating both Subcompounding and Cocompounding in the same morphological level. This simplification is significant in that it eliminates the need for a loop between the two levels. Mohanan (1982, 1986) had argued for a loop between Level 2 (Subcompounding) and Level 3 (Cocompounding) on the grounds that either type of compound can be embedded within the other; there is no extrinsic ordering between the processes.

In a 1995 overview of Malayalam lexical phonology, Mohanan responds to the prosodic reanalysis, arguing that reference to prosodic structure does not simplify the Level Ordering system. Mohanan cites evidence from complex compounds with three or more members that prosodic structure is not sufficient to distinguish Subcompounding and Cocompounding. Examples of compounds with complex embedding relations (some repeated from Chapter 7) are given in (14):

(14)   a. Cocompound within Subcompound (Mohanan 1986: 123)

        jaatimátawidwéeṣam

        L H L H   L   H

        [[jáaṯi + máṯam]$_{Co}$ + widwéeṣam]$_{Sub}$

         L H   L H   L   H

        caste   religion   hatred

        'hatred of religion and caste'

    b. Subcompounds within Cocompound within Subcompound (Mohanan 1982: 50; tone and stress not marked in source)

        maaṯrəsneehapaṯniwiḏweeṣawikaaŕaŋŋalə

        [[[maaṯr   + sneeham]$_{Sub}$ + [paṯni + wiḏweeṣam]$_{Sub}$]$_{Co}$

          mother   love   wife   hatred

        + wikaaŕam]$_{Sub}$ -kaḷ

         emotion   -PL

        'the emotions of mother love and wife hatred'

Mohanan's general argument is this: on an analysis in which each tone and stress domain is a Prosodic Word, compounds like those in (14) would have the following prosodic structure:

(15)   a. [[jáaṯi + máṯam]$_{Co}$ + widwéeṣam]$_{Sub}$

       {jáaṯi}$_\omega$ {máṯam}$_\omega$ {widwéeṣam}$_\omega$

    b. [[[maaṯr + sneeham]$_{Sub}$ + [paṯni   + wiḏweeṣam]$_{Sub}$]$_{Co}$

       {maaṯr sneeham}$_\omega$ {paṯni   wiḏweeṣam}$_\omega$

      + wikaaŕam]$_{Sub}$

      {wikaaŕam}$_\omega$

As seen in (15), when an existing Cocompound is subcompounded with another word (*widwéeṣam*, in (15a), or *wikaaŕam*, in (15b)), that word does not join into a tone and stress domain with its sister Cocompound; instead, it acquires its own stress and tone melody, suggesting that it forms its own Prosodic Word. This would be consistent with Itô and Mester's Prosodic Homogeneity Principle, which requires sisters in a compounding structure to have equal prosodic status.

As Mohanan (1995) points out, however, the Prosodic Word account leaves unexplained the fact that gemination behaves differently from stress and tone. Gemination applies across the internal boundary of Subcompounds but not across the internal boundary of Cocompounds, regardless of the Prosodic Word structure diagnosed by tone and stress assignment. In the three-word compound in (16a), for example, gemination applies to the third word, reflecting the fact that it is subcompounded with the constituent formed by the first two (Mohanan 1995: 52; stress added). Even though, due to the Prosodic Homogeneity Principle, the third word is ostensibly a Prosodic Word of its own, gemination still applies just as it does across the internal boundary of Subcompounds that form a single Prosodic Word, like that in (16b) (Mohanan 1995: 49; stress added):

(16)   a. [[A B]$_{Co}$ C]$_{Sub}$ {méeša}$_\omega$ {pétti}$_\omega$ {**kk**asáala}$_\omega$
               table   box   chair
               'chairs made from tables and boxes'

       b. [A B]$_{Sub}$ {méeša   **pp**étti}$_\omega$
               table   box
               'table-boxes'

If the internal Prosodic Word boundary in the [A B] Cocompound in (16a) is responsible for the lack of gemination within the Cocompound, then the Prosodic Word analysis is at a loss to explain why gemination does apply *across* the Prosodic Word boundary between words B and C.

This example, and others like it, show that Prosodic Word structure is not by itself sufficient to account for the application of gemination. Instead, Mohanan argues, strata are still necessary; introducing Prosodic Word structure does not eliminate the need for (other types of) morphological conditioning of phonology. This example shows the value in looking more deeply into a dataset, a point to which we will return in the conclusion to this chapter.

10.2.4 Interim summary

To wrap up this limited survey of cases in which prosodic structure has been invoked to explain the behavior of compounds, we have seen that characterizing compounds as one vs. two prosodic constituents can correlate with the application or nonapplication, respectively, of phonological patterns to the compound as a whole. The necessity for invoking prosodic structure is somewhat of a theory-internal matter, as was seen by the discussion of Indonesian, and the success of the approach also depends on how well it is integrated with all of the phonology, as opposed to just one pattern of interest, as was seen in the discussion of Malayalam.

10.2.5 Cohering vs. noncohering affixes

Paralleling prosodic differences across types of compounds are prosodic differences across affixes. Booij (1984) was one of the first to highlight the distinction between "cohering" and "noncohering" affixes and to model that distinction using prosodic structure: cohering affixes form a single Prosodic Word with the base of affixation, while noncohering affixes form a separate Prosodic Word.

In Dutch, 'cohering' affixes syllabify with the stem they combine with. Noncohering affixes syllabify separately. Non-native suffixes, and all prefixes, are all of the noncohering type. The difference between the two types of suffix in Dutch is illustrated in (17) with a pair of suffixes, both of which are semantically equivalent to English '-ish' (Booij 1984: 152):

(17) 'reddish' *rod-ig*   {*rod-ig*}$_\omega$ (ro)$_\sigma$(dəx)$_\sigma$ [Dutch]
      rood-achtig {*rood*}$_\omega$ {*-achtig*}$_\omega$ (rot)$_\sigma$ (ax)$_\sigma$ (təx)$_\sigma$

When the cohering suffix *-ig* combines with a consonant-final stem like *rod*, the stem-final consonant syllabifies as the onset of the syllable containing *-ig*, as evidenced by the failure of coda devoicing to apply to the /d/ of *rod*. By contrast, a noncohering suffix like *-achtig* forms its own domain for syllabification. The preceding stem-final consonant has to syllabify as a coda (as it would if no suffix were present) and exhibits coda devoicing as a result. Booij models this difference in behavior with Prosodic Word structure, as seen in (17). Syllabification operates within, but not across, Prosodic Word boundaries.

Booij (1984, 2002a: 172, 2002b) connects the prosodic asymmetry posited in examples like (17) to an interesting asymmetry in coordination constructions in Dutch. As seen in (18), noncohering Dutch suffixes like *-achtig* allow deletion under identity in coordination constructions. If two words end in the same noncohering suffix, the suffix is omissible from the first conjunct (18a–c) (Booij 1984: 151–2). The same is true of two compounds ending in the same stem (18d–f) (1984: 146):[1]

---

[1] The set of participating constructions is slightly broader, also including 'either ... or' constructions such as *hetzij hoofdaccent, hetzij nevenaccent* → *hoof, hetzij nevenaccent* 'either main stress or secondary stress' (Booij 1984: 148) as well as coordinated prefixed

(18) a. *stormachtig en regenachtig*   ~ *storm en regenachtig*
          'stormy and rainy'

      b. *zwangerschap en moederschap*   ~ *zwanger en moederschap*
          'pregnancy and motherhood'

      c. *eerzaam en deugdzaam*   ~ *eer en deugdzaam*
          'respectable and virtuous'

      d. *wespensteken en bijesteken*   ~ *wespen en bijesteken*
          'wasp and bee stings'

      e. *landbouw en tuinbouw*   ~ *land en tuinbouw*
          'agriculture and horticulture'

      f. *een elfjarige, twaalfjarige jonge*   ~ *een elf, twaalfjarige jonge*
          'an eleven-year-old, twelve-year-old boy'

Booij (1984) unites these patterns by observing that noncohering affixes and members of compounds form individual Prosodic Words. His description of the deletion rule (p. 151) can be paraphrased as: "Delete a phonological word if it is adjacent to a conjunction, has an identical counterpart in the other conjunct, and if the remnant of deletion is also a phonological word."

Deletion under identity fails when any of these conditions is not met. As shown in (19), deletion *cannot* target a cohering suffix like *-ig*, which does not constitute a phonological word (Booij 1984: 149) (19a,b).

(19) a. *blauig en rodig*   ~ **blau en rodig*
          'blueish and reddish'

      b. *absurditeit en banaliteit* ~ **absurd en banaliteit*
          'absurdity and banality'

English, of course, also has a version of this pattern, as illustrated by coordinations like *pre- and postwar, over- and underapplication*. On deletion under morphological identity in other languages, see e.g. Booij (1984) on German, Orgun (1996) and Kabak (2007) on Turkish, and Vigário and Frota (2002) on Portuguese.

---

words (*ontwikkelingen en verwikkelingen* → *ont en verwikkelingen* 'developments and complications' (p. 154). In Dutch, an identical initial element can also delete from the second conjunct under coordination: *regelordening en regeltoepassing* → *regelordening en toepassing* 'rule ordering and rule application' (p. 148).

10.3 Affix clusters forming prosodic domains

More dramatic than examples of individual affixes constituting their own prosodic domains are cases in which a cluster of adjacent affixes together forms a prosodic domain which excludes the base of affixation. We will review three apparent cases of this phenomenon here. These cases provide the most dramatic mismatch thus far between the presumed morphological constituent structure of the word and the parsing of the word into prosodic domains within which phonological patterns are imposed. In these cases, the coexisting prosodic and morphological structures seem to contradict each other, a possibility predicted by their autonomous existences.

10.3.1 Nimboran

In Nimboran, evidence from stress assignment and vowel harmony shows that suffixed verbs have bipartite prosodic structure: the root forms one prosodic domain, and all of the suffixes together form another. A Papuan language of Irian Jaya, Nimboran (Anceaux 1965) is heavily suffixing; its position class morphology has been analyzed in Inkelas (1993).

Most Nimboran verbs exhibit two stresses: one on the root, and one somewhere within the suffix complex. Root stress is apparently lexicalized, but stress within the suffix complex is clearly rule governed. If no suffix has its own lexical stress, then stress falls on the final vowel of the suffix complex (20). Page numbers come from Anceaux (1965):

(20)   No lexically stressed suffixes: default final stress in suffix complex
                                                            [Nimboran]
   a. [ŋedóu]p-[k-be-k-u]p   →   [ŋedóu]p[kebekú]p   p. 189
       draw-DU.SUBJ-6LOC-   'We two drew from
       PAST-1   here to above'
   b. [ŋedóu]p-[k-se-p-am]p   →   [ŋedóu]p[kesepám]p   p. 189
       draw-DU.SUBJ-7LOC-   'They two (m.) drew
       RPAST-3M   recently from here to there'

If one or more suffixes has a lexical stress, then the rightmost of these stresses surfaces; the others delete (21).[2]

---

[2] In inputs (to the left of the arrow in these examples), uppercase 'N' represents an underlyingly placeless nasal.

(21)   a. [ŋgedóu]p-[k-bá-k-u]p   → [ŋgedóu]p[kebáku]p p. 187
            draw.DU-DU.SUBJ-2LOC-   'We two drew above'
            PAST-1

        b. [ŋgedóu]p-[k-rár-k-u]p   → [ŋgedóu]p[kráku]p   p. 203
            draw.DU-DU.SUBJ-M.OBJ-   'We two drew him (here)'
            PAST-1

        c. [ŋgedóu]p-[k-rár-bá-k-u]p   → [ŋgedóu]p[krebáku]p p. 203
            draw.DU-DU.SUBJ-M.OBJ-   'We two drew him above'
            2LOC-PAST-1

        d. [ŋgedúo]-[rár-maN-ná-r-ám] → [ŋgedúo][remanarám] p. 204
            draw.SG-M.OBJ-INC.DU.SUBJ-   'You and I (sg.) will draw
            5LOC-FUT-INC   him far away'

        e. [ŋgedúo]-[maN-ná-r-ám]   →[ŋgedúo][manarám]   p. 188
            draw.SG-INC.DU.SUBJ-5LOC-   'You (sg.) and I will draw far
            FUT-INC   away'

The only verbs not to exhibit exactly two stresses are those in which either the suffix complex (22a,b) or the root (22c–e) is monomoraic. Default final stress assignment, seen applying in (20), does not apply to monomoraic domains:

(22)   Unaccented monomoraic suffix complex:
        a. [ŋgedúo]p-[p-am]p   →   [ŋgedúo]p[pam]p   p. 187
            draw.SG-RPAST-3M   'He drew recently (here)'

        b. [sá]p-[Na-d-u]p   →   [sá]p[ndï]p   p. 126
            drive away.SG-PART-FUT-1 'I will drive away from (here)'

        Unaccented monomoraic root:
        c. [dḯ]p-[k-d-u]p   →   [dḯ]p[kedú]p   p. 87
            roast-DU.SUBJ-FUT-1   'We two will roast (here)'

        d. [krḯ]p-[k-rár-d-u]p   →   [krḯ]p[kráru]p   p.129
            build-DU.SUBJ-PART-FUT-1 'We two will build (here)'

        e. [i]p-[bá-k-e]p   →   [i]p[báke]p   p. 156
            bathe-2LOC-PAST-2   'You bathed above'

The fact that both root and suffix complexes are subject to the same stress constraints (one stress is required unless the constituent is monomoraic) points to a structural symmetry, which Inkelas (1993) captures by positing that both are equivalent prosodic domains.[3]

---

[3] Inkelas (1993) in fact argues that the suffixes form a morphological constituent, not just a prosodic one, and that this is not a case of morphology-phonology mismatch at all. If so, then Nimboran is structurally unusual in a very different way.

Vowel harmony respects the internal boundary between the prosodic constituents diagnosed by stress assignment. As Anceaux states and as is illustrated by the data in this section, about 25 percent of Nimboran verbal suffixes are harmony triggers. Anceaux terms the harmony pattern Apophonicity; in the examples, Apophonicity-triggering suffixes are double-underlined in the forms to the left of the arrow, and the harmonic span is double-underlined in the forms to the right of the arrow. The minimal pair in (23a,b) illustrate a verb without Apophonic suffixes (23a), compared to one with nearly homophonous suffixes, one of which (underlined) is an Apophony trigger (23b):

(23) a. [ŋgedúo]p-[maN-se-d-ám]p   →[ŋgedúo][mansedám]p. 188
         draw.SG-INC.DU.SUBJ-7LOC-   'You and I will draw from
         FUT-INC   here to there'

      b. [ŋgedúo]p-[maN-sa-d-ám]p   →[ŋgedúo][mensedím]p. 188
         draw.SG-INC.DU.SUBJ-8LOC-   'You and I will draw from
         FUT-INC   here to below'

The harmony pattern fronts non-final vowels (e.g. $a \rightarrow e$) and raises final vowels (e.g. $e \rightarrow i$, $a \rightarrow i$). The important observation about Apophonicity is that it is bidirectional, affecting suffixes to either side of the trigger, but only within the suffix complex. Roots are never affected by the presence of an Apophonic suffix:

(24) a. [ŋgedúo]p-[maN-sa-d-ám]p   → [ŋgedúo][mensedím]p. 188
         draw.SG-INC.DU.SUBJ-8LOC-   'You and I will draw from
         FUT-INC   here to below'

      b. [iáN]p-[k-máN-bá-k-e]p   → [iáŋ][kemembéki]   p.141
         ask-DU.SUBJ-MO.PART-LOC-   'You two asked him above'
         PAST-2

      c. [príb]-[tem-ŋkát-t-u]   → [príp][temgétï]   p. 109
         throw-DUR-ITER-PRES-1   'I am throwing repeatedly
                                            here'

This behavior is consistent with the proposed prosodic structure: harmony applies within, but not across, a prosodic domain.

The fact that two phonological patterns—stress assignment and vowel harmony—both respect the same prosodic domains is what makes the postulation of prosodic domains more convincing in the Nimboran case than, say, in Malayalam, where they captured some but not all of the morphological conditioning of phonology in compounding.

10.3.2 Athapaskan

Various researchers have proposed, for several Athapaskan languages, that the highly prefixing Athapaskan verb is parsed into more than one Prosodic Word.

In Tahltan, for example, Alderete and Bob (2005) propose that the verb stem forms one Prosodic Word and the preceding span of prefixes forms another. The proposal is based on the distribution of stress. Drawing from a 1983 corpus assembled by Pat Shaw, Alderete and Bob (2005) note that stress tends to be alternating in the verb and that stress clash is avoided, with one principled exception: stress clash is tolerated across the prefix-stem boundary. Alderete and Bob attribute this to the bipartite Prosodic Word structure of Tahltan verbs. Stress is assigned within the Prosodic Word. Prosodic Words are parsed into feet, accounting for these two generalizations: "the stem syllable is always stressed," and "there is always a stressed syllable that precedes the stem syllable" (p. 374).

In the following examples, all prefixes are lumped into a single Prosodic Word. Within the prefixal Prosodic Word, stress is generally alternating and does not occur on adjacent syllables, showing that a prohibition on stress clash is active in the language. However, stress clash does occur across Prosodic Word boundaries; a monosyllabic prefix followed by a stem with initial stress produces clash, as seen in (25b) (Alderete and Bob 2005: 374–9):

(25) a. {mè-}{detɬ'óy}   'his/her pelts'   [Tahltan]
         {ʔùdes-}{ʔúːt}   'I whistled'
         {mèʔe-}{k'áhe}   'his/her fat'
         {ʔudèθiː-}{dlét}   'we (dual) melted it'
         {ʔàkayíː-}{gìdða}   'did she wring it out?'

      b. {mè-}{láʔ}   'his/her hand'
         {kàː-}{ts'ét}   'I scratched it out'
         {ʔès-}{θóne}   'my star'

Similar symmetries between prefix spans and stems have been noted for other Athapaskan languages, including Navajo (McDonough 1990, 2000), Tsek'ene (Halpern 1992), Slave (Rice 1989, 1993), and Witsu-wit'en (Hargus 2007). In Slave, for example, coda consonants are allowed in two places: stem-finally and at the end of the span of conjunct prefixes (those in the zone closest to the stem) (Rice 1989).

In Witsuwit'en, it is coda clusters that have this same distribution (Hargus 2007: 586). Rice and Hargus both observe that this pattern could be accounted for by proposing that (conjunct) prefixes form one prosodic domain, while stems form another. Codas (in Slave) or coda clusters (in Witsuwit'en) are limited to domain-final position.

In an interesting discussion, Hargus (2007) notes that while prosodic domains can be invoked in Witsuwit'en, they are not of broad utility in the language, tending instead to be used for morpheme-specific purposes. Hargus observes that the prosodic domain containing prefixes does not have the same properties as the domain containing the stem, and proposes (p. 587) that the two domains not be identified as equals.

For example, [w] is prohibited at the end of the Prefix domain but allowed at the end of the Stem domain (p. 586). Post-glottal schwa deletion applies only when its environment is completely contained within a Prefix domain, and not otherwise (pp. 586, 625). Hargus enumerates a number of conditions of this sort that seem to support the existence of a prosodic domain containing only prefixes. However, Hargus also notes that even invoking a prosodic domain used uniquely for the prefix span does not fully account for the morphological conditioning of Witsutwit'en phonology, a point similar to that made by Mohanan (1986) regarding gemination in Malayalam. Hargus cites as one example the case of /s/ voicing. Several s-prefixes—the s-conjugation, s-negative, and s-qualifier prefixes—voice to [z] when in the onset position internal to a Prefix domain (26a). The prefixes surface as [s] when domain-initial (26b) or in coda position. Examples are given here, from Hargus 2007: 590–91; the relevant prefix is underlined:

(26) a. s-prefix realized as [z]: Prefix domain-   [Witsuwit'en]
internal onset

    i. naabəz̲əcłkʷəz   'I drove them around'   (s-conjunct)
    ii. ts'eneweebəz̲əcłdzit 'I haven't woken them up'(s-negative)
    iii. həbəz̲icłyi   'I killed them'   (s-qualifier)

b. s-prefix realized as [s]: Prefix domain-initial
    i. s̲ecłyu   'I killed it'   (s-qualifier)

c. s-prefix realized as [s]: coda
    i. c'əs̲dətbəz   'we (du.) stretched it'   (s-conjunct)
    ii. nəwetos̲dəldił   'let's (du.) not throw it   (s-negative)
                    (rope, pl.) away'

However, Hargus observes, it is not sufficient to say that /s/ voicing is determined by position within the Prefix domain. There are morphologically conditioned counterexamples. For example, when preceded by the qualifier or unspecified prefix *c'-*, the *s*-conjunct and *s*-negative prefixes are voiceless, even when in a domain position correlated with voicing (p. 591):

(27)   c'əsəstəł   'I kicked something'   (*s*-conjunct)
        wec'əsəs?atl 'I haven't eaten'   (*s*-negative)

There are more details, but these examples suffice to illustrate Hargus's conclusion: "Within the [Prefix] domain to s-voicing, the failure of *c'-* to pattern with other conjunct prefixes is surprising. However, if the context for s-voicing is determined by particular morphemes, then the facts...can be accommodated." (p. 591). Hargus points out (e.g. p. 600) that a great deal of Witsuwit'en phonology, even internal to the Prefix domain, is highly morphologically conditioned, and comes to the same general conclusion suggested by Mohanan for Malayalam: even if invoking prosodic domain structure improves the account of some phenomena in the language, it does not obviate the need for (other kinds of) morphological conditioning of phonology.

10.3.3 Internal access: Prosodic Roots, Stems, and Words

The introduction of prosodic structure, independent of though conditioned by morphological structure, makes it possible to derive effects in which "late" phonological processes appear sensitive to very deeply embedded morphological structure. This occurs when "early" or deeply embedded morphological constituents occasion the construction of a Prosodic Root, Stem, or Word, which persists throughout the rest of the derivation.

The question of Bracket Erasure was discussed in Chapter 7, in the context of the interleaving of phonology and morphology. It is clear that phonological patterns imposed concomitantly with a given affixation construction can make reference to the boundary between the input stem and that affix, but it has been an open question whether this kind of access to internal morphological structure is also true of phonological patterns imposed, for example, by higher affixes, or at the word level. Strict theories of Bracket Erasure (e.g. Chomsky and Halle 1968; Pesetsky 1979) say no; weaker theories say yes. In Chapter 7 we examined several cases in which a weaker version of Bracket Erasure seemed to be motivated.

However, all bets are off if prosodic structure can be used as a proxy for morphological structure. If, in languages like Nimboran and Slave, the root is always demarcated with a prosodic domain boundary, phonological patterns triggered by outer affix constructions will have no problem in detecting even a deeply embedded root boundary. Such examples appear to exist (as was discussed in Chapter 7). Intriguing evidence suggests that indeed the access is mediated, at least in some cases, by prosodic structure. These are cases in which the internal boundary which is accessed by the phonology of an outer affix is not perfectly coincident with a morphological boundary, but is offset by a bit, apparently in service of the well-formedness of a prosodic domain. All of the examples discussed here involve "exfixation," the term applied by Downing (1997b, 1998b, 1999b) to the phenomenon of apparent internal root reduplication which targets not the root per se but rather a prosodic domain consisting of the root and some immediately adjacent phonological material. Exfixation was also discussed in Chapter 6, since it involves infixing reduplication.

10.3.4 Exfixation

In a number of cases, a late morphological process of reduplication targets the root, even when the root has already undergone significant affixation. Aronoff (1988) refers to these as "head operations," and Booij and Lieber (1993) propose that they involve reference to a prosodic constituent which matches the morphological root. These operations are of special interest when the targeted prosodic constituent does not perfectly match the morphological root, but incorporates adjacent material into it. In the cases we will examine, this material is a consonant which supplies the prosodic constituent with a needed syllable onset or syllable coda. Cases of this kind, termed "exfixation" in Downing's (1997b, 1998b, 1999b) comprehensive surveys and discussed in Inkelas and Zoll (2005), are found in a variety of languages, including Kihehe, Eastern Kadazan, Samala, Tagalog, and Javanese. Many of these cases were already discussed in Chapter 5. Here, we present just one illustrative example from Kihehe.

In Kihehe, a process of verbal reduplication meaning 'do X a little bit' targets the morphological verb stem, i.e. the root plus any following suffixes (Odden and Odden 1985; Downing 1997b, 1998b, 1999b; Hyman 2009). This is a very common pattern throughout the Bantu family; we saw examples in Chapter 5 of the range of morphological restrictions placed on verb stem reduplication in various Bantu languages. In Kihehe the process is straightforward (28a–c), with one principled exception: prefixes which syllabify with the root are also included in reduplication (28d–f). The data in (28) are taken from Hyman (2009: 192), citing Odden and Odden (1985):

(28) a. kú-fi-gúl-a   → kú-fi-[gul-a]-[gúl-a]   [Kihehe]
          INF-3PL.OBJ-buy-FV   'to buy a bit of them'

      b. kú-tov-a   → kú-[tov-a]-[tóv-a]
          INF-beat-FV   'to beat a bit'

      c. tu-gul-iite   → tu-[gul-iite]-[gúl-iite]
          1PL.SUBJ-buy-PERF   'we shopped a bit'

      d. kú-mw-iimb-il-a   → kú-[mw-iimb-il-a]-[mw-iimb-íl-a]
          (< kú-mu-imb-il-a)
          INF-3SG.OBJ-sing-APPL-FV   'to sing a bit to him'

      e. kw-íimb-a (< kú-imb-a) → [kw-íimb-a]-[kw-iímb-a]
          INF-sing-FV   'to sing a bit'

      f. n-gw-iítite   → [n-gw-itite]-[n-gw-iítite]
          1SG.SUBJ-OBJ-poured   'I poured it a bit'

On Downing's (1997b, 1998b, 1999b) analysis, Kihehe reduplication is not actually morphological stem reduplication. Instead, it is Prosodic Stem reduplication. Downing proposes that in Kihehe, a Prosodic Stem is constructed in each verb. Its left edge coincides with the beginning of the syllable containing the root-initial segment. For consonant-initial roots like those in (28a–c), the Prosodic Stem and the morphological stem coincide. For vowel-initial roots like those in (28d–f), the Prosodic Stem begins earlier in the word. The verbs in (28) are repeated, in (29), with Prosodic Stems indicated with curly brackets:

(29) a. kú-fi-{gúl-a}   → kú-fi-[gul-a]-[gúl-a]

      b. kú-{tov-a}   → kú-[tov-a]-[tóv-a]

      c. tu-{gul-iite}   → tu-[gul-iite]-[gúl-iite]

      d. kú-{mw-iimb-il-a}   → kú-[mw-iimb-il-a]-[mw-iimb-íl-a]

      e. {kw-íimb-a}   → [kw-íimb-a]-[kw-iímb-a]

      f. {n-gw-iítite}   → [n-gw-itite]-[n-gw-iítite]

With Prosodic Stem structure in place throughout the derivation, reduplication can be a very late process but still appear to be targeting (more or less) the root. Reference to Prosodic Stem structure makes it possible to maintain the position that the reduplication process does not need direct access to information about the morphological allegiance of individual segments. While it may seem a trivial technical point, there are advantages to not having to specify morphological allegiance of segments. For example, even in these examples, it is not always easy to know where to place the morpheme boundaries. In *kwíimba* (29e), from /ku-imb-a/ 'INFINITIVE-sing-FV', gliding and vowel lengthening result in a long [íi]. Does that entire long vowel belong to the root, even though its first mora arguably comes from the prefix? Is the vowel split between two different morphemes, even though its quality comes entirely from the root? These questions don't have to be asked if, instead of targeting the root morpheme specifically, reduplication targets the Prosodic Stem or Root.

10.4 Conclusion

We have seen two kinds of motivation for parsing morphologically complex words into prosodic domains, rather than having phonology be directly conditioned by morphology. One motivation, more on the empirical side, comes from mismatches between the domains that phonology applies in and the constituents of morphological structure. The other, more theoretical, comes from the desire to simplify the way in which phonology accesses morphology, by making the Prosodic Hierarchy the middleman. Once prosodic domains are in place, one might hypothesize that phonology never has direct access to morphology, but that access is mediated through the parsing of (potentially morphologically complex) words into prosodic constituents such as Prosodic Root, Stem, Word, and Clitic Group, to which individual phonological patterns are sensitive.

Both of these motivations played a large role in the development of the prosodic hierarchy in the literature on the phonology-syntax interface. In the apparent absence of phonological phenomena making direct reference to syntactic and semantic features such as case or agreement, and faced with evidence that postlexical phonological rule domains are not always coextensive with syntactic constituents, Selkirk (1978) and Nespor and Vogel (1986) proposed a widely adopted theory in which sentences are parsed into the higher-order constituents of the Prosodic Hierarchy. Phonology applies within, and references, these constituents, not syntactic ones (see also Hayes 1989 and the papers in

Inkelas and Zec 1990). Insofar as prosodic constituents like Prosodic Root, Prosodic Stem, and Prosodic Word have been linked to the levels or strata of Lexical Morphology and Phonology or Stratal OT, then theories of Level Ordering can be restated in prosodic terms; this point is elaborated in Inkelas (1989).

In this chapter we have focused on mismatch evidence in exploring uses for the lower-end prosodic units. Still open is the question raised by Mohanan, for Malayalam, and by Hargus, for Witsuwit'en, about whether prosodic structure really mediates between morphological structure and phonology in the way that it has been said to do in the syntax-phonology interface.

The answer to this question is almost certainly 'no'. A review of the types of morphologically conditioned phonology and process morphology from Chapters 2 and 3 shows a much richer range of phonological sensitivity to morphological information than can be captured by reducing the information in a morphologically complex word information to a tree of prosodic constituents. It has been claimed, for example, that postlexical phonology is insensitive to syntactic category (see e.g. Nespor and Vogel 1986); this claim could never be made about lexical phonology, given the strong evidence that phonology applies differently to nouns and verbs (Chapter 2). It has been claimed that postlexical phonology is insensitive to lexical differences beyond notions such as function vs. content word (often captured prosodically) and perhaps head vs. nonhead. In the case of the morphology-phonology interface, however, this claim could never be made, given the fact that different affixes are associated with different phonological patterns in the same language.

Thus the role of prosodic structure in the morphology-phonology interface is supplementary, rather than a replacement for a direct connection between morphological constructions and phonological patterns.

This may ultimately be shown to be the case for the syntax-phonology interface, as well. As increasing attention is paid to the association between semantics and intonation, and as more attention is paid to the phonological details of particular languages, more evidence may emerge showing that the syntax-phonology interface is also more complicated than the parsing of syntactic structures into trees consisting of the Prosodic Word, the Phonological Phrase, and the Intonational Phrase.

11

Paradigmatic effects

It has often been suggested that word formation and the phonological interpretation of words can be influenced not only by properties of the word in question, but also by other words. Some research in this area is motivated by the theoretical stance that morphology (and, therefore, morphologically conditioned phonology) is word-based, with generalizations stated over words rather than over their subconstituents. Work inspired by this theoretical commitment has striven to prove that inter-paradigmatic constraints, relating words to one another, are sufficient to account for the effects attributed to the interleaving phonology and morphology in morphologically complex words (discussed in Chapter 7). An additional motivation to approach the phonology-morphology interface with paradigms in view is the mounting empirical evidence that the phonological (and morphological) shape of words can be influenced by other words in the same paradigm even when neither of the interacting words is a subconstituent of the other. A recent collection of articles espousing this approach can be found in Downing et al. (2005). Work on paradigmatic influences on the phonology-morphology interface has focused on two angles: intra-paradigmatic uniformity (including Base-Identity) and intra-paradigmatic contrast (anti-homophony).

In straightforward cases like the ones we will look at in section 11.1, interleaving and Base-Identity make the same predictions and the difference between the analyses is almost notational. In more complex examples of paradigmatic correspondence (section 11.2), the cyclic and the para-digmatic approaches diverge radically, making very different predictions about the ways in which related words can influence each other.

11.1 Interleaving as paradigmatic correspondence: Base-Identity

Paradigm Uniformity is the situation in which the stem of every form in a morphological paradigm has the same shape. This situation is interesting to the analyst when allegiance to stem shape interferes with the otherwise "normal" application of phonology. For example, in Indonesian, stress is highly regular, but the stress of a monomorphemic word is different from that of a suffixed word (Cohn 1989) because the stem preserves aspects of the metrical footing that it exhibits in unsuffixed words. In Chapter 7 we saw that many such effects could be modeled on an interleaving, or cyclic, approach: stem shape is derived on the stem cycle and is then preserved across subsequent cycles.

Recent literature has suggested that at least some cyclic effects can be reanalyzed in terms of Paradigm Uniformity. It is not necessary to have cycles of phonology applying to the same word in order to preserve stem shape under affixation; instead, pan-paradigmatic constraints can enforce stem shape uniformity across related words. Benua (1997), Kenstowicz (1996, 1997, 2002), McCarthy (2005), and Downing (2005), among others, appeal to the paradigmatic constraint of Base-Identity to explain the common kind of interleaving effect in which a phonological property of a bare stem (or word) is exhibited in words in which that stem (or word) is a subconstituent.

11.1.1 Sundanese

As an illustrative example of Base-Identity in action, consider Sundanese plural infixation (Anderson 1972: 255), discussed earlier in Chapter 7. Recall the basic facts: nasal harmony applies progressively from a nasal consonant to an uninterrupted string of vocoids, but is halted by consonants. However, in words containing the plural infix /-aR/ (which surfaces either with an [l] or [r]), a nasal-initial stem will nasalize not only the vowel of the infix, which immediately follows the triggering nasal, but also the string of vowels immediately following the infix.

(1)

gloss	UR of root stem		plural	[Sundanese]
'seek'	/moekɤn/	[mõẽkɤn]	[mã̱rõẽkɤn]	
'say'	/naur/	[nãũr]	[nã̱lãũr]	
'to cool oneself'	/niis/	[nĩʔĩs]	[nã̱rĩʔĩs]	
'to know'	/ɲaho/	[ɲãhõ]	[ɲã̱rãhõ]	
'to eat'	/dahar/	[dãhãr]	[(di)dã̱lãhãr]	

On a cyclic account, nasal harmony applies both "before" infixation, i.e. to the input stem, and also "after" infixation; i.e. it applies to both the embedded and the inflected stem:

(2)   Cyclic account of overapplication of Sundanese nasal harmony

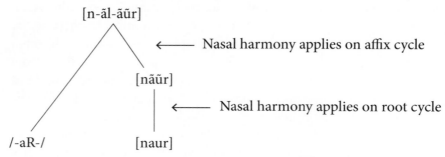

[n-āl-āũr]

⟵ —— Nasal harmony applies on affix cycle

[nāũr]

⟵ —— Nasal harmony applies on root cycle

/-aR-/   [naur]

Benua (1997) offers an alternative, noncyclic analysis in which harmony (like all other phonology) applies only to morphologically complete words. The key element of the analysis is a Base-Identity constraint requiring the segments of affixed words to be featurally identical to their counterparts in the unaffixed form of the word:

(3)   Sundanese Paradigmatic Overapplication (adapted from Benua 2000: 243)

Base-Identity

[nāũr]   →   [n-<u>āl</u>-āũr]

IO Identity, Nasal Harmony ↑   ↑   IO Identity, Nasal Harmony

/naur/   /n-al-aur/

The same nasal harmony constraint applies in the mapping of both words to surface form, and is responsible for the nasality on strings of vowels which immediately follow nasals. The nonlocal harmony in the infixed form is due not to the nasal harmony constraint directly but rather to Base-Identity:

(4)   [n - āl- āũr]

                                ↑   ↑

Nasal because of adjacency to [n]   Nasal because of identity to base [nāũr]

Because the nasal harmony of the base is perfectly preserved on the cyclic analysis, cyclicity and Base-Identity generate exactly the same outcome.

11.1.2 English flapping and aspiration

Another well-known case that has been analyzed as a paradigmatic identity effect is the famous contrast between flapped and aspirated /t/ in the words *militaristic* and *capitalistic* (Withgott 1982; Steriade 2000; cf. Davis 2005). In American English, flapping and aspiration are allophonic alternations conditioned by stress and syllable structure: /t/ is aspirated when foot-initial (word-initial or in the onset of a stressed syllable), and /t/ is flapped when it is the intervocalic onset of an unstressed syllable (see e.g. Kahn 1976; Zue and Laferriere 1979; Gussenhoven 1986). The words *militaristic* and *capitalistic* have the same stress pattern and syllable structure, yet flapping and aspiration apply differently (Withgott 1982):

(5) *militarístic* [ˌmɪ lə t̪ʰə ˈɹɪs tɪk]   (aspiration)
    càpitalístic [ˌkʰæ pə ɾə ˈlɪs tɪk]   (flapping)

While *militaristic* and *capitalistic* are stress-wise parallel, the contrast in the realization of /t/ in the two forms is apparently due to stress differences in the words to which they are paradigmatically related:

(6) *military* [ˈmɪlə ˌt̪ʰɛɹi]   (aspiration)
    cápital   [ˌkʰæpə ɾəl]   (flapping)
    cápitalist [ˌkʰæpə ɾə lɪst]   (flapping)

Steriade (2000) captures this insight using Paradigm Uniformity, observing that the paradigm containing *militaristic* (*militaristic, militant, military*) is made more consistent phonologically by preserving the aspirated [tʰ] that is phonologically conditioned in the word *military*. The paradigm based on *capital* is stress-invariant and so is phonologically consistent without the need to appeal to uniformity constraints.[1]

This kind of paradigmatic influence can be replicated in a cyclic or interleaving model, but at a cost. In order for *military* to influence *militaristic*, it is necessary to assume a cycle of stress assignment on *military* which feeds the cyclic application of aspiration, and to assume that aspiration—normally allophonic in English—persists in the representation even after stress shifts to a different syllable upon suffixation with *-istic*. Allowing aspiration to persist in the representation challenges the standard assumption that aspiration is not lexically contrastive in English and should not be present in lexical representations.[2]

---

[1] Davis (2005) presents an interesting alternative analysis, contending that the stress patterns of English predict the aspirated [tʰ] in *militaristic* and that it is the flapped /t/ in *capitalistic* that requires explanation. Davis does appeal to Paradigm Uniformity in his analysis of *capitalistic*, however; even on his analysis, the data provide support for interparadigmatic correspondence.

[2] This assumption about English has been challenged on other grounds; as many have observed, lexical frequency is a significant factor in rate of aspiration (see e.g. Rhodes 1992 and Patterson and Connine 2001 on words like *winter*, with a high likelihood of /t/ flapping, vs. *banter*, with a high likelihood of /t/ aspiration).

11.1.3 Cibemba

Benua (1997) offers a paradigmatic analysis of the Cibemba double mutation phenomenon for which a cyclic analysis was presented in Chapter 7. Recall the basic facts, from Hyman (1994, 2002) and Hyman and Orgun (2005): the causative suffix mutates (palatalizes, spirantizes) an immediately preceding root-final consonant (7a). If the applicative suffix intervenes, mutation is seen both on the root and the applicative suffix:

(7) a. Plain verb stem   Causative verb stem   [Cibemba]

   leep-a   'be long'   leef-y-a   'lengthen'   < /leep-i̜-a/
   fiit-a   'be dark'   fiiš-y-a   'darken'   < /fiit-i̜-a/
   buuk-a   'get up (intr.)'   buuš-y-a   'get (s.o.) up'   < /buuk-i̜-a/

   b. Applicative verb stem   Causative applicative verb stem

   leep-el-a 'be long for/at'   leef-eš-y-a 'lengthen   </leep-il-i̜-a/
                                               for/at'

   fiit-il-a 'be dark for/at'   fiiš-iš-y-a 'darken   < /fiit-il-i̜-a/
                                               for/at'

   buuk-il-a 'get up (intr.)   buuš-iš-y-a 'get (s.o.)   </buuk-il-i̜-a/
               for/at'   up for/at'

Hyman (and Orgun) develop a cyclic analysis in which the causative affixes directly to the root, triggering mutation, on the first cycle; to derive the verbs in (7b), the applicative is infixed between the root and the application suffix, undergoing mutation itself as a result of its proximity to the causative suffix:

(8)   Cyclic derivation of *leef-eš-y-a* 'lengthen for/at' (7b)

Causative suffixation cycle	leep + /-i̜/
Mutation	leefi̜
Applicative infixation cycle	leefi̜ + /-il-/
Mutation	leefeši̜
Output	leefešya

The essential problem presented by Cibemba is the opaque "over-application" of mutation in the causative applicatives. The root mutation is not conditioned on the surface, and in Hyman's analysis is transparent only on the inner, causative, suffixation cycle.

Benua proposes that the overapplication of mutation in applicativized Cibemba causatives is due not to cyclicity but to paradigm identity effects: the consonants of causative applicatives are constrained to be identical to their correspondents in plain causatives. The plain causative stem is presumed (as on the interleaving account in (8)) to be the base of the applicativized causative:

(9)   Cibemba Paradigmatic Overapplication (adapted from Benua 2000: 243)

Base-Identity

[CV-leef-į-a] → [CV-leef-es-į-a]

IO Identity, Local Mutation   ↑   ↑   IO Identity, Local Mutation

/CV-leep-į-a/   /CV-leep-il-į-a/

'lengthen'   'lengthen for/at'

The Input-Output (IO) mappings in the two words shown side-by-side in (9) are responsible for the local mutations of the consonants immediately adjacent, in surface form, to the triggering [į] vowel of the causative suffix. The Base-Identity mapping between the surface forms of the two words is responsible for the nonlocal mutation in the applicativized causative. It is there in order to preserve identity with the mutated root consonant of the base, i.e. the word on the left, "lengthen":

(10)   [CV - leef - es - į - a]
                              ↑   ↑

Mutated because of identity to base [leef-į-a]   Mutated because of adjacency to [į]

Base-Identity is not, of course, always the highest priority in a derivation. In fact, the correspondence between the derived form /leep-į-a/ [leef-į-a] and its base /leep-a/ [leep-a] violates Base-Identity. That is because the imperative to mutate an adjacent consonant outranks Base-Identity. Base-Identity only compels *overapplication* of mutation; it does not compel underapplication in Cibemba. This asymmetry is due to the ranking of the Base-Identity constraint below the constraints responsible for mutation but above Input-Output Identity.

11.1.4 Jita

A similar analysis is given by Downing (2005) to related facts in Jita (Bantu, E.25), in which the palatalization attributable to the short causative suffix -*y* occurs multiple times in multiply suffixed causative stems. In example (11), stems are shown without inflectional prefixes, which attach outside the stem and are not relevant to the duplication of causative -*y*:

(11) a. root gloss Plain stem +Caus   + Caus, Recip   [Jita]

       'do'   kór-a   kós-y-a kos-y-áːn-y-a

    b. root gloss Plain stem + Caus   + Caus, PERFECTIVE

       'run'   βilim-a   βilim-y-a   βilim-iːs-y-e
                         (<βilim-y-is-y-e) (<βilim-y-is-y-e)

    c. root gloss Plain stem+ Caus + Caus, Appl   + Caus, Appl, Recip

       'buy'   gur-a   gus-y-a gus-iːs-y-a   gus-iːs-y-aːn-y-a
                      (<gur-y-is-y-a) (<gur-y-is-y-an-y-a)

Downing summarizes the ubiquity of the causative *y* formative as follows: "When other suffixes are added to a causative stem, the /-y/ is repeated. It occurs not only in its semantically motivated position, but also after the final consonant of every subsequent morpheme in the stem." Downing's analysis of these facts appeals to two factors: the requirement that the Causative suffix appear in the linearly last suffix position, and Paradigm Uniformity. Templatic ordering, which Downing captures using an Align-Right constraint, is responsible for the linearly final instance of Causative *y*. Paradigm Uniformity is responsible for the others. Downing proposes the following paradigmatic constraints, named "Optimal Paradigm-Causative Stem (OP-CS)," borrowing McCarthy's (2005) "Optimal Paradigms" term for the use of Optimality-Theoretic cross-word correspondence constraints to achieve Paradigm Uniformity:

(12) OP-CS: MAX/DEP-OP Causative Stem
    The Causative Stem common to all paradigm members must contain all the segments (MAX) and only the segments (DEP) found in the corresponding position in the other paradigm members.

Align-Right-/-y/ requires the short causative to be the final derivational suffix in the verb stem. OP-CS requires the short causative to appear in the stem common to all paradigm members. In the case of a word containing a causative plus one other derivational suffix, the only way to satisfy both constraints is for the causative to appear twice. To see how these constraints work in tandem, consider a reciprocalized causative, as in (13a). Based in part on semantic scope facts, Downing treats the causative stem on the left, i.e. root 'do' + causative /-y/, as the base of the reciprocalized causative stem on the right:

(13)   OP-CS

[kos-y-a]   →   [kos-y-an-y-a]
↑   ↑
/kor-y-a /   /CV-kor-y-an-a /

(Causative stem)   (Reciprocalized Causative stem)

Output [kos-y-an-y-a] has two instances of /-y/, one at the end of the derivational stem in satisfaction of ALIGN-Right, and one next to the root, in satisfaction of OP-CS.

Downing is careful to point out that Paradigm Uniformity is specific to the Causative paradigm. It does not extend to the derivatives of other forms, such as Passive stems. As Downing shows, the Passive suffix is, like the Causative, also subject to an ALIGN-Right constraint. It is always the final suffix in the Derivational Stem.[3] Unlike the Causative, however, the Passive does not double when other derivational suffixes are present (Downing 2005: 129):

(14)   Applicative stem + Passive
a. 'build for'   uːmbak-ir-a   uːmbak-ir-w-a   *uːmbak-w-ir-w-a
b. 'cook'   teːk-er-a   teːk-er-w-a   *teːk-w-er-w-a

Downing observes that Paradigm Uniformity is not the only possible analysis of these data, and states that a cyclic analysis for Jita, along the lines of the one developed for Cibemba by Hyman, could also work. However, Downing notes, Causative duplication would be the only evidence for cyclicity in Jita. In cases like this, where cyclicity and Paradigm Uniformity yield similarly effective analyses, the choice often comes down to a theoretical one: is cyclicity independently needed in the theory? Is Paradigm Uniformity?

---

[3] The phonological requirement that the Passive occur as far to the right as possible is so rigid that it even results in the Passive apparently ex-fixing into the final disyllabic Perfective suffix -ire: sik-a 'bury', sik-w-a 'be buried', siːk-ir-w-e 'was buried'.

11.2 Divergences between interleaving and Paradigm Uniformity

Cyclicity (interleaving) and Paradigm Uniformity do not always make the same predictions. We will examine several cases in which one set of assumptions accounts for phenomena that the other does not. We begin with a case of cyclicity which does not result in an increase in Paradigm Uniformity. The dramatic overapplication of consonant mutation in Nyamwezi (Bantu, F.25) differs from the application of consonant mutation in Cibemba (section 11.1.3) in a crucial way. In Nyamwezi, the cyclic effects of mutation cannot be subsumed under Paradigm Uniformity. This discussion of Nyamwezi is drawn from Hyman (2002), based on Maganga and Schadeberg (1992).

Nyamwezi has a causative suffix (-i̧) with a super-high vowel, just like Cibemba, and it triggers mutation on a preceding consonant, like the causative suffixes do in Cibemba and Jita. For purposes of the following discussion it is important to note that with some Nyamwezi consonants the mutation is neutralizing, while with others it is allophonic, as shown here:

(15) a. Neutralizing palatalization before -i̧:   l, g → j [=ʤ]   [Nyamwezi]
          nz, ŋg → ɲj
          nh, ŋh → ŋh

      a. Non-neutralizing palataliza-   k → č
          tion before -i̧:   s → š
          n → ɲ

      c. No palatalization before -i̧:   p, β, t, d, m, mb, nd, mh, h

Nyamwezi exhibits the same basic facts as Cibemba, but with a twist: infixation of the applicative *-il* (or *-el*, by vowel harmony) inside the causative suffix *-i̧* produces a phonotactic violation, due to the double mutation effects that result: /gul-i̧-il/ → *guj-ij-i̧*. As in Cibemba, the causative suffix *-i̧* combines with the root on the first cycle, producing palatalization, and then the applicative suffix is infixed inside *-i̧*, undergoing its own process of patalalization. According to Hyman, Nyamwezi does not tolerate palatalized consonants in successive syllables; furthermore, the outcomes of neutralizing palatalization, namely *j*, *ɲj*, and *ɲh*, are not licensed before vowels other than *-i̧*, making it impossible for them to surface intact once the *-il* applicative is infixed after them. The phonological repair that resolves this cyclically derived situation is unusual. The mutated root-final consonant is replaced with [g] (16a):

(16)

gloss	root	root-CAUS	root-CAUS-APPL
a. 'buy'	gul-	guj-į-	gug-ij-į-
'wash'	kaánz-	kaáɲj-į-	kaáŋg-ij-į-
'bathe'	og-	oj-į-	og-íj-į-
b. 'see'	βon-	βoɲ-į-	βon-íj-į-
'hide'	βįs-	βįš-į-	βįs-íj-į

When patalization is non-neutralizing, i.e. allophonic, the same outcome is observed, except that instead of being restored to [g], the palatalized root-final consonant is restored to its nonpalatal counterpart (16b). Hyman provides a cyclic account in which replacement of the palatal consonant with [g] is driven by a phonological constraint against successive palatals.[4] The cyclic derivation that Hyman provides for the data in (16) is represented in (17), where it is compared with a noncyclic derivation:

(17)   Cyclic vs. noncyclic derivations of /gul, -į, -il-, -a/ [[[[buy]-CAUS]-APPL]-FV] 'sell for/at':

	Cyclic	Noncyclic
Input to Cycle 1:	gul	gul-il-į-a
Palatalization, repair of *jįa to ja		gulija
Input to Cycle 2:	gul + -į	
Palatalization	gujį	
Input to Cycle 3:	gujį + -il-	
Palatalization, repair of *jijį to gijį	gugijį	
Input to Cycle 4:	gugijį + –a	
Repair of *jįa to ja	gugija	
Output	gugija	*gulija

[4] As to why the replacive consonant is [g], Hyman offers, among other possible hypotheses, the suggestion that [g] became established as the nonpalatal counterpart of [j] at an earlier historical stage at which the [g]~[j] alternation was non-neutralizing. Subsequent introduction of [l]→[j] palatalization obscured this earlier bijective relationship, but the depalatalization of [j] to [g] persisted in the system.

The outcome of cyclic palatalization is still overapplication of palatalization, as in Cibemba, but it is opacified in Nyamwezi by the depalatalizing repair process which the cyclic application of palatalization feeds.

While Paradigm Uniformity provides a very plausible alternative to cyclicity in the case of Cibemba and what Downing (2005) characterizes as a superior alternative to cyclicity in the case of Jita, it is at a disadvantage in the case of Nyamwezi, in which the alternation that needs to be accounted for does not increase Paradigm Uniformity. Instead, for stems undergoing neutralizing palatalization, the depalatalization alternation triggered when the causative combines with another suffix introduces a potentially new stem shape into the paradigm of the verb. As seen in (17), the root 'buy' takes the forms *gul* (its basic form) and *guj* (preceding a palatalizing suffix). What, on a non-cyclic analysis that appeals to Paradigm Uniformity, could compel the introduction of a new root allomorph *gug* when the applicative is followed by a causative?

Whatever the answer may be in a non-interleaving analysis of these facts, it cannot be Paradigm Uniformity per se. Nyamwezi teaches us that the effect that the application of phonology to an inner stem can have on the form of an outer stem—i.e. the impact that interleaving or cyclicity can have—is more complex than the faithful inheritance of derived phonological structures. We will return to this issue in section 11.4, in a discussion of anti-homophony considerations.

11.2.1 Spanish diminutives

Another difference between cyclicity and Paradigm Uniformity emerges in cases in which there is an apparent phonological relationship between two words, neither of which is a subconstituent of the other. Such a case is presented by Kenstowicz (2005). Spanish diminutives are formed by adding -*cito* [sito] (for masculines) or -*cita* [sita] (for feminines) when the base ends in [n] or [r], and by adding -*ito*/-*ita* (masc./fem.) when the base ends in a vowel.[5] Examples include *limon* 'lemon (m.)' → *limon-cito*, *barco* 'ship (m.)' → *barc-ito*, *corona* 'crown (f.)' → *coron-ita*.

---

[5] This is the approximate generalization, as stated by Kenstowicz; the actual picture is more detailed, in ways not material to the point made here. See e.g. Butt and Benjamin (1988).

For nouns that have feminine and masculine gender counterparts, like *raton* 'mouse (m.)', *raton-a* 'mouse (f.)', the surface conditions for attachment of the *-cita/-cito* diminutive formatives are met by the *n*-final masculine but not by the *a*-final feminine. On Kenstowicz's assumption that the form of the nondiminutive noun determines the dimunitive suffix allomorph that is added, the feminine diminutive of 'mouse' should be *raton-ita,* based on *ratona,* whereas the masculine diminutive of 'mouse' should be *raton-cito,* based on *raton.* In fact, however, both diminutives have the diminutive formative triggered by an *n*-final input: *ratoncito, ratoncita.* Kenstowicz proposes a paradigm uniformity analysis, which he attributes to Calixto Agüero-Bautista, according to which masculine and feminine diminutives are required to have the same surface stem shape. Masculine *raton* transparently selects *-cito* (*raton-cito*). By Paradigm Uniformity, the feminine *ratona* is required to select the *-cita* allomorph as well. Paradigm Uniformity favors *ratoncita,* while transparency of suffix selection favors *ratonita;* Paradigm Uniformity wins out.

There is an alternative to invoking paradigm uniformity in this case. It is possible to propose that a gender-unspecified stem *raton* serves directly as input to *raton-cito, raton-cita,* and *raton-a.* On this analysis, the allomorphy would be transparent. Paradigm Uniformity would not need to be invoked. The argument for Paradigm Uniformity as a constraint in the analysis of these Spanish facts is thus only as strong as the argument that nouns are always gender-marked in the input to diminutivization. Since the diminutive endings themselves encode gender, this assumption could well be questioned.

11.2.2 Romanian

Steriade (2008) cites several examples from Romanian that illustrate the ability of two words to influence one another's surface form even when neither is a subconstituent of the other. In Romanian, whether or not a given stem undergoes phonologically conditioned suffix-triggered Assibilation (t→ts, d→z) and S-Palatalization (s→ʃ, z→ʒ) in its inflectional paradigm is a predictor, Steriade (2008) finds, of whether or not it will undergo Assibilation and S-Palatalization before a phonologically comparable derivational suffix. As shown in (18), the inflectional class of a noun determines which inflectional endings it combines with. Inflectional endings beginning with [i] trigger Assibilation; inflectional endings beginning with other vowels do not (Steriade 2008: 338):

(18)   Assibilation/S-Palatalization triggered by *i*-initial inflectional suffixes [Romanian]

gloss	Singular	Plural (masc.)
'brother'	frát-e	fráts-i̦
'green'	vérd-e	vérz-i̦
'subject'	supús	supúʃ-i̦
'brave'	viteáz	vitéʒ-i̦

Assibilation before inflectional endings is phonologically straightforward. But before derivational endings, Assibilation applies only if the same root also undergoes Assibilation when inflected (19a). If no Assibilated allomorph of the root exists in its inflectional paradigm, Assibilation cannot apply in derivation (19b). This is not a matter of idiosyncratic root exceptionality to Assibilation, according to Steriade (p. 339); it is a matter of which inflectional endings a root happens to combine with, itself a result of the inflectional class the noun happens to belong to:

(19)   Assibilation/S-Palatalization (ASP) blocked before denominalizing (-i) when absent in inflection

	gloss	Base (singular)	Base + Inflection (plural)	Base + Derivation (-i)	
				ASP *applies*	ASP *blocked*
a.	'wide'	lat-(u)	lats-i̦	lʌts-í	
	'wise'	kumínte	kumínts-i̦	kumints-í	
	'step'	pás	páʃ-i̦	pʌʃ-í	
	'healthy'	sʌnʌtós	sʌnʌtoʃ-i̦	in-sʌnʌtoʃ-í	
b.	'in mind'	amínte	—		amint-í
	'rest'	popas	popás-uri̦		popos-í
	'six'		ʃás-e		in-ʃes-í

The nominals illustrated in (19b) exhibit apparently opaque under-application of Assibilation/S-Palatalization. Steriade notes that some nouns which inflect like those in (19b) combine with a different denominal suffix, e.g. *-u*, thereby circumventing the problem of opaque underapplication of palatalization before denominal *-i*.

Steriade attributes the facts in (19) to Lexical Conservatism (Steriade 1999), the general constraint that a surface allomorph must match an allomorph which independently exists in another word. A statement of the constraint schema, from Steriade (2008: 331), is given in (20):

(20)   IDENT$_{lex}$[αF]: For any segment *s* in a subconstituent C of an expression under evaluation, if *s* is [αF] then *s* has an [αF] correspondent in a listed allomorph of C.

In Romanian, IDENT$_{lex}$ is applied differentially in derivation, where it holds, and in inflection, where it does not.

This analysis makes crucial reference to the inflectional paradigm of a stem in predicting the outcome of derived forms of that same stem. This paradigmatic dependency is illustrated in (21) for the stem *popas* 'rest':

(21)   IDENT$_{lex}$:   any allomorph here ... ... must exist here

Derivation	Inflection	
Verbalizer	*Singular*	*Plural*
[popas-í]	[popas]	[popás-ur̦i]
*[popaʃ-í]		

As Steriade observes, there is no way to recapitulate this kind of paradigmatic dependence in a framework where interleaving is the only means of enforcing phonological relationships among related forms of the same word. The key forms of a stem that influence its shape under derivational affixation in Romanian are not subconstituents of the derived word in question.

11.2.3 English stress

English derivational morphology provides another illustration of Lexical Conservatism and, therefore, another argument in favor of intra-paradigmatic correspondence. Steriade (1999) cites several examples from English that illustrate the ability of two words to influence one another's surface form even when neither is a subconstituent of the other. In a discussion of the English derivational suffixes *-ism* and *-able*,

Steriade notes that the suffixes are sometimes stress-shifting, as in (22a), and sometimes stress-preserving, as in (22b):[6]

(22)   a.   búreaucrat   buréaucrat-ism   (cf. *buréaucracy*)
            démonstrate   demónstr-able   (cf. *demónstrative*)
            rémedy   remédi-able   (cf. *remédiate*)

       b.   ínvalid   ínvalidism   (**inválidism*)
            admínister   admínistr-able   (**admínistrable*)
            párody   párodi-able   (**paródiable*)

Steriade accounts for the difference in behavior by appealing to the derivational paradigms of the words involved. The words in (22a) possess derivatives with stress in the position to which *-ism* and *-able* would shift it: e.g. *búreaucrat ~ buréaucracy*. However, neither *invalid* nor *administer* have relatives with stem-final stress. Steriade proposes that the stress-shifting tendencies of *-ism* and *-able* are impeded by Lexical Conservatism, which prohibits the creation of a stem allomorph that does not already exist independently in a member of the paradigm of the word in question. Because *demónstrative* exists, the allomorph *demónstr-* is available for use by the suffix *-able*, which prefers a stress-shifted allomorph if it can get one. Because no allomorph *admínistr-* exists, the suffix *-able* is limited to the existing allomorph *admínistr* and can't shift stress when it forms *admínistrable* (**admínistrable*).

Lexical Conservatism is an intra-paradigmatic correspondence constraint requiring the surface form of a stem to have an identical correspondent somewhere else in the paradigm. Not all cells of the paradigm are subject to this condition—if they were, no stem alternations would take place—but certain cells, such as those derived by *-ism* and *-able*, fall under its authority.

It would be difficult to account for this same dependency in an interleaving framework without access to paradigmatic relations. The words which are the source of influence—*buréaucrac-y* and *demónstrative*—are not subconstituents of the words which are influenced, namely *buréaucrat-ism* and *demónstr-able*. In this case, intraparadigmatic correspondence does not merely recapitulate the effects of interleaving (as in Sundanese and Cibemba) but can account for data that is beyond the scope of an interleaving account of the phonology-morphology interface.

---

[6] Steriade notes that there is a word *inválidism* but it is based on the negated adjective *in-válid*, not on the noun *invalid*. Only members of the same paradigm can influence the phonological shape of a word.

11.3 Summary: Paradigm constraints vs. interleaving

A major difference between interleaving and paradigmatic correspond-ence theory has to do with directionality. In interleaving theory, there is only one possible direction of influence between the phonological mappings associated with different layers of morphology. The output of the inner layer is always the input to the outer layer, and never the reverse. The architecture of the theory forces this "inside-out" asym-metry. However, in paradigmatic correspondence theory, it is not necessary for the arrows in the given derivations to point in only one direction. While it is possible to invoke a Base-Identity constraint, in which affixed forms respect the surface form of the unaffixed base, it would be equally possible to invoke a constraint going in the other direction, in which the base conforms to the surface form of its affixed counterpart, or for that matter a constraint relating the phonological form of two words neither of which is a subconstituent of the other.

The situation in which a base conforms to the surface form of its affixed counterpart is difficult to diagnose synchronically, but does correspond to the well-known historical phenomenon of leveling, in which it is possible for a phonological alternation triggered at the stem-affix boundary to be fossilized on the stem even when it occurs without the triggering affix. This is the standard diachronic account given to well-known cases like Latin *honos > honor. The evidence for a syn-chronic situation of this kind would be elusive, since it would not be supported by alternations, but the logical possibility should not be discounted.

From its origins in historical leveling and its synchronic counter-parts, the Base-Identity and Lexical Conservatism constraints, current research in paradigmatic correspondence is increasingly being extended to other ways in which designated cells of a paradigm are most likely to influence other cells. For example, in a discussion of paradigmatic gaps in Chapter 9, we noted that Albright (2003, 2009) has proposed that gaps can arise when speakers lack information about the cells in a word's paradigm that contain key information about the phonological makeup of the stem of the word. Albright's work suggests that morphophonemic alternations are determined, potentially dir-ectly, by knowledge of what we may call these "morphophonemic principal parts." McCarthy (2005) has proposed that faithfulness con-straints obtain among all the members of an inflectional paradigm. One consequence of this assumption is what McCarthy has termed "majority rules" effects, in which a phonological structure occurring in a majority of cells of a paradigm acts as an "attractor." If n cells exhibit one phonological value and m cells exhibit the complement value, then uniformity is best achieved by changing the smaller subset of cells, whether it is n or m, to match the larger set of cells. McCarthy provides the instructive example of Moroccan Arabic, in which, in nouns, the distribution of [ə] inside what would otherwise be CCC clusters is predictable from the sonority of the surrounding consonants. If C2 is more sonorous than C3, or if C2C3 is a geminate, [ə] occurs between C1 and C2 (23a). Otherwise, i.e. if the sonority of C2 is equal to or less than C3 (and C2C3 is not a geminate), then [ə] occurs between C2 and C3 (23b):

(23)   a.   kəlb   'dog'   [Moroccan Arabic]
             bərd   'wind'
             dənb   'sin'
             mʷəxx   'brain'
             ləʕb   'game'
       b.   rʒəl   'leg'
             ktəf   'shoulder'
             bɣəl   'mule'
             kfən   'shroud'
             wtəd   'peg'

In verbs, however, the distribution of [ə] is affected by Paradigmatic Uniformity and sometimes violates the phonotactic constraints obeyed by nouns (namely, in the tableau in (24), *ə]$_\sigma$, *CCC, and SON CON). The tableau in (24), adapted from McCarthy (2005), illustrates the perfective paradigm of the verb, 'drink', shown in the 3rd person masculine singular (-Ø), 1st person c. singular (-t), 1st person c. plural (-na), 2nd person c. singular (-ti), 2nd person c. plural (-tu), 3rd person c. plural (-u), and 3rd person feminine singular (-ət). The resulting verbs would, without [ə], assume these shapes: CCC, CCC-C (-t), CCC-CV (-na, -ti, -tu), CCC-V (-u), CCC-VC (-ət). [ə] must appear somewhere within the CCC(C) strings. The question is where. Specifically, the question for this tableau is whether the root for 'drink' surfaces in these inflected verbs as *ʃərb* or as *ʃrəb*. Paradigm candidates (24a) and (24b) both exhibit uniform paradigms, satisfying the Paradigm Uniformity constraint OP-MAX-V. But these candidates lose on phonotactic grounds to the paradigms in (24c) and (24d), each of which exhibits two different stem shapes:

(24)

	/ʃərb/ + {-Ø, -t, -na, -ti, -tu, -u, -ət}	*ə]$_\sigma$	*CCC	OP-MAX-V	SON CON
a.	<ʃərb, ʃərbt, ʃərbna, ʃərbti, ʃərbtu, ʃərbu, ʃərbət>		*!***		
b.	< ʃərb, ʃrəbt, ʃrəbna, ʃrəbti, ʃrəbtu, ʃrəbu, ʃrəbət>	*!*			*
☞ c.	< ʃrəb, ʃrəbt, ʃrəbna, ʃrəbti, ʃrəbtu, ʃrəbu, ʃərbət>			20	*
d.	< ʃərb, ʃrəbt, ʃrəbna, ʃrəbti, ʃrəbtu, ʃrəbu, ʃrəbət>			24!	

Although paradigm (24c) violates the SON CON phonotactic constraint on the positioning of schwa in CCC clusters (*ʃrəb* vs. *ʃərb*), it bests paradigm (24d) because of the "majority rules" effect. The number of violations of OP-MAX-V causes this to happen. McCarthy calculates OP-MAX-V violations in terms of the number of ordered pairs in the paradigm whose stems differ according to the position of [ə]. Candidate (24c) has five [ʃrəb] and two [ʃərb] stems, for a total of $5^*2^*2 = 20$ ordered mismatched pairs (e.g. <ʃrəb, ʃərbu>), while paradigm candidate (24d) has three [ʃərb] and four [ʃrəb] stems, for a total of 4^*3^*2 ordered mismatched pairs (e.g. <ʃərb, ʃrəbtu>). Candidate paradigm (24c) has a bigger majority (five *ʃrəb* stems vs. two *ʃərb* stems) and hence fewer OP-MAX-V violations, and this is why it wins in this tableau. This case is interesting because it is not a simple choice between a level and a nonlevel paradigm, but rather a gradient scale of combinatoric possibilities.

Besides paradigm uniformity (measured as binary or as n-ary), a second major way in which cells in a paradigm can influence one another is through anti-homophony considerations holding throughout the paradigm. We turn to this phenomenon in the next section.

11.4 Anti-homophony

Not all paradigmatic influences involve identity. A large number of examples in the literature point to the opposite kind of interaction among cells in a paradigm, namely paradigmatic distinctiveness or what is often referred to as *anti-homophony* effects. The generalization found in this literature is that morphology and phonology can conspire to avoid producing new word forms that are homophonous with some other word in the language (or paradigm). Prominent examples of

recent work in this area include Crosswhite (1999) and Kurisu (2001).
Ichimura (2006) provides a useful survey of effects in which a neutralizing alternation is claimed to be blocked by a constraint against
homophony. We will examine several cases here: the blockage of
phonological alternations that would delete entire affixes (section
11.4.1), the blockage of phonological alternations that would merge
competing affixes (sections 11.4.2, 11.4.3), and the disruption of normal
phonological alternations with the goal of keeping different stems
phonologically distinct (section 11.4.4).

11.4.1 Avoidance of affix deletion

A number of cases have been documented in which regular phonological deletion rules are blocked in case they would delete an entire
affix, rendering the affixed word homophonous with the base of affixation. For example, in a discussion of the Lesvian dialect of Greek
which is otherwise devoted to documenting Paradigm Uniformity
effects, Gafos and Ralli (2001: 42) mention that the usual rule of
unstressed high vowel deletion (25a,b) fails to apply when the deletion
would result in a loss of morphological information. In (25b),
unstressed *i*-deletion applies to presumed input /kóv-i/, yielding [kov]
'(he/she) cuts', but *u*-deletion is prevented from applying to /kóv-o/ '(I)
cut' and /pín-o/ 'I drink':

(25)   *Lesvian dialects*   *Standard Greek*   [Greek]

    a. Unstressed high vowel deletion

      [vnó], [vúnarus]   [vunó]   'mountain',
                                                  'big mountain'

      [pitnós], [pitínarus]   [petinós], [petínaros] 'rooster',
                                                 'big rooster'

      [épna]   [épina]   'I was drinking'

    b. Unstressed high suffix vowel: deletion inhibited

      [kóv]   [kóv-i]   '(he/she) cuts'
      [kóv-u] (*[kóv])   [kóv-o]   '(I) cut'
      [pín-u] (*[pín])   [pín-o]   'I drink'

Gafos and Ralli attribute the existence of opaque [kóv-u] (vs.
expected [kóv]) and [pín-u] (vs. [pín]) to the prohibition on phonologically merging the 1st and 3rd singular forms of the verb. Deriving
[kóv] from both /kóv-i/ and /kóv-o/ would produce homophony.

Ichimura (2006) describes a similar example in Japanese. The negative suffix -*nai* triggers a complex process in which the preceding vowel drops and a resulting /rn/ cluster is simplified to [nn]. Ichimura terms this process "Nasal Assimilation." Its application appears to be influenced by anti-homophony considerations. The data in (26a–d) show Nasal Assimilation applying across a variety of stem shapes.[7] The data in (26e) show, however, that Nasal Assimilation is blocked when the vowel that would be deleted represents the entire phonological substance of an affix. Examples (26d) and (26e) provide a convincing minimal pair:

(26) a. wakar-anai   → wakannai   [Japanese]
          CVCVC
          'understand-NEG'

      b. tari-nai   → tannai
          CVCV
          'suffice-NEG'

      c. kure-nai   → kunnai
          CVCV
          'give (me)-NEG'

      d. tor-anai   → tonnai
          CVC
          'take-NEG = does not take'

      e. tor-e-nai   → torenai (*tonnai)
          CVC
          'take-POTEN-NEG = cannot take'

Citing the "Realize-Morph" constraint of Kurisu (2001) and others, Ichimura proposes that the failure of Nasal Assimilation to apply in (26e) is due to a constraint compelling the surface realization of phonological material representing every morpheme. If Nasal Assimilation were to cause the deletion of the vowel [e] in /tor-e-nai/, producing [tonnai], the potential suffix /-e/ would not be realized on the surface. Moreover, homophony would be created with the plain negative form, /tor-anai/ → [tonnai].

---

[7] Data sources are as follows: (26a) = Ichimura (2006: 66), citing Umemura (2003: 133). (26b) = Ichimura (2006: 66), citing Otsubo (1982: 51). (26c) = Ichimura (2006: 66), citing Toki (1990: 231). (26d) = Ichimura (2006: 112–14). (26e) = Ichimura (2006: 112).

A particularly intricate example of the avoidance of affix deletion comes from Kiyaka (Bantu, H.31), via Hyman (1998). The Kiyaka perfective, applicative, and causative suffixes display an unusual type of infixation known in the Bantu literature as "imbrication" (see e.g. the discussion of imbrication in Tiene in chapters 4 and 6). Under the specific phonological conditions listed in (28), these suffixes infix into and fuse phonologically with the final VC of the verb stem. (The assimilation of the penultimate vowel to the final vowel in such cases is due, according to Hyman 1998, to a ban on the [wi] sequences that would result from imbrication.) Imbrication is illustrated in (27aii, bii, cii), using data from Hyman (1998: 43–56):

(27)　a. Causative (*-is*)　　　　　　　　　　　　　　　　　[Kiyaka]
　　　　　i. Non-imbrication environment
　　　　　　　'(make) strike out'　　　kik-a　　　kik-is-a
　　　　　　　'(make) deforest'　　　　sol-a　　　sol-is-a
　　　　　ii. Imbrication environment
　　　　　　　'(make) open'　　　zib-ul-a　zibwas-a (< /zibul, -is-, -a/)
　　　　　　　'(make) separate'　yek-ul-a　yekwas-a (< /yekul, -is-, -a/)

　　　　b. Applicative (*-il*)
　　　　　i. Non-imbrication environment
　　　　　　　'strike out (for)'　kik-a　　　kik-il-a
　　　　　　　'bind (for)'　　　　kas-a　　　kas-il-a
　　　　　ii. Imbrication environment
　　　　　　　'begin (by)'　　　butul-a　　butwal-a (< /butul, -il-, a/)
　　　　　　　'remind (for)'　　yubul-a　　yubwal-a (< /yubul, -il-, -a/)

　　　　c. Perfective (*-il-e*, subject to vowel harmony and *l→d* hardening before *i*)
　　　　　i. Non-imbrication environment
　　　　　　　'erase'　　　　kik-a　　　kik-idi
　　　　　　　'be pierced'　tob-uk-a　　tob-ok-ele
　　　　　ii. Imbrication environment
　　　　　　　'save'　　　　　hul-ul-a　　hulwel-e　(< /hulul, -el-, -e/)
　　　　　　　'turn round'　keembil-a　keembel-e (< keembil, -el-, -e/)

The conditions under which the Perfective, Applicative, and Causative imbricate are slightly different (Hyman 1998: 57):

(28)

	Perfective	Applicative	Causative
The base of affixation must be at least two syllables	✓	✓	✓
The base of affixation must end in /l/ or /n/	✓	✓	✓
The vowel preceding the base-final consonant must be /u/		✓	✓

If imbrication were simply infixing, its environment would not be unusual in the context of what we know about infixation cross-linguistically (see Chapter 6); imbricated affixes go inside the stem-final consonant, and then some phonological alternations apply. (The Perfective would have to be analyzed as bimorphemic -il-e, with only the first part infixing.) However, imbrication displays sensitivity to internal morphological structure in a way that is relevant to the present discussion of anti-homophony. As Hyman observes, Perfective imbrication is blocked from applying to stems containing an applicative suffix if the result would be the wholesale deletion of the material contributed by that suffix. Compare (29b), in which the perfective combines directly with the root, and (29c), in which the applicative combines directly with the root, with (29d), in which the perfective combines directly with the applicativized stem:

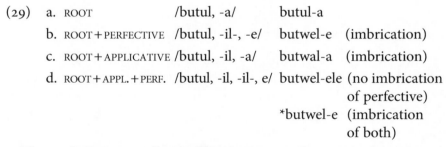

(29) a. ROOT   /butul, -a/   butul-a
      b. ROOT+PERFECTIVE /butul, -il-, -e/ butwel-e (imbrication)
      c. ROOT+APPLICATIVE /butul, -il, -a/   butwal-a (imbrication)
      d. ROOT+APPL.+PERF. /butul, -il, -il-, e/ butwel-ele (no imbrication
                                                            of perfective)
                                            *butwel-e (imbrication
                                                       of both)

The perfective normally would imbricate inside a stem of the shape butwVl-, the outcome of applicative imbrication (29c); the only obstacle to imbrication in (29d) is the homophony that would result with the stem in (29b).

11.4.2 Avoidance of affix conflation

Crosswhite (1999) argues on the basis of evidence in the Trigrad dialect of Bulgarian that the otherwise general rule of vowel reduction is blocked from applying just in case it would cause the merger of two words in the same paradigm. In Trigrad Bulgarian, unstressed /o/ and /ɔ/ surface as [a], merging with /a/ (p. 50):

(30)   a. /o/ /rog-ave/   ['rogave]   'horns'   [Trigrad Bulgarian]
               /rog-ave-te/   [raga'vete]   'the horns'

       b. /ɔ/ /sɔrp-ave/   ['sɔrpave]   'sickles'
               /sɔrp-ave-te/ [sarpa'vete]   'the sickles'

       c. /o/ /dɔrv-o/   ['dɔrva]   'tree'
               /dɔrv-o-to/   [dar'vota]   'the tree'

Crosswhite observes that unstressed /o/ fails to reduce when reduction would produce homophony with a close morphological relative. Consider, for example, the neuter nouns in (31). The singulars take the ending -o, which should reduce when unstressed to [a]. Reduction applies normally to the first group of nouns, but fails to apply to the second group (p. 52):

(31) | Neuter nouns: | Singular /-o/ | Plural /-a/ |
       | --- | --- | --- |
       | a. 'hoof' | Ka'pita | kapi'ta |
       | 'globe' | 'klɔba | kla'ba |
       | 'rib' | 'rebra | re'bra |
       | b. 'grain' | 'zɔrno | 'zɔrna |
       | 'horseshoe'| 'petalo | 'petala |
       | 'cigarette'| tsiga'rilo | tsiga'rila |

Crosswhite attributes the differential reduction of suffixal -o in (31) to anti-homophony considerations in the paradigm. The key factor in (31) is stress. When stress is the same in the singular and plural forms, o-reduction would produce homophony, and is blocked (31b). When, however, stress falls on different syllables in the two inflected forms, anti-homophony is already established and o-reduction is free to take place (31a).

Anti-homophony considerations also impede vowel reduction in the -o suffix marking predicative adjectives. In Trigrad Bulgarian, attributive adjectives are marked with the ending -a, while predicative adjectives end in -o. From Crosswhite (1999: 6–7):

(32) a. Predicative Adjectives (adjectives in **bold**): marked with /-o/
      i. **'bolno** (si sam)   '(I am) sick'
      ii. madʒɔs nʲɔ je **'glanno**   'the man is not hungry'
      iii. **vi'dɛlo** ga xubaf mɔʃ   '(a) handsome man saw him'

    b. Attributive adjectives (adjectives in **bold**): marked with /-a/
      i. **'slepa** 'oka   'blind eye'
      ii. **'xubava** 'sɛna   'good hay'
      iii. **'bɛla** 'platna   'white linen'

As Crosswhite observes, vowel reduction fails in predicative adjectives for the same reason that it fails in nominative masculine forms. The minimal difference between attributive and predicative adjectives would be neutralized if the -o predicative ending underwent vowel reduction to [a].

As many who have pointed out cases of anti-homophony in other languages have also observed (see e.g. Kurisu 2001; Ichimura 2006), Crosswhite notes that Trigrad Bulgarian tolerates plenty of homophony elsewhere in the system. Consider, for example, the four forms in (33). Within each mini-paradigm, vowel reduction is blocked in order to avoid homophony. However, each word (including those whose o fails to reduce) has a homophone in the other paradigm:

(33)   <u>noun</u>   <u>adjective</u>
    a. 'blago 'benefit'   c. 'blago 'sweet' (predicative)
    b. 'blaga 'benefits'   d. 'blaga 'sweet' (attributive)

The generalization in this case and others discussed in the literature is that homophony is more likely to be actively avoided when the ambiguity it would create is likely to cause confusion. Thus merger of words in the same part of speech (e.g. nouns) is more costly, and more likely to be avoided, than merger of words across different parts of speech (e.g. nouns and adjectives).

11.4.3 Dissimilation triggered to avoid affix homophony

A case of Romanian, discussed by Steriade (2009), bears a resemblance to the Bulgarian example except that instead of impeding neutralization reduction, anti-homophony considerations trigger a process of dissimilation. In one of the Romanian verb conjugations, a theme vowel which would be expected to surface as [a] dissimilates to [ʌ] in order to prevent the 3rd person perfect and imperfect verbs from being homophonous.

The relevant background is briefly presented here, following Steriade (2009). In Romanian verb conjugations, the verb stem assumes the same [root+theme vowel] form in tensed perfect verbs as it does in the present participle. The 3rd person singular ending is null, so that 3rd person singular perfect verbs should consist of root + theme vowel. This is true of most conjugations, e.g. those illustrated in (34):

(34)   2nd conjugation ('see'; participle = vʌz-ú-t)

	Perfect (sg)	Perfect (pl)
1st person	vʌz-ú-i	vʌz-ú-rʌ-m
2nd person	vʌz-ú-ʃi	vʌz-ú-rʌ-tsi
3rd person	vʌz-ú	vʌz-ú-rʌ

4th conjugation ('hear'; participle = auz-í-t)

	Perfect (sg)	Perfect (pl)
1st person	auz-í-i	auz-í-rʌ-m
2nd person	auz-í-ʃi	auz-í-rʌ-tsi
3rd person	auz-í	auz-í-rʌ

In the 1st conjugation, however, with theme vowel -a, the 3rd person singular shows an unexpected dissimilation to -ʌ:

(35)   1st conjugation ('see'; infinitive = ved-eá̯, participle = vʌz-ú-t)

	Perfect (sg)	Perfect (pl)
1st person	lʌud-á-i	lʌud-á-rʌ-m
2nd person	lʌud-á-ʃi	lʌud-á-rʌ-tsi
3rd person	lʌud-ʌ́ (*lʌud-á)	lʌud-á-rʌ

According to Steriade, this dissimilation occurs under pressure of anti-homophony with the imperfect form of the verb. Example (36) illustrates 3rd person singular imperfect and perfect verbs for all four verb conjugations:

(36)

	Imperfect	Perfect	
1st conjugation:	lʌud-á	lʌud-á-rʌ	'praise'
2nd conjugation:	ved-eá̯	vʌz-ú-rʌ	'see'
3rd conjugation:	ard-eá̯	árs-e	'burn'
4th conjugation:	auz-eá̯	auz-í	'hear'

Only in the 1st conjugation would the perfect and imperfect stems of 3rd person singulars be homophonous, were the 1st conjugation to follow the same pattern as the other conjugations. Steriade argues that these data motivate a prioritization of paradigmatic distinctiveness over inflectional regularity. Vowel dissimilation is the repair for what would otherwise be a merger of two distinct cells in the inflectional paradigm of 1st conjugation verbs.

11.4.4 Stem alternations blocked to avoid homophony

Anti-homophony effects have also been claimed to hold across related stems. We discuss two cases here: Tunisian Arabic and Tonkawa, both of which are discussed in Blevins (2005).

In Tunisian Arabic, as presented by Wise (1983), unstressed high vowels (and, optionally, nonhigh vowels) syncopate in a two-sided open syllable environment: $[\ldots \sigma$ C__CV(C)$]_{Wd}$. Syncope is illustrated in (37) with data from Wise (1983: 166–7). The same root is shown in each row of the example in two morphological contexts, one in which syncope is triggered and one in which it is not. (Note: the feminine suffix is /-it/ on possessed ("construct state") nouns, otherwise /-a/; /-na/ is 1st person plural possessive, and /-i/ is 1st person singular possessive):

(37)

Syncope not applicable		Syncope applicable	[Tunisian Arabic]
a. símiħ 'beautiful (masc.)'		símħ-a 'beautiful (fem.)'	(< /símiħ-a/)
b. ɣáaliT 'wrong (masc.)'		ɣálT-a 'wrong (fem.)'	(< /ɣáaliT-a/)
c. kúrkub 'carroway'	kurkúb-na 'our carroway'	kúrkb-i 'my carroway'	(< /kúrkub-i/)
d. škáar-a 'sack (fem.)'	škaar-ít-na 'our sack (fem.)'	škáar-t-i ~ škár-t-i 'my sack (fem.)'	(< /škáar-it-i/)
e. qáhw-a 'coffee (fem.)'	qahw-ít-na 'our coffee (fem.)'	qáhw-t-i 'my coffee (fem.)'	(< /qáhw-it-i/)

The evidence for anti-homophony comes from the data in (38), in which syncope is blocked. These are verbs in which the syncope environment occurs within a cluster of three identical consonants (Wise 1983: 169):

(38) a. xammim-u   *xammmu, *xammu
          'they worried'

      b. ɣaššiš-u   *ɣaššššu, *ɣaššu
          'they angered'

      c. xaffif-u   *xafffu, *xaffu
          'they alleviated'

Wise speculates (p. 170) that syncope is blocked because its output would render homophonous CVCCVC verb stems like *xammim* and the CVCC stems that they are frequently related to—in this case, *xamm*. Blevins (2005) summarizes the situation as follows: "Many of the $CVC_iC_iVC_i$ verbs in question are causative forms of CVC_iC_i stems. Given this, the consequence of syncope + degemination is to essentially undo the templatic morphology associated with causative formation" (p. 212).

It is important to note that the problem with the starred forms in (38) is not simply that they involve the creation of a $C_iC_iC_i$ cluster. Tunisian Arabic has a mechanism for dealing with such clusters, which can arise through ordinary suffixation (c). Both C_iC_iC and $C_iC_iC_i$ clusters undergo degemination, producing a licit C_iC_i cluster (Wise 1983: 158):

(39) a. zawwiz   zawz-u   (< /zawwiz-u/)
         'he brought in' 'they brought in'

      b. fumm   fumm-i   fum-ha   (< /fumm-ha/)
         'mouth'   'my mouth'   'her mouth'

Further evidence that the blockage of syncope in (38) is due to anti-homophony comes from nouns, adjectives, and participles in which $C_iC_iC_i$ clusters are created via syncope, and reduce, by the same process illustrated already, to a simple C_iC_i geminate:

(40) a. mSammim   mSamm-a   (< /mSammim-a/)
         'determined (masc.)' 'determined (fem.)'

      b. mħaTT-a   mħaTT-it-na   mħaTT-i (< /mħaTT-it-i/)
         'stop (fem.)'   'our stop (fem.)' 'my stop (fem.)'

      c. mityaššiš   mityašš-a   (< /mityaššiš-a/)
         'angry (masc.)' 'angry (fem.)'

Due to paradigmatic differences between nouns and verbs, homophony is not an issue in the examples in (40).

Blevins (2005) cites a similar case from Tonkawa, in which rules of syncope and degemination are blocked from applying if the result of their application would be a word which is homophonous to the base from which it is morphologically derived. The data in (41) illustrate a syncope process which is similar to that of Tunisian Arabic (Blevins 2005: 216):

(41) Underlying stem   Syncope   gloss   [Tonkawa]

    a. /notoxo-/   notxo?   (< /notoxo-o?/)   'he hoes it'
    b. /picena-/   picno?   (< /picena-o?/)   'he cuts it'
    c. /yakapa-/   yakpo?   (< /yakapa-o?/)   'he hits him'
    d. /topo-/   ketpo?   (< /ke-topo-o?/) 'he cuts me'

The data in (42) show that syncope is blocked from applying to reduplicated verbs. The reason, explains Blevins, is that the result of syncope in CVC_iV_j-C_iV_j reduplicated stems would be a geminate consonant (C_iC_i) that would have to degeminate: thus $CVC_iV_jC_iV_j \rightarrow$ $CVC_iC_iV_j \rightarrow CVC_iV_j$. The result of syncope and degemination would therefore be a form identical to the prereduplicated input:

(42)   Reduplicated stems: no syncope

Base	RED with hypothetical syncope + degemination	gloss
a. /hewa-/	/hewawa-/ > hewwa- > *__hewa__	'to die'
b. /ham'a-/	/ham'am'a-/ > ham'm'a > *__ham'a__	'to burn'
c. /CV-topo-/	/CV-totopo-/ > CV-ttopo > *__CV-topo-__	'to cut'

The resulting homophony, Blevins suggests (p. 218), is intolerable, and Tonkawa chooses to block the syncope process instead.

11.4.5 Stem alternations triggered by anti-homophony

Kurisu (2001) further develops the idea that considerations against homophony can trigger dissimilatory phonological alternations, interpreting a number of stem alternations previously described as process morphology (see Chapter 3) as resulting from the requirement that input and output forms be distinct. This particularly affects base words and their would-be zero-derived relatives. Two examples cited by Kurisu are given in (43): the use of ablaut to mark plurality in German (Kurisu 2001: 56; see also Marcus et al. 1995: 248), and the use of vowel deletion to derive deverbal nouns from infinitives in Icelandic (Kurisu 2001: 31, citing Orešnik 1978; Arnason 1980; Kiparsky 1984; Itô 1986; Benua 1995):

(43) a. *Vater* 'father'   → *Väter* 'fathers'   [German]
        Mutter 'mother'   → *Mütter* 'mothers'
        Acker 'field'   → *Äcker* 'fields'
        Apfel 'apple'   → *Äpfel* 'apples'
        Boden 'ground, bottom'   → *Böden* 'grounds, bottoms'

b. *klifra* 'climb (inf.)'   → *klifr* 'climbing'   [Icelandic]
   puukra 'conceal (inf.)'   → *puukr* 'concealment'
   kumra 'bleat (inf.)'   → *kumr* 'bleating'

Kurisu's analysis is that these constructions consist, morphologically, of zero-derivation, but that anti-homophony considerations compel the phonology to alter the output to avoid identity with the input. The fact that ablaut (in German) or vowel deletion (in Icelandic) are the preferred options, as opposed to any other imaginable changes, follows, in Kurisu's Optimality-Theoretic account, from the ranking of faithfulness constraints penalizing deletion, insertion, and/or featural changes. In German, the least costly repair is vowel change; in Icelandic, the least costly repair is vowel deletion.

A challenge for Kurisu's view comes from cases of morphologically conditioned phonological effects applying alongside affixation, e.g. German: *Gast ~ Gäst-e* 'guest(s)' or *Gaul ~ Gäul-e* 'pack horse(s)', with suffixation *and* ablaut (Kurisu 2001: 191). Since affixation alone suffices to make two forms distinct, what motivates the accompanying ablaut effect? Kurisu's answer is that these cases are instances of double morphological exponence resulting from morphological opacity: the affixes in these examples are essentially invisible to the principle that requires the singular and plural cells of the paradigm to be distinct. The "first" or visible layer of morphology is null, and phonology conspires to make the zero-marked plural stem (*Gäst*) distinct from the singular stem (*Gast*). The second layer of morphology, to which the phonology is blind, then double-marks the plural with a suffix: *Gäst-e*.

Of course, multiple (or extended) exponence is not limited to cases of this kind in which one exponent is arguably a phonological modification and the other is an overt affix. Languages are known to use two or more overt affixes, or a suppletive stem plus overt affix(es), to mark a single category as well. (On the phenomenon of multiple exponence, see e.g. Matthews 1972, 1974; Lehmann 2005; Harris 2008; for a variety of theoretical treatments, see e.g. Stump 1992, 2001; Bobaljik 2000, 2005; Anderson 2001; Blevins 2003; Xu and Aronoff 2011; Caballero and Inkelas 2013.) Thus it is not entirely clear that when ablaut is one of the two exponents, it is a phonological resolution to anti-homophony, or simply driven by whatever diachronic and synchronic morphological factors are responsible for multiple exponence more generally.

11.4.6 Anti-homophony in morphophonological context

Anti-homophony distinguishes between interleaving and paradigmatic correspondence theories insofar as the anti-homophony relationship involves words neither of which is a subconstituent of the other. Interleaving allows for anti-homophony constraints between input and output forms, and thus prevents a derived or inflected word from having the same phonological shape as the base to which the derivational or inflectional process is applying. By contrast, paradigmatic correspondence theories can block homophony between any two words in the same paradigm.

Thus far, the examples of anti-homophony effects we have seen fall into these two categories:

(44)   a. Stem can't merge with its affixed counterpart (Greek, Tunisian Arabic, Tonkawa, Kiyaka)

       b. Two different affixes in the same inflectional paradigm can't merge/be identical (Bulgarian, Romanian)

An interleaving approach can handle the facts in (44a) without reference to paradigms, by enforcing input-output anti-homophony constraints (as is done in Kurisu 2001). However, cases of the kind in (44b) support paradigmatic approaches to the morphology-phonology interface. In Bulgarian, for example, predicative adjectives (derived by the ending /-o/) can't merge phonologically with attributive adjectives (derived by the ending /-a/), although neither apparently serves as the derivational input to the other.

Thus anti-homophony effects potentially favor theories of the phonology-morphology interface which can directly model paradigms and constrain relationships among all kinds of paradigmatic cells (McCarthy 2005; Steriade 2008).

However, the evidence is only as strong as the principles of anti-homophony turn out to be. Anti-homophony principles seem to play an acutely subordinate role in synchronic grammars. Phonological alternations and neutralizations are rampant, as is the creation of homophony in paradigms. Even setting aside all cases of systematic syncretism within paradigms (see e.g. Baerman 2005), we still find numerous situations in which phonological neutralizations produce homophony that would not otherwise have existed. Examples of anti-homophony effects tend to be sporadic; for each case in a language in which merger is actively avoided, there seems to be another in which it is allowed. For example, German allows zero plurals without umlaut, e.g. *Knoten* 'knot(s)'. This class of plurals does not respect the anti-homophony constraint that Kurisu (2001) appeals to in deriving umlauting zero plurals such as *Bogen* 'floor', *Bögen* 'floors'.

Russian presents an interesting comparandum for Trigrad Bulgarian. Contemporary Standard Russian reduces unstressed /a/ and /o/ to [ə] after a plain consonant and to [i] after a palatalized consonant (*pálʲitʲ* 'speak', *vɨ-pəlʲitʲ*; *vɨ-tʲágivətʲ* 'stretch', *vɨ-tʲinutʲ* 'pull out') (Crosswhite 1999: 13). Reduction has the potential for creating homophony across different affixed forms of the same stem. In some cases homophony is tolerated; in others it is apparently avoided. In (45a), unstressed /a, o/ reduction produces homophony between the nominative/accusative and genitive forms of root-stressed neuter *o*-stems (Baerman 2005: 809).

(45)

	gloss	nom/acc (-o)	genitive (-a)	[Russian]
a. Ending stressed	'wine'	vin[ó]	vin[á]	
Root stressed	'place'	mést[ə]	mést[ə]	← Homophony created

	gloss	3rd singular (-it)	3rd plural (-at)	
b. Ending stressed	'speak'	gəvarʲít	gəvarʲát	
Root stressed	'place'	stávʲit	stávʲetʲ (*stávʲitʲ)	← Homophony avoided

In (45b), however, reduction of /a/ to [i] in the 3rd person plural suffix to root-stressed verbs is avoided, with /a/ instead reducing to [e] (Crosswhite 1999: 14). According to Crosswhite, this occurs in order to avoid the homophony that reduction of /a/ to [i] would produce between the 3rd singular and 3rd plural forms of these verbs.

In counterpoint to examples in which anti-homophony appears to inhibit affix deletion (section 11.4.1), there are also many examples in which a phonological deletion process entirely eliminates a morph. Michael (2008: 241) points to one example in Nanti (Kampan), in which VV hiatus in pre-root position is resolved by deleting the first vowel. This can result in the loss of an entire vocalic prefix. For example, the 3rd person nonmasculine singular prefix /o-/, illustrated in (46a,b), deletes before a vowel-initial root (46c,d):

(46) a. otsararaha   [Nanti]

         /o-   tsararah   -a/

         3NMS- horse.around   -REAL.A

         'Was she horsing around?' (p. 162)

b. oNteNtanaheri

/o-	N-	teNT	-an	-ah	-e	-ri/
3NMS-	IRREAL-	accompany	-ABL	-REG	-IRREAL.I	-3MO

'She would accompany him away (i.e. back to Marankehari)'

(p. 174)

c. aratehanake

/o-	arateh	-an	-ak	-i/
3NMS-	wade	-ABL	-PERF	-REAL

'She waded away' (p. 269)

d. oganaka

/o-	ogan	-ak	-a/
3NMS	be.mature	-PERF	-REAL.A

'It is mature (speaking of manioc)' (p. 270)

Vowel deletion can create homophony when the only difference between two prefixes is the deleted vowel. Thus, for example, the 3rd person masculine singular prefix (3MS) is /i-/. Normally /i-/ glides before another vowel, but before /i/, it deletes. Thus before an /i/-initial root, both 3rd person nonmasculine singular (3NMS) /o-/ and 3MS /i-/ delete, neutralizing the difference between masculine and nonmasculine 3rd singular subjects:

(47)   a. iragaka

/o-	irag	-ak	-a/
3NMS-	cry	-PERF	-REAL.A

'She cried' (p. 269)

b. iragaka

/i-	irag	-ak	-a/
3MS-	cry	-PERF	-REAL.A

'He cried' (p. 269)

(Michael points out that the homophony this creates is of little functional importance, since only one root begins with *i*, namely 'cry'.)

The apparently sporadic nature of anti-homophony effects is a puzzling challenge. It is possible that future work on language usage will turn up factors that will help predict when anti-homophony will be enforced and when it will not be. One possible hypothesis is that anti-homophony effects will be enforced when ambiguity is the most costly, i.e. when syntactic or other contextual factors are of little assistance in disambiguating an instance of homophony, and that anti-homophony effects will be tolerated much more readily when the potential for confusion in context is low.

11.5 Lexical distinctiveness

A growing literature is pointing to pressure within the lexicon to keep roots or words phonologically distinct. This pressure goes beyond the simple anti-homophony effects that we have seen. For example, Frisch et al. (2004) make a strong case that contrast plays an important role in the diachronic development, and thus the synchronic distribution, of Arabic root consonants.

Recall from Chapter 4 that Arabic roots are purely consonantal (mostly duples or triples); e.g., √ktb 'write'. Frisch et al. show that the distribution of consonants in Arabic triconsonantal roots is skewed to favor consonant sets that are phonologically internally disparate over those that are internally similar. Computing consonant co-occurrence rates within roots from Cowan's (1979) dictionary of Standard Arabic, Frisch et al. show that, for example, homorganic consonants (those with the same place of articulation) co-occur less often than would be expected if distribution were random. The chart in (48), adapted from Frisch et al. (p. 186), shows co-occurrence figures both for adjacent and for nonadjacent pairs of homorganic consonants. Coronals and gutturals are further subcategorized by manner:

(48)   Observed/expected (O/E) ratios of occurrence for homorganic consonant pairs:

Place	Consonants	O/E (Adjacent)	O/E (Nonadjacent)
Labial	b f m	0.00	0.30
Coronal plosives	t d tˤ dˤ	0.14	0.38
Coronal fricatives	θ ð s z sˤ zˤ ʃ	0.04	0.24
Coronal sonorants	l r n	0.06	0.67
Dorsal	k g q	0.02	0.07
Dorsal & guttural	χ ʁ	0.00	0.25
Guttural	ħ ʕ h ʔ	0.06	0.34

In all cases, but especially under "adjacency" (potentially across one intervening vowel), these pairs occur below the expected rate. The consequence is that within roots, it is more common than chance to find disparate consonants co-occurring. The "adjacent" pairs that occur at the highest rate are Labial-Coronal, Coronal-Guttural, and Coronal-Dorsal.

Frisch et al. suggest a diachronic path by which dissimilatory phonological pressures affect the lexicon: "...lexical items that avoid repetition will be easier to process, and so will be favored in acquisition, lexical borrowing, coining novel forms, and in active usage" (p. 221). Whether the pressures are purely diachronic or also synchronic is a question that future research is sure to focus on. Recent research has already turned up similar lexical effects in other languages. Frisch (2004: 347) writes that "similarity avoidance constraints for homorganic consonants like those in Arabic have been found in a wide range of languages, such as English, Javanese, and Ngbaka. Analogous constraints that apply to repeated laryngeal features rather than repeated place features are also attested across unrelated languages such as Sanskrit, Hausa, and Souletin Basque (MacEachern 1999). Further, in cases where lexical patterns have been analysed statistically, the co-occurrence patterns are gradient and quantitatively depend on similarity (Berkley 1995, 2000; Buckley 1997b; Frisch 1996; Pierrehumbert 1993)."

Pushing this idea even further, Ussishkin and Wedel (2002) have suggested that neutralizing phonological alternations can be inhibited if the words they would apply to exist in dense phonological lexical neighborhoods, i.e. if there are high numbers of phonologically similar words in the lexicon. If this hypothesis is correct, contrast preservation might inhibit phonological alternations not only when the words in question are in the same paradigm, but even when they are morphologically unrelated.

11.6 Summary

Theories of the phonology-morphology interface were initially constructed on the assumption that the imposition of phonological patterns in words would be guided by the internal constituent structure of those words. In Chapter 10 we observed cases in which phonological patterns sometimes respect prosodic constituent structure which can diverge from that of the morphology in principled ways. In this chapter we have seen that cross-word influences can also play a role. When the phonological makeup of word A influences the phonological makeup of word B, of which word A is a subconstituent, the effects are essentially indistinguishable from the predictions of a theory in which phonology applies only to words in isolation, interpreting them in a cyclic fashion (from most embedded subconstituent outwards). However, when two words influence each other in any other way, it becomes clear that phonology cannot interpret a given word in isolation. Discoveries of this sort have been mounting. The key questions for future research will be: is cross-word influence (of the kind not accounted for by interleaving) limited to members of the same inflectional paradigm (McCarthy 2005), or can any two words which share a root, or even an affix, be subject to identity or anti-homophony considerations? Are the effects observed among members of the same paradigm (however it is defined) similar to, or different form, those statistical patterns that researchers like Frisch et al. (2004), and Ussishkin and Wedel (2002), have suggested might hold throughout entire lexicons? The answers to these questions will illuminate our understanding of the phonology-morphology interface.

12

Conclusion

Phonology-morphology interaction is pervasive. Rather than being modular components of grammar, phonology and morphology are tightly intermingled. Early models of generative grammar assumed that the morphology would construct a word and then send it to the phonology, which would convert the underlying phonological representations of the morphemes in that word to surface forms, via the application of phonological rules that could be conditioned by morphological information either indirectly, by applying cyclically to morphological subconstituents from the bottom up, or directly, by referencing morphosyntactic or diacritic features of the morphemes in the word. However, evidence that phonological considerations can drive the choice of suppletive allomorphs, can block or trigger affixation, and can determine the order of morphemes show that the interaction of phonology and morphology is much more intimate than a unidirectional modular approach can accommodate.

Recent approaches to the morphology-phonology connection have adopted a less modular view. In Optimality-Theoretic analyses, phonological and morphological constraints often appear in the same tableau, ranked with respect to one another and thus able to cooperate efficiently in the production of a given word. In Construction Morphology, the phonological and morphosyntactic properties of a word-building construction are stated in the same construction, such that affixation has simultaneous phonological and morphological consequences.

The intimate interplay between phonology and morphology is significant to acknowledge, especially in light of the comparatively diminished interplay found between phonology and syntax. To date, the interplay is mostly one-sided: syntax produces configurations which phonology accepts and interprets, e.g. by assigning phonological phrasing to a given syntactic structure and applying accordingly. Effects of phonology on syntax are less often documented, consisting mainly of end-weight effects and subtle statistical effects of rhythmic well-formedness on the choice between competing, functionally equivalent syntactic constructions (see e.g. Shih 2014). While new discoveries are emerging with more advanced, corpus-based methods of investigation, it still appears to be the case that phonological considerations are generally much more subordinate to syntactic considerations than they are to morphological ones. The reason behind this asymmetry is as yet unknown, and is extremely important to address in future research. Is the difference related to the fact that words and sentences are intrinsically different? Is it related to the fact that the literature on the phonology-morphology interface is much more cross-linguistically diverse than the literature on the phonology-syntax interface, which is heavily based on European languages? Perhaps increasing the typological diversity of languages whose phonology-syntax interface has been closely studied will shed light on this question.

These are open questions. But one conclusion is clear: studying the interplay between morphology and phonology teaches us much more about each phenomenon than could be gained by studying them in isolation from one another. The morphology-phonology interplay sheds light on word-internal structure and on the ability for relatively unnatural phonological alternations to be productive, at least within a given morphological niche. Taking morphologically conditioned phonology *and* process morphology seriously is crucial for assessing universalist theories of phonology. Limiting our assessment of what is common (or "unmarked") and what is rare ("marked") to just those phonological processes which are not morphologically conditioned warps the data considerably. Especially in light of attempts to reduce all synchronic morphological patterns to syntax, or to reduce all synchronic phonological patterns to universal phonetic motivations, it is essential to have a solid understanding of how morphology and phonology operate in the context of one another.

References

Abbi, Anvita (1991). *Reduplication in South Asian languages: an areal, typological and historical study*. New Delhi: Allied Publishers Limited.

Ackema, Peter, and Ad Neeleman (2005). 'Word-formation in Optimality Theory', in Pavol Štekauer and Rochelle Lieber (eds), *Handbook of word-formation*. Dordrecht: Springer, 285–313.

Ahn, Sang-Cheol (1998). *An introduction to Korean phonology*. Seoul: Hanshin Publishing Co.

Albright, Adam (2003). 'A quantitative study of Spanish paradigm gaps', in G. Garding and M. Tsujimura (eds), *Proceedings of the 22nd West Coast Conference on Formal Linguistics (WCCFL)*. Somerville, MA: Cascadilla Press, 1–14.

Albright, Adam (2009). 'Lexical and morphological conditioning of paradigm gaps', in Curt Rice and Sylvia Blaho (eds), *Modeling ungrammaticality in Optimality Theory*. London: Equinox, 117–64.

Alderete, John (1999). 'Morphologically governed accent in Optimality Theory', Ph.D. dissertation, University of Massachusetts, Amherst.

Alderete, John (2001a). 'Dominance effects as transderivational anti-faithfulness', *Phonology* 18, 201–53.

Alderete, John (2001b). 'Root-controlled accent in Cupeño', *Natural Language and Linguistic Theory* 19: 455–502.

Alderete, John, Jill Beckman, Laura Benua, Amalia Gnanadesikan, John McCarthy, and Suzanne Urbanczyk (1999). 'Reduplication with fixed segmentism', *Linguistic Inquiry* 30: 327–64.

Alderete, John, and Tanya Bob (2005). 'A corpus-based approach to Tahltan stress' in Sharon Hargus and Keren Rice (eds), *Athabaskan prosody*. Amsterdam: John Benjamins, 369–91.

Alekseev, M. E. (1994). 'Budukh', in R. Smeets (ed.), *The indigenous languages of the Caucasus volume 4: North East Caucasian language part 2 presenting the three Nakh languages and six minor Lezgian languages*. Delmar, NY: Caravan Books, 259–96.

Allen, Margaret (1978). 'Morphological investigations', Ph.D. dissertation, MIT.

Álvarez, José (2005). 'Vocalic mora augmentation in the morphology of Guajiro/Wayuunaiki', in Lea Harper and Carmen Jany (eds), *Proceedings from the Eighth Workshop on American Indigenous Languages*. Santa Barbara, CA: Department of Linguistics, UC Santa Barbara, 78–93.

Anceaux, J. C. (1965). *The Nimboran language: phonology and morphology.* 'S-Gravenhage: Martinus-Nijhoff.

Anderson, Stephen R. (1969). 'An outline of the phonology of Modern Icelandic vowels', *Foundations of Language* 5: 53–72.

Anderson, Stephen R. (1972). 'On nasalization in Sundanese', *Linguistic Inquiry* 3: 253–68.

Anderson, Stephen R. (1975). 'On the interaction of phonological rules of various types', *Journal of Linguistics* 11: 39–62.

Anderson, Stephen R. (1992). *A-Morphous morphology.* Cambridge: Cambridge University Press.

Anderson, Stephen R. (2001). 'On some issues in morphological exponence', *Yearbook of Morphology* 2000: 1–18.

Anttila, Arto (1997). 'Deriving variation from grammar', in Frans Hinskens, Roeland Van Hout, and W. Leo Wetzels (eds), *Variation, change and phonological theory.* Amsterdam: John Benjamins, 35–68.

Anttila, Arto (2002). 'Morphologically conditioned phonological alternations', *Natural Language and Linguistic Theory* 20: 1–42.

Anttila, Arto (2006). 'Variation and opacity', *Natural Language and Linguistic Theory* 24: 893–944.

Anttila, Arto (2009). 'Derived environment effects in Colloquial Helsinki Finnish', in Kristin Hanson and Sharon Inkelas (eds), *The nature of the word: essays in honor of Paul Kiparsky.* Cambridge, MA: MIT Press, 433–60.

Anttila, Arto, and Adams Bodomo (2009). 'Prosodic Morphology in Dagaare', in Masangu Matondo, Fiona McLaughlin, and Eric Potsdam (eds), *Selected Proceedings of the 38th Annual Conference on African Linguistics.* Somerville, MA: Cascadilla Proceedings Project, 56–68.

Anttila, Arto, and Young-mee Yu Cho (1998). 'Variation and change in Optimality Theory', *Lingua* 104: 31–6.

Applegate, Richard (1972). *Ineseño Chumash grammar.* Berkeley: University of California, Linguistics.

Applegate, Richard (1976). 'Reduplication in Chumash', in Margaret Langdon and Shirley Silver (eds), *Hokan studies.* The Hague: Mouton, 271–83.

Archangeli, Diana (1983). 'The root CV-template as a property of the affix: evidence from Yawelmani', *Natural Language and Linguistic Theory* 1: 348–84.

Archangeli, Diana (1984). 'Underspecification in Yawelmani phonology and morphology', Ph.D. dissertation, MIT.

Archangeli, Diana (1991). 'Syllabification and prosodic templates in Yawelmani', *Natural Language and Linguistic Theory* 9: 231–83.

Archangeli, Diana (1997). 'Optimality Theory: an introduction to linguistics in the 1990s', in Diana Archangeli and D. Terence Langendoen (eds), *Optimality Theory: an overview.* Oxford: Blackwell, 1–32.

Archangeli, Diana, and D. Terence Langendoen (eds). (1997). *Optimality Theory: an overview*. Oxford: Blackwell.

Arnason, Kristján (1980). *Quantity in historical phonology: Icelandic and related cases*. Cambridge, MA: MIT Press.

Arnott, David W. (1970). *The nominal and verbal systems of Fula*. Oxford: Oxford University Press.

Aronoff, Mark (1988). 'Head operations and strata in reduplication: a linear treatment', *Yearbook of Morphology* 1: 1–15.

Aronoff, Mark (1994). *Morphology by itself: stems and inflectional classes*. Cambridge, MA: MIT Press.

Austin, Peter (1981). *A grammar of Diyari*. Cambridge: Cambridge University Press.

Baerman, Matthew (2005). 'Directionality and (un)natural classes in syncretism', *Language* 80: 807–27.

Baerman, Matthew (2007). 'Morphological reversals', *Journal of Linguistics* 43: 33–61.

Barker, Christopher (1989). 'Extrametricality, the cycle, and Turkish word stress', in Junko Itô and Jeff Runner (eds), *Phonology at Santa Cruz*. UC Santa Cruz: Syntax Research Center, 1–33.

Bates, Dawn, Thom Hess, and Vi Hilbert (1994). *Lushootseed dictionary*. Seattle: University of Washington Press.

Beckman, Jill (1997). 'Positional faithfulness, positional neutralization and Shona vowel harmony', *Phonology* 14: 1–46.

Benjamin, G. (1976). 'An outline of Temiar grammar', in Philip N. Jenner, Laurence C. Thompson, and Stanley Starosta (eds), *Austroasiatic Studies*. Honolulu: University of Hawaii Press, 129–87.

Benor, Sarah Bunin, and Roger Levy (2006). 'The chicken or the egg? A probabilistic analysis of English binomials', *Language* 82: 233–78.

Benton, R. A. (1971). *Pangasinan reference grammar*. Honolulu: University of Hawaii Press.

Benua, Laura. (1997). 'Transderivational identity: phonological relations between words', Ph.D. dissertation, University of Massachusetts. Revised version published in 2000 by Routledge.

Berkley, D. (1995). 'Variability in obligatory contour principle effects', *Proceedings of CLS 30*: 1–12. Chicago: Chicago Linguistic Society.

Berkley, D. (2000). 'Gradient OCP effects', Ph.D. dissertation, Northwestern University.

Bickel, Balthasar, Kristine Hildebrandt, and René Schiering (2009). 'The distribution of phonological word domains: a probabilistic typology', in Janet Grijzenhout and Barış Kabak (eds), *Phonological domains: universals and deviations*. Berlin: Walter de Gruyter, 47–75. <http://www.zora.uzh.ch/48994/>.

Blevins, James (2003). 'Stems and paradigms', *Language* 79: 737–67.

Blevins, Juliette (1996). 'Mokilese reduplication', *Linguistic Inquiry* 27: 523–30.

Blevins, Juliette (1997). 'Rules in Optimality Theory: two case studies', in Iggy Roca (ed.), *Derivations and constraints in phonology*. Oxford: Clarendon Press, 227–60.

Blevins, Juliette (1999). 'Untangling Leti infixation', *Oceanic Linguistics* 38: 383–403.

Blevins, Juliette (2004). *Evolutionary phonology*. Cambridge: Cambridge University Press.

Blevins, Juliette (2005). 'Understanding antigemination', in Zygmunt Frajzyngier, David Rood, and Adam Hodges (eds), *Linguistic diversity and language theories*. Amsterdam/Philadelphia: John Benjamins, 203–34.

Blevins, Juliette, and Sheldon P. Harrison (1999). 'Trimoraic feet in Gilbertese', *Oceanic Linguistics* 38: 203–30.

Bloomfield, Leonard (1933). *Language*. New York: Henry Holt.

Boas, Franz, and Ella Deloria (1941). 'Dakota grammar', *Memoirs of the National Academy of Sciences* 23, part 2.

Bobaljik, Jonathan (2000). 'The ins and outs of contextual allomorphy', *University of Maryland Working Papers in Linguistics, vol. 10*, ed. by K. K. Grohmann and C. Struijke.

Bobaljik, Jonathan (2005). 'Itelmen diminutives: a belated reply to Perlmutter 1998', *Yearbook of Morphology* 2004: 317–19.

Bochner, Harry (1992). *Simplicity in generative morphology*, Publications in Linguistic Sciences 37. Berlin: Walter de Gruyter.

Bogoras, Waldemar (1969). 'Chukchee', in Franz Boas (ed.), *Handbook of American Indian languages, Bureau of Ethnology Bulletin 40, part 2*. Washington DC: Government Printing Office, 639–903.

Bonet, Eulalia (2004). 'Morph insertion and allomorphy in Optimality Theory', *International Journal of English Studies* 4: 73–104.

Bonet, Eulalia, Maria-Rosa Lloret, and Joan Mascaró (2007). 'Allomorph selection and lexical preferences: two case studies', *Lingua* 117: 903–27.

Booij, Geert (1984). 'Coordination reduction in complex words: a case for prosodic phonology', in H. van der Hulst and N. Smith (eds), *Advances in non-linear phonology*. Dordrecht: Foris, 143–60.

Booij, Geert (1996). 'Cliticization as prosodic integration: the case of Dutch', *The Linguistic Review* 13: 219–42.

Booij, Geert (2002). 'Prosodic restrictions on affixation in Dutch', *Yearbook of Morphology* 2001, 183–201.

Booij, Geert (2010). *Construction morphology*. Oxford: Oxford University Press.

Booij, Geert, and Rochelle Lieber (1993). 'On the simultaneity of morphological and prosodic structure', in Sharon Hargus and Ellen Kaisse (eds), *Phonetics and Phonology 4: Studies in Lexical Phonology*. San Diego: Academic Press, 23–44.

Bradley, Travis (2002). 'Gestural timing and derived environment effects in Norwegian clusters', in Line Mikkelsen and Chris Potts (eds), *Proceedings of WCCFL 21*, 43–56.

Brame, Michael (1974). 'The cycle in phonology: stress in Palestinian, Maltese and Spanish', *Linguistic Inquiry* 5: 39–60.

Bright, William (1972). *The Karok language*. University of California Publications in Linguistics 13. Berkeley: University of California Press.

Broadbent, Sylvia (1964). *The Southern Sierra Miwok language*. Vol. 38. University of California Publications in Linguistics. Berkeley: University of California Press.

Broadwell, Aaron (1993). 'Subtractive morphology in Southern Muskogean', *International Journal of American Linguistics* 59: 416–29.

Broselow, Ellen, and John McCarthy (1983). 'A theory of internal reduplication', *The Linguistic Review* 3: 25–88.

Brown, Dunstan, and Andrew Hippisley (2012). *Network morphology: a defaults-based theory of word structure*. Cambridge: Cambridge University Press.

Browne, Wayles (1974). 'On the problem of enclitic placement in Serbo-Croatian', in R. Brecht and C. Chvany (eds), *Michigan Slavic Materials 10*. Ann Arbor: Department of Slavic Languages and Literatures, University of Michigan, 36–52.

Buckley, Eugene L. (1994). *Theoretical aspects of Kashaya phonology and morphology*. Dissertation in Linguistics Series. Stanford: CSLI Publications.

Buckley, Eugene L. (1997a). 'Explaining Kashaya infixation'. *Berkeley Linguistics Society 23*. Berkeley: Berkeley Linguistics Society, 14–25.

Buckley, Eugene L. (1997b). 'Tigrinya root consonants and the OCP', *Penn Working Papers in Linguistics* 4: 19–51.

Buckley, Eugene L. (1998). 'Integrity and correspondence in Manam double reduplication', in Pius Tamanji and Kiyomi Kusumoto (eds), *Proceedings of the North East Linguistic Society 28, Vol. 1*. Amherst: GLSA, 59–67.

Burzio, Luigi (1997). 'Cycles, non-derived environment blocking, and correspondence', in Joost Dekkers, Frank van der Leeuw, and Jeroen van de Weijer (eds), *The pointing finger: conceptual studies in Optimality Theory*. Oxford: Oxford University Press, 47–87.

Butt, John, and Carmen Benjamin (1988). *A new reference grammar of modern Spanish*. London, Baltimore: E. Arnold.

Bybee, Joan (1985). *Morphology: a study of the relation between meaning and form*. Amsterdam: John Benjamins.

Bye, Patrik (2007). 'Allomorphy: selection, not optimization', in Sylvia Blaho, Patrik Bye, and Martin Kraemer (eds), *Freedom of analysis*. Berlin: Mouton de Gruyter, 63–91.

Bye, Patrik, and Peter Svenonius (2012). 'Non-concatenative morphology as epiphenomenon', in Jochen Trommer (ed.), *The morphology and phonology of exponence Oxford Studies in Theoretical Linguistics* 41. Oxford: Oxford University Press, 427–95.

Caballero, Gabriela (2007). '"Templatic backcopying" in Guarijio abbreviated reduplication', *Morphology (2006)* 16: 273–89.

Caballero, Gabriela (2008). 'Choguita Rarámuri (Tarahumara) phonology and morphology', Ph.D. dissertation, University of California, Berkeley.

Caballero, Gabriela, and Sharon Inkelas (2013). 'Word construction: Tracing an optimal path through the lexicon', *Morphology* 23: 103–43

Cahill, Michael (2004). 'Tone polarity in Konni: an Optimality Theoretic account', *Ohio State University Working Papers in Linguistics* 51: 19–58.

Callaghan, Catherine A. (1987). *Northern Sierra Miwok dictionary.* Vol. 110. University of California Publications in Linguistics. Berkeley: University of California Press.

Cammenga, Jelle (2002). *Phonology and morphology of Ekegusii.* Köln: Rüdiger Köppe Verlag.

Carlson, Katy (1998). 'Sonority and reduplication in Nakanai and Nuxalk (Bella Coola)', in J. Austin and A. Lawson (eds), *Proceedings of the Fourteenth Eastern States Conference on Linguistics*, 23–33.

Carpenter, Robert (1992). *The logic of typed feature structures.* Cambridge: Cambridge University Press.

Carrier, Jill (1979). 'The interaction of phonological and morphological rules in Tagalog: a study in the relationship between rule components in grammar', Ph.D. dissertation, MIT.

Carstairs-McCarthy, Andrew (1998). 'Phonological constraints on morphological rules', in Andrew Spencer and Arnold Zwicky (eds), *Handbook of morphology.* Oxford: Blackwell, 144–8.

Casali, Roderic (1997). 'Vowel elision in hiatus contexts: which vowel goes?', *Language* 73: 493–533.

Childs, Tucker (1994). 'African ideophones', in Leanne Hinton, Johanna Nichols, and John Ohala (eds), *Sound symbolism.* Cambridge: Cambridge University Press, 278–304.

Cho, Taehong (1998). 'Intergestural timing and overlap in Korean palatalization: an Optimality-Theoretic approach', *Japanese/Korean Linguistics* 8: 261–76.

Cho, Young-mee Yu (2009). 'Derived environment effects in Korean', in Kristin Hanson and Sharon Inkelas (eds), *The nature of the word: essays in honor of Paul Kiparsky.* Cambridge, MA: MIT Press, 461–86.

Chomsky, Noam, and Morris Halle (1968). *The sound pattern of English.* New York: Harper and Row.

Clements, G. N. (1976). *Vowel harmony in nonlinear generative phonology.* Bloomington: Indiana University Linguistics Club.

Clements, G. N., and Jay Keyser (1983). *CV phonology: a generative theory of the syllable*. Cambridge, MA: MIT Press.

Clements, G. N, and Engin Sezer (1982). 'Vowel and consonant disharmony in Turkish', in Harry van der Hulst and Norval Smith (eds), *The structure of phonological representations, part II*. Dordrecht: Foris, 213–55.

Coetzee, Andries (2009). 'Learning lexical indexation', *Phonology* 26: 109–45.

Cohn, Abigail (1989). Stress in Indonesian and bracketing paradoxes. *Natural Language and Linguistic Theory* 7: 167–216.

Cohn, Abigail (1990). 'Phonetic and phonological rules of nasalization', Ph.D. dissertation, UCLA.

Cohn, Abigail (1992). 'The consequences of dissimilation in Sundanese', *Phonology* 9: 199–220.

Cohn, Abigail, and John McCarthy (1998). 'Alignment and parallelism in Indonesian phonology', *Working papers of the Cornell Phonetics Laboratory* 12: 53–137.

Cole, Jennifer S., and Charles W. Kisseberth (1997). 'Restricting multi-level constraint evaluation: opaque rule interaction in Yawelmani vowel harmony', *Proceedings of the 1995 Southwestern Workshop on Optimality Theory*. University of Arizona Linguistics Circle, 18–38.

Collins, Chris (1994). 'The factive construction in Kwa', *Travaux de recherche sur le créole haïtien* 23: 31–65.

Conathan, Lisa, and Jeffrey Good (2000). 'Morphosyntactic reduplication in Chechen and Ingush', *Proceedings of the Chicago Linguistic Society 36-2: the panels*, ed. by Arike Okrent and John P. Boyle. Chicago: Chicago Linguistic Society.

Condoravdi, Cleo, and Paul Kiparsky (1998). 'Optimal order and scope', paper presented at the Lexicon in Focus workshop, Wuppertal, August 17–19, 1998.

Conteh, Patrick, Elizabeth Cowper, and Keren Rice (1985). 'The environment for consonant mutation in Mende', in G. J. Dimmendaal (ed.), *Current approaches to African linguistics (vol. 3)*. Dordrecht: Foris Publications. 107–16.

Corbett, Greville (2007). 'Canonical typology, suppletion, and possible words', *Language* 83: 8–42.

Corston-Oliver, Simon (2002). 'Roviana', in John Lynch, Malcolm Ross, and Terry Crowley (eds), *The Oceanic languages*. Richmond: Curzon Press, 467–97.

Cowan, J. (1979). *Hans Wehr: A dictionary of modern written Arabic*. Wiesbaden: Harrassowitz.

Crosswhite, Katherine (1997). Avoidance of homophony in Trigrad Bulgarian vowel reduction. *Southwest Workshop on Optimality Theory*. University of California, Los Angeles.

Crosswhite, Katherine (1999). 'Intra-paradigmatic homophony avoidance in two dialects of Slavic', in Matthew K. Gordon (ed.), *UCLA Working Papers in Linguistics, vol. 1. Papers in phonology 2*. Los Angeles: UCLA Department of Linguistics, 48–67.

Crowhurst, Megan (1994). 'Foot extrametricality and template mapping in Cupeño', *Natural Language and Linguistic Theory* 12: 177–201.

Crowhurst, Megan (1998). '*Um* infixation and prefixation in Toba Batak', *Language* 74: 590–604.

Crowley, Terry (1998). *Oceanic linguistics special publication; no. 27*. Honolulu: University of Hawaii Press.

Crowley, Terry (2002). 'Sye', in John Lynch, Malcolm Ross, and Terry Crowley (eds), *The Oceanic languages*. Richmond: Curzon Press, 694–722.

Crysmann, Berthold (1999). 'Morphosyntactic paradoxa in Fox: an analysis in linearization-based morphology', *Constraints and resources in natural language syntax and semantics. Studies in constraint-based lexicalism*. Stanford: CSLI Publications.

Czaykowska-Higgins, Ewa (1993). 'Cyclicity and stress in Moses-Columbia Salish (Nxa'amxcin)', *Natural Language and Linguistic Theory* 11: 197–278.

Czaykowska-Higgins, Ewa (1998). 'The morphological and phonological constituent structure of words in Moses-Columbia Salish (Nxa?amxcin)', in Ewa Czaykowska-Higgins and M. Dale Kinkade (eds), *Salish languages and linguistics: theoretical and descriptive perspectives*. Berlin: Mouton, 153–96.

Dahlstrom, Amy (1997). 'Fox (Mesquakie) reduplication', *International Journal of American Linguistics* 63: 205–26.

Dai, Qingxia (1990a). 'Jingpo yu binglie jiegou xiaheci de yuanyin he xie [On the vowels and agreement of Jingpho coordinate compounds]', in Qingxia Dai (ed.), *Zang-Mian yuzu yuyan yanjiu [Research on Tibeto-Burman languages]*. Kunming: Yunnan Minzu Chuban She, 213–27.

Dai, Qingxia (1990b). 'Zang-Mian yu zu mou xie yuyan de jinjie dapei lu [Collocation rules of syllables in some Tibeto-Burman languages]', in Qingxia Dai (ed.), *Zang-Mian yuzu yuyan yanjiu [Research on Tibeto-Burman languages]*. Kunming: Yunnan Minzu Chuban She, 55–69.

Dai, Qingxia, and Xijian Xu (1992). *Jingpo yu yufa [The grammar of Kachin]*. Beijing: Zhongyang Minzu Xueyuan Chubanshe.

Davis, Stuart (2005). 'Capitalistic v. militaristic: the paradigm uniformity effect reconsidered', in Laura Downing, T. Alan Hall, and Renate Raffelsiefen (eds), *Paradigms in phonological theory*. Oxford: Oxford University Press, 107–21.

DeLacy, Paul (2012). 'Morpho-phonological polarity', in Jochen Trommer (ed.), *The morphology and phonology of exponence, Oxford Studies in Theoretical Linguistics* 41. Oxford: Oxford University Press, 121–59.

Dixon, Robert (1972). *The Dyirbal language of North Queensland*. Cambridge: Cambridge University Press.

Dixon, Robert (1988). *A grammar of Boumaa Fijian*. Chicago: University of Chicago Press.

Downing, Laura. (1995). Correspondence effects in Siswati reduplication. *Studies in the Linguistic Sciences* 25. <was 1997>

Downing, Laura (1997a). 'Morphological correspondence in Kinande reduplication', *Proceedings of the Berkeley Linguistics Society 23*. Berkeley: Berkeley Linguistics Society, 83–94.

Downing, Laura (1997b). 'Prosodic misalignment and reduplication', *Yearbook of Morphology 1997*: 83–120.

Downing, Laura (1998a). 'Morphological correspondence constraints on Kikerewe reduplication', in Emily Curtis, James Lyle, and Gabriel Webster (eds), *Proceedings of the 16th West Coast Conference on Formal Linguistics*. Stanford: CSLI Publications, 161–75.

Downing, Laura (1998b). 'Prosodic stem ≠ prosodic word in Bantu', in Tracy Hall and Ursula Kleinhenz (eds), *Studies on the phonological word*. Amsterdam: John Benjamins, 73–98.

Downing, Laura (1999a). 'Morphological constraints on Bantu reduplication', *Linguistic Analysis* 29: 177–206.

Downing, Laura (1999b). 'Onset motivated overcopy in reduplication', *Proceedings of the Xth Western Conference on Linguistics*. Fresno, 81–96.

Downing, Laura (1999c). 'Verbal reduplication in three Bantu languages', in Harry van der Hulst, René Kager, and Wim Zonneveld (eds), *The prosody-morphology interface*. Cambridge: Cambridge University Press, 62–89.

Downing, Laura (2000). 'Morphological and prosodic constraints on Kinande verbal reduplication', *Phonology* 17: 1–38.

Downing, Laura (2001). 'Ungeneralizable minimality in Ndebele', *Studies in African Linguistics* 30: 33–58.

Downing, Laura (2005). 'Jita causative doubling and Paradigm Uniformity', in Laura Downing, T. Alan Hall, and Renate Raffelsiefen (eds), *Paradigms in phonological theory*. Oxford: Oxford University Press, 122–44.

Downing, Laura (2006). *Canonical forms in Prosodic Morphology*. Oxford: Oxford University Press.

Downing, Laura, T. Alan Hall, and Renate Raffelsiefen (eds) (2005). *Paradigms in phonological theory*. Oxford: Oxford University Press.

Dressler, Wolfgang (1985). *Morphonology, the dynamics of derivation*. Edited by Kenneth C. Hill. Ann Arbor: Karoma Publishers.

Dryer, Matthew (2011). 'Prefixing vs. suffixing in inflectional morphology', in Matthew Dryer and Martin Haspelmath (eds), *The World Atlas of Language Structures Online*, Chapter 26: <http://wals.info/chapter/26>.

DuBois, John W. (1985). 'Incipient semanticization of possessive ablaut in Mayan', *International Journal of American Linguistics* 51: 396–8.

Dudas, Karen Marie (1976). 'The phonology and morphology of modern Javanese', Ph.D. dissertation, University of Illinois.

Durie, Mark (1985). *A grammar of Acehnese: on the basis of a dialect of North Aceh*. Dordrecht: Foris.

Elenbaas, Nina, and René Kager (1999). 'Ternary rhythm and the lapse constraint', *Phonology* 16: 273–329.

Ellington, John (1977). 'Aspects of the Tiene language', Ph.D. dissertation, University of Wisconsin, Madison.

Embick, David (2010). *Localism vs. globalism in morphology and phonology*. Cambridge, MA: MIT Press.

Emeneau, Murray (1955). *Kolami: a Dravidian language*. Berkeley: University of California Press.

England, Nora (1983). *A grammar of Mam, a Mayan language*. Austin: University of Texas Press.

English, Leo J. (1986). *Tagalog-English dictionary*. Manila: Congregation of the Most Holy Redeemer.

Everett, Daniel, and L. Seki (1985). 'Reduplication and CV skeleta in Kamaiurá', *Linguistic Inquiry* 16: 326–30.

Fabb, Nigel (1988). 'English suffixation is constrained only by selectional restrictions', *Natural Language and Linguistic Theory* 6: 527–39.

Fife, James, and Gareth King (1998). 'Celtic (Indo-European)', in Andrew Spencer and Arnold M. Zwicky (eds), *The handbook of morphology*. Oxford: Blackwell, 477–99.

Fitzgerald, Colleen M. (1997). 'O'odham rhythms', Ph.D. dissertation, University of Arizona.

Fitzgerald, Colleen M. (2000). 'Vowel hiatus and faithfulness in Tohono O'odham reduplication', *Linguistic Inquiry* 31: 713–22.

Fitzgerald, Colleen M. (2001). 'The Morpheme-to-Stress principle in Tohono O'odham', *Linguistics* 39: 941–72.

Fitzgerald, Colleen M. (2002). 'Tohono O'odham stress in a single ranking', *Phonology* 19: 253–71.

Fitzpatrick-Cole, Jennifer (1994). 'The prosodic domain hierarchy in reduplication', Ph.D. dissertation, Stanford University.

Flack, Kathryn (2007). 'Templatic morphology and indexed markedness constraints', *Linguistic Inquiry* 38: 749–58.

Ford, Alan, and Rajendra Singh (1983). 'On the status of morphophonology', in John F. Richardson, Mitchell Marks, and Amy Chukerman (eds), *Papers from the parasession on the interplay of phonology, morphology and syntax*. Chicago: Chicago Linguistic Society, 63–78.

Ford, Alan, and Rajendra Singh (1985). 'Towards a non-parametric morphology', in Mary Niepokuj, M. VanClay, N. Nikiforidou, and D. Feder (eds), *Papers from BLS 11*. Berkeley: Berkeley Linguistic Society, 87–95.

Frampton, John (2009). *Distributed reduplication*. Cambridge, MA: MIT Press.

Frank, Wright Jay (1999). 'Nuer noun morphology', Ph.D. dissertation, University of New York at Buffalo.

Freeland, Lynn (1951). *Language of the Sierra Miwok.* Supplement to *International Journal of American Linguistics*, Vol. 17, No. 1. Indiana University Publications in Anthropology and Linguistics Memoir 6. Bloomington: Waverley Press.

Freeland, Lynn, and Sylvia Broadbent (1960). *Central Sierra Miwok dictionary, with texts.* Vol. 23. University of California Publications in Linguistics. Berkeley: University of California Press.

Frisch, Stephan (1996). 'Similarity and frequency in phonology', Ph.D. dissertation, Northwestern University.

Frisch, Stephan (2004). 'Language processing and segmental OCP effects', in Donca Steriade, Bruce Hayes, Robert Kirchner (eds), *Phonetically-based phonology.* Cambridge: Cambridge University Press, 346–71.

Frisch, Stephan, Janet Pierrehumbert, and Michael Broe (2004). 'Similarity avoidance and the OCP', *Natural Language and Linguistic Theory* 22: 179–228.

Fukazawa, Haruka (1997). 'Multiple input-output faithfulness relations in Japanese', Rutgers Optimality Archive 260–0598. <http://roa.rutgers.edu/files/260-0598/roa-260-fukazawa-2.pdf.gz>.

Fukazawa, Haruka, Mafuyu Kitahara, and Mitsuhiko Ota (1998). 'Lexical stratification and ranking invariance in constraint-based grammars', in M. Catherine Gruber, Derrick Higgins, Kenneth S. Olson, and Tamra Wysocki (eds), *Proceedings of the Chicago Linguistic Society 34–2: The panels.* Chicago: University of Chicago Press, 47–62.

Fulmer, S. Lee (1991). 'Dual-position affixes in Afar: an argument for phonologically-driven morphology', in Aaron Halpern (ed.), *Proceedings of the Ninth Annual Meeting of the West Coast Conference on Formal Linguistics.* Stanford: CSLI Publications, 189–203.

Gafos, Adamantios (1998). 'A-templatic reduplication', *Linguistic Inquiry* 28: 515–27.

Gafos, Adamantios, and Angela Ralli (2001). 'Morphosyntactic features and paradigmatic uniformity in two dialectal varieties of the island of Lesvos', *Journal of Greek Linguistics* 2: 41–73.

Galloway, Brent (1993). *A grammar of Upriver Halkomelem*, University Publications in Linguistics 96. Berkeley: University of California Press.

Garrett, Andrew. (2001). 'Reduplication and infixation in Yurok: morphology, semantics, and diachrony', *International Journal of American Linguistics* 67: 264–312.

Göksel, A., and Celia Kerslake (2005). *Turkish: a comprehensive grammar.* Abingdon: Routledge.

Goldsmith, John (1976). An overview of autosegmental phonology. *Linguistic Analysis* 2: 22–68.

Goldsmith, John (1979). 'The aims of autosegmental phonology', in D. A. Dinnsen (ed.), *Current approaches to phonological theory*. Bloomington: Indiana University Press, 213–55.

Goldsmith, John (1992). 'Tone and accent in Llogoori', in Diane Brentari et al. (eds), *The joy of grammar*. Philadelphia: John Benjamins, 73–94.

Golston, Chris (1997). 'Direct Optimality Theory: representation as constraint violation', *Language* 73: 713–48.

Gomez-Imbert, Elsa, and Michael Kenstowicz (2000). 'Barasana tone and accent', *International Journal of American Linguistics* 66: 419–63.

Good, Jeff (2006). 'Rarum begets rarum: a rare clitic and morphosyntactic reduplication in Chechen and Ingush', paper presented at the Rara and Rarissima conference, Max Planck Institute for Evolutionary Anthropology, March 20, 2006.

Goodenough, Ward H., and Hiroshi Sugita (1980). *Trukese-English dictionary*. Philadelphia: American Philosophical Society.

Green, T. M. (1999). 'A lexicographic study of Ulwa', Ph.D. dissertation, MIT.

Greenberg, Joseph (1977). 'Niger-Congo noun class markers: prefixes, suffixes, both or neither', *Studies in African Linguistics* 7: 97–104.

Gurevich, Olya (2006). 'Constructional morphology: the Georgian version', Ph.D. dissertation, University of California, Berkeley.

Gussenhoven, Carlos (1986). 'English plosive allophones and ambisyllabicity', *Grammar* 10: 119–41.

Haas, Mary R. (1977). 'Nasals and nasalization in Creek', in Kenneth Whistler et al. (eds), *Proceedings of the third annual meeting of the Berkeley Linguistics Society*. Berkeley: Berkeley Linguistics Society, 194–203.

Haiman, John (1972). 'Ablaut in the Hua verb', *Oceanic Linguistics* 11: 32–46.

Haiman, John (1980). *Hua: a Papuan language of the Eastern Highlands of New Guinea*. Studies in Language Companion Series, vol. 5. Amsterdam: John Benjamins.

Haiman, John (1998). 'Repetition and identity', *Lingua* 100: 57–70.

Hale, Kenneth (1973). 'Deep-surface canonical disparities in relation to analysis and change: an Australian example', in T. A. Sebeok (ed.), *Linguistics in Oceania*, Current Trends in Linguistics 11. The Hague: Mouton, 401–58.

Hale, Kenneth, and A. Lacayo Blanco (1989). *Diccionario elemental del Ulwa (Sumu Meridional)*. Cambridge, MA: Center for Cognitive Science, MIT.

Hall, Robert A. (1953). 'Haitian Creole: grammar, texts, vocabulary', *Memoirs of the American Anthropological Association 64*. Menasha, WI: American Anthropological Association.

Hall, T. Alan (2006). 'Derived environment blocking effects in Optimality Theory', *Natural Language and Linguistic Theory* 24: 803–56.

Halle, Morris (1973). 'Prolegomena to a theory of word formation', *Linguistic Inquiry* 4: 3–16.

Halle, Morris and Alec Marantz (1993). 'Distributed Morphology and the pieces of inflection', in Kenneth Hale and Stephen Jay Keyser (eds), *The view from Building 20*. Cambridge, MA: MIT Press, 111–76.

Halle, Morris and Alec Marantz (1994). 'Some key features of Distributed Morphology', in Andrew Carnie and Heidi Harley (eds), *MITWPL 21*. Cambridge, MA: MIT, 275–88.

Halle, Morris, and K. P Mohanan. (1985). 'Segmental phonology of modern English', *Linguistic Inquiry* 16: 57–116.

Halpern, Aaron (1992). 'Topics in the syntax and placement of clitics', Ph.D. dissertation, Stanford University.

Hammond, Michael (1992). 'Morphemic circumscription', *Yearbook of Morphology 1991*: 195–209.

Han, Eunjoo (1994). 'Prosodic structure in compounds', Ph.D. dissertation, Stanford University.

Hankamer, Jorge (2011). 'Turkish vowel epenthesis', in Eser Taylan and Bengisu Rona (eds), *Puzzles of language: essays in honour of Karl Zimmer*. Wiesbaden: Harrassowitz, 55–69.

Haraguchi, Shosuke (1977). *The tone pattern of Japanese*. Tokyo: Kaitakusha.

Hardy, Heather, and Timothy Montler (1988). 'Imperfective gemination in Alabama', *International Journal of American Linguistics* 54: 399–415.

Hargus, Sharon (1988). *The lexical phonology of Sekani*. Outstanding dissertations in linguistics series. New York: Garland Publishing Co.

Hargus, Sharon (2007). *Witsuwit'en grammar: phonetics, phonology, morphology*. Vancouver and Toronto: UBC Press.

Hargus, Sharon, and Virginia Beavert (2006). 'High-ranking affix faithfulness in Yakima Sahaptin', *Proceedings of the 25th West Coast Conference on Formal Linguistics*. Somerville, MA: Cascadilla Press, 177–85.

Hargus, Sharon, and Siri Tuttle (1997). 'Augmentation as affixation in Athabaskan languages', *Phonology* 14: 177–220.

Harley, Heidi, and Maria Florez Leyva (2009). 'Form and meaning in Hiaki (Yaqui) verbal reduplication', *International Journal of American Linguistics* 75: 233–72.

Harley, Heidi, and Rolf Noyer (1999). 'Distributed Morphology', *GLOT international* 4: 3–9.

Harrikari, Heli (2003). 'Opaque consonant gradation in Finnish', in Roger Billerey and Brook Lillehaugen (eds), *Proceedings of the 19th West Coast Conference on Formal Linguistics*. Somerville, MA: Cascadilla Press, 191–203.

Harris, Alice (2000). 'Where in the word is the Udi clitic?', *Language* 76: 593–616.

Harris, Alice (2008). 'Explaining exuberant agreement', in Thorhallur Eythorsson (ed.), *Linguistic theory and grammatical change: the Rosendal papers*. Amsterdam: John Benjamins, 265–83.

Harrison, Sheldon P. (1973). Reduplication in Micronesian languages. *Oceanic Linguistics* 12: 407–54.

Harrison, Sheldon P. (1976). *Mokilese reference grammar*. Honolulu: The University Press of Hawaii.

Haspelmath, Martin, Matthew Dryer, David Gil, and Bernard Comrie (2005). *The World Atlas of Language Structures*. Oxford: Oxford University Press.

Haugen, Jason (2009). 'Three challenges for Morphological Doubling Theory', paper presented at the Workshop on the Division of Labor between Morphology and Phonology. Meertens Instituut, Amsterdam. Handout downloadable from <http://www.uni-leipzig.de/~exponet/Slides/Amsterdam/Haugen.pdf>.

Hayes, Bruce (1989). 'The prosodic hierarchy in meter', in Paul Kiparsky and Gilbert Youmans (eds), *Rhythm and meter*. Orlando: Academic Press, 201–60.

Hayes, Bruce (1995). *Metrical stress theory: principles and case studies*. Chicago: University of Chicago Press.

Hayes, Bruce, and Colin Wilson (2008). 'A maximum entropy model of phonotactics and phonotactic learning', *Linguistic Inquiry* 39: 379–440.

Hendon, Rufus (1966). *The phonology and morphology of Ulu Muar Malay (Juala Pilah District, Negri Sembilan, Malaya)*. Yale University Publications in Anthropology 40. New Haven: Yale University.

Hendricks, Sean Q. (1999). 'Reduplication without template constraints: a study in bare-consonant reduplication', Ph.D. dissertation, University of Arizona.

Hendricks, Sean Q. (2001). 'Bare-consonant reduplication without prosodic templates: expressive reduplication in Semai', *Journal of East Asian Linguistics* 10: 287–306.

Hill, Jane (1970). 'A peeking rule in Cupeño', *Linguistic Inquiry* 1: 534–9.

Hill, Jane (2005). *A grammar of Cupeño*. UC Publications in Linguistics 136. Berkeley: University of California Press.

Hinton, Leanne, Johanna Nichols, and John J. Ohala (eds) (1994). *Sound symbolism*. Cambridge: Cambridge University Press.

Hippisley, Andrew (1997). 'Declarative derivation: a network morphology account of Russian word formation with reference to nouns denoting "person"', Ph.D. dissertation, University of Surrey.

Hockett, Charles (1947). 'Problems of morphemic analysis', *Language* 24: 414–41.

Hockett, Charles (1954). 'Two models of grammatical description', *Word* 10: 210–34.

Horne, Elinor (1961). *Beginning Javanese*. New Haven: Yale University Press.

Horwood, Graham (2001). 'Anti-faithfulness and subtractive morphology', <http://roa.rutgers.edu/files/466-0901/466-0901-HORWOOD-0-0.PDF>.

van der Hulst, Harry (1982). 'Prosodic domains and opaque segments in autosegmental phonology', in Harry van der Hulst and Norval Smith (eds), *The structure of phonological representations. Part II*. Dordrecht: Foris, 311–36.

Hurlbut, Hope M. (1988). *Verb morphology in Eastern Kadazan*, Pacific Linguistics Series B, No. 97. Canberra: Department of Linguistics, Research School of Pacific Studies, The Australian National University.

Hyman, Larry M. (1981). 'Tonal accent in Somali', *Studies in African Linguistics* 12: 169–203.

Hyman, Larry M. (1994). 'Cyclic phonology and morphology in Cibemba', in Jennifer Cole and Charles Kisseberth (eds), *Perspectives in phonology*. Stanford: CSLI Publications, 81–112.

Hyman, Larry M. (1998). 'Positional Prominence and the "Prosodic Trough" in Yaka', *Phonology* 15: 41–75.

Hyman, Larry M. (2002). 'Cyclicity and base non-identity', in David Restle and Dietmar Zaefferer (eds), *Sounds and systems: studies in structure and change, a festschrift for Theo Vennemann*. Berlin: Mouton de Gruyter, 223–39.

Hyman, Larry M. (2003). 'Suffix ordering in Bantu: a morphocentric approach', *Yearbook of Morphology 2002*: 245–81.

Hyman, Larry M. (2006). 'Affixation by place of articulation: rare AND mysterious', *UC Berkeley Phonology Lab Annual Report* 2006: 51–72.

Hyman, Larry M. (2008). 'Directional asymmetries in the morphology and phonology of words, with special reference to Bantu', *Linguistics* 46: 309–50.

Hyman, Larry M. (2009). 'The natural history of verb-stem reduplication in Bantu', *Morphology* 19: 177–206.

Hyman, Larry M., and Sharon Inkelas (1997). 'Emergent templates: the unusual case of Tiene', in Viola Miglio and Bruce Moren (eds), *University of Maryland Working Papers in Linguistics: selected phonology papers from the Johns Hopkins Optimality Theory Workshop/Maryland Mayfest*. Baltimore: Department of Linguistics, University of Maryland, 92–116.

Hyman, Larry M., Sharon Inkelas, and Galen Sibanda (2009). 'Morphosyntactic correspondence in Bantu reduplication', in Kristin Hanson and Sharon Inkelas (eds), *The nature of the word: essays in honor of Paul Kiparsky*. Cambridge, MA: MIT Press, 273–309.

Hyman, Larry M., and Al Mtenje (1999). 'Prosodic Morphology and tone: the case of Chichewa', in René Kager, Harry van der Hulst, and Wim Zonneveld (eds), *The prosody-morphology interface*. Cambridge: Cambridge University Press, 90–133.

Hyman, Larry M., and C. Orhan Orgun (2005). 'Endocyclicity and paradigm non-uniformity', in C. Orhan Orgun and Peter Sells (eds), *Morphology and the web of grammar*. Stanford: CSLI Publications, 7–23.

Ichimura, Larry (2006). 'Anti-homophony blocking and its productivity in transparadigmatic relations', Ph.D. dissertation, Boston University.

Inkelas, Sharon (1989). 'Prosodic constituency in the lexicon', Ph.D. dissertation, Stanford University. Revised version published in 1990 by Garland Publishing Co.

Inkelas, Sharon (1993). 'Nimboran position class morphology', *Natural Language and Linguistic Theory* 11: 559–624.

Inkelas, Sharon (1998). 'The theoretical status of morphologically conditioned phonology: a case study from dominance', *Yearbook of Morphology* 1997: 121–55.

Inkelas, Sharon (2003). 'J's rhymes: a longitudinal case study of language play', *Journal of Child Language* 30: 557–81.

Inkelas, Sharon (2008a). 'The dual theory of reduplication', *Linguistics* 46: 351–401.

Inkelas, Sharon (2008b). 'The morphology-phonology connection', paper presented at the 34th annual meeting of the Berkeley Linguistics Society. To appear in *Proceedings of BLS 34*. Berkeley: Berkeley Linguistics Society.

Inkelas, Sharon (2011). 'Another look at velar deletion in Turkish, with special attention to the derived environment condition', in Eser Taylan and Bengisu Rona, *Puzzles of language: essays in honour of Karl Zimmer*. Berlin: Walter de Gruyter, 37–53.

Inkelas, Sharon, and William R. Leben (1991). 'Where phonology and phonetics intersect: the case of Hausa intonation', in John Kingston and Mary Beckman (eds), *Papers in laboratory phonology I: between the grammar and physics of speech*. Cambridge: Cambridge University Press, 17–34.

Inkelas, Sharon, and Cemil Orhan Orgun (1995). 'Level ordering and economy in the lexical phonology of Turkish', *Language* 71: 763–93.

Inkelas, Sharon, and Cemil Orhan Orgun (2003). 'Turkish stress: a review', *Phonology* 20: 139–61.

Inkelas, Sharon, Cemil Orhan Orgun, and Cheryl Zoll (1997). 'Implications of lexical exceptions for the nature of grammar', in Iggy Roca (ed.), *Constraints and derivations in phonology*. Oxford: Clarendon Press, 393–418.

Inkelas, Sharon, and Draga Zec (eds) (1990). *The phonology-syntax connection*. Chicago: CSLI Publications and the University of Chicago Press.

Inkelas, Sharon, and Cheryl Zoll (2005). *Reduplication: doubling in morphology*. Cambridge: Cambridge University Press.

Inkelas, Sharon, and Cheryl Zoll (2007). 'Is Grammar Dependence Real? A comparison between cophonological and indexed constraint approaches to morphologically conditioned phonology', *Linguistics* 45: 133–71.

Itô, Junko (1986). 'Syllable theory in prosodic phonology', Ph.D. dissertation, University of Massachusetts, Amherst.

Itô, Junko (1990). 'Prosodic minimality in Japanese', in Michael Ziolkowski, Manuela Noske, and Karen Deaton (eds), *Papers from the twenty-sixth regional meeting of the Chicago Linguistics Society. Volume 2: the parasession on the syllable in phonetics and phonology.* Chicago: Chicago Linguistics Society, 213–39.

Itô, Junko, and Jorge Hankamer (1989). 'Notes on monosyllabism in Turkish', in Junko Itô and Jeff Runner, *Phonology at Santa Cruz 1.* Santa Cruz: University of California, Santa Cruz Syntax Research Center, 61–9.

Itô, Junko, and Armin Mester (1992). *Weak layering and word binarity.* Linguistic Research Center report. University of California, Santa Cruz.

Itô, Junko, and Armin Mester (1995a). 'The core-periphery structure of the lexicon and constraints on reranking', *University of Massachussets Occasional Papers in Linguistics 18.* Amherst, MA: GLSA, 181–209.

Itô, Junko, and Armin Mester (1995b). 'Japanese phonology', in John Goldsmith (ed.), *The handbook of phonological theory.* Cambridge, MA: Blackwell, 817–38.

Itô, Junko, and Armin Mester (1996). 'Stem and word in Sino-Japanese', in Takashi Otake and Ann Cutler (eds), *Phonological structure and language processing: cross-linguistic studies.* Berlin: Mouton de Gruyter, 13–44.

Itô, Junko, and Armin Mester (1997). 'Sympathy Theory and German truncations', in Viola Miglio and Bruce Morén (eds), *University of Maryland Working Papers in Linguistics: Selected papers from the Hopkins Optimality Theory Workshop 1997/University of Maryland Mayfest 1997.* College Park, MD: Linguistics Department, University of Maryland, 117–39.

Itô, Junko, and Armin Mester (1999). 'The structure of the phonological lexicon', in N. Tsujimura (ed.), *The handbook of Japanese linguistics.* Malden, MA: Blackwell, 62–100.

Itô, Junko, and Armin Mester (2003). 'Weak layering and word binarity', in Shin-ichi Tanaka Takeru Honma, Masao Okazaki, and Toshiyuki Tabata (eds), *A new century of phonology and phonological theory: a festschrift for Professor Shosuke Haraguchi on the occasion of his sixtieth birthday.* 26–65.

İz, Fahir, H. C. Hony, and A. D. Alderson (1992). *The Oxford Turkish-English dictionary.* 3rd Vol. Oxford: Oxford University Press.

Jensen, J. T. (1977). *Yapese reference grammar.* Honolulu: University of Hawaii Press.

Johanson, Lars, and Eva Csato (1998). *The Turkic languages.* New York: Routledge.

Johnston, R. (1980). *Nakanai of New Britain: the grammar of an Oceanic language.* Pacific Linguistics, Series B 70. Canberra: The Australian National University.

Kabak, Barış (2007). 'Turkish suspended affixation', *Linguistics* 45: 311–47.

Kabak, Barış, and Anthi Revithiadou (2009). 'An interface approach to prosodic word recursion', in Janet Grijzenhout and Barış Kabak (eds), *Phonological domains: universals and deviations.* Berlin: Mouton de Gruyter, 105–33.

Kabak, Barış, and Irene Vogel (2001). 'The phonological word and stress assignment in Turkish', *Phonology* 18: 315–60.

Kager, René (1996). 'On affix allomorphy and syllable counting', in Ursula Kleinhenz (ed.), *Interfaces in phonology*. Berlin: Akademie Verlag, 155–71.

Kager, René (1999). *Optimality Theory*. Cambridge: Cambridge University Press.

Kahn, D. (1976). *Syllable-based generalizations in English phonology*, distributed by IULC, Indiana University, Bloomington: MIT.

Kaisse, Ellen (1985). *Connected speech: the interaction of syntax and phonology*. Orlando: Academic Press.

Kaisse, Ellen, and Patricia Shaw (1985). 'On the theory of Lexical Phonology', *Phonology Yearbook* 2: 1–30.

Karlsson, Fred (1983). *Suomen kielen äänne- ja muotorakenne [The phonological and morphological structure of Finnish]*. Helsinki: Werner Söderström Osakeyhtiö.

Kawahara, Shigeto (2002). 'Similarity among variants: output-variant correspondence', BA thesis, International Christian University.

Kean, Mary-Louise (1973). 'Non-global rules in Klamath phonology', *Quarterly Progress Report, MIT Research Laboratory in Electronics* 108: 288–310.

Kean, Mary-Louise (1974). 'The strict cycle in phonology', *Linguistic Inquiry* 5: 179–203.

Keane, Elinor (2001). 'Echo words in Tamil', Ph.D. dissertation, Oxford University.

Kennedy, Robert (2003). 'Confluence in phonology: evidence from Micronesian reduplication', Ph.D. dissertation, Rutgers University.

Kenstowicz, Michael (1996). 'Base Identity and Uniform Exponence: alternatives to cyclicity', in Jacques Durand and Bernard Laks (eds), *Current trends in phonology: models and methods*. Manchester: University of Salford Publications, 363–93.

Kenstowicz, Michael (1997). 'Uniform Exponence: extension and exemplification', in Viola Miglio and Bruce Moren (eds), *University of Maryland Working Papers in Linguistics: selected phonology papers from the Johns Hopkins Optimality Theory Workshop/Maryland Mayfest*. Baltimore: Department of Linguistics, University of Maryland, 139–55.

Kenstowicz, Michael (2002). 'Paradigmatic uniformity and contrast', *MIT Working Papers in Linguistics: Phonological answers (and their corresponding questions)* 42: 141–64.

Kenstowicz, Michael (2005). 'Paradigmatic uniformity and contrast', in Laura Downing, Tracy Hall, and Renate Raffelsiefen (eds), *Paradigms in phonological theory*. Oxford: Oxford University Press, 170–210.

Kenstowicz, Michael, and Charles Kisseberth (1979). *Generative phonology*. New York: Academic Press.

Key, Gregory (2013). 'The morphosyntax of the Turkish causative construction', Ph.D. dissertation, University of Arizona.

Keyser, Samuel J., and Paul Kiparsky (1984). 'Syllable structure in Finnish phonology', in Mark Aronoff and Richard Oehrle (eds), *Language sound structure*. Cambridge, MA: MIT Press, 7–31.

Kidima, Lukowa (1990). 'Tone and syntax in Kiyaka', in Sharon Inkelas and Draga Zec (eds), *The phonology-syntax connection*. Chicago: Chicago University Press, 195–216.

Kim, Yuni (2008). 'Topics in the phonology and morphology of San Francisco del Mar Huave', Ph.D. dissertation, University of California, Berkeley.

Kimball, Geoffrey (1991). *Koasati grammar*. Lincoln, NE: University of Nebraska Press.

Kimenyi, Alexandre (2002). *A tonal grammar of Kinyarwanda: an autosegmental and metrical analysis*. Lewiston, NY: E. Mellen Press.

Kiparsky, Paul (1968). *Explanation in phonology*. Dordrecht: Cinnaminson (also published by New Jersey: Foris).

Kiparsky, Paul (1982a). 'How are the levels linked?' ms, Stanford University.

Kiparsky, Paul (1982b). 'Lexical morphology and phonology', in I.-S. Yang (ed.), *Linguistics in the morning calm*. Seoul: Hanshin, 3–91.

Kiparsky, Paul (1982c). 'Word-formation and the lexicon', in Frances Ingemann (ed.), *1982 Mid-America linguistics conference papers*. Lawrence, KS: University of Kansas, 3–32.

Kiparsky, Paul (1984). 'On the lexical phonology of Icelandic', in Claes-Christian Elert, Iréne Johansson, and Eva Strangert (eds), *Nordic prosody II: papers from a symposium*. Umeå: University of Umeå, 135–64.

Kiparsky, Paul (1985). 'Some consequences of lexical phonology', *Phonology Yearbook* 2: 85–138.

Kiparsky, Paul (1993). 'Blocking in non-derived environments', in Sharon Hargus and Ellen Kaisse (eds), *Phonetics and Phonology 4: Studies in Lexical Phonology*. San Diego: Academic Press, 277–313.

Kiparsky, Paul (2000). 'Opacity and cyclicity', *The Linguistic Review* 17: 351–67.

Kiparsky, Paul (2003). 'Finnish noun inflection', in Diane Nelson and Satu Manninen (eds), *Generative approaches to Finnic and Saami linguistics*. Stanford: CSLI Publications, 109–61.

Kiparsky, Paul (2008). 'Fenno-Swedish quantity: contrast in Stratal OT', in Bert Vaux and Andrew Nevins (eds), *Rules, constraints, and phonological phenomena*. Oxford: Oxford University Press, 185–220.

Kiparsky, Paul (2010). 'Reduplication in Stratal OT', in Linda Uyechi and Lian Hee Wee (eds), *Reality exploration and discovery: pattern interaction in language and life*. Stanford: CSLI Publications, 125–42.

Kiparsky, Paul, and Morris Halle. (1977). 'Towards a reconstruction of the Indo-European accent', in Larry Hyman (ed.), *Studies in stress and accent*. Los Angeles: Department of Linguistics, University of Southern California, 209–38.

Kiyomi, Setsuko (1993). 'A typological study of reduplication as a morpho-semantic process: evidence from five language families (Bantu, Australian, Papuan, Austroasiatic and Malayo-Polynesian)', Ph.D. dissertation, Indiana University.

Kiyomi, Setsuko (1995). 'A new approach to reduplication: a semantic study of noun and verb reduplication in the Malayo-Polynesian languages', *Linguistics* 33: 1145–67.

Klavans, Judith (1985). 'The independence of syntax and phonology in cliticization', *Language* 61: 95–120.

Klein, Thomas (2003). 'Syllable structure and lexical markedness in creole morphophonology: determiner allomorphy in Haitian and elsewhere', in Ingo Plag (ed.), *The phonology and morphology of creole languages*. Tübingen: Max Niemeyer, 209–28.

Klein, Thomas (2005). 'Infixation and segmental constraint effects: UM and IN in Tagalog, Chamorro and Toba Batak', *Lingua* 115: 959–95.

Klokeid, Terry J. (1976). 'Topics in Lardil grammar', Ph.D. dissertation, MIT.

Koenig, Jean-Pierre, and Daniel Jurafsky (1995). 'Type underspecification and on-line type construction in the lexicon', in Raul Aranovich, William Byrne, Susanne Preuss, and Martha Senturia, *Proceedings of the thirteenth West Coast Conference on Formal Linguistics*. Stanford: CSLI Publications, 270–85.

Kornfilt, Jaklin (1997). *Turkish*. London: Routledge.

Koul, Omkar (2008). 'Reduplication in Kashmiri', ms, Indian Institute of Linguistics, <http://koausa.org/iils/pdf/Reduplication.pdf>.

Koutsoudas, Andreas (1980). 'The question of rule ordering: some common fallacies', *Journal of Linguistics* 16: 19–35.

Krause, Scott (1980). 'Topics in Chukchee phonology and morphology', Ph.D. dissertation, University of Illinois.

Kroeger, Paul (1990). 'Discontinuous reduplication in vernacular Malay', *Proceedings of the Berkeley Linguistic Society 15*. Berkeley: Berkeley Linguistics Society, 193–202.

Kurisu, Kazutaka (2001). 'The phonology of morpheme realization', Ph.D. dissertation, University of California, Santa Cruz.

Kurisu, Kazutaka, and Nathan Sanders (1999). 'Infixal nominal reduplication in Mangarayi', *Phonology at Santa Cruz* 6: 47–56.

Langdon, Margaret (1994). 'Noise words in Guarani', in Leanne Hinton, Johanna Nichols, and John J. Ohala (eds), *Sound symbolism*. Cambridge: Cambridge University Press, 94–103.

Lappe, Sabine (2003). 'Monosyllabicity in Prosodic Morphology: the case of truncated personal names in English', *Yearbook of Morphology 2002*: 135–86.

Leben, William R. (1978). 'The representation of tone', in V. A. Fromkin (ed.), *Tone: a linguistic survey*. New York: Academic Press, 177–219.

Lees, Robert (1961). *The phonology of Modern Standard Turkish*. Bloomington: Indiana University Publications.

Lefebvre, Claire, and A. M. Brousseau (2002). *A grammar of Fongbe*. Berlin:
Mouton de Gruyter.

Lehmann, Christian (2005). 'Pleonasm and hypercharacterisation', *Yearbook
of Morphology 2005*: 119–54.

Lewis, Geoffrey (1967). *Turkish grammar*. Oxford: Oxford University Press.

Li, Fengxiang, and Lindsay J. Whaley (2000). 'Emphatic reduplication in
Oroqen and its Altaic context', *Linguistics* 38: 1–18.

Lichtenberk, Frantisek (1983). *A grammar of Manam*. Honolulu: University of
Hawaii Press.

Lidz, Jeffrey (2001). 'Echo-reduplication in Kannada and the theory of word
formation', *The Linguistic Review* 18: 375–94.

Lieber, Rochelle (1980). 'On the organization of the lexicon', Ph.D.
dissertation, MIT.

Lombardi, Linda, and John McCarthy (1991). 'Prosodic circumscription in
Choctaw morphology', *Phonology* 8: 37–72.

Łubowicz, Anna (2002). 'Derived environment effects in Optimality Theory',
Lingua 112: 243–80.

Łubowicz, Anna (2007). 'Paradigmatic contrast in Polish', *Journal of Slavic
Linguistics* 15: 229–62.

Lynch, John (1978). *A grammar of Lenakel*. Pacific Linguistics B55. Canberra:
Australian National University.

McCarthy, John (1979). 'Formal problems in Semitic phonology and morphology', Ph.D. dissertation, MIT.

McCarthy, John (1981). A prosodic theory of non-concatenative morphology.
Linguistic Inquiry 12: 373–418.

McCarthy, John (1982). 'Prosodic structure and expletive infixation', *Language* 78: 574–90.

McCarthy, John (1999). 'Sympathy and phonological opacity', *Phonology* 16:
331–99.

McCarthy, John (2000). 'Faithfulness and prosodic circumscription', in
J. Dekkers, F. van der Leeuw, and J. van de Weijer (eds), *Optimality Theory:
phonology, syntax, and acquisition*. New York: Oxford University Press,
151–89.

McCarthy, John (2002). *A thematic guide to Optimality Theory*. Cambridge:
Cambridge University Press.

McCarthy, John (2003a). 'Comparative markedness', *Theoretical Linguistics*
29: 1–51.

McCarthy, John (2003b). 'OT Constraints are categorical', *Phonology* 20:
75–138.

McCarthy, John (2004). *Optimality Theory in phonology: a reader*. Cambridge,
MA: Blackwell.

McCarthy, John (2005). 'Optimal paradigms', in Laura Downing, T. Alan Hall, and Renate Raffelsiefen (eds), *Paradigms in phonological theory*. Oxford: Oxford University Press.

McCarthy, John (2007). *Hidden generalizations: phonological opacity in Optimality Theory*. London: Equinox, 170–210.

McCarthy, John (2008). *Doing Optimality Theory*. Malden, MA and Oxford, UK: Blackwell.

McCarthy, John, Wendell Kimper, and Kevin Mullin (2012). 'Reduplication in harmonic serialism', *Morphology* 22: 173–232.

McCarthy, John, and Alan Prince (1990). Foot and word in Prosodic Morphology: the Arabic broken plural. *Natural Language and Linguistic Theory* 8: 209–82.

McCarthy, John, and Alan Prince (1993). 'Generalized alignment', in Geert Booij and Jaap van Marle (eds), *Yearbook of Morphology 1993*. Dordrecht: Kluwer, 79–153.

McCarthy, John, and Alan Prince (1994a). 'The emergence of the unmarked', in Mercè Gonzàlez (ed.), *Proceedings of NELS 24*. Amherst, MA: GLSA, 333–79.

McCarthy, John, and Alan Prince (1994b). 'Two lectures on Prosodic Morphology', OTS/HIL Workshop on Prosodic Morphology. Downloadable from <http://works.bepress.com/john_j_mccarthy/58>.

McCarthy, John, and Alan Prince (1995). 'Faithfulness and reduplicative identity', in Jill Beckman, Laura Dickey, and Suzanne Urbanczyk (eds), *University of Massachusetts Occasional Papers in Linguistics 18: Papers in Optimality Theory*. Amherst, MA: GLSA, 249–384.

McCarthy, John, and Alan Prince (1996). *Prosodic Morphology 1986*. Rutgers University Center for Cognitive Science.

McCarthy, John, and Alan Prince (1999a). 'Faithfulness and identity in Prosodic Morphology', in René Kager, Harry van der Hulst, and Wim Zonneveld (eds), *The prosody-morphology interface*. Cambridge: Cambridge University Press, 218–309.

McCarthy, John, and Alan Prince (1999b). 'Prosodic Morphology (1986)', in John Goldsmith (ed.), *Phonological theory: the essential readings*. Malden, MA: Blackwell, 238–88.

McCarthy, John, and Matthew Wolf (2009). 'Less than zero: correspondence and the null output', in Curt Rice and Sylvia Blaho (eds), *Modeling ungrammaticality in Optimality Theory*. London: Equinox, 17–66.

McCawley, J. D. (1968). *The phonological component of a grammar of Japanese*. The Hague: Mouton.

McDonough, Joyce (1990). 'Topics in the phonology and morphology of Navajo verbs', Ph.D. dissertation, University of Massachusetts, Amherst.

McDonough, Joyce (2000). 'On the bipartite model of the Athabaskan verb', in T. B. Fernald and P. R. Platero (eds), *The Athabaskan languages:*

perspectives on a Native American language family. Oxford: Oxford Univeristy Press, 139–66.

MacEachern, Margaret (1997). 'Laryngeal cooccurrence constraints', Ph.D. dissertation, UCLA. Published in 1999 in the Outstanding dissertations in linguistics series, Routledge.

McLaughlin, Fiona (2000). 'Consonant mutation and reduplication in Seereer-Siin', *Phonology* 17: 333–63.

Maganga, Clement, and Thilo Schadeberg (1992). *Kinyamwezi: grammar, texts, vocabulary*. Cologne: Rüdiger Köppe Verlag.

Malkiel, Yakov (1959). 'Studies in irreversible binomials', *Lingua* 8: 113–60.

Malou, J. (1988). *Dinka vowel system*. Summer Institute of Linguistics Publications in Linguistics 82. Summer Institute of Linguistics and University of Texas Arlington.

Marantz, Alec (1982). 'Re reduplication', *Linguistic Inquiry* 13: 435–82.

Marcus, Gary, Ursula Brinkmann, Harald Clahsen, Richard Wiese, and Steven Pinker (1995). 'German inflection: the exception that proves the rule', *Cognitive Psychology* 29: 189–256.

Marlo, Michael (2008). 'Tura verbal tonology', *Studies in African Linguistics* 37: 153–243.

Martin, Jack (1988). 'Subtractive morphology as dissociation', in Hagit Borer (ed.), *Proceedings of the seventh West Coast Conference on Formal Linguistics*. Stanford, CA: Stanford Linguistics Association.

Martin, Jack, and Margaret McKane Mauldin (2000). *A Dictionary of Creek/ Muskogee, with notes on the Florida and Oklahoma Seminole dialects of Creek*. Lincoln/London: University of Nebraska Press.

Mascaró, Joan (1976). *Catalan phonology and the phonological cycle*. Bloomington: Indiana University Linguistics Club.

Mascaró, Joan (2007). 'External allomorphy and lexical representation', *Linguistic Inquiry* 38: 715–35.

Matthews, Peter H. (1972). *Inflectional morphology*. Cambridge: Cambridge University Press.

Matthews, Peter H. (1974). *Morphology*. Cambridge: Cambridge University Press.

Matthews, S., and Moira Yip (1994). *Cantonese grammar*. London/New York: Routledge.

Melvold, Janis (1986). 'Cyclicity and Russian stress', in Joyce McDonough and Bernadette Plunkett (eds), *Proceedings of NELS 17*. Amherst, MA: GLSA, 467–81.

Menn, Lise, and Brian MacWhinney (1984). 'The repeated morph constraint: toward an explanation', *Language* 60: 519–41.

Merlan, F. (1982). *Mangarayi*. Amsterdam: North-Holland.

Mester, Armin (1986). 'Studies in tier structure', Ph.D. dissertation, University of Massachusetts, Amherst.

Mester, Armin (1994). 'The quantitative trochee in Latin', *Natural Language and Linguistic Theory* 12: 1–61.

Michael, Lev (2008). 'Nanti evidential practice: language, knowledge, and social action in an Amazonian society', Ph.D. dissertation, University of Texas, Austin.

Miller, D. Gary (1975). 'On constraining global rules in phonology', *Language* 51: 128–32.

Miller, W. R. (1996). *Guarijio: gramática, textos y vocabularios*. Mexico: UNAM, Instituto de Investigaciones Antropológicas.

Mohanan, K. P. (1982). 'Lexical phonology', Ph.D. dissertation, MIT.

Mohanan, K. P. (1986). *Lexical phonology*. Dordrecht: Kluwer.

Mohanan, K. P. (1995). 'The organization of the grammar', in John Goldsmith (ed.), *The handbook of phonological theory*. Cambridge, MA: Blackwell, 24–69.

Mohanan, K. P., and Tara Mohanan (1984). 'Lexical phonology of the consonant system in Malayalam', *Linguistic Inquiry* 15: 575–602.

Moravcsik, Edith (1977). *On rules of infixing*. Bloomington: Indiana University Linguistics Club.

Moravcsik, Edith (1978). 'Reduplicative constructions', in Joseph Greenberg (ed.), *Universals of human language, vol 3 word structure*. Stanford: Stanford University Press, 297–334.

Moravcsik, Edith (2000). 'Infixation', in Gert Booij, Lehmann Christian, and Joachim Mugdan (eds), *Morphologie–Morphology*. Berlin: Walter de Gruyter, 545–52.

Mortensen, David (2006). 'Formal and substantive scales in phonology', Ph.D. dissertation, University of California, Berkeley.

Mtenje, Al (1988). 'On tone and transfer in Chichewa reduplication', *Linguistics* 26, 125–55.

Mtenje, Al (1992). 'Extralinguistic constraints on rule application in Chichewa and Chiyao', *African Languages and Cultures* 5: 65–73.

Muller, Jennifer (1999). 'A unified mora account of Chuukese', in Sonya Bird, Andrew Carnie, Jason Haugen, and Peter Norquest (eds), *Proceedings of the 18th West Coast Conference on Formal Linguistics*. Malden, MA: Cascadilla Press, 393–405.

Munro, Pamela, and P. Benson (1973). 'Reduplication and rule ordering in Luiseño', *International Journal of American Linguistics* 39: 15–21.

Munro, Pamela, and Jason Riggle (2004). 'Productivity and lexicalization in Pima compounds', *Proceedings of BLS*. Berkeley: Berkeley Linguistics Society.

Mutaka, Ngessimo, and Larry M. Hyman (1990). 'Syllable and morpheme integrity in Kinande reduplication', *Phonology* 7: 73–119.

Nelson, Nicole (2003). 'Asymmetric anchoring', Ph.D. dissertation, Rutgers University.

Nelson, Nicole (2005). 'Wrong-side reduplication is epiphenomenal: evidence from Yoruba', in Bernhard Hurch (ed.), *Studies in reduplication*. Berlin: Mouton, 135–60.

Nespor, Marina, and Irene Vogel (1986). *Prosodic phonology*. Dordrecht: Foris.

Nevins, Andrew (2005). 'Overwriting does not optimize in nonconcatenative morphology', *Linguistic Inquiry* 36: 275–87.

Newman, Paul (1986). 'Tone and affixation in Hausa', *Studies in African Linguistics* 17: 249–67.

Newman, Paul (1995). 'Hausa tonology: complexities in an "easy" tone language', in John Goldsmith (ed.), *Handbook of phonological theory*. Cambridge, MA: Blackwell, 762–81.

Newman, Paul (2000). *The Hausa language: an encyclopedic reference grammar*. New Haven: Yale University Press.

Newman, Paul (2001). 'Are ideophones really as weird and extra-systematic as linguists make them out to be?', in F. K. Erhard Voeltz and Christa Kilian-Hatz (eds), *Ideophones*. Amsterdam: John Benjamins, 251–8.

Newman, Stanley (1944). *Yokuts Language of California*. New York: Viking Fund Publications.

Newman, Stanley (1965). *Zuni grammar*. University of New Mexico publications in anthropology 14. Albuquerque: University of New Mexico.

Ngunga, Armindo (2000). *Phonology and morphology of the Ciyao verb*. Stanford Monographs in African Linguistics. Stanford: CSLI Publications.

Niepokuj, Mary Katherine (1991). 'The historical development of reduplication, with special reference to Indo-European', Ph.D. dissertation, University of California, Berkeley.

Noske, Roland (1985). 'Syllabification and syllable-changing processes in Yawelmani', in Harry van der Hulst and Norval Smith (eds), *Advances in nonlinear phonology*. Dordrecht: Foris, 335–61.

Noyer, Rolf (1994). 'Mobile affixes in Huave: Optimality and morphological wellformedness', in Erin Duncan, Donka Farkas, and Philip Spaelti (eds), *Proceedings of the Twelfth West Coast Conference on Formal Linguistics*. Stanford: Stanford Linguistics Association, 67–82.

Odden, David (1988). 'Anti antigemination and the OCP', *Linguistic Inquiry* 19: 451–75.

Odden, David (1990). 'Syntax, lexical rules and postlexical rules in Kimatuumbi', in Sharon Inkelas and Draga Zec (eds), *The phonology-syntax connection* Chicago: University of Chicago Press and CSLI Publications, 259–78.

Odden, David (1993). 'Interaction between modules in Lexical Phonology', in Sharon Hargus and Ellen Kaisse (eds), *Phonetics and Phonology 4: Studies in Lexical Phonology*. San Diego: Academic Press, 111–44.

Odden, David (1999). 'Typological issues in tone and stress in Bantu', in Shegeki Kaji (ed.), *Cross-linguistic studies of tonal phenomena: tonogenisis, typology, and related topics.* Tokyo: ILCAA, 187–215.

Odden, David, and Mary Odden (1985). 'Ordered reduplication in Kihehe', *Linguistic Inquiry* 16: 497–503.

Onn, Farid M. (1976). 'Aspects of Malay phonology and morphology: a generative approach', Ph.D. dissertation, University of Illinois.

Orešnik, Janez (1978). 'The age and importance of the Modern Icelandic type *klifr*', in John Weinstock (ed.), *The Nordic languages and modern linguistics.* Austin: University of Texas, 149–52.

Orgun, Cemil Orhan (1996). 'Sign-based morphology and phonology: with special attention to Optimality Theory', Ph.D. dissertation, University of California, Berkeley.

Orgun, Cemil Orhan, and Sharon Inkelas (2002). 'Reconsidering Bracket Erasure', *Yearbook of Morphology 2001*: 115–46.

Orgun, Cemil Orhan, and Ronald Sprouse (1999). From MParse to Control: deriving ungrammaticality. *Phonology* 16: 191–224.

Otsubo, Kazuo (1982). 'Shukuyakukei', in Ogawa Yoshio et al. (eds), *Nihongo kyoiku jiten.* Tokyo: Taishuukan shoten, 51–2.

Paster, Mary (2005). 'Pulaar verbal extensions and phonologically driven affix order', *Yearbook of Morphology 2005*: 155–99.

Paster, Mary (2006). 'Phonological conditions on affixation', Ph.D. dissertation, University of California, Berkeley.

Paster, Mary (2008). 'Optional multiple plural marking in Maay', in Franz Rainer, Wolfgang Dressler, Dieter Kastovsky, and Hans Christian Luschütsky (eds), *Variation and change in morphology.* Amsterdam: John Benjamins, 177–92.

Pater, Joe (2000). 'Non-uniformity in English secondary stress: the role of ranked and lexically specific constraints', *Phonology* 17: 237–74.

Patterson, D., and C. M. Connine (2001). 'A corpus analysis of variant frequency in American English flap production', *Phonetica* 58: 254–75.

Peperkamp, Sharon (1996). 'On the prosodic representation of clitics', in Ursula Kleinhenz (ed.), *Interfaces in phonology.* Berlin: Akademie Verlag, 104–28.

Pesetsky, David (1979). 'Russian morphology and lexical theory', ms, MIT.

Peterson, David (2001). 'The Ingush clitic ʔa: the elusive Type 5 clitic?', *Language* 77: 144–55.

Pierrehumbert, Janet (1993). 'Dissimilarity in the Arabic verbal roots', *Proceedings of the Northeastern Linguistics Society* 23. Amherst, MA: GLSA.

Pierrehumbert, Janet, and Mary Beckman (1988). *Japanese tone structure.* Cambridge, MA: MIT Press.

Piñeros, Carlos (2002). 'Truncamientos en español' [Truncated words in Spanish], *Bulletin of Hispanic Studies* 79: 437–59.

Plag, Ingo (1998). 'Morphological haplology in a constraint-based morpho-phonology', in Wolfgang Kehrein and Richard Wiese (eds), *Phonology and morphology of the Germanic languages*. Tübingen: Niemeyer, 199–215.

Poser, William J. (1984). 'The phonetics and phonology of tone and intonation in Japanese', Ph.D. dissertation, MIT.

Poser, William J. (1990). 'Evidence for foot structure in Japanese', *Language* 66: 78–105.

Poser, William J. (1992). 'Blocking out of the Lexicon', in I. Sag and A. Szabolsci (eds), *Lexical Matters*. Stanford: CSLI Publications, 111–30.

Prentice, D. J. (1971). *The Murut languages of Sabah*. Pacific Linguistics Series C 18. Canberra: Australian National University.

Prince, Alan (1980). 'A metrical theory for Estonian quantity', *Linguistic Inquiry* 11: 511–62.

Prince, Alan, and Paul Smolensky (1993). 'Optimality Theory: constraint interaction in generative grammar', ms, Rutgers University.

Prince, Alan, and Paul Smolensky (2004). *Optimality Theory: constraint inter-action in generative grammar*. Malden, MA: Blackwell.

Pulleyblank, Douglas (1986). *Tone in lexical phonology*. Dordrecht: D. Reidel.

Pycha, Anne (2008a). 'Morphological sources of phonological length', Ph.D. dissertation, University of California, Berkeley.

Pycha, Anne (2008b). 'Partial blocking', *Proceedings of the Chicago Linguistic Society 41*, 1: 415–30. Chicago: University of Chicago.

Rackowski, Andrea (1999). 'Morphological optionality in Tagalog aspectual reduplication', *Papers on Morphology and Syntax, Cycle Two: MIT Working Papers in Linguistics* 34. Cambridge, MA: MIT.

Raffelsiefen, Renate (1996). 'Gaps in word-formation', in Ursula Kleinhenz (ed.), *Interfaces in phonology*. Berlin: Akademie-Verlag, 193–208.

Raffelsiefen, Renate (2004). 'Absolute ill-formedness and other morpho-phonological effects', *Phonology* 21: 91–142.

Raimy, Eric (2000). *The phonology and morphology of reduplication*. Berlin: Mouton.

Regier, Terry (1994). *A preliminary study of the semantics of reduplication*. Berkeley: International Computer Science Institute.

Rhodes, Richard (1992). 'Flapping in American English', *Phonologica 1992*. Turin: Rosenberg & Sellier.

Rice, Curt (2005). 'Optimal gaps in optimal paradigms', *Catalan Journal of Linguistics* 4: 155–70. Available from <http://ling.auf.net/lingBuzz/000055>.

Rice, Curt, and Sylvia Blaho (eds) (2009). *Modeling ungrammaticality in Optimality Theory*. London: Equinox.

Rice, Keren (1989). *A grammar of Slave*. Berlin: Mouton de Gruyter.

Rice, Keren (1990). 'Predicting rule domains in the phrasal phonology', in Sharon Inkelas and Draga Zec (eds), *The phonology-syntax connection*. Chicago: University of Chicago Press and CSLI Publications, 289–312.

Rice, Keren (1993). 'The structure of the Slave verb', in Sharon Hargus and Ellen Kaisse (eds), *Studies in Lexical Phonology*. New York: Academic Press, 145–72.

Rice, Keren (2000). *Morpheme order and semantic scope: word formation in the Athapaskan verb*. Cambridge: Cambridge University Press.

Rice, Keren (2011). 'Principles of affix ordering: an overview', *Word Structure* 4: 169–200.

Rice, Keren, and Elizabeth Cowper (1984). 'Consonant mutation and auto-segmental morphology', in Joseph Drogo, Veena Mishra, and David Testen (eds), *Proceedings of CLS 20*. Chicago: Chicago Linguistic Society, 309–20.

Riehemann, Susanne (1998). Type-based derivational morphology. *Journal of Comparative Germanic Linguistics* 2: 49–77.

Riehemann, Susanne (2001). 'A constructional approach to idioms and word formation', Ph.D. dissertation, Stanford University.

Riggle, Jason (2004). 'Nonlocal reduplication', in Kier Moulton and Matthew Wolf (eds), *Proceedings of the 34th meeting of the North Eastern Linguistics Society*. Amherst: GLSA, 485–96.

Riggle, Jason (2006). Infixing reduplication in Pima and its theoretical conse-quences. *Natural Language and Linguistic Theory* 24: 857–91.

Roberts, John (1987). *Amele*. London: Croom Helm.

Roberts, John (1991). 'Reduplication in Amele', in Tom Dutton (ed.), *Papers in Papuan Linguistics* 1, Pacific Linguistics A 73: 115–46.

Robins, R. H. (1959). 'Nominal and verbal derivation in Sundanese', *Lingua* 8: 337–69.

Rose, Françoise (2005). 'Reduplication in Tupi-Guarani languages', in Bern-hard Hurch and Veronika Mattes (eds), *Studies on reduplication*. Berlin: Mouton de Gruyter, 351–68.

Rose, Sharon (2003). 'Triple take: Tigre and the case of internal reduplication', *San Diego Linguistic Papers* 1: 109–28.

Rose, Sharon, and Rachel Walker (2011). 'Harmony systems', in John Gold-smith, Jason Riggle, and Alan C. L. Yu (eds), *The handbook of phonological theory*, 2nd edition. Hoboken: Wiley-Blackwell, 240–89.

Rose, Suzanne (1981). 'Kyuquot grammar', Ph.D. dissertation, University of Victoria.

Rubach, Jerzy. (1984). *Cyclic and lexical phonology*. Dordrecht: Foris.

Rubach, Jerzy, and Geert E. Booij (1990). 'Edge of constituent effects in Polish', *Natural Language and Linguistic Theory* 8: 427–63.

Rubino, Carl (2005). 'Reduplication: form, function and distribution', in Bernhard Hurch and Veronika Mattes (eds), *Studies on reduplication*. Berlin: Mouton de Gruyter, 11–29.

Rubino, Carl (2013). 'Reduplication', in Matthew Dryer and Martin Haspel-math (eds), *The World Atlas of Language Structures Online*, Chapter 27: Available online at <http://wals.info/chapter/27>.

Ryan, Kevin (2010). 'Variable affix order: grammar and learning', *Language* 86: 758–91.

Saeed, John (1999). *Somali*. Amsterdam: John Benjamins.

Samek-Lodovici, Vieri (1992). 'A unified analysis of crosslinguistic morphological gemination', *Proceedings of CONSOLE-1*. Utrecht.

Schachter, Paul, and Fe Otanes (1972). *Tagalog reference grammar*. Berkeley: University of California Press.

Selkirk, Elisabeth (1978). 'On prosodic structure and its relation to syntactic structure', in T. Fretheim (ed.), *Nordic prosody II*. Trondheim: TAPIR, 111–40.

Selkirk, Elisabeth (1982). *The syntax of words*. Cambridge, MA: MIT Press.

Selkirk, Elisabeth (1986). 'On derived domains in sentence phonology', *Phonology Yearbook* 3: 371–405.

Selkirk, Elisabeth (2011). 'The syntax-phonology interface', in John Goldsmith, Jason Riggle, and Alan C. L. Yu (eds), *The handbook of phonological theory*, 2nd edition. Oxford: Blackwell, 435–84.

Sezer, Engin (1981). 'The k/Ø alternation in Turkish', in G. N Clements (ed.), *Harvard Studies in Phonology*. Bloomington: Indiana University Linguistics Club, 354–82.

Shaw, Patricia A. (1980). 'Theoretical issues in Dakota phonology and morphology', *Outstanding dissertations in linguistics*. New York: Garland.

Shaw, Patricia A. (2009). 'Inside access', in Kristin Hanson and Sharon Inkelas (eds), *The nature of the word: essays in honor of Paul Kiparsky*. Cambridge, MA: MIT Press, 241–72.

Shih, Stephanie (2014). 'Towards optimal rhythm', Ph.D. dissertation, Stanford University.

Sibanda, Galen (2004). 'Verbal phonology and morphology of Ndebele', Ph.D. dissertation, University of California, Berkeley.

Siegel, Dorothy (1974). 'Topics in English morphology', Ph.D. dissertation, MIT.

Singh, Rajendra (1987). 'Well-formedness conditions and phonological theory', in Wolfgang Dressler, H. C. Luschützky, O. E Pfeiffer, and J. E. Rennison (eds), *Phonologica 1984*. Cambridge: Cambridge University Press, 273–84.

Singh, Rajendra (1996). 'Natural phono(morpho)logy: a view from the outside', in Bernhard Hurch and Richard Rhodes (eds), *Natural phonology: the state of the art. Papers from the Bern Workshop*. Berlin: Mouton, 1–38.

Singh, Rajendra (2005). 'Reduplication in Modern Hindi and the theory of reduplication', in Bernhard Hurch (ed.), *Studies on reduplication*. Berlin: Mouton de Gruyter, 263–82.

Skinner, Tobin (2008). 'Morphological opacity in reduplication: a lowering account', in Charles Chang and Hannah Haynie (eds), *Proceedings of the*

26th West Coast Conference on Formal Linguistics. Somerville, MA: Cascadilla Press, 420–8.

Smith, I., and S. Johnson (2000). 'Kugu Nganhcara', in R. M. A. Dixon and B. J. Blake (eds), *The handbook of Australian languages vol. 5: grammatical sketches of Bunuba, Ndjebbana and Kugu Nganhcara.* Oxford/New York: Oxford University Press, 357–489.

Smith, Jennifer (1997). 'Noun faithfulness: on the privileged status of nouns in phonology', ms, University of Massachusetts, Amherst. Rutgers Optimality Archive #242-1098. <http://www.unc.edu/~jlsmith/home/pdf/nfaith97.pdf>.

Smith, Jennifer (1999). 'Noun faithfulness and accent in Fukuoka Japanese', in Sonya Bird, Andrew Carnie, Jason Haugen, and Peter Norquest (eds), *Proceedings of WCCFL XVIII.* Somerville, MA: Cascadilla Press, 519–31.

Smith, Jennifer (2001). 'Lexical category and phonological contrast', in Robert Kirchner, Joe Pater, and Wolf Wikely (eds), *Papers in Experimental and Theoretical Linguistics 6: Workshop on the lexicon in phonetics and phonology.* Edmonton: University of Alberta, 61–72.

Smith, Jennifer (2011). 'Category-specific effects', in Marc van Oostendorp, Colin Ewen, Beth Hume, and Keren Rice (eds), *Companion to phonology.* Malden, MA: Wiley-Blackwell, 2439–63.

Smolensky, Paul, and Géraldine Legendre (2006). *The harmonic mind: from neural computation to Optimality-Theoretic grammar.* Cambridge, MA: MIT Press.

Spencer, Andrew (1998). 'Morphophonological operations', in Andrew Spencer and Arnold Zwicky (eds), *Handbook of morphology.* Oxford: Blackwell, 123–43.

Spencer, Andrew, and Ana Luís (2013). 'The canonical clitic', in Dunstan Brown, Marina Chumakina, and Greville Corbett (eds), *Canonical morphology and syntax.* Oxford: Clarendon Press, 123–50.

Sproat, Richard (1986). 'Malayalam compounding: a non-stratum ordered account', in Mary Dalrymple, Jeffrey Goldberg, Kristin Hanson, Michael Inman, Chris Piñon, and Stephen Wechsler (eds), *Proceedings of the fifth West Coast Conference on Formal Linguistics.* Stanford: Stanford Linguistics Association, 268–88.

Stairs, E. F., and Barbara Hollenbach (1969). 'Huave verb morphology', *International Journal of American Linguistics* 35: 38–53.

Stemberger, Joseph (1981). 'Morphological haplology', *Language* 57: 791–817.

Steriade, Donca (1988). 'Reduplication and syllable transfer in Sanskrit', *Phonology* 5: 73–155.

Steriade, Donca (1999). 'Lexical conservatism in French adjectival liaison', in Marc Authier, Barbara Bullock, and Lisa Reed (eds), *Formal perspectives on Romance linguistics.* Amsterdam: John Benjamins, 243–70.

Steriade, Donca (2000). 'Paradigm uniformity and the phonetics-phonology boundary', in Janet Pierrehumbert and Michael Broe (eds), *Papers in Laboratory Phonology V: acquisition and the lexicon.* Cambridge: Cambridge University Press, 313–34.

Steriade, Donca (2008). 'A pseudo-cyclic effect in Romanian morphophon-ology', in Asaf Bachrach and Andrew Nevins (eds), *Inflectional identity*. Oxford: Oxford University Press, 313–60.

Stevens, Alan M. (1977). 'On local ordering in Sundanese', *Linguistic Inquiry* 8: 155–62.

Stevens, Alan M. (1985). 'Reduplication in Madurese', *Proceedings of the Second Eastern States Conference on Linguistics*. Columbus: Linguistics Department, the Ohio State University.

Stonham, John (1994). *Combinatorial morphology*. Amsterdam: John Benjamins.

Stonham, John (2007). 'Nuuchahnulth double reduplication and Stratal Opti-mality Theory', *Canadian Journal of Linguistics* 52: 105–30.

Stonham, John (2009). 'Level ordering in Nootka', in Kristin Hanson and Sharon Inkelas (eds), *The nature of the word: essays in honor of Paul Kiparsky*. Cambridge, MA: MIT Press, 225–40.

Struijke, Caro (2000). 'Existential Faithfulness: a study of reduplicative TETU, feature movement, and dissimilation', Ph.D. dissertation, University of Massachusetts, Amherst.

Stump, Gregory (1992). 'On the theoretical status of position class restric-tions', in Geert Booij and Jaap van Marle (eds), *Yearbook of Morphology 1991*. Dordrecht: Kluwer, 211–41.

Stump, Gregory (2001). *Inflectional morphology: a theory of paradigm struc-ture*. Cambridge: Cambridge University Press.

Sumukti, Rukmantoro Hadi (1971). 'Javanese morphology and phonology', Ph.D. dissertation, Cornell University.

Taylan, Eser (2011). 'Is there evidence for a voicing rule in Turkish?', in Eser Taylan and Bengisu Rona (eds), *Puzzles of language: essays in honour of Karl Zimmer*. Wiesbaden: Harrassowitz, 71–91.

Toki, Satoshi (1990). 'Nihongo no goikousei niyoru oto no heni', in Nihongo Kyoiku Gakkai (ed.), *Nihongo Kyoiku Handobukku*. Tokyo: Taishuukan shoten.

Topping, Donald (1973). *Chamorro reference grammar*. Honolulu: University of Hawaii Press.

Trommer, Jochen (2012). 'Zero-exponence', in Jochen Trommer (ed.), *The morphology and phonology of exponence*. Oxford: Oxford University Press, 326–54.

Trommer, Jochen, and Eva Zimmerman (2010). 'Generalized mora affixation', paper presented at the 28th *West Coast Conference on Formal Linguistics*. Slides downloadable from <http://www.uni-leipzig.de/~zimmerma/Talks/wccfl28_slides.pdf>.

Tsujimura, Natsuko (1996). *An introduction to Japanese linguistics*. 1st edition Cambridge, MA: Blackwell.

Tsujimura, Natsuko, and Stuart Davis (2011). 'A construction approach to innovative verbs in Japanese', *Cognitive Linguistics* 22: 799–825.

Tucker, A. N. (1994). *A grammar of Kenya Luo (Dholuo)*. Cologne: Rüdiger Köpper Verlag.

Uhrbach, Amy (1987). 'A formal analysis of reduplication and its interaction with phonological and morphological processes', Ph.D. dissertation, University of Texas, Austin.

Ultan, Russell (1978). 'A typological view of metathesis', in Joseph Greenberg (ed.), *Universals of human language*. Stanford, California: Stanford University Press, 367–402.

Umemura, Osamu (2003). 'Nihongo no choukai shidou - kikitorio youinisuru "chishiki" towa nanika –', *Teikyou daigaku bungakubu kiyou kyouikugaku* 28: 117–43.

Underhill, Robert (1976). *Turkish grammar*. Cambridge, MA: MIT Press.

Urbanczyk, Suzanne (1996). 'Patterns of reduplication in Lushootseed', Ph.D. dissertation, University of Massachusetts, Amherst.

Urbanczyk, Suzanne (1999). 'A-templatic reduplication in Halq'eméylem', in Susan Blake, Eun-Sook Kim, and Kimary Shahin (eds), *Proceedings of the 17th West Coast Conference on Formal Linguistics*. Stanford: CSLI Publications, 655–69.

Urbanczyk, Suzanne (2006). 'Reduplicative form and the root-affix asymmetry', *Natural Language and Linguistic Theory* 24: 179–240.

Urbanczyk, Suzanne (2011). 'Root-affix asymmetries', in Marc van Oostendorp, Colin J. Ewen, Elizabeth Hume, and Keren Rice (eds), *Blackwell companion to phonology, volume IV: phonological interfaces*. Malden, MA: Blackwell, 2490–515.

Ussishkin, Adam (1999). 'The inadequacy of the consonantal root: Modern Hebrew denominal verbs and Output-Output correspondence', *Phonology* 16: 401–42.

Ussishkin, Adam, and Andrew Wedel (2002). 'Neighborhood density and the root-affix distinction', in Masako Hirotani (ed.), *Proceedings of NELS 32*. GLSA.

Vaux, Bert (1996). 'Abkhaz Mabkhaz: m-reduplication in Abkhaz and the problem of melodic invariance', unpublished ms, Harvard University.

Vaux, Bert (1998). *The phonology of Armenian*. Oxford: Clarendon Press.

Vaux, Bert (2003). 'Syllabification in Armenian, Universal Grammar, and the lexicon', *Linguistic Inquiry* 34: 91–125.

Vigário, Marina, and Sónia Frota (2002). 'Prosodic word deletion in coordinate structures', *Journal of Portuguese Linguistics* 1: 241–64.

Voegelin, Charles F. (1935). 'Tübatulabal grammar', *University of California Publications in American Archaeology and Ethnology* 34: 55–90.

Voeltz, F. K. Erhard, and Christa Kilian-Hatz (eds) (2001). *Ideophones*. Amsterdam: John Benjamins.

Weber, David J. (1989). *A grammar of Huallaga (Huánuco) Quechua*. Berkeley: University of California Press.

Weber, David J., and Peter N. Landerman (1985). 'On the interpretation of long vowels in Quechua', *International Journal of American Linguistics* 51: 94–108.

Wee, Lionel (1995). '"Discontinuous reduplication" in Ulu Muar', in Mark Alves (ed.), *Papers from the third annual meeting of the Southeast Asian Linguistics Society (1993)*. Arizona State University, 221–34.

Weeda, Donald Stanton (1987). 'Formal properties of Madurese final syllable reduplication', *Papers from the 23rd Annual Regional Meeting of the Chicago Linguistics Society*. Part II: Parasession on autosegmental and metrical phonology, 403–17.

Weeda, Donald Stanton (1992). 'Word truncation in prosodic morphology', Ph.D. dissertation, University of Texas, Austin.

Weigel, William (1993). 'Morphosyntactic toggles', *Papers from the 29th Regional Meeting of the Chicago Linguistics Society*. Chicago: Chicago Linguistics Society, 467–78.

Wells, Margaret (1979). *Siroi grammar*. Pacific Linguistics Series B, vol. 51. Canberra: Dept. of Linguistics, Research School of Pacific Studies, Australian National University.

Wilbur, Ronnie (1973). *The phonology of reduplication*. Bloomington: Indiana University Linguistics Club.

Wilkinson, Kay (1988). 'Prosodic structure and Lardil phonology', *Linguistic Inquiry* 19: 325–34.

Willard, Rainbow (2004). 'Dominance effects in a dialect of Mam Maya', ms, UC Berkeley.

Williams, Edwin (1976). 'Underlying tone in Margi and Igbo', *Linguistic Inquiry* 7: 463–84.

Wise, Hilary (1983). 'Some functionally motivated rules in Tunisian phonology', *Journal of Linguistics* 19: 165–81.

Withgott, Margaret (1982). 'Segmental evidence for phonological constraints', Ph.D. dissertation, University of Texas, Austin.

Wolf, Matthew (2008). 'Optimal interleaving: serial phonology-morphology interaction in a constraint-based model', Ph.D. dissertation, University of Massachusetts, Amherst.

Xu, Zheng, and Mark Aronoff (2011). 'A realization Optimality-Theoretic approach to extended morphological exponence', *Journal of Linguistics* 47: 1–35.

Yip, Moira (1991). 'Coronals, coronal clusters and the coda condition', in C. Paradis and J.-F. Prunet (eds), *Phonetics and Phonology 2: the special status of coronals*. New York: Academic Press, 61–78.

Yip, Moira (1992). 'Reduplication with fixed melodic material', *Proceedings of NELS 22*. Amherst: GLSA, 459–76.

Yip, Moira (1998). 'Identity avoidance in phonology and morphology', in Steven LaPointe, Diane Brentari, and Patrick Farrell (eds), *Morphology and its relations to phonology and syntax*. Stanford: CSLI Publications, 216–46.

Yu, Alan C. L. (2000). 'Stress assignment in Tohono O'odham', *Phonology* 17: 117–35.

Yu, Alan C. L. (2005a). 'Quantity, stress and reduplication in Washo', *Phonology* 22: 437–75.

Yu, Alan C. L. (2005b). 'Toward a typology of compensatory reduplication', in John Alderete, Chung-hye Han, and Alexei Kochetov (eds), *Proceedings of the 24th West Coast Conference on Formal Linguistics*. Somerville, MA: Cascadilla, 397–405.

Yu, Alan C. L. (2007). *A natural history of infixation*. Oxford: Oxford University Press.

Zec, Draga, and Sharon Inkelas (1990). 'Prosodically constrained syntax', in Sharon Inkelas and Draga Zec (eds), *The phonology-syntax connection*. Chicago: CSLI publications and the University of Chicago Press, 365–78.

Zepeda, Ofelia (1983). *A Papago grammar*. Tucson: University of Arizona Press.

Zepeda, Ofelia (1984). 'Topics in Papago morphology', Ph.D. dissertation, University of Arizona.

Zimmer, Karl, and Barbara Abbott (1978). 'The k/Ø alternation in Turkish; some experimental evidence for its productivity', *Journal of Psycholinguistic Research* 7: 35–46.

Zoll, Cheryl (1993). 'Directionless syllabification and ghosts in Yawelmani', Rutgers Optimality Workshop I. Rutgers University.

Zoll, Cheryl (1995). 'Consonant mutation in Bantu', *Linguistic Inquiry* 26: 536–45.

Zoll, Cheryl (2001). 'Constraints and representations in subsegmental phonology', in Linda Lombardi (ed.), *Segmental phonology in Optimality Theory*. Cambridge: Cambridge University Press, 46–78.

Zue, Victor, and Martha Laferriere (1979). 'Acoustic study of medial /t, d/ in American English', *Journal of the Acoustical Society of America* 66: 1038–50.

Zuraw, Kie Ross (2000). 'Exceptions and regularities in phonology', Ph.D. dissertation, University of California, Los Angeles.

Zuraw, Kie Ross (2002). 'Aggressive reduplication', *Phonology* 19: 395–439.

Zuraw, Kie Ross, and Yu-an Lu (2009). 'Diverse repairs for multiple labial consonants', *Natural Language and Linguistic Theory* 27: 197–224.

Zwicky, Arnold, and Geoffrey Pullum (1983). 'Cliticization vs. inflection: English n't', *Language* 59: 502–13.

Index of languages

Index of authors

Index of subjects

Printed and bound by CPI Group (UK) Ltd, Croydon, CR0 4YY